Understanding Dying, Death, and Bereavement

MICHAEL R. LEMING
St. Olaf College

GEORGE E. DICKINSON
Morehead State University

HOLT, RINEHART AND WINSTON
New York   Chicago   San Francisco   Philadelphia
Montreal   Toronto   London   Sydney
Tokyo   Mexico City   Rio de Janiero   Madrid

Photo credits: Cover photo by Tom Kingrey, courtesy of the Minnesota Association of Homes for the Aging; *p. 2 (top, right)*, R. Wheeler *(top, left and bottom)*, Michael Leming: *p. 26*, © 1983, C. Racioppo; *p. 46*, Michael Leming; *p. 77*, R. Wheeler; *p. 104*, © Vivienne della Giotta, 1980/Photo Researchers, Inc.; *p. 138*, R. Wheeler; *p. 173*, Michael Weisbrot and Family; *p. 208*, Michael Leming; *pp. 234, 262*, Bettmann Archive, Inc.; *p. 298*, Michael Weisbrot and Family; *p. 326*, R. Wheeler.

Acknowledgments: *p. 3*, excerpt from "Sweeney Agonistes: Fragments of an Agon," in *Collected Poems, 1909–1962* by T. S. Eliot, copyright 1936 by Harcourt Brace Jovanovich, Inc., copyright © 1963, 1964 by T. S. Eliot. Reprinted by permission of the publisher; *pp. 8–9*, reprinted with permission from the *Minneapolis Star and Tribune*; *pp. 19–20, 28*, used by permission of The Associated Press; *pp. 31–32*, copyright ©1973 Concordia Publishing House and used by permission; *pp. 36, 91*, used by permission of Judson Press; *pp. 50–51*, excerpts adapted from R. M. Coe, *Sociology of Medicine*, copyright ©1970 McGraw-Hill Book Co., New York, and reprinted by permission; *pp. 51, 54–56*, used by permission of Macmillan Publishing Co. Inc. from *On Death and Dying* by Elisabeth Kubler-Ross, copyright © 1969 by Elisabeth Kubler-Ross; *pp. 60–62*, excerpted and adapted from *The Social System* by Talcott Parsons, copyright © 1951 by Talcott Parsons and reprinted by permission of Macmillan Publishing Co., Inc.; *p. 66*, reprinted by permission of W. B. Saunders Company *p. 66*, reprinted by permission of America Press, Inc., 106 West 56th Street, New York, NY, © 1981, all rights reserved; *pp. 86–87*, copyright © 1980 the Boston Globe Newspaper Company/Washington Post Writers Group and reprinted by permission; *pp. 92–94*, used by permission of The Associated Press; *p. 105*, from *Talking About Death: A Dialogue Between Parent and Child*, rev. ed., by Earl R. Grollman, copyright © 1976 by Earl R. Grollman and reprinted by permission of Beacon Press; *pp. 111–114*, reprinted with permission of the *Minneapolis Star and Tribune*; *pp. 132–133*, excerpt from "A Matter of Life and Death" by Harlene Galen reprinted by permission from *Young Children* (1972), Vol. 27, No. 6: 351–356, © 1972 by the National Association for the Education of Young Children, 1834 Connecticut Ave., N. W., Washington, DC 20009; *pp. 152–154*, copyright 1965 Time Inc., and reprinted by permission from TIME; *pp. 155–156*, reprinted by permission of G. K. Hall & Co., Twayne Publishers Division; *p. 157*, reprinted by permission of Judson Press; *p. 175*, epigraph reprinted by permission of the authors; *pp. 192–196 passim*, copyright © 1978 by Princeton University Press and reprinted by permission of Princeton University Press; *pp. 214–216*, reprinted by permission of *The Philadelphia Inquirer*; *pp. 226–230*, copyright © 1981 by Judy Sklar Rasminsky and reprinted by her permission; copyright © 1981 The Reader's Digest Association, Inc.; *pp. 246–247*, reprinted by permission of The Associated Press; *pp. 272–273*, reprinted by permission of *The Boston Globe*; *p. 280*, © 1969 United Artists Music Co., Inc., rights assigned to CBS Catalogue Partnership, all rights controlled and administered by CBS U Catalogue, Inc., all rights reserved, international copyright secured, used by permission; *pp. 281–284*, excerpts from "Grave Remarks" from *The People's Almanac* by David Wallechinsky and Irving Wallace. Copyright 1975 by David Wallechinsky and Irving Wallace. Reprinted by permission of Doubleday & Co., Inc.; *pp. 292–293*, copyright © 1971 by Wendell Berry, reprinted from his *The Country of Marriage*, by permission of Harcourt Brace Jovanovich, Inc.; *pp. 302–303*, reprinted by permission of The Associated Press; *pp. 303–305*, copyright 1965 Time Inc., and reprinted by permission from TIME; *pp. 314–315*, reprinted by permission of The Associated Press; *pp. 318–319*, reprinted by permission of *Us*, a trademark of Peters Publishing Co., a division of Concentric Enterprises, Inc.; *pp. 330–331*, adapted by permission of International Universities Press, Inc.; *p. 329*, copyright 1979 by Family Service Association of America, New York, and reprinted by permission.

Library of Congress Cataloging in Publication Data

Leming, Michael R.
  Understanding dying, death, and bereavement.

  Includes bibliographies and index.
  1. Death—Social aspects—United States. 2. Death—
Psychological aspects. 3. Bereavement—Social aspects
—United States. 4. Bereavement—Psychological aspects.
5. Funeral rites and ceremonies—United States.
I. Dickinson, George E. II. Title.
HQ1073.5.U6L45   1985   306'.9   84-15640

ISBN 0-03-069824-3

CBS COLLEGE PUBLISHING
Holt, Rinehart and Winston
The Dryden Press
Saunders College Publishing

PREFACE

WITH MORE THAN twenty-five books on the subject of dying and death appearing within the last five years, one might well ask, "Why add another text to the dying and death bookshelf?" The answer is that the subject has never been covered as it is here. Most of the books currently on the market deal exclusively with either the dying patient, death meanings, or the bereavement process. We believe there is a need for a book that is informational, practical, takes a multidisciplinary approach, and is concerned with the major foci of the interdisciplinary subject of social thanatology—the study of dying, death, and bereavement.

Understanding Dying, Death, and Bereavement is designed to provide the reader with the necessary information to both *understand* and *cope* with the social processes of dying, death, and bereavement. Having taught courses on this subject for a decade, we realize that every student approaches this subject with both academic and personal agendas. For this reason, we have brought together nine authorities with extensive academic experience and personal involvement in their respective topics. Our coauthors include persons from the academic areas of sociology, psychology, social work, history, mortuary science, and theology. Each author possesses a doctorate or the equivalent in his or her respective field.

The Uniqueness of This Book

At present there are four types of books published on the subject of social thanatology. The first is the popular "self-help" psychological approach that includes the Kubler-Ross books, *On Death and Dying* and *Death: The Final Stage of Growth,* and the many books by Grollman such as *Concerning Death, Explaining Death to Children,* and *Talking About Death.* "Pop" psychology books of this type are appropriate for general audiences but of limited use in academic settings. The second type—prevalent in the field—is the

iii

focused book that deals with only one of the topics of dying, death, or bereavement. Books of this kind, while academic in scope, are limited in their coverage and tend to be too specialized for general college and university audiences.

The third type of book is the analytical textbook written from the perspective of a single academic discipline. Books in this category include Vernon's *The Sociology of Death* (sociology), Charmaz's *The Social Reality of Death* (sociology), Kastenbaum's *Death, Society, and Human Experience* (psychology), Schulz's *Psychology of Death, Dying, and Bereavement* (psychology), and Kalish's *Death, Grief, and Caring Relationships* (psychology). The major criticism directed at books of this type is that they focus primarily on academic issues to the exclusion of personal concerns; for many, this approach is rather esoteric.

The last type of dying and death book, of which there are so many, is the collection of readings. The most popular of these is Herman Feifel's *The New Meaning of Death*. While this type of book is multidisciplinary, the problem is in its being a book of readings; the articles do not relate well to each other, there is no attempt to integrate the ideas found in the specific articles, there is a lack of unity found throughout the work, and many of the articles are too specific to be of general interest.

Understanding Dying, Death, and Bereavement is a multiauthored college level text that is significantly different from all existing books because it combines the strengths of the four types of thanatology books currently available. It is multidisciplinary. It is comprehensive, in that it deals with the full range of topics in social thanatology. It is scholarly and academically sound because the persons writing the chapters are academicians and scholars in their own right. It is a unified effort because the coauthors have participated in the formation of the format of the book, and the content of each chapter was coordinated and edited by the primary authors. Finally, it is of practical value because it is concerned with personal issues relating to an individual's ability to cope with the social and psychological processes of dying, death, and bereavement.

This book is directed primarily at undergraduate and graduate university students, although it also would be appropriate for use in professional courses in medicine, nursing, mortuary science, social work, and pastoral counseling. The book could be used in sociology, psychology, nursing, social work, physical education, religion, health science, and education courses. It could also be used as a primary or a supplementary text in courses on gerontology, health, human development, counseling, and medical sociology. We believe that the book's potential audience is great, not only because of its wide adoptability on college and university campuses, but also because of its practical implications for all persons who must cope with dying, death, and bereavement.

Special Features

The following features have been added to the book to make it more interesting and personally relevant: (1) boxed inserts of readings of special interest; (2) chapter summaries that outline the important points of each
chapter; (3) applications that provide practical information students can
apply to the material in the chapters; (4) discussion questions that highlight
important issues in the chapters; (5) annotated bibliographies for students
who wish to do further reading; and (6) glossaries of the unfamiliar terms
contained within chapters. There is also an instructor's manual available
from Holt, Rinehart and Winston that includes audiovisual aid recommendations and test bank items.

The authors would welcome suggestions and feedback from readers that
might improve future editions of this book. We would also appreciate correspondence from instructors concerning pedagogy related to the teaching
of this subject.

Acknowledgments

When we look back over the past five years, it is obvious that this book is
the result of a large team effort. Our contributing authors were extremely
diligent in their research and writing efforts. They were also very accepting
of our editing and rewriting of their work as we attempted to provide
continuity throughout the book. Many editors of multiauthored textbooks
claim they could have written a better book, with less trouble, and in a
shorter period of time if they had done it by themselves. Such was not the
case with *Understanding Dying, Death, and Bereavement*. This project was
greatly enhanced by the contributions of our coauthors. We could not have
produced a book of this quality without their valuable knowledge and insights.

We are also indebted to Andrew Paprocki, Marie Schappert, Barbara
Heinssen, Herman Makler, and the supporting staff personnel at Holt,
Rinehart and Winston for their work in making the production of the manuscript possible, and for the confidence and encouragement they invested
in this project.

Our appreciation is extended to the psychologists, sociologists, geron-
tologists, and social thanatologists who reviewed the manuscript in its several drafts and who contributed to its improvement, coherence, and overall
refinement. They are Meredith McGuire, Montclair State University; Carol
Nowak, State University of New York at Buffalo; Paul Rosenblatt, University of Minnesota; and Sylvia Zaki, Rhode Island State College.

M.R.L. / G.E.D.

CONTENTS

PART TWO
UNDERSTANDING DEATH ATTITUDES

PART THREE
COPING WITH DYING AND DEATH

THE CONTRIBUTORS

John W. Abbott   *(Chapter 8)*

Director of Educational Services and Public Information for The Connecticut Hospice, the first hospice founded in the United States. In the seventeen years before joining the staff of The Connecticut Hospice he was with the National Council of Churches in New York City.

Robert Bendiksen   *(Chapter 7)*

Associate Professor of Sociology at the University of Wisconsin (La Crosse) and Research Associate of the Center for Death Education and Research at the University of Minnesota. He has collaborated with Robert Fulton in editing *Death and Identity* (1976). He currently serves as a trustee of La Crosse Lutheran Hospital, as well as a hospice volunteer and member of the hospital's Institutional Review Board.

George E. Dickinson   *(Chapters 1, 3, 9, and 12)*

Professor and Head of the Department of Sociology, Social Work, and Corrections at Morehead State University in Morehead, Kentucky. He has completed a post-doctoral fellowship in gerontology at Pennsylvania State University and has authored over twenty-five articles in professional journals in dying and death, family, adolescence, and corrections.

James J. Farrell   *(Chapter 10)*

Assistant Professor of History and Coordinator of American Studies at St. Olaf College in Northfield, Minnesota. He is the author of *Inventing the American Way of Death, 1830–1920,* published by Temple University Press in 1980. He is currently involved in research on nuclear war and megadeath experiences.

Nils C. Friberg   *(Chapter 5)*

Associate Professor of Pastoral Care at Bethel Theological Seminary in St. Paul, Minnesota. He has degrees in psychology of religion and theology, and has served as a chaplain in state hospitals in both the United States and Brazil.

Michael R. Leming   *(Chapters 1, 3, 6, and 12)*

Associate Professor of Sociology and Director of the Social Research Center of St. Olaf College in Northfield, Minnesota. He has been actively involved as researcher, writer, and lecturer in social thanatology on a national level for the past ten years and is currently a hospice volunteer involved in death education.

Ann L. Overbeck   *(Chapter 4)*

Associate Professor and Coordinator of Social Treatment Concentration at the Western Michigan University School of Social Work in Kalamazoo, Michigan. Her clinical social work positions include appointments at Massachusetts General Hospital (Boston) and the Langley Porter Neuropsychiatric Institute in San Francisco. She has also taught at Pennsylvania State University and The Smith College School for Social Work, where she continues as Visiting Associate Research Professor.

Robert C. Slater   *(Chapter 11)*

Professor and Director of the Department of Mortuary Science at the University of Minnesota in Minneapolis. He is a licensed funeral director and embalmer and is a member of the Committee of Examiners in Mortuary Science for the Minnesota Department of Health. He has published over fifty articles in professional journals and is the coauthor of *The Funeral Director and His Role as a Counselor* (1975).

Glenn M. Vernon   *(Chapter 2)*

Professor of Sociology at the University of Utah in Salt Lake City. He has authored more than fifty articles in professional journals and a number of books, including *Sociology of Death* (1970) and *A Time to Die* (1977). He is currently engaged in research on near-death experiences.

ONE

Understanding Dying and Death

Chapter 1

THE AMERICAN WAY OF DYING

Birth, and copulation, and death. That's all the facts when you
come to brass tacks—Birth, copulation, and death.

T. S. Eliot, Sweeney Agonistes

NOTE THE REACTIONS of others when someone says he or she is a funeral
director, works in a nursing home, or is an oncology nurse (one who works
with patients with tumors, often cancerous). Reactions like "How can you
do that?" often result. Better still, how do your friends and relatives respond when they hear that you are taking a course dealing with dying and
death? From the reactions that most people have to these death-related
issues, it appears that in contemporary society, death discussions are considered in bad taste and something to be avoided.

Dying in the United States today occurs "offstage," away from the arena
of familiar surroundings of kin and friends. Currently, over 70 percent of
deaths in the United States occur in institutional settings—hospitals and
nursing homes. Grandfather seldom dies at home where he has spent
years living in an environment he appreciates and feels is his own. The
removal of death from the usual setting prompted Dumont and Foss
(1972:2) to raise the following question: "How is the modern American able
to cope with his own death when the deaths he experiences are infrequent,
highly impersonal, and viewed as virtually abnormal?"

THE CURRENT INTEREST IN THANATOLOGY

The realization of this problem in the early 1970s brought about a concerted
effort to talk about and study dying and death. The movie industry began
to produce films revolving around the theme of death. For example, in *Love
Story* one of the two main characters was dying—and did die before the
movie concluded. She was not the "bad guy," who in the end was killed by
people with "white hats," but was *the star* of the movie—the "good guy."

3

Movies such as this are unlike earlier movies where right always prevailed and the evil character received his or her just reward—death.

In the late 1970s and early 1980s prime time television comedy series such as "Benson," "Archie's Place," "M*A*S*H," and "The Jeffersons" dealt with death. While "Benson," "Archie's Place," and "M*A*S*H" viewed death in a serious vein, "The Jeffersons" literally took a tongue-in-cheek attitude toward death.

Numerous television specials in the 1970s and 1980s have discussed dying and death in one- and two-hour programs. An NEH-sponsored program, entitled "Dying," aired in the late 1970s depicted how four cancer patients related to their situation. For two hours this special very sensitively portrayed these individuals, ranging in age from the late twenties to the early seventies—interacting with others, and others responding to them. A PBS documentary, produced in 1979, showed the last three years of Joan Robinson's life. This three-hour film documented the experience of a woman and her husband as they attempted to live with her cancer of the breast and uterus.

Other programs such as ABC's "The Right to Die" addressed moral questions of mercy killing and suicide. "Living With Death" presented various death-related situations observed by a reporter. More recently, CBS's "A Time For Dying" discussed support groups for the dying. All of the major television networks have now aired special programs concerned with dying and death.

Along with the mass media, the interdisciplinary study of dying, death, and bereavement—called "thanatology"—flourished in the academic world in the 1970s. Literally hundreds of courses on dying and death were offered in high schools and colleges. Indeed, three professional journals on the subject were started — *Omega: The Journal of Death and Dying*, *Advances in Thanatology* (formerly *Journal of Thanatology*), and *Death Education*. The number of articles on dying and death also expanded considerably in nursing, education, social work, psychology, and sociology journals.

Why this increased emphasis on dying and death in the 1970s? Certainly death, like sex, was not a new event, but both had been rarely discussed openly. Sex, as a subject of discussion, came "out of the closet" in the 1960s followed by death in the 1970s.

As noted earlier, most persons in the United States today die in a nursing home or hospital—this was not the case at the turn of the century, when most people died at home. Also, at the turn of the century, more Americans lived in rural environments where the direct observation of birth and death was an everyday event. In this time period, children were brought up surrounded by the alpha and omega of the life cycle. Kittens, puppies, piglets, calves, and colts were born and also died. Thus, it was commonplace to make observations of death and to deal with these situations accordingly.

Today, with less than 10 percent of the United States population living on farms, these birth and death scenes have largely been removed from the personal observations of most individuals. Kavanaugh (1972) conducted an extensive poll among college students and found that 92 percent had yet to witness a death. For most of us, our most frequent experience of death comes from the evening news as reporters attempt to bring us as close to the scene of death as availability and "good taste" will allow. However, since we are unlikely to know the people who have died, the effect of this "death news" upon us is minimal. Kavanaugh (1972:13) makes the following observation that demonstrates this problem.

> Over a two-week period of nighttime [television] viewing, I counted an average of 34 deaths at close range, countless more at a distance. Not one death raised as much as a slight tremor in me. Television feeds our fantasy of forever being a spectator. Even a bloody nose or a fainting spell by a fellow viewer would have aroused more emotion in me than a hundred deaths on the tube.

Perhaps the removal of frequent observations of the complete life cycle, as the population of the United States became more urbanized, contributed to a desire to learn more about the events of birth and death. Somewhat paralleling the increased emphasis in dying and death in the 1970s has been a change in birthing procedures. More and more fathers are now allowed to be present at the births of their children. Midwives are also becoming recognized as legitimate in hospitals as they add a more personal touch to the birthing process.

Another reason for an increased emphasis on dying and death can be attributed to a prolongation of life. Medical technology has advanced to the point where people are literally kept alive by machines. Organ transplants have allowed individuals who might have died to continue life at a normal pace. The development of penicillin and other antibiotics has also helped prevent death. Thus, the norm today is to die away from home in an institutional setting largely because of advances in medical technology.

By itself, the prolongation of life (due to medical progress) would not have lead to talk and research on dying and death, if highly publicized cases such as Karen Ann Quinlan's had not alerted the public to moral and legal questions on death. Whether or not to "pull the plug" and disconnect one from life-supporting machines posed questions for which ready answers were not found. The whole issue of when death occurs evolves from these medical developments. The question of who determines when one is alive or dead has been addressed by physicians, lawyers, philosophers, and theologians. These questions, along with the controversy over abortion rights, were a few of the significant ethical issues of the 1970s that provided an open forum for discussion and debate concerning the topic of dying and death.

While dying and death have now become issues of intellectual concern, our society has done little to formally socialize its members to deal with death on the personal and emotional levels. Hospitals have traditionally excluded visitors under the age of fourteen. Parents have often tried to shield their "innocent" children from death scenes. Medical and theology schools, which train persons who will work with the dying, have not had significant curricular offerings to prepare their students for this death-related work. Overall, our socialization to dying and death situations has been unsystematic and ineffective.

MORTALITY STATISTICS

Ask a number of people the following question: "When your time comes, how would you wish to die?" With the exception of the comical reply "When I am ninety-two, at the hands of a jealous lover," most people will respond "At home, unexpectedly, in my own bed, when I am asleep, and when I am very old—but with my full mental and physical capabilities." Unfortunately for most of us, we will not die as we would like, and for some this may be a source of apprehension and anxiety. From what we have stated earlier, most Americans die in institutionalized settings and not at home as they would like. A small percentage of persons die of acute diseases. Most of us (76 percent) will die of one of the following chronic diseases: heart disease, cancer, liver, kidney, and lung diseases, and diabetes. With these chronic diseases, deaths are usually prolonged and are anything but sudden and unexpected as most people would desire. In the remainder of this chapter we will describe the ways in which Americans die, and discuss some of the problems associated with creating and compiling mortality statistics.

Certain "vital events" are collected, recorded, and compiled by the Bureau of Vital Statistics. Principal among these events are live births, fetal deaths, marriages, divorces, and deaths. According to Stockwell (1976), the most important functions of death statistics include: (1) analysis of present demographic data and potential growth; (2) supplying administrative and research needs of public health agencies; (3) determining administrative policy and action regarding government agencies other than public health; and (4) providing information on population changes in relation to professional and commercial activities.Death statistics are useful in analyzing past population changes in order to make population projections. Such projections are useful in such areas as developing plans for expanding housing, educational facilities, and industry, as well as various governmental programs.

Please Notify

A lecturer was about to address a business association in Los Angeles when the association director reminded its members: "Every week we pay return postage for mail that goes to our members and is not deliverable because you have moved, changed your post office box number, or died without letting us know."

Source: *Mountaineer*, Waynesville, N.C., April 11, 1980.

Defining death for statistical purposes is very difficult. Back in the 1950s, the United Nations and the World Health Organization proposed the following definition of death: "Death is the permanent disappearance of all evidence of life at any time after birth has taken place" (United Nations, 1953). Thus, as death can take place only after a birth has occurred, any deaths prior to a (live) birth cannot be included in this definition. The latter is called a fetal death and is defined (Stockwell, 1976) as:

> Death (disappearance of life) prior to the complete expulsion or extraction from its mother of a product of conception irrespective of the duration of pregnancy; the death is indicated by the fact that after such separation the fetus does not breathe or show any other evidence of life, such as beating of the heart, pulsation of the umbilical cord, or definite movement of voluntary muscles.

Not all countries follow the definition of death recommended by the United Nations. In some countries, infants dying within twenty-four hours after birth are classified as stillbirths rather than deaths, or are disregarded altogether. In some other countries infants born alive, who die before the end of the registration period (which may last several months), are considered stillbirths or are excluded from all tabulations. Thus, one is not "alive" until officially registered, and one cannot be legally "dead" if never alive! This whole question of life and death is more complicated than might initially appear on the surface.

Kass (1971:699) simply defines death as "the transition from the state of being alive to the state of being dead." Simple enough, yet, the issue is clouded by many factors. Traditionally, death has clinically meant "the irreparable cessation of spontaneous cardiac activity and spontaneous respiratory activity" (Ramsey, 1970:59). The functions of heart and lungs must cease before one is pronounced dead by this definition. However, in 1968 a committee of the Harvard Medical School (Beecher, 1968) claimed that the ultimate criterion for death is brain activity rather than the functioning of heart and lungs. The Harvard Report notes that death should be understood in terms of "a permanently nonfunctioning brain" for which there are many tests.

With a lack of consensus regarding the definition of death, determining death continues to be controversial. Kansas was the first state to legislate a definition of death in 1970. Since then, seventeen other states have enacted definition of death laws (Backer, Hannon, and Russell, 1982:178–179).

Is Death, Like Pregnancy, an All-or-Nothing Thing?

Lewis Cope

By traditional definitions, death is when heartbeat and breathing stop. But medical advances, particularly in the past decade, have made this heartbeat definition of death obsolete. Here's why:

Hundreds of people living today would have to be considered to have once died under the old definitions of death. Their hearts stopped beating and their breathing stopped as a result of heart attacks. But because they were being cared for in a hospital's coronary care unit, electrical paddles placed on their chests were able to restart their heartbeats. And once their heart was beating again, pushing an ample supply of blood through the section of the brain that controls respiration, normal breathing returned.

With respirators to artificially breathe for a patient, along with intravenous feeding that infuses nutrients into the body through a vein, many lives are saved. Patients sometimes can be kept alive until their own bodily systems recover.

But is a patient still alive when consciousness and brain control are permanently gone, and blood flow and breathing continue only by grace of machines? The diagnosis of "brain death" allows respirators to be turned off when the brain is "totally and irreversibly" dead.

According to Dr. Shelley Chou, chief of neurosurgery at the University of Minnesota Hospitals, with brain death the body would never be able to breathe on its own, because breathing is controlled in the brain. The body would never be able to think or remember or have any form of consciousness. In short, when the entire brain is dead, any artificially induced heartbeat is merely pumping blood through a dead body.

If heartbeat alone were the essence of life, mind-boggling questions would rise in this era of heart transplants. Would the living recipients of transplanted hearts have to be considered dead, because their own hearts would no longer be beating? Would a man who received a heart from a deceased person become that donor?

"Ultimately, all deaths are brain deaths," said Dr. Ronald Cranford, a neurologist at Hennepin County Medical Center. When death is declared on the basis of cessation of breathing and heartbeat, the brain is deprived of blood supply and dies within a matter of minutes. The death of the brain is what's really final and absolute, he explained.

On the other hand, some people lose all brain function, but it's not *irreversible,* Cranford said, for example, a person who has taken an overdose of barbiturates may have a temporary absence of any signs of brain activity. But this is not brain death either, because it is *reversible.*

Physicians have an extensive battery of tests to use to detect any signs of brain activity. They search for any hint of normal brain-controlled reflexes. They turn the head, and even put cold water in the ear, to look for any sign of movement. They search for any sign of whether the eye pupils respond to light. One of the many tests is to touch the cornea of the eye and see whether this triggers a blink. The respirator is also stopped briefly to see whether there's any sign of spontaneous breathing.

Even after all such signs indicate brain death, Chou and Cranford explained, the tests are repeated at least 12 hours later to make certain that the absence of these life signs is not temporary.

Source: *Minneapolis Tribune,* June 22, 1978, pp. 1A, 6A.

In discussing the American way of dying, it is noted in Table 1–1 that major causes of death in the United States have changed significantly since 1900. While accounting for only 17 percent of all deaths in 1900, heart disease, cancer, and accidents now cause more than 76 percent of all deaths in the United States. Currently, the third leading cause of death is accidents—with motor vehicle accidents most frequent (half of which are alcohol-related), followed by falls, and drownings.

Life expectancy has increased considerably since 1920, as is shown in Table 1–2. Life expectancy for males in the United States has increased from fifty-four years to nearly seventy years over the past half century, while females' life expectancy during this same time period has increased from fifty-five to seventy-seven years. Whites live nearly five years longer than blacks in the United States.

While Table 1–2 concludes that males in the United States do not live as long as females, data shows that the shorter life expectancy for males is to some extent attributable to aggressive behaviors (careless and other-

**TABLE 1–1.   Ten Leading Causes of Death in the United States
(In Death Rates per 100,000 Population), 1900 and 1978**

Causes of Death	Death Rates Per 100,000 Population	Percent of All Deaths
*1900**		
1. Pneumonia	191.9	12.5
2. Consumption (Tuberculosis)	190.5	12.5
3. Heart Disease	134.0	8.3
4. Diarrheal Diseases	85.1	5.6
5. Diseases of the Kidneys	83.7	5.5
6. All Accidents	72.3	4.7
7. Apoplexy	66.6	4.3
8. Cancer	60.0	3.9
9. Old Age	54.0	3.5
10. Bronchitis	48.3	3.2
All Other Causes		36.0
1978		
1. Major Cardiovascular Diseases	442.7	50.5
2. Malignancies	181.9	20.8
3. Accidents	48.4	5.5
4. Influenza and Pneumonia	26.7	3.0
5. Diabetes Mellitus	15.5	1.8
6. Cirrhosis of the Liver	13.8	1.6
7. Suicide	12.5	1.4
8. Certain Diseases in Infancy	10.1	1.2
9. Bronchitis, Emphysema, and Asthma	10.0	1.1
10. Homicide	9.4	1.1
All Other Causes		12.0

*These data are limited to the registration area that includes ten registration states and all cities having at least 8,000 inhabitants. In 1900 this composed 38 percent of the entire population of the continental United States. Since accidents were not reported in the 1900 census, this rate was taken from Lerner (1970).

Sources: *Abstract of the Twelfth Census of the United States,* 1900. Table 93. Washington, D.C.: U.S. Government Printing Office, 1902, and *Statistical Abstract of the United States,* 1981. Table 113. Washington D.C.: U.S. Government Printing Office, 1981.

wise) and perhaps to job related toxins. Sex mortality ratios for all major causes of death reveal males' aggressive behaviors through homicide, suicide and accidents to be much higher than for females. Also, respiratory problems leading to death are much greater for males; these could certainly be related to jobs traditionally occupied by males.

Why females outlive males is a long debated topic. This pattern tends to

**TABLE 1–2. Expectation of Life at Birth:
in the United States, 1920–1978**

Year	TOTAL			WHITE			BLACK AND OTHER		
	Total	Male	Female	Total	Male	Female	Total	Male	Female
1920	54.1	53.6	54.6	54.9	54.4	55.6	45.3	45.5	45.2
1930	59.7	58.1	61.6	61.4	59.7	63.5	48.1	47.3	49.2
1940	62.9	60.8	65.2	64.2	62.1	66.6	53.1	51.5	54.9
1950	68.2	65.6	71.1	69.1	66.5	72.2	60.8	59.1	62.9
1960	69.7	66.6	72.8	70.6	67.4	74.1	63.6	61.1	66.3
1970	70.9	67.1	74.8	71.7	68.0	75.6	65.3	61.3	69.4
1978	73.3	69.5	77.2	74.0	70.2	77.8	69.2	65.0	73.6

Source: *Statistical Abstract of the United States:* 1981. Table 105. Washington, D.C.: U.S. Government Printing Office, 1981.

exist in most parts of the world except for a few nonliterate societies where a high maternal mortality rate exists. In answering this question about mortality rates in the United States, one could suggest that females have traditionally been engaged in less strenuous work. (However, traditional housework involves the lifting of many pounds of laundry, daily picking up and keeping up with children, the handling of foodstuffs, and walking several miles within the house performing daily chores.) Women probably watch their diet more carefully than males due to their traditional knowledge about food and a special concern and emphasis upon figure maintenance. As Montagu (1968) suggests, women also have a superior use of emotions, because men restrain from crying, causing them to develop psychosomatic disorders such as peptic ulcers.

On the biological side of the argument, the conception ratio (projected to be higher than 120 males per 100 females) favors males as does the sex ratio at birth (105 males per 100 females). In the early teens the sex ratio levels off; after age eighty the ratio is less than fifty males per 100 females. Perhaps females simply have better built bodies. Their bodies must be capable of carrying and supporting a fetus/embryo. Thus they are the "Porsche" model whereas males are the more "thrown-together" model.

The debate goes on. Whether females outlive males in the United States because of biological or cultural reasons, we will not settle here. The fact is—females outlive males. As sex roles continue to change and females are found in greater numbers and in greater variety of nontraditional occupations and males share more in domestic tasks, stresses and strains of jobs should be more equally distributed between the sexes. The argument of biology versus behavior as influencing life expectancy by sex can then be better addressed.

TABLE 1–3.   Death Rates, by Age, Sex, and Race, 1978 (Number of deaths per 100,000 population in specified group)

Sex and race	All ages[1]	Under 1 year	1–4	5–14	15–24	25–34	35–44	45–54	55–64	65–74	75–84	85 and over
						MALE						
White	994	1,592	78	41	174	193	314	797	1,906	4,185	9,385	17,259
Black and other	1,000	1,360	72	39	169	167	268	734	1,819	4,136	9,421	18,100
	960	2,709	108	52	202	377	659	1,305	2,730	4,633	8,992	10,678
						FEMALE						
White	778	1,270	60	26	61	80	168	433	976	2,138	5,863	13,541
Black and other	797	1,070	53	25	58	69	146	394	914	2,064	5,810	14,079
	665	2,207	90	32	76	143	308	719	1,535	2,822	6,514	8,449

[1]Includes unknown age.

Source: *Statistical Abstracts of the United States*, 1981. Table 109. Washington, D.C.: U.S. Government Printing Office, 1981.

Table 1–4 depicts death rates by age, sex, and race in 1978. It is noted that if one survives the first year of life, chances of living to adulthood are very high. Table 1–5 gives the number of additional years one might expect to live according to race, sex, and age. In this table we can see that a white male at birth can expect to live to the age of seventy, while a white male, age sixty-five, can expect to live to be seventy-nine.

As noted in Table 1–1, in the United States homicide is the tenth leading cause of death today. In 1980, for every 100,000 people in the United States, approximately ten were murder victims. There were 23,044 persons murdered in the United States in 1980 according to the Uniform Crime Report (1981). The most frequently used murder weapon was the handgun (50 percent), followed by a stabbing device (17 percent), clubs and poison (13 percent), shotguns (7 percent), hands, fists, and feet (6 percent), and rifles (5 percent). Fifty-one percent of the murders were perpetrated by relatives or persons acquainted with the victims. Forty-five percent of all murders were the result of arguments, while 18 percent occurred as a result of felonious activities such as robbery and rape.

Suicide as a cause of death in the United States has climbed since 1900. While suicide was the twenty-eighth leading cause of death in 1900 (11.8 per 100,000 population), it was seventh (12.5 per 100,000 population) in 1978. However, while the suicide rates have increased, the main reason suicide has climbed in the rankings is due to the fact that other causes of death have declined. Suicide is more prevalent among people who fall into the following social categories: whites, males, unmarried and formerly married persons, unemployed persons, and older persons. Currently, suicide rates are highest for white males (20.2 per 100,000 population), second for black males (10.8), third for white females (6.9), while black females are last (2.8) in 1978 (Statistical Abstracts of the United States, 1981).

As noted in Table 1–5, firearms (as is true of homicides) are most often used in committing suicide in the United States; poisoning is second; and hanging or strangulation is third.

The suicide rate per 100,000 population in the United States (Statistical Abstract of the United States, 1981) has risen for white males from 18.0 in 1970 to 20.2 in 1978 as well as for black males (from 8.0 to 10.8). Females have a lower rate of suicide and this rate changed slightly during this eight-year period. Rates for white females dropped from 7.1 in 1970 to 6.9 per 100,000 in 1978; for black females it went from 2.6 to 2.8 in the same time period. According to Backer et al. (1982), suicide rates gradually rise during adolescence, increase sharply in early adulthood, and parallel advancing age up to the age bracket seventy-five to eighty-four, when it reaches a rate of 27.9 suicides per 100,000.

As in our discussion of the definition of death, the meaning of suicide is likewise problematic. Theodorson and Theodorson (1969:427) classify as suicide any "death resulting either from a deliberate act of self-destruction

TABLE 1–4. Expectation of Life by Race, Age, and Sex, 1978

| | EXPECTATION OF LIFE IN YEARS | | | | |
| Age (years) | | WHITE | | BLACK AND OTHER | |
	Total	Male	Female	Male	Female
At birth	73.3	70.2	77.8	65.0	73.6
1	73.3	70.1	77.6	65.5	74.0
2	72.4	69.2	76.7	64.6	73.1
3	71.5	68.3	75.7	63.7	72.1
4	70.5	67.3	74.8	62.8	71.2
5	69.5	66.3	73.8	61.8	70.2
6	68.6	65.4	72.8	60.8	69.3
7	67.6	64.4	71.8	59.9	68.3
8	66.6	63.4	70.8	58.9	67.3
9	65.6	62.4	69.9	57.9	66.3
10	64.6	61.5	68.9	57.0	65.4
11	63.7	60.5	67.9	56.0	64.4
12	62.7	59.5	66.9	55.0	63.4
13	61.7	58.5	65.9	54.0	62.4
14	60.7	57.5	64.9	53.1	61.4
15	59.7	56.6	64.0	52.1	60.4
16	58.8	55.6	63.0	51.1	59.5
17	57.8	54.7	62.0	50.2	58.5
18	56.9	53.8	61.1	49.3	57.5
19	56.0	52.9	60.1	48.3	56.6
20	55.0	52.0	59.1	47.4	55.6
21	54.1	51.1	58.2	46.5	54.7
22	53.2	50.2	57.2	45.7	53.7
23	52.2	49.3	56.2	44.8	52.8
24	51.3	48.4	55.3	43.9	51.8
25	50.4	47.5	54.3	43.1	50.9
26	49.5	46.5	53.5	42.2	49.9
27	48.5	45.6	52.4	41.4	49.0
28	47.6	44.7	51.4	40.5	48.1
29	46.6	43.8	50.4	39.7	47.1
30	45.7	42.8	49.5	38.8	46.2
31	44.8	41.9	48.5	37.9	45.2
32	43.8	41.0	47.5	37.1	44.3
33	42.9	40.0	46.6	36.2	43.4
34	41.9	39.1	45.6	35.4	42.5
35	41.0	38.2	44.6	34.5	41.5
36	40.1	37.2	43.7	33.7	40.6

TABLE 1–4   *(continued)*

Age (years)	EXPECTATION OF LIFE IN YEARS				
		WHITE		BLACK AND OTHER	
	Total	Male	Female	Male	Female
37	39.1	36.3	42.7	32.9	39.7
38	38.2	35.4	41.8	32.0	38.8
39	37.3	34.5	40.8	31.2	37.9
40	36.4	33.6	39.9	30.4	37.0
41	35.5	32.6	38.9	29.6	36.1
42	34.6	31.7	38.0	28.9	35.3
43	33.7	30.8	37.1	28.1	34.4
44	32.8	29.9	36.1	27.3	33.5
45	31.9	29.1	35.2	26.5	32.7
46	31.0	28.2	34.3	25.8	31.8
47	30.1	27.3	33.4	25.0	31.0
48	29.3	26.5	32.5	24.3	30.2
49	28.4	25.6	31.6	23.5	29.3
50	27.6	24.8	30.7	22.8	28.5
51	26.7	24.0	29.8	22.1	27.8
52	25.9	23.2	29.0	21.4	27.0
53	25.1	22.4	28.1	20.8	26.2
54	24.3	21.6	27.3	20.1	25.5
55	23.5	20.8	26.4	19.5	24.7
56	22.7	20.1	25.6	18.9	24.0
57	22.0	19.3	24.7	18.3	23.3
58	21.2	18.6	23.9	17.7	22.5
59	20.5	17.9	23.1	17.1	21.8
60	19.7	17.2	22.3	16.5	21.2
61	19.0	16.5	21.5	16.0	20.5
62	18.3	15.8	20.7	15.5	19.9
63	17.6	15.2	19.9	15.1	19.3
64	17.0	14.6	19.2	14.6	18.6
65	16.3	14.0	18.4	14.1	18.0
70	13.1	11.1	14.8	11.6	14.8
75	10.4	8.6	11.5	9.8	12.5
80	8.1	6.7	8.8	8.8	11.5
85 and over	6.4	5.3	6.7	7.8	9.9

Source: *Statistical Abstract of the United States,* 1981. Table 107. Washington, D.C.: U.S. Government Printing Office, 1981.

TABLE 1–5.   Suicides, by Method Used, 1960–1978

Method	MALE				FEMALE			
	1960	1970	1975	1978	1960	1970	1975	1978
Firearms[1]	7,879	9,704	12,185	12,830	1,138	2,068	2,688	2,557
Poisoning[2]	2,631	3,299	3,297	3,105	1,699	3,285	3,129	2,912
Strangulation[3]	2,576	2,422	2,815	2,759	790	831	846	753
Other	1,453	1,204	1,325	1,494	875	667	778	884
Total	14,539	16,629	19,622	20,188	4,502	6,851	7,441	7,106

[1]Includes explosives.
[2]Includes solids, liquids, and gases.
[3]Includes suffocation and hanging.

Source: *Statistical Abstract of the United States,* 1981. Table 121. Washington, D.C.: U.S. Government Printing Office, 1981.

or from inaction when it is known that inaction will have fatal consequences." From this definition, we could possibly classify the following persons as engaging in *suicidal* behavior:

1. A person who smokes cigarettes, knowing that the Surgeon General has determined that smoking is an important cause of lung cancer.
2. A race car driver who drives even though he or she knows that in any given race there is a good chance that someone will be killed.
3. A person who takes a bottle of sleeping pills, hoping to call attention to self—as one who has personal needs which are not being met.
4. A person who mistakenly takes an overdose of a prescribed drug.
5. A person who continues to eat fatty foods after having suffered a heart attack.
6. A person in the advanced stages of cancer who refuses chemotherapy or surgery.

Probably, most of us would not consider the above list of actions as suicidal behaviors. Rather, we would be concerned with the intent of the person in question—"Was this person deliberately trying to kill him or herself?" In classifying deaths as suicides, it is difficult to determine the motivations of a person who is no longer living.

There is a qualitative difference between a "suicide gesture" and a "successful suicide." Women are more likely to attempt suicide, yet men are more successful in their attempts. Suicide gestures are motivated by a need for aid and support from others, while successful suicides are acts of resignation. At this point, we have a problem of tautology—suicide gestures that mistakenly end in death are classified as intentional suicides, and unsuccessful suicide attempts are considered "suicide gestures."

In compiling statistics on suicides, we have another dilemma. There is a social stigma ascribed to suicidal deaths. Many surviving family members feel a special type of guilt when one of their loved ones commits suicide. They may feel that they could have done something to prevent the death, or that they caused the person to commit suicide. Consequently, many suicides are classified as accidents or "natural deaths" as a favor to family members or as a method of "providing a more positive view" of the deceased. Consequently, there are deaths resulting from intentional acts of self-destruction which are recorded as "natural deaths," and there are suicidal gestures which accidently end in death and are classified as suicide. The problems in defining and recording suicide are enormous!

A Few Words on Suicide:
Don't Try It!

A few months ago, I tried to commit suicide. The reason I did this was that I could no longer find happiness within me. I know that sorrow and pain are parts of life, but so are joy and laughter. I wasn't getting enough of the happiness that should be in everyone's life. I felt that, no matter how hard I tried to be a good, kind, thoughtful person, I failed. My best just wasn't good enough for people. This was making me miserable, and a miserable person is a burden to others. I didn't want to live the rest of my life feeling the way I was feeling, so I decided to end it all and find out what my Lord thought of me. It was wrong. I know that society thinks it's wrong. That's why, when I made the decision to commit suicide, I really wanted to die. Having to survive and face the music, so to speak, seemed worse than death itself.

I'm hoping now, though, that you won't make me feel as though I should be ashamed of myself. You see, I'm really glad to be alive, and I even believe I have a bright future. Someday I might even have children, and I don't want them to think badly of me. I know they won't if you don't.

I've learned to be stronger: I've done this by becoming a little more selfish. But that is necessary, or else you'll lose yourself to others and become their puppet. I've also learned to make demands of others. The big one I'm making now is that you just keep giving me affection.

Sincerely,
Don't Try Suicide

Source: *Boston Globe*, June 7, 1981, p. B13.

Coping with the American Way of Dying

Before concluding this chapter, we should mention that human beings do not respond to all deaths in the same manner. As will be discussed in Chapter 2, humans ascribe meanings to death and then respond to these meanings. The American way of dying places higher values on some causes of deaths and ascribes less status to other causes (see Chapter 2). Likewise, coping with the death of a loved one will be influenced by the cause of the death.

While there are some special problems associated with deaths caused by a chronic disease (e.g., heart disease, cancer, and diabetes), there are some real advantages also. The following is a partial list of the opportunities provided by a slow death caused by a chronic disease:

1. The dying person is given an opportunity to attend to unfinished business—make out a will, complete incompleted projects.
2. The dying person and his or her family can attempt to heal broken family relationships, they can say their final farewells, and they can all participate in constructing a meaningful and dignified death.
3. Funerals and other arrangements can be made with the consent and participation of the person who is dying.
4. Anticipatory grief on the part of the survivors and dying patient can take place.

Deaths due to acute diseases (e.g., pneumonia), accidents, and suicide also provide special problems and advantages to survivors. For all quick deaths there is the problem of being unprepared for the death. Some of the grieving that has preceded the death due to a chronic disease cannot be expressed in deaths of this type. Consequently, grief is usually more intense when the dying takes place in a short period of time. Survivors may also experience more intense guilt—"If only I had done something they wouldn't have died." Suicide creates special problems for survivors because they can become stigmatized by having a relative commit suicide—"They drove them to it." Finally, when people die without warning, survivors often are troubled because they did not have a chance to mend a broken relationship or say good-bye.

On the other hand, survivors of deaths due to acute diseases, accidents, and suicide are spared the following problems associated with chronic diseases:

1. Dying persons may not be willing to accept death, and when learning of their fates, may act in unacceptable ways.
2. Families may also be unwilling to accept the death of a loved one.
3. The dying process may be a long and painful process, not only for the dying patient but for the family as well.

4. The cost of dying from a chronic disease can be, and usually is, very expensive. The entire assets of a family can be wiped out by the medical bills of a chronically ill patient.

After 60 Years of Marriage, Couple Decides to Leave World Together

Julia Saunders, 81, had her hair done. Her husband, Cecil, 85, collected the mail one final time and paused to chat with a neighbor. Inside their mobile home, they carefully laid out a navy blazer and a powder-blue dress.

After lunch, the Saunderses drove to a rural corner of Lee County and parked. As cows grazed in the summer heat, the couple talked. Then Cecil Saunders shot his wife of 60 years in the heart and turned the gun on himself.

Near the clothes they had chosen to be buried in, the couple had left a note:

"Dear children, this we know will be a terrible shock and embarrassment. But as we see it, it is one solution to the problem of growing old. We greatly appreciate your willingness to try to take care of us.

"After being married for 60 years, it only makes sense for us to leave this world together because we loved each other so much."

On the floorboard of the car, Cecil and Julia Saunders had placed typewritten funeral instructions and the telephone numbers of their son and daughter.

Then they consummated their suicide pact, becoming two of the more than 4,000 elderly Americans authorities say will commit suicide this year.

"What struck all of us was how considerate, how thoughtful they were to all concerned about killing themselves," said Sheriff's Sgt. Richard Chard, who investigated the August 19 murder-suicide. "They didn't want to impose or be a bother to anyone. Not even in dying."

Julia's dimming eyesight, heart congestion and a stroke had driven Cecil to place his wife in a nursing home earlier this year. But she became hysterical over what she said was poor care there, and Cecil brought her home, said neighbors at the mobile home park where the couple had lived since 1974.

"You never saw him without her," said Vera Whittimore, 67. "If there ever was true love, they had it. I think they were just tired of living and couldn't wait for God to take them."

The Saunderses had hot dogs and beans for lunch, then drove their Caprice to pastureland 5½ miles from their mobile home, parking on the grassy shoulder.

As thunderstorms rumbled in the distance, they talked.

"I can picture in my mind them sitting there," Chard said. "Maybe they spoke about how things were when they were young. Then he leaned over and gave her a farewell kiss."

The bodies were found by workers from nearby Owl Creek Boat Works, who called the police.

In Philadelphia, a police officer stood by as the Saunderses' son, Robert, 57, was told of his parents' death. His parents wanted no tears shed over their decision to die. The note they left for Robert and his sister, Evelyn, 51, ended with a wish:

"Don't grieve because we had a very good life and saw our two children turn out to be such fine persons. Love, Mother and Father."

Source: *Minneapolis Star and Tribune,* October 4, 1983, p. 12A.

CONCLUSION

While the American way of dying is being discussed and researched more today than in previous decades, discussion often poses as many questions as answers. The following questions do not have simple and straightforward answers: "When does death take place?", "Who should determine the timing of a particular death?", "Who in society should be responsible for defining the meaning of life and death?", and "When is a death an accident and when is it a suicide?"

Americans have developed a paradoxical relationship with death—we know more about the causes and conditions surrounding death, but we have not equipped ourselves emotionally to cope with dying and death. The American way of dying is such that avoiding direct confrontation with dying and death is a real possibility for many persons. What we need is the ability to both understand and cope with dying and death. The purpose of this book is to provide an understanding of dying, death and bereavement that will assist individuals to better cope with their own deaths and with the deaths of others.

Summary

1. The American way of dying is typically confined to institutional settings and removed from usual patterns of social interaction.
2. American society has done little to formally socialize its members to deal with dying and death on the personal and emotional levels.

3. The "thanatology movement" was a concerted effort in the 1970s to bring about an open discussion and awareness of behaviors and emotions related to dying, death, and bereavement.

4. The issue of when death occurs is a difficult one to resolve because consensus does not exist in America regarding the meaning of life and death.

5. The American way of dying has changed considerably in the last eighty years. Relative to earlier times, Americans are less likely to die of acute diseases. Currently more than 75 percent of the deaths that take place in America can be attributed to the chronic diseases.

6. Life expectancy has increased twenty-four years since 1920. With the increase in life expectancy, there have been many effects upon Americans' understanding and ability to cope with dying and death.

7. Difficulties exist in being able to determine when a death is a suicide. These difficulties are a function of the following problems: families are stigmatized when one of their members commits suicide; it is difficult to determine the motivations of a person who is no longer living; and it is impossible to distinguish between a successful suicide and an unsuccessful suicide gesture.

8. The manner in which an individual dies will influence the way in which his or her survivors cope with the death. Chronic and acute diseases each have advantages and disadvantages for the coping abilities of dying patients and their families.

APPLICATION: VERIFYING THE FACTS

At the end of each of the chapters in this book we have provided an application section. These applications will vary in their format and content, but each has the objective of giving practical information that can be applied to the material of the respective chapter.

In this first chapter we have discussed life expectancy, using as our source of information data collected by the Bureau of Vital Statistics on all of the fifty states. To check the validity of our generalizations as they apply to your city of residence, you can fill out the following table from information gathered in a local cemetery.

You and/or a group of fellow students can go to a cemetery and survey different areas within the cemetery. Write down the age at death and sex (M or F) for all of the grave markers you survey. You will record the information under the year the person died. The two examples that have been recorded in the chart are of a woman of sixty-seven who died in 1947, and of a boy of fourteen who died in 1922. (The ideas for this application were adapted from Cemetery Data Collection Record in *Perspectives on Death: Student Activity Book* by David W. Berg and George G. Daugherty, 1972.)

				YEAR OF DEATH				
1900– 1910	1911– 1920	1921– 1930	1931– 1940	1941– 1950	1951– 1960	1961– 1970	1971– 1980	1981– Present
		14 M		67 F				

If you are unable to collect information in a local cemetery, go to your school library and record the same information from the obituaries of a local newspaper for the years 1900 and 1978. After you have pooled your data with that collected by others, answer the following questions:

1. What was the average age at death for each of the nine time periods?
2. On the average did women live longer than men? Did these differences,

with respect to gender, hold for each of the nine time periods or just for some?

3. Were there any time periods in which an exceptionally large number of people died? What explanations can you give for these deaths?
4. Did you notice any changes in infant mortality over the nine time periods?
5. How does your information compare with that presented in this chapter? What explanations can you give for any differences discovered between the data you collected on the local level and that collected by the Bureau of Vital Statistics?

Discussion Questions

1. What factors have contributed to the American avoidance of death and dying?
2. Why did death "come out of the closet" in the 1970's? What events related to the "thanatology movement" helped change the American awareness of dying and death?
3. What is the present American way of dying? How has it changed in the last century?
4. How has the definition of death changed in the last thirty years? What complications has this created for the American way of dying?
5. What are the differences between successful suicides and unsuccessful suicide gestures? What criteria would you use to classify a death as a suicide? Why is it necessary to identify suicidal deaths?
6. Compare and contrast the relative advantages and disadvantages of dying from acute and chronic diseases. What effects do each of these causes have on the abilities of families to cope with the death of a family member?

Glossary

ACUTE ILLNESS: A communicable disease caused by a number of microorganisms including viruses, fungi, and bacteria. Acute illnesses last for a relatively short period of time and either result in a cure or death. Examples of acute illnesses include the following: small pox, malaria, cholera, influenza, and pneumonia.

CHRONIC ILLNESS: A noncommunicable self-limiting disease from which the individual rarely recovers, even through the symptoms of the disease can often be alleviated. Chronic illnesses usually result in deterioration of organs and tissues, making the individual vulnerable to other diseases, often leading to serious impairment and even death. Examples of chronic illnesses include the following: cancer, heart disease, arthritis, emphysema, and asthma.

SEX RATIO: The number of males per 100 females.

SOCIALIZATION: The social process by which individuals are integrated into a social group by learning its values, goals, norms, and roles. This is a lifelong process that is never completed.

SUICIDE: A deliberate act of self-destruction or intentional inaction when it is
  known that inaction will lead to death.
SUICIDE GESTURE: A life-threatening action that is taken to force others to inter-
  vene and recognize the individual's loneliness, alienation, anger, or despair.
THANATOLOGY: The interdisciplinary study of death-related behavior including
  actions and emotions concerned with dying, death, and bereavement.

References

Abstract of the Twelfth Census of the United States: 1900. 1981. Table 93. Washington,
  D.C.: U. S. Government Printing Office.
Backer, Barbara A., Natalie Hannon, Noreen A. Russell. 1982. *Death and Dying:
  Individuals and Institutions.* New York: Wiley.
Beecher, Henry K. 1968. "A Definition of Irreversible Coma." *Journal of the American
  Medical Association,* 205 (August 5): 85–88.
Dumont, Richard G., and Dennis C. Foss. 1972. *The American View of Death: Accept-
  ance or Denial?* Cambridge, Mass.: Schenkman.
Kass, L. R. 1971. "Death as an Event: A Commentary on Robert Morison." *Science*
  173: 698–702.
Kavanaugh, Robert E. 1972. *Facing Death.* Baltimore: Penguin Books.
Lerner, Monroe. 1970. "When, Why, and Where People Die," in *The Dying Patient.*
  ed. by O. Brim et al. New York: Russell Sage Foundation.
Montagu, Ashley. 1968. *The Natural Superiority of Women,* Rev. Ed. New York: Col-
  lier Books.
Ramsey, Paul. 1970. *The Patient as Person: Explorations in Medical Ethics.* New Haven:
  Yale University Press.
Statistical Abstracts of the United States: 1981. 1981, Table 122. Washington, D.C.: U.S.
  Government Printing Office.
Stockwell, Edward G. 1976. *The Methods and Materials of Demography,* Condensed
  Edition. New York: Academic Press.
Theodorson, George A., and Achilles G. Theodorson. 1969. *Modern Dictionary of
  Sociology.* New York: Thomas Y. Crowell Company.
Uniform Crime Report, 1981. 1981. Washington, D.C.: U. S. Department of Justice.
United Nations. 1953. *Principles for a Vital Statistics System,* Statistical Papers, Series
  M, No. 19 (August): 6.

Suggested Readings

Charmaz, Kathy. 1980. *The Social Reality of Death.* Reading, Mass.: Addison-Wesley.
  Provides an excellent discussion of the problems of identifying suicide. Also describes theoretical and clinical perspectives on suicide and suggests that there is a
  need to understand the perspective of the person who has committed the act.
Dumont, Richard G., and Dennis C. Foss. 1972. *The American View of Death: Acceptance or Denial?* Cambridge, Mass.: Schenkman.
  Discusses American attitudes and experience related to the fear of death. Provides an analysis and comparison of the attitudes of those who accept the reality
  of their own deaths and those who deny that reality. Suggests that Americans
  must both accept and deny death simultaneously.

Kubler-Ross, Elisabeth. 1969. *On Death and Dying.* New York: Macmillan.
  Provides an understanding of the feelings and experiences of dying patients. More than any other books, this book created a national interest and concern for needs of the dying patient and greatly influenced the thanatology movement.
Kavanaugh, Robert E. 1972. *Facing Death.* Baltimore: Penguin Books.
  An important early book in the thanatology movement which suggests that a growing awareness of death can contribute to a more meaningful and peaceful life.
Stannard, David E., ed. 1974. *Death in America.* Philadelphia: University of Pennsylvania Press.
  This anthology is concerned not merely with death as individual crisis and fate but also with attitudes toward death as a dimension of American Culture.

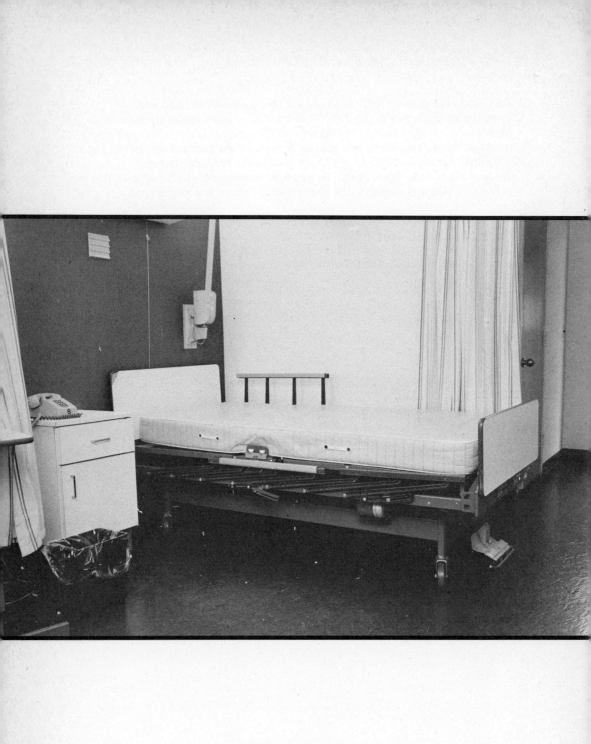

Chapter 2

THE SOCIAL MEANING OF DYING AND DEATH

The symbols of death say what life is and those of life define what death must be. The meanings of man's fate are forever what he makes them.

W. Lloyd Warner, The Living and the Dead

THIS CHAPTER FOCUSES attention upon the basic theme of the book—meaning. Meaning is interpreted as the most important component of every aspect of dying and death considered in this text. If dying is perceived to be primarily a biological process, then classifying or locating the meaning of death on the edge of the biological "core" would seem to be appropriate. Most people would likely agree with the "biology-is-primary, meaning-is-secondary" interpretation. We do not.

Dying, in fact, is much more than a biological process. No living biological human body exists in a vacuum or outside a socio-symboled context. Biological bodies are not isolated things. When a person dies, many things other than internal biological changes take place.

In that every act of dying influences others, it is social or shared. The dying occurs in a larger arena or situation to which meanings are ascribed. Physically, everyone dies in some place and that place is given a meaning by those involved. Consequently, every act of dying has three interconnected characteristics—it is *shared, symboled and situated.*

This chapter counters the widespread tendency to interpret dying as primarily a biological process—something the body does to the person. We are concerned with what people do about these processes. Attention is called to the fact that biologists and medical personnel (or anyone else, including social scientists) respond to the meaning of the biology rather than to the biology per se. Physicians' decisions are made on the basis of what the biological condition means to the physician. Making a medical diagnosis is the process by which the physician decides the meaning of the biological factors to which he or she is attending. The diagnosis is the process of transposing biological factors into meaning factors. Whatever is realized is real to the physician, and the consequences of such reality are equally real. Thus, a self-fulfilling prophecy exists.

A reoccurring dramatic illustration of the fact that the behavior of the physician and others stems from the meaning rather than from the biology per se can be seen when the news media periodically report that a "corpse" in the morgue has "come back to life" after wrongly being pronounced dead by the "expert." The fact that the physician believes a body is dead does not guarantee that it is. Behavior follows from the meaning, not from the biological factors per se—a *living* body was sent to the morgue.

Blink Saves "Dead" Man from Grave

MILWAUKEE, Wis. (AP)—S. William Winogrond, a heart attack victim who was certified dead and scheduled for surgery to remove some of his organs, remained in critical but stable condition today.

Winogrond, 46, a University of Wisconsin-Milwaukee administrator, was declared clinically dead by doctors after a massive heart attack earlier this week.

His doctors told doctors at Columbia Hospital to remove his eyes and kidneys for possible donations and then remove the mechanical life support systems which were keeping his heart beating.

However, just as doctors were about to begin surgery to remove the organs—nearly 12 hours after the heart attack—Winogrond blinked his eyes and doctors rushed him back in the intensive care ward.

Hospital officials said his condition has been steadily but slowly improving.

Death-related meaning has experienced extensive change since the early 1970's. With reference to past knowledge about death, it is accurate to say that much of what was known was not true or does not harmonize with contemporary knowledge. Ignorance causes problems. Greater problems, however, stem from what people "know" is not so. Yet the sociological truism made popular by W.I. Thomas applies—whatever one believes to be true is real in its decision-making consequences.

THE NATURE OF MEANING

To understand the role of meaning in death-related behavior, it is necessary to understand the influence of meaning in all human behavior and the critical involvement of symbols in all meaning. Accordingly, we will briefly consider the nature of meaning symbols.

We use words to tell ourselves and each other what something means. This book consists of words about dying and death. Words consist of configurations of symbols. The words or symbols are not somehow embedded in the things named. We do not somehow extract words or meaning from the things we see as meaningful. Rather we create symbols or words to represent the things named.

The fact that all symbols are empirical means that they can potentially be shared by more than one person. For example, the meaning of a flower can be shared by many—the flower per se cannot. Meaning is created from symbols that are socially constructed, transmitted, and used.

Some symbols have empirical referents. These are the symbols (especially names or labels) that people use to identify, talk, or think about the aspects of the empirical world. Some symbols, however, do not refer to anything empirical. These types of symbols would include beauty, humor, indignity, and evil. Such nonempirically referential words have an exceptionally meaningful impact upon behavior because they are involved in the human process of making choices. To engage in social behavior, we employ both types of symbols or meanings.

Thus, we have attempted to recognize distinct differences between the empirical world and the meaning world. We have attempted to emancipate the words (symbols or meaning) from the world. Most people do just the reverse in their conceptualizing and thinking. They enslave the words by joining, locking, or laminating them to the empirical world so strongly that their separate identity is lost or hardly recognized.

Most discussions of words (symbols or meaning) involve people who think primarily in terms of "the world." They have an empirical-world bias, even though they are talking to each other about things that are not physically present and about things that have no empirical existence. They effectively execute a "symbol by-pass."

Creating and Changing Meaning

Biological bodies are created, born, live, and die. Bodies of meaning are also created, live, and die. Biological continuity occurs through a process of biological transmission or transference. Meaning (culture) continuity occurs through a process of social-symboled transmission. The socialization process is the process by which biological bodies are transformed into social beings. In the socialization process we teach our children how to behave in what our society considers to be a human way.

Creation of new meaning is always possible. Death-related meaning is no different from any other type of meaning. It is important to remember that this meaning is also created by humans, and is not discovered in "the world." All meanings, including death-related meaning, are subject to change. The history of humans is a history of meaning change. However, well established meaning is difficult to change. Meaning is frequently defined as sacred and, therefore, more likely to be protected and perpetuated than changed. Crises or traumatic conditions may be necessary for the acceptance of change in death-related meaning.

As noted in Chapter 10, many of the contemporary death-related meanings, including the rituals involved in adjustment, were created by our ancestors who experienced dying in quite different social situations and circumstances than those found in contemporary society. Furthermore, considering the dramatic changes in health, longevity, and health-care, it would not be inaccurate to say that our ancestors experienced death in somewhat different biological bodies. Therefore it is not surprising that discontinuities have developed in American death-related meanings and experiences.

Any aspect of death-related behavior can be changed if there is enough societal (or sub-societal) support. One person can change death-related meaning for him or herself, but it is difficult to maintain and sustain the new "vision" if significant others do not support, legitimate, or validate this meaning system.

As in the waves caused by dropping a stone into the lake, changes in death-related meaning will inevitably have consequences that penetrate or move into other areas of living. Change in the "sacred" components of dying and death may come in through the back door, so to speak. Cremation may gain increased acceptance, not as a direct result of changes in religion, but as a result of the availability of space for earth burials. Changes in life-prolonging, or death-prolonging procedures may result more from availability of technological devices than from changes in religion or mores.

MEANING AND DEATH-RELATED BEHAVIOR

The foundation of symbolic interaction theory is that symbols (meaning) are a basic component of human behavior. The symbolic interactionist perspective is summarized in what has been called the ISAS paradigm statement—*Individual-level behavior* is in response to *Symbols*, relative to the *Audience* and to the *Situation*. "ISAS" stands for the four basic components (See Vernon and Cardwell, 1981). Death-related behavior of the one dying, and of those who care about that person, is in response to meaning, relative to the audience and to the situation. Death-related behavior is shared, symboled (given meaning), and situated. It is socially created and not biologically predetermined.

Symbols

Interaction is a dynamic, flexible, and socially created phenomenon. Meaning is socially created and socially perpetuated. Meaning is preserved in symbols or words. However, preserved words have to be rediscovered and reinterpreted if they are to be continually used in human interaction. Generation after generation repeats the process with a somewhat different content—no book means the same to every reader. Death-related behavior and meanings are dynamic phenomena.

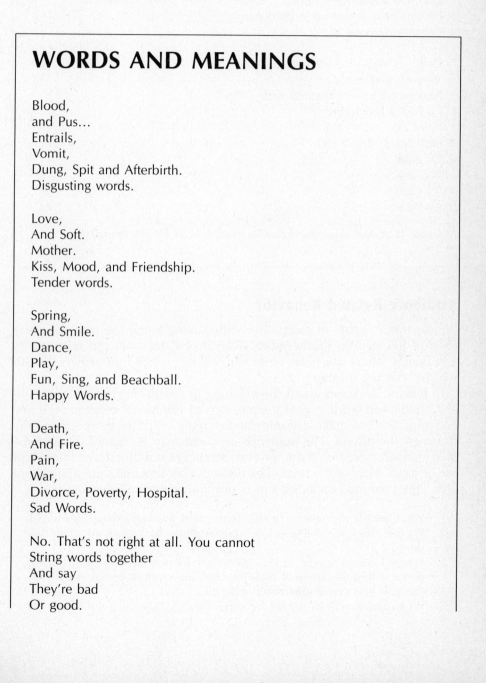

WORDS AND MEANINGS

Blood,
and Pus...
Entrails,
Vomit,
Dung, Spit and Afterbirth.
Disgusting words.

Love,
And Soft.
Mother.
Kiss, Mood, and Friendship.
Tender words.

Spring,
And Smile.
Dance,
Play,
Fun, Sing, and Beachball.
Happy Words.

Death,
And Fire.
Pain,
War,
Divorce, Poverty, Hospital.
Sad Words.

No. That's not right at all. You cannot
String words together
And say
They're bad
Or good.

Where are the verbs?
Who are we talking about?
What are the circumstances?

Vomit is beautiful to a mother whose child
Had just swallowed a pin.
Love is pain if you are a third party,
Outside, looking in.

Death is very nice for someone very old,
Very ill, and ready.
And surely you've danced with a clod.
Or had a sad spring.

No, Words aren't sad
Or glad.
You are.
Or I am.
Or he is.

Source: W. A. Armbruster, *Bag of Noodles* (St. Louis: Concordia Publishing House, 1972), p. 8.

Audience-Related Behavior

We constantly relate to each other with talking being the most common form of interaction. Furthermore, even if one does not put meaning in words that others can hear, he or she still has to tell him or herself with words what the meaning is.

In making decisions about the meaning of death, one can in effect consult established words, other people, self, or situational conditions. If one is dying, one can make decisions about dying behavior by observing the treatment by others. The audience involved may be family, physicians, clergypersons, nurses, peers, or even strangers walking down the hall of the hospital. How one is treated by these people tells one something about self. This treatment includes, but is not limited to the following:

1. What people are willing to talk about with me—and what they avoid.
2. Whether they are willing to touch me, and how they touch me when they do.
3. Where I am, or maybe where others have located me—hospital, nursing home, intensive care unit, isolation unit, my room at home.
4. Tangible and verbal gifts others give me.
5. What people will let me do, or expect me to do, or will not let me do.

6. The tone of voice people use when they talk to me.
7. Frequency and length of visits from others.
8. Excuses these people make for not visiting.
9. The reactions of others to my prognosis.

Dying with dignity or self respect does not always happen. Self meaning can be created and sustained with the help of others. Dying as an unloved person makes the dying an extremely difficult experience.

How you treat one also influences how he or she treats you. If one thinks you are "leveling" with him or her, he or she will treat you one way. If one thinks you want to engage in a game of "let's pretend" one may be willing to play, as a favor to you. In death-related behavior, as in all behavior, one watches others for cues in deciding how to act.

The audience to which the dying person relates may also be supernatural. Symbol users are not restricted to the natural-empirical world. Neither are they restricted to the world of the living. If a person realizes that those who have died have an existence in another realm, or that there is a life after death, this belief is real to that person and has consequences for his or her behavior.

The person who is approaching death may involve him- or herself in a gradual replacement of a living audience with a supernatural, or other-world audience. As we have demonstrated, the dying person relates to many audiences.

The Situation

Where a person dies is also given meaning. As the patient comes to grips with the terminal condition, the manner in which he or she defines the situation (and responds to it) will have a tremendous impact upon the experiences in the dying process. Dying in a nursing home or hospital is different from dying in one's home, in one's bed, surrounded by feelings of belonging and a loving family. If the patient views the institutional death setting as a supportive environment, it may aid the patient's coping behavior. On the other hand, if the patient feels all alone, and if he or she has defined the place of dying as a foreign environment, adjustment will not be facilitated (Leming et al., 1977).

Like other meanings, the definition of the situation is an attempt by the individual to bring meaning to the world. Since the situational definition always involves selective perception, the terminal patient will assign meaning to the environment and will respond to this symbolic reality. The thing to which the patient responds does not have existence independent of his or her definition. Therefore, each terminal patient will interpret the dying environment differently. This accounts for the different experiences of dying patients (Leming et al., 1977). This point will be elaborated upon further in the next chapter.

Conflicting Death-Related Meanings

Some Believe:

They are dying when they are not.
They are not dying when they are.

They should refuse to let some people die who want to die.
They, or maybe the state, should kill some people who want to live.

It would be good for a specific person to die.
It would be wrong for that specific person to die.

Dying is caused by the moral condition of the person dying.
Dying has nothing to do with the moral condition of a person.

God causes particular deaths.
God created universal death (thus everyone dies at some time) but does
    not influence particular deaths.

Wishing another person to die caused that death.
Wishing it were so cannot make it so.

Death is terminal—there is nothing beyond death.
Death is transition—it involves movement from one to another type of
    existence.

There is nothing for the person beyond death.
Death is transition—it involves movement to another type of existence.

An individual's dying time is predestined—a person dies when his or her
    time is up.
An individual's dying time is emergent—a person's time is up when
    death occurs.

Every person should fight to stay alive.
You should not fight that which is inevitable.

Dying is the worst thing that can happen to a person.
Certain types of living, such as living in an incapacitated and dependent
    state are worse than dying.

Keeping the biological body alive is the greatest value.
Humans in fact have a God-given instinct for such preservation.
The well-being of the person is of greater value than just keeping the body alive.

Quantity of biological life is an overriding value.
Quality of life is an overriding value.

Nothing is of greater value than preserving one's life.
Everyone has something for which they would give their life.

They can help the dying most by telling them the "real" meaning of death—"Let me tell you what dying should mean to you."
They can help the dying most by helping them decide what dying means to them—"Let me help you live fully while you are dying."

Dying is inherently fearful.
Dying can be welcomed and may be beautiful.

If death could be eliminated from our society, it would be wonderful—a step toward the creation of heaven on earth.
If death could be, (and were) eliminated from our society it would be awful—a step toward the creation of a hell on earth.

A genuine concern with the dying person qualifies one as an effective care-giver.
Good intentions alone do not automatically qualify one as an effective care-giver.

Death would be welcomed—they want to die.
Death would be undesirable—they do not want to die.

THE SOCIAL MEANING OF DEATH

Dying biologically is one of the most individual things that can happen to the body. What happens takes place exclusively within the skin of the one person. However, with reference to the *meaning* of dying, the dying process is one of the most social experiences one can have.

A popular cliche suggests that "one does not appreciate the water till the well runs dry." The taken-for-granted social meaning of life loses some of its "just accepted" or "just there" aspects in a life-time review (for a discussion of the concept of life review see Lindemann, 1979). It may well be that as biological death approaches, the person becomes acutely aware of the social nature of being human. This awareness refers not only to the terminal period, but also the entire lifetime preceding it. This review of prior events may highlight the social aspects of life previously ignored or taken for granted.

The sociological perspective emphasizes the social-symbolic nature of human interaction. The key or critical factor that unites biological entities into a social group or multiperson entity is shared meaning. Many of the goals one person wants to achieve, and many of the experiences a person wants to have, require shared and coordinated meanings and situations. The death of one person has extensive social consequences.

Who or What Dies? One Person and Multiperson Consequences

A specific death has meaning wherever the deceased had meaningful relationships. With a death in a husband-wife dyad, half of that entity dies. If the couple has two children, one fourth of the family dies. One 30,000th of the community dies, and one two hundred fifty-millionth of a nation dies. Each type of death has distinctive meanings.

The Free Fall

When I die, my husband loses his wife, his lover, his confidante. My children lose their mother. Each friend loses me as a friend. But I lose all human relationships. That's the meaning of the free fall. That's the meaning of being alone.

Source: JoAnn Kelley Smith (a dying person), *Free Fall* (Valley Forge, Pa.: Judson Press, 1975), p. 36.

The elimination or departure of a person from the ranks of "the living" leaves a hole or vacuum in the midst of the living. Certain meaning is lost, while new meaning is added. After the person's death, behavior that previously involved him or her is literally no longer possible—it also died or ceased to exist. Established interaction or behavior systems are disrupted, and such disruption calls for attention. Potential social disruption is reduced by the use of established funeral rituals—so long as the rituals are acceptable to those involved.

The living are not only concerned with the death of a person, but also with what happens to the living as a result of that death. What happens to survivors when their loved ones die? The biological person may be gone, but the meaning remains just as long as the living grant the "symboled immortality" or "meaning immortality" to the deceased (Lifton and Olson, 1974).

The granting or creating of such immortality is one of the things symbol-using beings can do. In fact, a given person may even take on more significance after dying than was granted by the living before the death. For the bereaved, changing the meaning of lost relationships is essential and may be done with varying degrees of ease, depending upon the nature of the relationship.

If we answer the "who question" by identifying the various roles or positions held by one person, our answer is usually that many roles or positions are vacated. Therefore, "many persons" or role occupants die in a single death.

One biological body is what dies but ownership of that body is difficult to determine. "Who owns my body?" is a question often posed by persons who are dying. Related to the basic ownership question is "Who is qualified to make decisions about *my* body?" If I am the one who is dying, what right do any others have to tell me what to do with my body? Since humans are social animals, ownership is a creation of symbol-using persons. Joint ownership patterns are created and exist for most persons. Therefore, body ownership might be considered shared and the decisions related to it would be joint decisions.

SOCIETAL MEANING

An individual has a personal biography that applies only to this one person. It is that person's personal history. However, the events and behavior recorded in that biography are generally social experiences. The biography recounts the manner in which the person has related to, or has been involved with, others. The total configuration is uniquely that person's, yet many people are also involved in creating the biography.

A group—such as a family, a church, or a society—also has a unique biography. However, the group's biography is also the "property" of each of its members. The biography of my family is also my biography—my family biography. Evaluations made of the family—past, present, or future—are evaluations that are significant to its members, because all group members share that biography.

The death of one member of a group, and the meanings related to it, become a part of that group's biography. In sharing the group's name, we also share the group's consequences. The meaning of my death becomes an important part of the meaning of my group. Therefore, the meanings ascribed to death have both individual and group influences.

Society's Heroes

The death of an individual brings about a change in influence that person has over the members of their group or society. Heroes are more likely to come from the ranks of the dead rather than the living.

Hero meaning is a symboled-meaning component. One cannot become a hero by oneself. The society bestows the "rank" of hero only upon certain of its members. This is but one type of symboled immortality. A death may be part of the process by which heroes are born. When something dies, something else is born or created. The death of a Jesus Christ has had consequences which have expanded in significance over the years. It is likely that Christ's death has had greater impact upon humanity than his life. The Roman Catholic Church only grants sainthood to persons who have been dead for many years. Conversely, a government may grant pardons to convicted persons who died many years ago. Meaning is a flexible, yet powerful thing.

A number of interesting speculative questions arise. If there is an afterlife (in which those who are dead have some type of post-earth living), and all of the heroes will become our contemporaries (assuming we make it, too), what would this do to their hero status? In such a situation, would the hero category be retained? Would such a person have to meet new hero qualifications? Would everyone in that "kingdom" be heroes? What would a society of heroes be like? Would the hero category be meaningful?

Relative Death Meanings in Society

One of the most feared, distressful, and anxiety-producing deaths is a death that is perceived as being relatively meaningless. A lifetime is spent searching for and creating meaning. The search for meaning is a task that all people share. Furthermore, significant others are involved in the process attempted by individuals in creating meaning for themselves. In many respects, the meaning created turns out to be meaning for the group or society.

As the dying of martyrs dramatically illustrates, a death may be willingly entered into if it is meaningful. Given the right configuration of ISAS components, NOT to die would be more difficult. For example, dying may be preferable to defining oneself, and being defined by others, as being a coward or a traitor.

Dying is acceptable if it furthers "the cause." People may, in fact, literally work themselves to death in order to obtain a promotion, an artistic achievement, or public recognition. Whatever the specific content, the key factor of concern is the meaning involved. If the meaning is right, dying may be evaluated as a worthwhile thing.

Within a given society there are high-status types of death, as well as low-status types. Giving one's life in defense of family or country is generally conceived as being in the high-status category. In times past, dying in childbirth was considered to be a high-status death for females.

In summary, it is society's contextualized meaning of death that is important. It is the meanings of self, others, and situation that enable individuals and groups to make sense of dying and death.

LIVING WHILE DYING

Dying is a living process. It is a living person who dies. The processes of living are not suspended in the terminal stage of living. The same model that helps us understand behavior in general can be used to understand dying behavior.

Dying may be (and frequently is) a difficult process, but it is not necessarily the most difficult experience in life. There is certainly nothing inherent in the process of dying that automatically makes it the top-level problem. It may, depending upon the configuration of ISAS elements involved, be just the reverse—a welcome change or an experience for which one expectantly waits. Furthermore, some efforts to relate to persons who are dying seem to operate on the premise that one hour, one day, or one week of living, while in a dying condition, is somehow of more worth than such time periods for those who are not "actively" dying. It may, however, be just the reverse.

While it is often assumed that meaning of death and dying is inherent, empirical research has found no one meaning for dying that is universal. It seems apparent that it is the unique configuration of symbols, people (the audience), and situations that determine the meaning of dying.

THE MEANING OF NOT DYING

One of the fascinating things humans can do is take negatives into account. We can give meaning to what does not exist, does not happen, or maybe never could happen. We can do this largely because symbols allow us to anticipate non-existent futures. From the symbols we can create a model of a future that could exist, and then compare our present situation with this potential future. Any differences discovered in this comparison become that which we are *not experiencing now*. An example of the experience of the "non-existent" is the use of the concept zero in our number system. Zero is an empirical nothing, but a symboled something.

In the area of dying and death, the most salient illustration of a meaningful negative is an unactualized expected death. The fact that a person does not die can be given significance. The actuality of not dying is particularly meaningful when it is related to an expectation of dying. In a hypothetical case, the mother in the hospital has been told that she has a limited time to live. The husband and family members have also been told of this time table. The family can engage in anticipatory grieving and may essentially complete some of the grieving process before the death occurs. Such anticipatory behavior is a frequent human experience in other areas of life. To have meaningfully anticipated a death facilitates adjustment to that death. In their thinking, the mother is "as good as dead." They have already prepared themselves for the death and engaged in anticipatory behavior concerning their own futures without the mother. (For a further discussion of anticipatory bereavement see Lindemann, 1944.)

The miraculous recovery and the return home have been called the "resurrection syndrome." Adjustment to such a nondeath may be very difficult. In some cases it is so difficult that families are broken as a result of the multifaceted problems engendered or activated by the "resurrection."

Another dramatic—and at times traumatic—"nondeath" is the case where two friends are involved in an accident or in combat experience. One is killed, the other is not. The family of the one not killed may interpret this fact, frequently in public, from a moral causative perspective.Their son was saved from "certain death" (which obviously was not "certain") because he was too good to die, or was morally worthy to live. God saved him because God loved him so much. He was saved because the parents had prayed for his well-being, and God was answering their prayers.

For the family of the one who was killed, however, the consequences of accepting such an interpretation and generalizing it to the death of their own son may be traumatic. By the same logic, their son was killed or not saved because he was not good enough to live. He was morally deficient. God did not save him because God did not love him that much, or he was not worthy of God's saving action.

Another nondeath interpretation occurs when a child is told "Mommy went to be with God because she was so good." The child's process of creating meaning may lead to the conclusion "I guess I'm not very good" or "Why should I be good?" With such an interpretation of the mother's death the child may also conclude, "If that is the way God behaves, I'm not sure I can love God." If such an interpretation is not shared with others, living with it can be a source of many problems for the child.

This obviously was the concern of the little girl who wrote the following letter to God (Marshall and Hemple, 1967):

Dear God,

Do good people have to die young? I heard my mommy say that. I am not always good.

Yours truly,
Barbara

Not dying has no inherent meaning. However, it can be given meaning of various types. Most people are glad they are not dying. However, not dying may be a problem for people who wish to die. Nursing-home workers frequently encounter such persons. However, to wish for death is largely frowned upon in our society. We desire to live forever, unlike many African groups who know when it is right to die. While the Swedish government supports a program to discuss suicide as a possible alternative to living, such a program is not likely to be accepted in the United States in the near future. For nursing home residents who desire death, living is a difficult circumstance with which to cope.

CONCLUSION

Cultural anthropology emphasizes the importance of symbols in distinguishing humans from the rest of the animal kingdom. Stories (Singh and Zingg, 1942) of feral children (raised in isolation from other human beings), Kingsley Davis' account (1947) of Anna and Isabelle, and the remarkable autobiography of Helen Keller illustrate the importance and significance of symbols. Without the ability to assign meaning, we are no different from other animals.

Without the ability to assign meaning to death, would death then have any significance for us? In general, it is agreed that animals other than humans do not have a concept of death. The absence of such a concept is contributed to the inability to use oral symbols (words). Some linguists would go so far as to say "in the word was the beginning." It is through words (meanings or symbols) that one's perception is largely shaped. Words are learned through interaction with others. Our perception of the color spectrum is slanted according to the number of colors described in our language. To have only three colors in one's language would give one a different view from a person whose language had a color spectrum of six. Similarly, time perceptions will vary if one has no past or future tenses in the language. Thus, words (meanings or symbols) are crucial in determining how one perceives color, time, death, or whatever.

The idea of societal meaning and society's heroes is functional to a social system as a form of social control. By making heroes out of the deceased (highlighting their "good qualities" and emulating their behavior), we are helping to establish order—social control—by affective reinforcement. We are saying: Let's follow the behavior exemplified by this deceased hero. Thus through death, something else is born—a role model whose "good" is accentuated.

Summary

1. The goal of this chapter is to emphasize the extensive involvement of meaning in what many consider to be primarily a biological process— i.e., dying.
2. Meaning consists of symbols that are socially created and socially used. Some symbols refer to something else or have an empirical referent. Some do not. The major function of both types of symbols is to permit humans to relate to each other and thus create shared behavior and meaning.
3. Death-related meaning permits sharing death-related behavior. The death-related behavior of the one dying, and those who are significant to that person, is in response to meaning, relative to the audience and to the situation. It is a phenomenon that is socially created, not biologically predetermined.
4. Since most people participate in various social groups, they are involved in many different interaction patterns. Consequently, even though it is but one biological body that dies, many "role holes" or vacancies are left with the death of a single individual. Bodies die, but so do social relationships and social networks.
5. Death-meaning includes evaluations of whatever those involved decide to evaluate. Evaluators may include values believed to be absolute, abstract, and situational. Defining values such as "living is always preferable to dying," as abstract rather than absolute helps explain the relativity of situational values and likely leads to fewer adjustment problems when confronting dying.
6. Dying is a social process. The person who is dying is living and is involved in living experiences with others.
7. Changing death meanings are part of the general cultural changes taking place in contemporary society. Much of this change is centered around a discounting of biological influences upon social behavior.

APPLICATION:
WHAT CAREGIVERS SHOULD NOT ASSUME ABOUT THE DYING

For the terminally ill person, the significant meaning that is taken into account in decision-making concerning self and others is the meaning she or he realizes. It is suggested that priority attention be given to meaning in any confrontation with death. Likewise the caregiver's behavior is influenced by the meaning the caregiver realizes. The same is also true of all people who are in social situations where dying and death occur.

Working from this perspective, it may be helpful to identify some frequently accepted assumptions that need to be questioned. It is accordingly suggested that those working with the dying and the bereaved should *not* assume that:

1. Those with whom you work necessarily share your meaning of death.
2. Meanings that were helpful to earlier generations are equally functional today.
3. Meaning remains constant and does not change.
4. Dying biologically is all that is happening.
5. Knowing about the biological aspects of dying will in and of itself provide knowledge about how humans expect to behave in death-related situations.
6. Pretension or deception, which you believe will help you cope with those who are dying, will help those with whom you are working.
7. The terminal patient is the only person who has death adjustment problems.
8. Persons facing bereavement have to wait until the death actually occurs before they can start working on their bereavement—meaning adjustment.
9. The person who is dying has somehow stopped meaningful living during the terminal period.
10. A death that is defined as meaningless, from the perspective of the person dying, cannot be given meaning in the last stages.
11. The terminal period without an extended future is necessarily one of no hope.
12. Talking is the only way for the caregiver to communicate "I care."

Discussion Questions

1. Discuss the differences between biological and symbolic death.
2. What arguments are offered in rejection of the premise: In death, biology is primary, meaning is peripheral? Evaluate and discuss.
3. It is stated that each act of dying has three interconnected characteristics: shared, symboled, and situated. How does this relate to his statement that more dies than a biological body?
4. Answer the question "Who or what dies?"
5. Discuss the implications of the following quote: "Even though it is but one biological body which dies, many 'role holes' or vacancies are left with the death of that one person."
6. In making decisions about death meaning, how does the treatment of the dying patient affect that patient's understanding of death and his or her role in the dying process?

7. As one faces imminent death, one becomes increasingly aware of the social nature of life. This change in awareness can lead to a life review where the individual realizes how extensively he or she lives with, through, and for others. Speculate as to why this change in perspective takes place.
8. Discuss the implications of the following quote: "I die for whatever it was for which I lived."
9. What are some of the meanings of "Not Dying?"

Glossary

ANTICIPATORY GRIEF: Grieving prior to the death of a significant other.

DYAD: Two units regarded as a pair (e.g., a husband and wife).

ISAS: A shorthand presentation of the paradigm statement: Behavior of the Individual is in response to Symbols, relative to the Audience and relative to the Situation.

MORES: Ways of society felt to be for the good of society. "Must" behaviors which have stronger sanctions than a folkway (e.g., eating three meals per day) but not as severe as a law.

SELF-FULFILLING PROPHECY: When a situation is defined as real, it becomes real in its consequences when individuals act to make it so.

SIGNIFICANT OTHER: A person to whom special significance is given in the process of reaching decisions.

SYMBOL: Anything to which socially created meaning is given.

References

Davis, Kingsley. 1947. "Final Note on a Case of Extreme Isolation." *American Journal of Sociology*, Vol. 52: 432–437.

Leming, Michael R., Glenn M. Vernon, and Robert M. Gray. 1977. "The Dying Patient: A Symbolic Analysis." *International Journal of Symbology*, Vol. 8 (July):77–86.

Lifton, Robert J., and E. Olson. 1974. *Living and Dying*. New York: Praeger Publishers.

Lindemann, Edward. 1944. "Symptomatology and Management of Acute Grief." *American Journal of Psychiatry*, Vol. 101: 141–148.

Lindemann, Edward. 1979. *Beyond Grief: Studies in Crisis Intervention*. New York: Jason Aronson.

Marshall, Eric and Stuart Hemple. 1967. *More: Children's Letters to God*. New York: Simon and Schuster.

Singh, J.A.L., and R. M. Zingg. 1942. *Wolf Children and Feral Man*. New York: Harper and Row.

Vernon, Glenn M., and Jerry D. Cardwell. 1981. *Social Psychology: Shared, Symboled, Situated Behavior*. Washington, D.C.: University Press of America.

Suggested Readings

Feifel, Herman, ed. 1977. *New Meanings of Death*. New York: McGraw Hill.
  Eighteen articles emphasizing the meaning of a wide variety of various aspects of death-related behavior.
Thompson, Ian, ed. 1979. *Dilemmas of Dying*. Edinburgh: Edinburgh University Press.
  Reports on a British study of ethical dilemmas confronted by professionals relating to terminal patients.
Vernon, Glenn M. 1970. *Sociology of Death*. New York: Ronald Press.
  A sociological analysis focusing upon meaning, social, and situational components of death-related behavior.

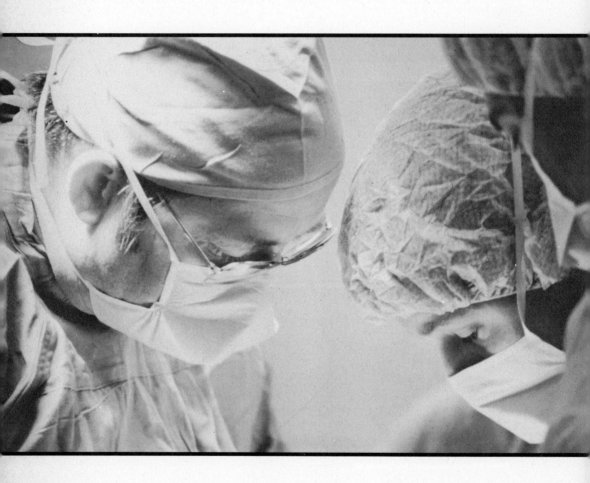

Chapter 3

THE DYING PROCESS

I'm not afraid of dying. I just don't want to be there when it happens.

Woody Allen

OF ALL OF THE EVENTS of our lives, dying can be the most stressful. Many factors will contribute to and alleviate stress related to the dying process. Primarily we are concerned with the physical and social factors.

Among other things, dying is a process that happens to the physical body of the individual. Although the determination of the timing of death is problematic, there is a qualitative difference between a live and a dead human being. For the most part, the cause of death is ultimately attributed to physiological factors. However, the biological aspect of dying means less to us than the meaning we place upon the events that take place during the dying process.

DEATH MEANINGS AND THEIR EFFECT UPON THE DYING PROCESS[1]

The meaning of our dying will depend to a great extent upon the social context in which the dying takes place. As discussed in the second chapter of this book, meanings are the basic component of human behavior because individuals respond to the meanings of phenomena rather than to the phenomena themselves. Meanings are both socially created and socially perpetuated.

The major types of meanings to which individuals respond in death-related situations are the following: time meanings, space meanings, norm and role meanings, value meanings, object and self meanings, and meanings of social situations (Vernon, 1972). We will now look at each of these types of meanings and their effects upon the dying process.

[1]Much of the material in this section was taken from "The Dying Patient: A Symbolic Analysis" by Michael R. Leming, Glenn M. Vernon, and Robert M. Gray, *International Journal of Symbology*, Vol. 8, No. 2 (July), 1977: 77–86.

Time Meanings

> Even if I live for 100 years, I'll be dead a lot longer.
> *Richard Pryor*

In thinking about the dying process, the first thing that comes to our awareness is the concept of time. We are confronted with the fact that time, for the terminal patient, is running out. Yet, when does the dying process begin? Are we not all dying, with some reaching the state of being dead before others? From the moment of our births, we are approaching the end of our lives. We assume that terminal patients will experience death before nondying individuals, but this is not always the case.

Guest Lecturer

I invited to class a woman who had been diagnosed as a terminal cancer patient. Deeply impressed by the visitor's positive outlook on the time left to her, one student on the following day noted, "When I came into the session I expected to meet someone who was dying. Instead, I realize that woman is more alive than I am. The discussion wasn't about dying at all, it was about living."

Source: Joan M. Boyle, "Dialectic on Dying," in M. M. Newell et al., eds. *The Role of the Volunteer in the Care of the Terminal Patient and the Family* (New York: The Foundation of Thanatology/Arno Press), pp. 182–89.

Since it is possible to diagnose a disease from which most people die, we can assume that patients with these diseases are "more terminal" than individuals without them. The terminal patient is very much concerned with the time dimension of his or her physical existence. Many surveys (see Glaser and Strauss, 1965) have demonstrated that as many as 80 percent of patients want to be told if their illness is terminal. However, doctors are not always prepared to tell their patients of a terminal diagnosis.

While many doctors in the past (see Kasper, 1959) have not been in favor of telling their patients, Kubler-Ross (1969) claims that it is not a question of whether the patient should be told, but of how the patient is told. Krant (1972:106) gives the following advice:

Communication should be the responsibility of someone familiar and deeply committed to the patient and family. Time must be allowed for the facts to sink in and for questions to arise. The art of telling is the art of supporting.

Should patients be told the amount of time they have left? Kubler-Ross (1969) wisely suggests that specifying an amount of time dispels hope and serves no more function than telling the patient that the condition is very serious and life threatening. If the patient presses for time specificity, a range of time should be given such as the following statement: "Sixty percent of the patients with your disease live as long as three to five years." This statement provides hope without deluding the patient. Furthermore, it is honest. Medical science cannot say with any certainty that a person will live one year—some die sooner and others live longer (some even outlive the doctor!).

Sharing the Experience of Dying

Some of the most beautiful human interactions I have witnessed have occurred between dying patients and supportive families. Sometimes the quality of human interactions in the terminal phase far exceeds anything the patient or family experienced prior to diagnosis.

I strongly feel the dying patient should be told as much as he or she wants to know. The family should also be encouraged to share feelings with the patient in an open manner. *Nothing* is worse than dying alone. The terminal patient whose family won't broach the subject, or who is afraid to upset his or her family or doctors with fears and feelings, *does* die alone.

Source: A physician's comment from a survey of 1093 physicians conducted by Dickinson and Pearson, 1980–81.

Space Meanings

Even when the patient has not been told of his or her terminal condition, he or she will eventually become aware of it. Many times factors related to social space will give the patient clues that he or she is terminal. Within the hospital, there are areas where the very ill are treated. When one is placed in the intensive care unit or on an oncology (cancer) ward, it becomes obvious that all is not well and that death is a real possibility.

Confinement to a health care institution conveys a tremendous amount of meaning to the patient. For the most part, he or she is alone. The patient is told through spatial meanings that he or she is removed from those things that give life meaning and purpose—family, friends, and job. For the terminal patient, this is the first stage of social disengagement.

The following statement by Hale (1971) demonstrates the significance of the space when applied to the dying patient:

> As for the patient himself, he faces his life's ultimate crisis in a foreign place— the hospital. Usually, he dies alone, not in the presence of anyone who cares. Often the family is allowed to visit even the dying only during the hours set by the hospital. And since hospital visits usually lack privacy, they are of little comfort either to the patient or to the relatives who are entering the period of "anticipatory grief." There is little room or opportunity for sharing that most poignant moment of a lifetime—death! There is little opportunity for dignity in those settings.

Within any health care setting the patient's confinement serves to diminish his or her social and personal power. According to Coe (1970), three processes occur within the institution to accomplish this—"stripping," control of resources, and restrictions on mobility.

The process of *stripping* takes place when the patient is issued a hospital gown and stripped of any valuables for safe keeping. In doing this the patient's identity is also stripped. Most factors that differentiate patients with regard to status in the larger society are taken from the patient and create the primary status of patient—all patients look alike. According to Coe (1970:300); "every distinctly personalizing symbol, material or otherwise, is taken away, thus reducing the patient to the status of just one of many." (This may be one of the reasons why physicians are known to be such bad patients—they are forced to relinquish their physician status when they are admitted to the hospital.)

The second process is the *control of resources*. When the patient is denied access to his or her medical records and important information about the events of the hospital, personal power is greatly diminished. Personal power is the ability to make decisions that determine the direction of one's own life. Without all the information concerning oneself and the place of one's confinement, it may not be possible to make important decisions. One method used by hospitals in controlling resources is to deny all patients and their families access to medical charts and records.

The third process is the *restriction on mobility*. Not being able to leave one's room or bed further reduces the patient's personal power. The patient is put in a position of dependency upon others. Confinement of this type greatly affects the patient's autonomy. It also makes it possible for others to withdraw from the patient.

Social space is very important in the process of patient disengagement. This disengagement can be accomplished by two methods—the patient can withdraw from others and others can withdraw from the patient. If the patient is debilitated by illness, he or she may not have the energy to continue normal patterns of social interaction. The loss of physical attractiveness can also cause the patient to withdraw. Some patients, knowing that they are terminal, may disengage as a coping strategy to avoid having to see all that their death will take from them. They may also disengage as a sign of their acceptance of social death—"I'm as good as dead" (anticipatory death).

When persons significant to the patient withdraw, patient disengagement will also take place. In this situation the process of disengagement is something beyond the patient's control. Family members and friends can refrain from visiting the patient as a sign of their acceptance of social death. The terminal label can stigmatize the patient, and others may treat the individual differently.

Orville Kelly, founder of "Make Each Day Count" (a support group for persons with cancer), tells the story of being invited by a friend to dinner. The table was set with the finest china and silverware—with one exception. His place setting consisted of a paper plate and plastic fork, spoon, and knife. He was the guest with cancer! Many people do not know how to relate to the dying and therefore withdraw as a method of coping with their inadequacy.

Norm and Role Meanings

Norms are defined as plans of action or expected behavior patterns felt to be appropriate for a particular situation. Likewise, roles are plans of action or expected behavior patterns specifying what should be done by persons who occupy particular social positions. Applied to the death-related behavior of the dying patient, norm definitions would involve the general expectation that the dying patient should be brave and accept the fact that life will soon end. The patient is not supposed to cry or become verbal in regard to feelings about his or her death. Nurses often sanction such behavior by giving less attention to patients who deviate from this norm. Kubler-Ross (1969:56–57) gives the following example of one such deviant:

> The patient would stand in front of the nurses' desk and demand attention for herself and other terminally ill patients, which the nurses resented as interference and inappropriate behavior. Since she was quite sick, they did not confront her with her unacceptable behavior, but expressed their resentment by making shorter visits to her room, by avoiding contact, and by the briefness of their encounters.

Role meanings differ from norm meanings in that they specify, in a detailed fashion, what behavior is expected for persons who occupy specific social positions. For example, if a husband-father is dying, it is expected that he do all that he can before he dies to provide for the financial needs of his family. It would probably be expected that he make arrangements for his funeral, insure that his bills are paid, finalize his will, and establish a trust fund for his children.

One of the important aspects of norm and role meanings is its relationship to the process of societal disengagement (see Cumming and Henry, 1961; and Newell, 1961). Societal disengagement is the process by which the society withdraws from, or no longer seeks, the individual's efforts (Atchley, 1977). The individual can also withdraw from societal participation and choose not to perform the roles he or she performed before the terminal diagnosis. The type of disengagement of which we are speaking goes beyond withdrawing from interaction patterns with others, it refers to a withdrawal from the social structure—i.e. quitting one's job and taking a trip around the world.

Role disengagement has many consequences for the patient as well as for his or her family members. Gaspard, (1970:78) notes:

> If the father is ill, the mother must generally become the breadwinner and children who are able often must take over household tasks sooner than they otherwise might. Each person in such a situation may feel both guilt and resentment at such a change whereby they can no longer adequately fulfill the expectations they have had of themselves. Conversely, if the mother is ill, household help may be hired, and problems may arise with regard to the mother's maintaining, in so far as is possible, her self-image in relation to caring for her family.

In addition to the disengagement process, patients are expected to acquire the sick role (see Parsons, 1951). They are expected to want to get better—to want to seek more treatment—even though everyone realizes that such treatment only prolongs death and not life. This role disengagement can create conflict within the family, especially when the patient has accepted his or her death (and even longs for it), while family members are unwilling to let the patient go. As Kubler-Ross (1969) documents, families many times cannot comprehend that a patient reaches a point when death comes as a great relief, and that patients die easier if they are allowed and helped to detach themselves slowly from all the responsibilities and meaningful relationships in their lives.

Value Meanings

Values, like all other meaning systems, are socially created. They are not inherent in the phenomena, they are applied by humans to the phenomena. Death per se is neither good nor evil. However, humans do ascribe value to the different types of deaths. Each of these value meanings has important behavioral consequences.

Most people in our society view death as being intrinsically evil and therefore something to fear. We tend to see death as an intruder—the spoiler of our best plans. Therefore, in the past, the medical profession has attempted to delay death in favor of life. We keep people on machines to prolong life even if death is inevitable. We assume that people who wish to die are mentally ill or irrational because death is seen as something to be avoided. Yet, the terminally ill eventually come to view death as a great blessing, when they have finally accepted the fact that they are going to die. This is possible because humans are able to create hierarchies of values where value meanings take on relative meanings. To the terminally ill patient, dignity is more highly valued than is life with pain, indignity, and suffering. Consequently, death may be ascribed positive value for the dying patient who has accepted the inevitability of his or her death.

Christmas Tree Ornament Received with Enclosed Letter from Elderly Friend circa July

My Dear Children,

This seems a strange *gift* for this time of the year. This lovely ball was given me by the friend who made it and I want it to hang for many years on your happy tree. If I live until another Christmas, I would be 97 which is too long to stay in this devastated world which my generation has made. I am ready to depart any time. God has been wonderfully good to me. I have had all any one could ask for. Love and care and now every comfort in this shadowing time. I say with Cardinal Newman: "So long thy hand hath led me, Sure it will lead me on."

I know that you are leading lives full of meaning and my blessings go with this bright ball. I believe a circle has no beginning and no end.

Sincerely your friend

(The writer died before another Christmas.)

Object and Self Meanings

Thus far we have focused our attention upon meanings that have been applied to an object—the dying patient. From a biological perspective the person is a living organism—a physical object. From a social-psychological perspective, the patient is a social object—a self.

Many patients who are defined as having a terminal condition begin to view themselves as being "as good as dead." They have accepted the terminal label, applied it to their understanding of who they are, and have experienced anticipatory death. Families also come to see their loved ones as being in bereavement. This symbolic definition of the patient is reinforced by the role disengagement process, the spatial isolation of the dying patient, and the terminal label placed upon the patient by the physician and other medical personnel. The patient seems to take on a status somewhere between the living and the dead.

Don't Abandon the Patient

When I say I feel as comfortable with a dying patient as with any other, and that I do not find treating a dying patient unpleasant, I do not mean that I am anaesthetized to the fact that they are dying, and do not have feelings about that patient which are different from my feelings about a patient whom I know will get well. Anaesthasion of feeling is the method which we physicians employ initially in dealing with the pain—ours and theirs—involved in treating a dying patient. But this passes, and when one accepts the patient as part of life, and not someone who is no longer a real part of the world (or a frightening part of the world), then caring for the dying patient, becomes (though often sad) neither unpleasant nor something one wishes to avoid. To abandon the dying patient is the *worst* thing that can be done—both for the patient and the doctor.

Source: A physician's comment from a survey of 1093 physicians conducted by Dickinson and Pearson, 1980–81.

Kubler-Ross (1969:116) says that the terminally ill have a need to detach themselves from the living to make dying easier. The following example illustrates this point:

She asked to be allowed to die in peace, wished to be left alone—even asked for less involvement on the part of her husband. She said that the only reason that kept her still alive was her husband's inability to accept the fact that she had to die. She was angry at him for not facing it and for so desperately clinging on to something that she was willing and ready to give up. I translated to her that she wished to detach herself from this world, and she nodded gratefully as I left her alone.

When an individual's condition has been defined by self and others as terminal, all other self meanings take on less importance. While a given patient may be a lawyer, Republican, mother, wife, Episcopalian, etc., she tends to think of herself primarily as a terminal patient. The terminal label, in this instance, is what sociologists refer to as a master status, because it dominates all other status indicators. Consequently, most of the symbolic meanings we have previously explored become incorporated into the individual's self meaning.

Acquiring the terminal label as part of the self definition is not an easy task for the individual. Elizabeth Kubler-Ross, in her best-selling book *On Death and Dying* (1969), delineated the following five stages that she believes all patients go through in accepting their terminal self meaning: *denial, anger, bargaining, depression, and acceptance.*

In the first stage the patient attempts to deny that his or her condition is fatal. The patient may seek additional medical advice in hope that the terminal diagnosis will be proven false. When the diagnosis is verified, the patient may often retreat into self-imposed isolation. The second stage—anger—is a natural reaction for most patients. The patient may vent anger at a number of individuals—at the doctor because he or she is not doing enough, at relatives because they will outlive the patient, at other patients because their condition is not terminal, and at God for allowing the patient to die.

When the individual has begun to incorporate the terminal label into his or her self meaning, he or she may attempt to bargain for a little more time. There may be promises made to God in exchange for an extension of life, followed by the wish for a few days without pain or physical discomfort. This bargaining always includes an implicit promise that the patient will not ask for more if the one postponement is granted. The promise is very rarely, if ever, kept according to Kubler-Ross (1969:84).

The fourth stage is one of depression. The patient begins to realize that with death approaching he or she will lose the meaningful things of life—family, physical appearance, personal accomplishments, and often a sense of dignity.

In the final stage, the patient accepts death as a sure outcome. This acceptance, while not happy, is not terribly sad either. The patient is able to say "I have said all of the words that have to be said. I am ready to go."

While the analysis of the dying patient's behavior in terms of concrete stages is very attractive due to its specificity and simplicity, many scholars have cast doubt on its validity (see Charmaz, 1980; Garfield, 1978; and Pattison, 1977).

Kathy Charmaz (1980:153), in concluding that the stages emanate from preconceived psychiatric categories *imposed* upon the experiences rather than emerging from the data, gives the following statement by Ted Rosenthal: "It's fiendish. No matter what you say, they all say uh hum, just what we thought you'd say." Charmaz notes that "what originated as *description* of a reality often becomes *prescription* for reality."

Another criticism (Charmaz, 1980) of Kubler-Ross' stages is based upon the idea that the stages do not take adequately into consideration the perspective of the patient. For example, anger may be vented at others because they have withdrawn from the patient as their attempt to cope with the loss of someone they care about. The bargaining behavior of the patient may be motivated by a need for moral and social support from caregivers, rather than a hope for an extension of time (Gustafson, 1972). Depression may be a function of the severity of the physical condition of the patient rather than an emotional response to the terminal condition (Charmaz, 1980). As the disease progresses, the strength of the patient will diminish and be evaluated by others as psychological depression. In actuality, the patient may be depressed not by dying, but by the physical effects of the illness.

Finally, there are a number of critiques that reject the developmental nature of the sequential stage approach. Some have criticized the stage analysis of Kubler-Ross because it lacks universality—not all patients manifest all five types of behaviors. Others have noted that the stages are not mutually exclusive—some patients may bargain, be depressed, and angry at the same time. Finally, many have observed that the order of the stages is more arbitrary than Kubler-Ross would have us believe—dying patients may go from denial to acceptance, followed by depression and anger.

With regard to the stages of dying, we must conclude that dying behavior is more complex than five universal, mutually exclusive, and linear

The Care of the Dying Patient

No matter how we measure his worth, a dying human being deserves more than efficient care from strangers, more than machines and septic hands, more than a mouth full of pills, arms full of tubes and a rump full of needles. His simple dignity as man should merit more than furtive eyes, reluctant hugs, medical jargon, ritual sacraments or tired Bible quotes, more than all the phony promises for a tomorrow that will never come. Man has become lost in the jungle of ritual surrounding death.

Source: Robert E. Kavanaugh, *Facing Death* (Baltimore: Penguin Books, 1972), p. 6.

stages. However, Kubler-Ross has helped us in understanding that each of the five behaviors is a "normal" coping strategy employed by dying patients. It may be that it is the social situation that accounts for the similar coping strategies of dying patients, and that in other cultural settings different patterns of behavior will be found.

Meanings of the Situation

As the dying patient comes to grips with his or her terminal condition, the manner in which he or she defines the social situation in which the dying takes place will have a tremendous impact upon the process of dying. If the hospital is viewed as a supportive environment, patient coping may be facilitated. On the other hand, if the patient feels all alone in his or her place of confinement, and if the hospital is defined as a foreign place, personal adjustment to dying and death will be hindered.

Like all other meaning systems, the definition of the social situation is an attempt by the individual to bring order to his or her world. Since situational meaning always involves selective perception, the terminal patient will create the meaning for the social environment and will respond to this meaning and not to the environment itself. Each terminal patient will not only experience death in a different environment, but will have a unique interpretation of his or her social situation. This accounts for the different experiences of dying patients. The hospice movement (described in Chapter 8) is an attempt to create a more positive and supportive social situation in which dying can take place.

PHYSICIANS AND THE DYING PATIENT

In Chapter 1 we suggested that Americans are poorly socialized with regard to issues of dying and death. One might expect that the early socialization experiences of physicians would be similar to other members of our society. This is illustrated by a story told to the authors by Dr. Charles Huggins, a Nobel recipient and professor of medicine at the University of Chicago. Dr. Huggins noted that when he entered medical school as a first year student, he felt ill-prepared for dealing with death. After the instructor finished the initial lecture on gross anatomy, the class went to the laboratory to begin work on their cadavers. Dr. Huggins said that his cadaver was a female. He recounted that upon taking one look at the body—having never seen either a naked or a dead woman—he said to himself, "I should have gone to law school after all." Even though this Nobel recipient entered medical school several decades ago, many first year medical students of today have had similar experiences and feelings. (See the application at the end of this chapter.)

Historically, medical education has offered limited assistance to the medical student encountering death for the first time (Rabin and Rabin, 1970). For many students, like Dr. Huggins, the first exposure to death is an impersonal experience in an anatomy laboratory. Physicians are trained to work with bodies, but rarely with people (Neale, 1973).

According to Barton (1972), there is the frequently not verbalized, but subtly perpetuated idea in the medical profession, that the death of the patient represents a failure. Death and some of the aspects of the dying process contradict the physician's professional goals and objectives. Olin (1972) suggests that death represents a failure to the medical student instead of being valued as a dignified human event. Much of the literature suggests that the medical profession does not recognize death as a legitimate outcome of treatment regardless of the circumstances under which it occurs (Becker, 1961; Levine and Scotch, 1970; Rabin and Rabin, 1970).

Perhaps physicians are expected to be all things to all people. The medical training of most doctors, however, seems to be primarily concerned with the patient's physical state rather than social-psychological needs. From the point of view that the physician is a defender of life, sworn to use the best judgment in protecting patients, death is the enemy. From this perspective, the dying patient is a lost cause from the beginning (Tarnower, 1969).

According to Hackett (1976), physicians have been taught how to pronounce the patient dead but not how to ease the psychological distress of the dying. A more equal balance of training to deal with both the physical and psychological aspects of dying would seem to be appropriate.

Feeling confident with respect to tasks of reassurance and control in relating to a dying patient might be an intrinsic quality that only certain medical students possess (when reinforced by clinical experience), or it might be a skill that all medical students can learn if they are given proper instruction and guidance. In a survey of 1093 physicians, Dickinson and Pearson (1980–81) found that the medical students who took an entire course devoted exclusively to the subject of relating to dying patients were better able to relate to patients and families than those medical students who did not include this course in their medical education. This would suggest that relating to dying patients and their families is a skill that can be developed or improved upon.

If this is true, how widespread are thanatology courses in medical curricula? Surveys of more than 100 United States medical schools in 1975 and 1980 (Dickinson, 1981) showed that the number of full courses on dying and death increased from 6 to 13 percent. Eighty percent of the medical schools in both 1975 and 1980 offered death education in the form of an occasional lecture or minicourse. However, death education is relatively new to medical school curricula in the United States. Seventy-three percent of the schools offering such courses reported that death and dying courses were in their curricula for less than five years (Dickinson, 1976). With few exceptions, most medical specialties will involve dying patients, yet, the thrust in medical school has not generally prepared students for these encounters.

In a recent study of 1012 physicians, Dickinson and Pearson (1979a) concluded that those with a high probability of relating to dying patients (oncologists) were more open with their patients than physicians who practiced medicine in areas where there was a lower probability of dealing with death (obstetricians and gynecologists). Since this study suggests that differences exist among medical specialties in relating to dying patients, it is possible that one factor influencing the selection of a medical specialty is the medical student's personal understanding and feelings concerning dying and death issues.

In this same study, Dickinson and Pearson (1979b) found that female physicians related better to dying patients and their families than did male physicians. Perhaps the traditional "feminine characteristics" of gentleness, expressiveness, responsiveness, and kindness help to explain these differences. If more physicians and other medical personnel were to display these "human qualities," with a greater frequency, patients might receive more help and support in their dying.

DYING AS DEVIANCE IN THE MEDICAL SETTING[2]

The student entering the medical profession comes with certain attitudes and feelings toward patients that will be shaped, molded, and continually processed until their attitudes comply with those of the medical profession itself. The medical profession's attitudes toward patients, in particular the dying patient, are functional to the reinforcement of the view of "the physician as healer" and functional with respect to maintenance of order in the medical subculture.

The dying patient is a deviant in the medical subculture because death poses a threat to the image of the "physician as healer." It also creates embarrassing and emotionally upsetting disruptions in the scientific objectivity of the medical social system. Hence, the disruption caused by death in the medical social system, if not controlled, could lead to a great deal of conflict.

A major school of thought explaining deviance is the labeling perspective. This perspective does not focus on the act or actor, but rather on the

[2]Much of the material from this section was taken from three unpublished manuscripts by Alban L. Wheeler: "The Dying Person: A Deviant in the Medical Subculture," "Dying as Deviance: A Reinforcement of Society's Norms in the Medical Profession," and "On Becoming a Physician: The Care of the Dying Patient" (the latter two with Christine Larson-Kurz and George E. Dickinson).

audience observing them. According to Kai Erikson (1962) the critical variable in the study of deviance is the social audience rather than the individual
person. Therefore, deviance is not a property inherent in certain forms of
behavior, but is a property conferred upon acts or actions by the audiences
which directly or indirectly witness them.

When a person is labeled deviant, that individual is stigmatized.
Goffman (1963) describes the stigmatized individual as a person who is
reduced in the minds of others from a "whole" and "usual" person to
a "tainted" and "discounted" one. Therefore, the key to the identification
of deviance is found in the audiences that label the individual or act as
deviant. Hence, in analyzing the dying person as deviant in the medical
subculture, the medical audiences, who interact with and participate in the
labeling of the patient, must be examined.

When a person is labeled deviant, an entire interactional framework is
created within which the "normals" relate to the "deviant." Regardless of
whether or not the individual is responsible for the deviant label, the label
stigmatized individual is still discredited and is treated with less respect
than other people.

Thus, according to Freidson (1972:236), when a person is labeled deviant, the stigma interferes with normal interaction. While people may not
hold the deviant responsible for his or her stigma, they are nonetheless
"embarrassed, upset or even revolted by it," says Freidson. Therefore, the
assumption can be made that the deviant person elicits certain aversive
attitudes from the audience with whom interaction occurs. These aversive
attitudes may be of sufficient strength to elicit attempts to manage them
and to decrease aversion through avoidance behavior.

Employing a model created by Talcott Parsons (1951) to understand the
nature of role expectations, we can analyze the physician's role in contemporary society as being based upon the following characteristics: *univer-
salism, performance, affective neutrality, and specificity.* The physician in the
contemporary organizational context does not view the patient in a holistic
sense, but rather views him or her as someone with a particular disease or
ailment needing treatment. The physician's goal, therefore, is purely instrumental. The task is to utilize expertise and cure the patient's disease by
returning to health.

Secondly, with regard to performance, the physician views the patient
not by what he or she is but by what he or she does. The concern is not
with the patient's life, history, or social background, but with pulse rate,
respiration and other vital signs. Hence, the concern is with external indicators of the patient's progress.

Thirdly, the physician takes an affectively neutral stance when dealing
with patients. The goal in the medical social system is the instrumental task
of returning the patient to normal role functioning. Instrumentalism and
the corresponding subordination of expressive interests are the predomi-
nate traits of the physician's role.

The final characteristic describing the physician's role is that of specificity. The physician's relationship with the patient is purely on a professional level. The relationships of physician and patient are secondary relationships with little or no personal involvement.

Parsons (1951) states that health is included in the functional needs of the society, thus, too high an incidence of illness is dysfunctional for societal maintenance. To assure that the normal functioning of society continues and that sufficient numbers of individuals fulfill their role expectations of "staying healthy," there must be positive and negative sanctions for conformity and nonconformity, respectively.

Parsons (1958) extends his analysis of illness as deviance by enumerating the functions of the health-illness role structure. The sick person is restricted in his or her interaction with those who are not sick. This restriction is not so much for the sick person but because the illness may be contagious to others.

The primary reaction, therefore, to deviance of any type is punishment of some sort. Durkheim (1961) points out that the primary purpose of punishment is not for the deviant himself or herself, but to affirm in the face of the offense, the rule the offense would deny. If we take Parsons' conceptualization, illness is a rejection of the societal value of health.

The interpretation by Parsons of society's role expectation regarding the sick person dictates that the sick role be a temporary one. The sick person is exempted temporarily and expected to cooperate with medical personnel and get well. The key to Parsons' conceptualization of illness, as a form of deviance, is the temporal aspect of the condition. The individual who is ill, but who with the correct type of medication can get well, is granted temporary legitimation of his or her illness. Therefore, the individual with a "treatable" illness is exempted temporarily from normal role responsibilities.

The God of Physical Health

Characterizing the American deification of physical health, the hospital, and the physician, Kavanaugh (1972:8) makes the following statement:

> Our universal deity, Physical Health, is the major god currently [worshipped]. His demands for untold dollars in tribute are incessant. Every day it costs more to worship at his shrine (the hospital), yet the devout seem only too willing to scrape and to pay. They sit uncomplainingly for endless hours in the offices of His high priests (physicians), and will purchase any drug or pill or lotion the priests prescribe, in any combination. In His shrine, *the dying are excommunicated, the dead are damned.*

A problem arises when Parsons' conceptualization of illness as deviance is applied to the dying person, since the dying person defies the role expectations of the culture in general and the medical subculture in particular. Parsons assumes that illness is by definition undesirable, and therefore, carries with it the obligation to get well. The dying person, however, can seldom assume normal role functioning, although he or she views the illness as undesirable and has tried to cooperate with medical personnel to get well. The dying person, therefore, is permanently cast into a deviant role due to the inability to respond to treatment and get well.

RELATING TO DYING PATIENTS

The significance of physicians' attitudes on dying and death becomes apparent in Pine's (1975) analysis of institutionalized communication. Doctors and nurses are intricately entwined in dealing with dying patients because it is the doctor who defines when the patient is "dying" and "dead." The nursing staff must wait for an "official" message from the physician. The patient is then treated as if there were little chance for recovery. This alteration in treatment is predicted by the physician's decision but is not carried out until he or she communicates it.

Am I Dead?

Once upon a time a patient died and went to heaven, but was not certain where he was. Puzzled, he asked a nurse who was standing nearby, "Nurse, am I dead?" The answer she gave was: "Have you asked your doctor?"

Anonymous (circa 1961)

The importance of communication between medical personnel and patients is stressed by Glaser and Strauss (1965) who define the awareness context as what each interacting person knows of the patient's defined status, along with the recognition of the others' awareness of his or her own definition. According to Glaser and Strauss (1965), four awareness contexts exist: closed, suspicion, mutual pretense, and open. *Closed awareness* is usually the first context. In order to maintain the patient's trust and yet keep him or her unaware of the terminal condition, the staff must consistently construct a fictional future biography. Since many physicians choose not to tell the patient about a terminal condition, the burden of

The Dying Person's Bill of Rights

I have the right to be treated as a living human being until I die.

I have the right to maintain a sense of hopefulness, however changing its focus may be.

I have the right to be cared for by those who can maintain a sense of hopefulness, however changing this might be.

I have the right to express my feelings and emotions about my approaching death in my own way.

I have the right to participate in decisions concerning my care.

I have the right to expect continuing medical and nursing attention even though "cure" goals must be changed to "comfort" goals.

I have the right not to die alone.

I have the right to be free from pain.

I have the right to have my questions answered honestly.

I have the right not to be deceived.

I have the right to have help from and for my family in accepting my death.

I have the right to die in peace and dignity.

I have the right to retain my individuality and not be judged for my decisions which may be contrary to the beliefs of others.

I have the right to expect that the sanctity of the human body will be respected after my death.

I have the right to be cared for by caring, sensitive, and knowledgeable people who will attempt to understand my needs and will be able to gain some satisfaction in helping me face my death.

Source: Karen C. Sorenson and Joan Luckmann, *Basic Nursing: A Psychophysiologic Approach* (Philadelphia: W. B. Saunders, 1979).

telling the unaware patient falls on the nursing staff. Since most patients are able to recognize death-related situational and spatial clues, this context tends to be unstable and the patient usually moves to suspicion or full awareness contexts.

Suspicion awareness is a contest for control between the patient and medical staff. The patient suspects that he or she is dying but receives no verification from the staff. Nurses must use teamwork to refute this challenge. *Mutual pretense* often follows and requires subtle interaction with both patient and staff "acting correctly" to maintain the pretense that the patient is not approaching death. If not sustained, *open awareness* follows with many ambiguities. The patient is obligated to not commit suicide and to die "properly." If the patient is dying in an unacceptable manner, then difficulties are faced when trying to negotiate for things from the staff. Dying "properly" is difficult, however, for as Blauner (1966) points out, the nurses expect "proper" dying but the patient has no model to follow.

In a study of nurses, Pearlman, Stotsky, and Dominick (1969) found that those having had more experience with dying patients were more likely to avoid the dying than nurses with less experience. Since the physician usually directs the medical team, nurses are often forced to work in a closed awareness context regardless of their own view. Ashley-Cameron and Dickinson (1979) found that nurses working with dying patients seem to be comfortable in this awareness context. Since nurses spend more time than physicians on the wards with patients, a closed awareness context may produce a more comfortable setting for the nurse.

Whether a nurse or a physician, coping with dying patients does not come easily. Traditionally, society has not prepared one for such interaction. Some obviously react better than others. The key to good relations with dying patients is coming to grips with death in one's own mind. In addition, good communication skills are of utmost importance. If only the dying patient could be viewed as a person—not the "malignant brain tumor" in Room 719—and treated as a human being, rather than a physical body, certainly the trauma of the dying process would be eased. In the end, both medical personnel and patient would benefit.

THE RIGHT TO DIE

In 1976 the state of California passed the Natural Death Act. This bill legally recognized a patient's "right to die" by honoring requests for the withholding or withdrawal of life-sustaining procedures from adults who have a terminal condition. Since that time, at least ten other states have passed similar legislation and many others have drafted but not approved equivalent bills. While being the subject of legal controversy, the question of a right to die is better understood as a social and moral dilemma revolving around the following question: "What constitutes life before death?"

In order to better understand the current predicament regarding the timing of death, one must have a limited view of the history of medicine in the American society. The hospital, the health care institution in which presently over 60 percent of all deaths take place, was originally structured as an institution for the practice of charity rather than as a place primarily devoted to physical healing. With this emphasis, early hospitals cared for not only the sick but also anyone in need of shelter. It was not until the latter part of the nineteenth century that the hospital became primarily a healing and comforting institution, and even then most persons viewed the hospital as a place where people went to die (Coe, 1970).

Even the medical professionals in the earlier part of the twentieth century could do no more than promise their patients a 50 percent chance of being helped by their efforts. Medicine as an effective scientific enterprise is a relatively recent phenomenon. The technological advances of scientific medicine in the latter half of the twentieth century have given rise to a classic example of what sociologists call "cultural lag." This condition was created by rapid medical technological developments and relatively static definitions of biological life and death. Medical practice today can prolong life (or postpone death) without having a precise definition of a point at which death has occurred. As discussed in Chapter 1, consensus does not exist within the medical community with regard to a specific definition of death. Currently, patients are certified to be dead when there is agreement among the attending medical personnel that life no longer exists. This would be of little significance if medical science were not able to maintain some biological functioning of the individual with artificial means, but such is not the case.

The condition of cultural lag is not only currently a situation of social concern but, given the progress in medical technology, promises to become one of the major social issues of this decade. It is not surprising that many patients request that their doctors allow them to die and not be kept alive by artificial means or heroic measures in the event of a terminal illness. "For them contemplating modern medicine's ability to prolong life, death itself is welcomed compared to the terrors of senility and protracted terminal treatment" (Fletcher, 1977:355).

A typical American occurrence of death finds the patient in a sedated and comatose state—betubed nasally, abdominally, and intravenously—and far more like a manipulated object than like a moral subject (Fletcher, 1977). Fletcher goes on to contrast this situation to the historical deathbed scene where the elderly "pass on," surrounded by their families and friends, making their farewell speeches and *meeting* death instead of being overtaken or snatched by it. In the face of such a contrast, one may wonder if the efforts to delay death clinically and biologically actually hastens social death by stripping the patient of any sense of self-possession and conscious integrity. To postpone death without considering the type of life that is prolonged is to consider all physiological life to be of primary importance. This position is not supported by most people who are concerned with preserving their social-self identities.

Why should patients be forced to allow the death anxieties of persons who have the power to prolong biological life, keep them from death, when social death has already occurred? It is understandable to want to hold on to life and to our relationships with people we love; yet, sooner or later, we realize that life in its fullest meaning includes death. The only real question open to a patient in the final stages of dying is how the death comes—as a good death (euthanasia) or as a bad death (dysthanasia)? Those favoring euthanasia would assert that the social worth of the individual must be maintained by protecting his or her integrity and dignity.

A Living Will

I wish to live a full and long life, but not at all costs. If my death is near and cannot be avoided, and if I have lost the ability to interact with others and have no reasonable chance of regaining this ability, or if my suffering is intense and irreversible, I do not want to have my life prolonged. I would then ask not to be subjected to surgery or resuscitation. Nor would I then wish to have life support from mechanical ventilators, intensive care services, or other life prolonging procedures, including the administration of antibiotics and blood products. I would wish, rather, to have care which gives comfort and support, which facilitates my interaction with others to the extent that this is possible, and which brings peace.

In order to carry out these instructions and to interpret them, I authorize _____ to accept, plan and refuse treatment on my behalf in cooperation with attending physicians and health personnel. This person knows how I value the experience of living, and how I would weigh incompetence, suffering, and dying. Should it be impossible to reach this person, I authorize _____ to make such choices for me. I have discussed my desires concerning terminal care with them, and trust their judgment on my behalf.

In addition, I have discussed with them the following specific instructions regarding my care:

Date_____

Signed_____

Witnessed by_____ and

_____.

Source: Sissela Bok (1976), cited by John J. Paris and Richard A. McCormick, "Living-Will Legislation Reconsidered," *America*, September 5, 1981, p. 89.

An important question remains for those who are concerned about protecting the integrity and dignity of dying patients: How can the patient's right to die be preserved and carried out? First, patients and their families need to be supported in their decisions to choose death rather than sustaining biological life which has lost its meaning. When patients and their families have made the moral choice to "pull the plug" and stop extraordinary life sustaining efforts, they will need the emotional support of friends and other members of the community.

Secondly, patients and their families may need an advocate against the powerful health care institution that functions primarily to heal rather than to comfort individuals as they approach death. Patients by themselves cannot fight against the technology that modern medicine provides. Individuals acting as political groups can serve a prophetic function in a society where mechanistic progress is an unquestioned value. This may involve supporting state and national legislation relative to the legal establishment of a living will.

Finally, concerned people can help to make the dying person's remaining moments as meaningful as possible by creating an ambience of love for both the patient and his or her family. This can be accomplished by acts of charity and being physically present to offer compassion and concern. If we are to assure a meaningful life before death, then we must protect the right of any patient to be permitted to die with dignity.

THE AUTOPSY

Examining the body after death is an autopsy. The pathologist performing the autopsy assumes a mechanical, physical cause for the death. A *complete autopsy* refers to an examination of the organs of the three major cavities of the body—the abdomen, chest, and head. An autopsy is at the discretion of the next of kin unless the death is a medical examiner's (coroner) case. Then it is performed as a matter of law (Korndorffer, 1978).

Hospital autopsy rates (number of autopsies performed in a hospital divided by the number of hospital deaths) in the United States have declined from 41 percent in 1964 to 22 percent in 1975 (Roberts, 1978:332). The decline is attributed to a decrease in the absolute number of autopsies performed and to an increase in the number of deaths in hospitals. Physicians, hospital administrators, and families of the deceased have shown reduced interest in autopsies. Autopsies also create difficulties for funeral directors in that it complicates the embalming process and can postpone funeral arrangements if the medical examiner delays the release of the body.

Roberts (1978:332–3) cites the following as the purposes of an autopsy:

1. A check on the accuracy of the clinical diagnoses and historical data.
2. A check on the appropriateness of medical and surgical therapy.
3. Helps gather data on new and old diseases and surgical procedures.
4. Obtains information beneficial to the deceased's family.
5. Can provide organs, tissues, and extracts for the benefit of the living.
6. Clarifies real or potential medicolegal deaths.

In teaching hospitals associated with medical schools, the faculty and students often meet regularly to discuss a death. For the attending physician this can be somewhat threatening in that after he or she presents a case study of the patient, the pathologist then presents the autopsy report to the group. A crucial role is served by the pathologist in that the report could confirm the medical efforts of the attending physician or show that other medical applications should have been performed. To appear competent to one's colleagues is especially important to physicians. Thus, the pathologist may serve as a counselor by consoling the physician if the autopsy report reveals a negative action on behalf of the physician.

> "Doctor," complained the patient, "all the other physicians called in on my case seem to disagree with your diagnosis."
> "Yes, I know they do," said the doctor, "but the autopsy will prove that I'm right."

CONCLUSION

Since the thought of dying is stressful, it seems appropriate that we be aware of dying and death; with more awareness, hopefully a greater acceptance of dying and death will result. Through a better understanding of death meanings, our coping with dying and death should be enhanced. It is difficult to relate to the dying if we ourselves have not been sensitized to our own death.

Traditionally, medical schools have had very limited offerings in death education. On the job training may only enforce one's anxieties about the dying. It is encouraging that medical schools seem more concerned about the social and psychological aspects of their patients today. While death education does not constitute a significant place in current medical curricula, the situation is improving.

With dying patients being viewed as deviants in the medical subculture, the treatment of the dying is not always the most humane. After all, death is counter to what physicians learn in medical school. They take an oath to prolong life and relieve suffering (sometimes the two are contradictory). To lose a patient is a failure.

We often play games in communicating with a dying patient. We know, the physician and nurse know, and the patient knows (probably whether told or not) when the condition is terminal, but we often exist in a closed awareness context. No one lets the other know that he or she knows. Death talk remains taboo.

Patients do not always wish to be kept alive but our society has difficulty fulfilling such a request. Moral, religious, and legal questions cloud the whole issue of the right to die. It is important to remember that patients (even dying patients!) have rights. A meaningful life before death must be assured. We must remember that one is living even though he or she may have a terminal disease.

Summary

1. The meaning of dying is dependent upon the social context in which it takes place.
2. Time, space, norm, role, value, self, and situational meanings are important components of the meaning of our dying.
3. One may go through stages in accepting his or her terminal self meaning.
4. Physicians have limited education concerning issues of dying and death.
5. The dying patient is *viewed* as a deviant in the medical setting; therefore, the dying patient is *treated accordingly*.
6. Different awareness contexts exist between medical personnel, patients, and the patients' families.
7. A growing concern about the rights of the patient is evolving in the United States as is evidenced by the living will and euthanasia issues now prominent in the news headlines.
8. Autopsies are sometimes performed after death to aid in determining the cause of death.

APPLICATION: AN AUTOPSY OBSERVED AND EXPERIENCED

The following essay was written by Elizabeth Maxwell, who as a college sophomore at St. Olaf College visited a medical center during a health science internship experience. In this essay, Elizabeth discusses her observations of the autopsy and her emotional reactions to it. While it is difficult to generalize from one experience, it is possible that her first encounter with the autopsy is not unlike that of first year medical students.

We stepped into the autopsy room wondering what to expect. I was nervous for we had just been told that we might feel sick, and if we did we should leave the room so we would not faint and hurt ourselves. The sights and smells overwhelmed my senses. The mixed odors were of form-aldehyde and old blood, and the air was thick with that scent. I was won-dering how long I would last in this environment when we were offered surgical masks to wear. "I nearly fainted from the smell when I watched my first autopsy. Those masks help a little," said the resident who was working on the case. She was right about that.

The room was lined with stainless steel shelves and drawers. These con-tained countless preserved specimens from "interesting or unusual cases" to be studied in the future or used as references for curious medical stu-dents. Two large rectangular steel tables were in the center of the room. Each table had a gutter and tilted into a draining area leading to a sink. The water was always running to wash down the blood.

If what I've described so far is all there was, the room itself would not have been too bad. But there was more to the scene. On the top of one of the steel tables lay a large, naked, old, male body. That was my second shock (after the smell) and the major cause for my alarm. Fearing that I would pass out, I stood as far away from the tables and other people as I could. I took deep breaths and I stood with my legs spread apart for better balance, but I did not faint.

This man on the table seemed so vulnerable. I tried to think of him only as a body. Despite my efforts I began imagining myself in his position—a resident, a medical student, and an autopsy specialist cutting, probing, and making comments about my physical condition; other interested peo-ple coming into the room now and then to check out the progress; and six more students curiously watching the whole procedure. I did not like this situation, and I felt sympathy for the autopsy victim. Yet I was curious enough to stay and try to survive the whole autopsy.

When we had become accustomed to our surroundings, the resident told us about the "patient." This fifty-five year old white male had come to the hospital to get his foot treated. He had an ulcer (an open sore common to diabetics like himself) on his foot. "He was very lucky to have come in when he did, his foot ulcer was getting bad and it could have led to gan-grene," said the resident. His accident happened as he was dressing to leave the hospital after getting treatment for the ulcer. He fell and broke his hip. His surgeon operated, making a large incision from the upper thigh to his waist. He replaced the joint and sent him into recovery. The surgeons thought he was doing well, but he died the next day. (Hip operations are not usually life-threatening.)

This man had a good heart and did not smoke. He was not fat and he seemed to be in good health. What went wrong? The autopsy team was instructed to look for possible blood clots or other problems in the internal organ system.

When we began observing, the autopsy specialist was finishing the job of resuturing the long incision in the victim's hip. A blood clot the size of a big potato had been extracted. It was soft and jello-like and looked like a raw liver. When I asked, they told me that it was a small clot and that it was not the main reason for this poor man's death.

The next part of the autopsy process again unnerved me—and again I did not faint though I thought I would. The autopsy specialist made a huge Y-shaped incision from the lower abdomen to the lower chest branching out to the shoulders. The layer just below his skin was yellow and fatty, and the strong muscle layer was dark red. The upper layer peeled away from the muscle, but the muscle stuck tight to the ribs. The specialist then hacked through the muscle and ribs around the outside of the chest cavity with a curved pruning shears that had long handles for good leverage. Then he pulled away that layer to expose the heart and lungs.

The centrally located heart was at least as big as two of my fists. The lungs were located high in the chest region, starting at the top of the shoulders and going down only halfway to the lower ribs. They were pink and porous, and I wondered how such small organs could take in enough air for a man his size.

The heart, lungs, liver, and the rest of the smaller organs were then removed and put aside to be studied by the resident medical student, Kris. While Kris "breadsliced" (cut lengthwise at one-inch intervals to study the inside of the organ) the liver, lungs, and digestive system, the autopsy specialist started his electric saw; I wondered what he was planning to do with it. The noise was alarming. He cut a one-foot segment of the backbone out of the man's back and then cut that lengthwise down the middle. Then he extracted the spinal cord and laid it on the table for us to see. I touched it. The finger-thick cord was made up of hundreds of tiny nerves. To see and touch all of these incredible impulse messengers awed me.

The specialist was not done with the saw. While we were watching the dissection of the organs, the patient's scalp was cut at the base of his head and peeled forward so his scalp lay inside out over his face. I was glad that I could not see his face. The saw started again and cut away a portion of his skull at the back of his head. I looked inside the hole at the body's mastermind—the brain. The resident told me that the brain was too soft to cut right then, so they would store it in formaldehyde for several days until it "firmed up."

As we were examining the organs on another table, two more male medical students arrived. They planned to practice inserting a vein catheter. To practice they used our patient's leg veins. They worked at cutting a small hole and inserting the catheter tube (which drains out blood). They saw that there were some young, female observers in our group so they wanted to be noticed. They joked about how they were going to save him now. I was appalled at this crude behavior. I wondered how anyone could joke in a situation like this one. I tried to remind myself that it was a horrible place to work and that these students used humor to relieve their tensions and make their work more manageable.

We had to leave soon after that incident. We thanked the resident and autopsy specialist and left the room. It was nice to take off the gloves, masks and aprons we had been wearing. Fresh air was welcome, too. But I began thinking about what I had seen that morning. I was upset by the whole situation: an innocent, older man suddenly dies, and with the loss of his life, he loses his identity and dignity. He was just a body for anatomical study. He was not a person, though he was still wearing his wedding ring.

As I contemplated this paradox, I thought again of the whole autopsy process, and was dismayed again. It had been so brutal. It was nothing like the delicate surgery I had expected. Since an autopsy must show every detail, huge incisions must be made. Nothing needs replacement, so little care is taken to keep the parts intact. This carelessness upset me.

I tried to sort everything out in my mind—the patient, the tragic accident, the brutal procedure, the stoic autopsy specialist, the helpful and concerned medical student (Kris), and the joking male medical students. All of this was too much for me to comprehend.

All that day and night, I kept smelling the autopsy odor in various places I went; I could not escape it! The next morning I wrote down my feelings in my journal concerning what I had seen and felt. I also talked with people about my frustrated emotions for several weeks. With the passing of time I can now talk easily about it, but sometimes I think about that old man.

Discussion Questions

1. What does it mean to you to say that the meaning of dying will depend upon the social context in which the dying takes place?
2. Would you prefer to live with a person with a terminal disease or a person who is chemically dependent? Discuss the advantages and disadvantages of each.
3. How might steps be taken to overcome the diminished social and personal power of the hospital patient? Are such limitations on patients necessary for an orderly hospital?
4. Discuss the statement: The terminally ill eventually come to view death as a blessing.
5. You have just been told that you have inoperable cancer. Discuss how you think you would react. In what ways might you change your life?

6. If a patient's death does represent a failure to a physician, how might medical schools assist in creating an attitude of acceptance of death as the final stage of growth?
7. List as many types of deviant individuals as you can. Do you include the dying patient as deviant? Why or why not?
8. Deviance may vary with time and place. What is meant by this statement?
9. Discuss Glaser and Strauss' four awareness contexts. Which do you think most often exists in a medical setting with a dying patient?
10. Since a dying person is often unable to help him or herself and is often dependent on others, why should he or she have any rights?
11. Should the living will be legalized by the Congress of the United States? Why or why not?
12. What, in your opinion, can be gained from observing an autopsy as Elizabeth Maxwell did?

Glossary

AUTOPSY: A medical examination of the organs of the body after death by a pathologist to determine the cause of death.

AWARENESS CONTEXT: What each interacting person knows of the others' defined status and the recognition of the others' awareness of his or her own definition.

CULTURAL LAG: Not all aspects of a culture change at the same rate of speed; typically nonmaterial aspects (e.g., attitudes and values) change more slowly than material aspects (e.g., technological innovations).

DISENGAGEMENT: The process by which an individual withdraws from society or society withdraws from or no longer seeks the individual's efforts.

EUTHANASIA: A means for producing a gentle and easy death. Literally "the good death."

LABELING THEORY: The significance of how an act is viewed is on the audience observing rather than on the act itself or the actor.

MASTER STATUS: The status (position) that dominates all other statuses in the mind of an individual.

NORM: A plan of action or expected behavior pattern thought to be appropriate for a particular situation.

ROLE: Specified behavior expected for persons occupying specific social positions.

References

Ashley-Cameron, S., and George Dickinson. 1979. "Nurses' Attitudes Toward Working with Dying Patients." Paper presented at the Alpha Kappa Delta Research Symposium, Richmond, Va. February.

Atchley, Robert C. 1977. *The Social Forces in Later Life: An Introduction to Social Gerontology,* 2d ed. Belmont, Calif.: Wadsworth.

Barton, D. 1972. "The Need for Including Instruction on Death and Dying in the Medical Curriculum." *Journal of Medical Education,* Vol. 47:169–175.

Becker, Howard S. 1961. *Boys in White.* Chicago: University of Chicago Press.

Blauner, R. 1966. "Death and Social Structure." *Psychiatry,* Vol. 29:378–394.

Charmaz, Kathy. 1980. *The Social Reality of Death.* Reading, Mass.: Addison-Wesley.

Consumer Reports. 1977. *Funerals: Consumers' Last Rights,* pp. 199–206. Mount Vernon, N.Y.: Consumers Union.

Coe, Rodney M. 1970. *Sociology of Medicine.* New York: McGraw-Hill.

Cumming, Elaine, and William E. Henry. 1961. *Growing Old: The Process of Disengagement.* New York: Basic Books.

Dickinson, George E. 1976. "Death Education in U. S. Medical Schools." *Journal of Medical Education,* Vol. 51:134–136.

Dickinson, George E., and A. A. Pearson. 1979a. "Differences in Attitudes Toward Terminal Patients Among Selected Medical Specialties of Physicians." *Medical Care,* Vol. 17:682–685.

Dickinson, George E., and A. A. Pearson. 1979b. "Sex Differences of Physicians in Relating to Dying Patients." *Journal of the American Medical Women's Association,* Vol. 34:45–47.

Dickinson, George E., and A. A. Pearson. 1980–81. "Death Education and Physicians' Attitudes Toward Dying Patients." *Omega,* Vol. 11:167–174.

Dickinson, George E. 1981. "Death Education in U. S. Medical Schools: 1975–1980." *Journal of Medical Education,* Vol. 56:111–114.

Durkheim, Emile. 1961. *Moral Education.* Glencoe, Ill.: The Free Press.

Erikson, Kai. 1962. "Notes on the Sociology of Deviance." *Social Problems,* Vol. 9 (Spring):307–314.

Fletcher, Joseph. 1977. "Elective Death," in *Understanding Death and Dying,* pp. 352–367, ed. by Sandra Wilcox and Marilyn Sutton. New York: Alfred Publishing Co.

Freidson, Elliot. 1972. *Profession of Medicine.* New York: Dodd Mead.

Garfield, Charles A. 1978. *Psychosocial Care of the Dying Patient.* New York: McGraw-Hill.

Gaspard, N. J. 1970. "The Family of the Patient with Long-Term Illness." *Nursing Clinics of North America,* Vol. 5, No. 1:77–84.

Glaser, Barney, and Anselm Strauss. 1965. *Awareness of Dying.* Chicago: Aldine.

Goffman, Erving. 1963. *Stigma.* Englewood Cliffs, N.J.: Prentice-Hall.

Gustafson, Elizabeth. 1972. "Dying: The Career of the Nursing Home Patient." *Journal of Health and Social Behavior,* Vol. 13:226–235.

Hackett, T. P. 1976. "Psychological Assistance for the Dying Patient and His Family." *Annual Review of Medicine,* Vol. 5:371–378.

Hale, R. 1971. "Some Lessons on Dying." *Christian Century* (September):1076–1079.

Kasper, A. M. 1959. "The Doctor and Death," in *The Meaning of Death,* pp. 259–270, ed. by Herman Feifel. New York: McGraw-Hill.

Kavanaugh, Robert E. 1972. *Facing Death.* Baltimore: Penguin Books.

Korndorffer, W. E. 1978. "Medical Examiner's Office," in *Death and Dying: Principles and Practices in Patient Care,* pp. 288–303, ed. by R. G. Benton. New York: D. Van Nostrand.

Krant, M. J. 1972. "The Organized Care of the Dying Patient." *Hospital Practice* (January): 101–108.

Kubler-Ross, Elizabeth. 1969. *On Death and Dying.* New York: Macmillan.

Larson-Kurz, C., A. L. Wheeler, and G. E. Dickinson. 1979. "Dying as Deviance: A

Reinforcement of Society's Norms in the Medical Profession." Paper presented at the annual meeting of the Midwest Sociological Society, Minneapolis, Minn., April 25.

Larson-Kurz, C., A. L. Wheeler, and G. E. Dickinson. 1979. "On Becoming a Physician: The Case of the Dying Patient." Paper presented at the annual meeting of the Southern Sociological Society, Atlanta, Ga., April.

Leming, Michael R., Glenn M. Vernon, and Robert M. Gray. 1977. "The Dying Patient: A Symbolic Analysis." *International Journal of Symbology*, Vol. 8 (July): 77–86.

Levine, S., and N. A. Scotch. 1970. "Dying as an Emerging Social Problem," in *The Dying Patient*, ed. by Orville Brim et al. New York: Russell Sage Foundation.

Neale, Robert E. 1973. *The Art of Dying*. New York: Harper and Row.

Newell, David S. 1961. "Social Structural Evidence for Disengagement," in *Growing Old*, ed. by Elaine Cumming and W. E. Henry. New York: Basic Books.

Olin, H. S. 1972. "A Proposed Model to Teach Medical Students the Care of the Dying Patient." *Journal of Medical Education*, Vol. 47:564–567.

Parsons, Talcott. 1951. *The Social System*. New York: The Free Press.

Parsons, Talcott. 1958. "The Definitions of Health and Illness in the Light of American Values and Social Structure," in *Patients, Physicians, and Illness*, ed. by E. Gartly Jaco. New York: The Free Press.

Pattison, E. Mansell. 1977. *The Experience of Dying*. Englewood Cliffs, N.J.: Prentice-Hall.

Pearlman, J., B. A. Stotsky, and J. R. Dominick. 1969. "Attitudes Toward Death Among Nursing Home Personnel." *Journal of Genetic Psychology*, Vol. 114:63–75.

Pine, V. 1975. "Institutionalized Communication About Death and Dying." *Journal of Thanatology*, Vol. 3:1–12.

Rabin, D. L., and L. H. Rabin. 1970. "Consequences of Death for Physicians, Nurses, and Hospitals. *The Dying Patient*, pp. 171–190, ed. by Orville Brim et al. New York: Russell Sage Foundation.

Roberts, W. C. 1978. "The Autopsy: Its Decline and a Suggestion for its Revival." *The New England Journal of Medicine*, Vol. 299 (August 17):332–338.

Tarnower, W. 1969. "The Dying Patient." *Kansas City American Academy of General Practice*, Vol. 40:97–102.

Vernon, Glenn M. 1972. *Human Interaction*. New York: Ronald Press.

Wheeler, Alban L. 1973. "The Dying Person: A Deviant in the Medical Subculture." Paper presented at the Southern Sociological Society Meeting, Atlanta, Ga., April.

Suggested Readings

Brim, Orville G., Howard E. Freeman, Sol Levine, and Norman A. Scotch. 1970. *The Dying Patient*. New York: Russell Sage Foundation.
 These fourteen original articles examine the problems of dying and medical conduct from the perspectives of sociology, economics, medicine, and law.

Glaser, Barney, and Anselm Strauss. 1965. *Awareness of Dying*. Chicago: Aldine.
 Uses the approach of awareness to deal with the practical and theoretical aspects of interaction between terminal patients, their families, and hospital personnel.

Kavanaugh, Robert E. 1972. *Facing Death*. Baltimore: Penguin Books.
  Excellent coverage of death and dying from the perspective of a psychologist and former priest.
Kubler-Ross, Elizabeth. 1969. *On Death and Dying*. New York: Macmillan.
  Kubler-Ross elaborates on the five common emotional stages observed in her work with terminal patients. She concludes that if relatives and hospital personnel are unable to deal with death in their own lives, they will be unable to face death calmly and helpfully with the patient. Includes interviews with terminal patients and focuses on what we can learn from them.
Neale, Robert E. 1971. *The Art of Dying*. New York: Harper and Row.
  Presents problems of dying by placing the reader in the role of the dying person.
Quint, Jeanne C. 1967. *The Nurse and the Dying Patient*. New York: Macmillian.
  Based on a six-year investigation of five nursing schools in the San Francisco area, this book reports on what happens to student nurses during and after their encounters with death and shows how the death of a patient is handled as an occupational fact.
Schoenberg, Bernard, et al. 1981. *Education of Medical Students in Thantology*. New York: Arno Press.
  An anthology describing the status of death education for the medical profession.
Sudnow, David. 1967. *Passing On: The Social Organization of Dying*. Englewood Cliffs, N.J.: Prentice-Hall.
  Explores the sociological structure of certain aspects of death in a hospital setting.

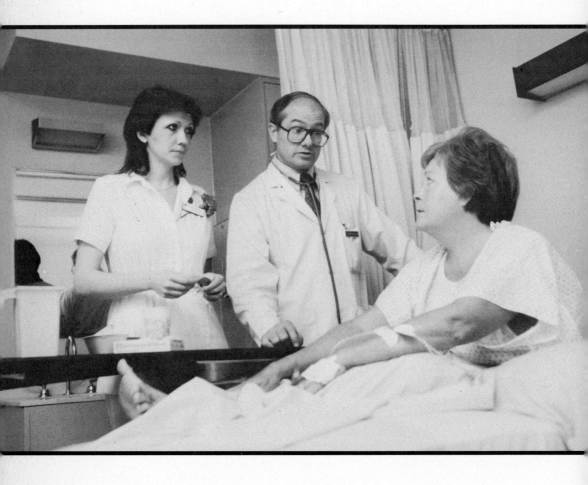

Chapter 4

PERSONAL COPING WITH DYING AND DEATH

Is this dying? Is this all? Is this what I feared when I prayed
against a hard death? Oh, I can bear this! I can bear it!!
Cotton Mather (1663–1728), American clergyman, on his deathbed

AUNT MIRA DIED as she had lived. At ninety-two she was still a respected
historian and colorful single woman who wore rubbers every day to protect herself from falling, breaking a hip, and dying. When the nurse
brought her breakfast, she asked, "Is today the day I go?" The nurse re-
plied, "Yes," referring to our later outing for lunch. When I arrived, I
learned that she had eaten her breakfast, read the *New York Times,* and died
before the nurse could return for the tray. Few of us will be as fortunate as
Aunt Mira who neither welcomed nor dreaded death.

The intent of this chapter is to focus on life and living in the face of
inevitable death; to provide a context in which we can assess our lives as
finite; and to contemplate a course of dying supportive of our own needs,
those of our family, and those of persons caring for us.

This topic is important because with purposeful study we may be able to
avoid overwhelming fears or dysfunctional denial of death, conserving
energy for the pursuit of a meaningful life. Rather than romanticizing or
intellectualizing, we can become death-reality oriented, appreciating both
the uniquenesses and commonalities of the complex intrapersonal, social,
and cultural experience associated with death. This chapter will attempt to
provide an understanding for deaths that are anticipated, planned for, and
thoughtfully experienced—deaths that are consistent with most people's
goals.

Specifically, this chapter will present a theoretical framework for understanding the processes of personal death awareness and coping, of "getting one's house in order" in preparation for death, and of helping the
dying to cope with their situation. A discussion of support groups to assist
those with mutual death concerns will conclude the chapter.

Overall, this chapter is about adaptation—to living, to dying, and to grieving. Adaptation, the goodness-of-fit between person and environment, is used synonymously with coping to connote "active mastery," and not just "adjustment." Adaptation is a two-way process in which we are able to change our environment, be changed by it, and/or remove ourselves from it entirely.

Stress is a concept used here to signify an event, a process, or accumulated inputs placing an adaptive demand on a person or family system. Dying is a stress process made up of many small, and not so small, stressors that evoke a host of adaptive maneuvers.

Contemplating "personal" death forces us to retreat at times from our theoretical world of rational thought, intellectual illusions, and statistical descriptions to the real world of people who struggle with ultimate challenges. Therefore, we will be addressing the topic of dying and death at the point where it intersects with real lives.

Aunt Mira came into my life when she was admitted to the psychiatric ward for an acute psychotic episode associated with taking too much of an antacid. As the ward social worker, I was asked to help her find a new place to live since the manager of her residence club would not allow her to return. Fortunately, we located a warm and secure place for her to live out her last two years. Since she had no family, I continued seeing her on a regular basis. We never had to sit and wait for death since she was too busy even to get ill. On the last day perhaps she knew, and the nurse inadvertently confirmed, that she was going to die, but she made the best of those last few moments available to her.

A THEORETICAL FRAMEWORK FOR UNDERSTANDING THE PROCESS OF DEATH AWARENESS AND COPING WITH DYING AND GRIEVING

In trying to cope with death, it is important to develop a theoretical framework for understanding this process of death awareness. A review of the literature suggests that coping with the various stress situations surrounding death (both before and after it occurs) takes place in a process of stages. As discussed in Chapter 3, "stages" are not always followed in one-two-three order. Indeed, one might skip from stage one to five or any other such combination. Stages are not sacred. They are simply a theoretical scheme for helping to understand and predict behavior.

Hans Selye (1956), a physiologist, proposes a general adaptation syndrome—a response to all stressors—characterized by the following distinct stages: an alarm response, resistance, and exhaustion. Although describing a physiological process, Selye's stages have much in common with the formulation of other "stage-developers" such as Lindemann (1944) on acute grief, Kubler-Ross (1969) on the dying process, and Weisman (1974) on fatal illness. Just as these writers have proposed stages for explaining reactions to death, we will present a conception of an adaptive response in stages. The process of dying and grieving occurs within the greater context of a particular life. We distort our understanding if we treat dying as a distinct, isolated event. The following sections explore the stages in stress adaptation: anticipation, onset of a stressful event, disorganization, organization, and resolution.

Anticipation

Prior to the onset of a stressor may come an early stage of anticipation; we are alert to the possibility of danger and start mobilizing our personal resources. Most of us anticipate, at least intellectually, that death lies ahead. The elderly have probably had many experiences with death, but few mature adults, and even fewer children have experienced the death of a loved one. Therefore, anticipation of dying and death may be based on ignorance and fear of the unknown. Children attempt to master this "death anxiety" through play, while adults use mental imagery, avid attention to obituaries, or active participation in the dying of others in their anticipation of dying and death. Through modeling and rehearsal, one prepares for the stress.

Onset of a Stressful Event

The second stage of stress adaptation occurs at the onset of a stressful event or events—the experience of an alarming symptom, frightful diagnosis, threat of imminent loss of an important person, or a decline in one's physical, emotional, or social functioning. If denial results, it may insulate a person from being overwhelmed so that reality will only slowly impinge on awareness.

Disorganization

As awareness increases, disorganization occurs—an alarming bio-psychosocial process characterized by physical distress, breakdown of logical thought and feeling, and a change in customary roles and social relationships. Acute grief is a hallmark of this stage, a signal that adaptation has begun. Most people find it impossible to ignore a person in acute distress and they respond to the pain and suffering with a desire to "do something, anything!" Although our efforts to help at this stage may be awkward, they do communicate our care and concern. Silent sufferers are adaptively vulnerable in that they do not elicit the necessary support from others. Most people do not have the energy to sustain intense suffering without "risking" deterioration, disability, or even death.

Organization

In the next stage of adaptation, we begin to inventory resources and chart an adaptive course to "normal functioning." We send clearer messages for the kind of help that will be useful to us, and we resist attempts of others to be helpful who are actually detrimental to our ultimate well-being. Persons facing their own death have work to do, and they want to do it in a way that is most compatible with their customary life style. They will look for models of adaptive coping from others who have suffered similar experiences and have been successful in mastering them. They will also search their prior experiences for clues on other ways to cope. Organization and reorganization will continue until adequate resolution is approached.

Resolution

With mastery comes a sense of exhilaration and achievement; we feel that we will never again be vulnerable. However, when overtaxed or having fewer supports, resolution may be in process, with a general sense of relief but without final accomplishment. Persons who have been relatively unable to reach resolution, come from the experience feeling defeated and deteriorated.

In summary, judgments on adaptive success—such as assessing the attainment of an "appropriate" death awareness (Weisman, 1974)—are difficult to make since different value orientations and/or cultural expectations distort objectivity. The appearance of control over the situation, adequate support given by others, and apparent open and honest communication can serve as objective criteria of successful adaptation. But in the end, only the persons involved can really know the success of their coping efforts.

The Problem of Personal Death Awareness

Death awareness is a complex process. It is a function of one's level of cognitive, affective, and social development, as well as the social and cultural context of the experience. Humans both approach and avoid an awareness of their finite destiny. Freud (1915) proposed that individuals cannot consciously contemplate their own nonbeing, generating strenuous defenses against this anxiety-provoking awareness. Erikson (1980) suggests that it is the young and the old who live closer to the "shadow of nonbeing," and who are most keenly aware of death. However, the child's conception of death gradually shifts from an overwhelming (though partial and reversible) loss, brought on by egocentric omnipotence, to a death seen as permanent and universal (see for example Bluebond-Langer, 1977; Sahler, 1978; and Stillion and Wass, 1979).

Culturally, death is viewed as "defeat," with the dying and grieving as "victims." Because the dying and dead are hidden, we are unable to deal directly with our fears until such a time as we are confronted by a personally relevant death. On becoming more aware of the brevity of our life, we are better able to consciously adapt to the experiences of our last living days.

The Life Context of the Dying

The life context of the dying is not only the here-and-now physical setting (inhabited by people and events), it is the historical past and the anticipated future. A nurturing and stimulating context promotes adaptive death awareness, whereas a toxic context complicates adaptation. Of pivotal importance are prior, current, and anticipated experiences with loss, grief, and dying. These experiences give to the individual a unique meaning of the dying and death (Bowlby, 1980).

Karen, age twenty-three, experienced mild neurological symptoms similar to those of her grandmother and great grandmother who had died tragically of belatedly diagnosed brain tumors. Her physician supported a wait-and-see stance. For this family, the doctor's approach recapitulated the circumstances of the prior deaths and generated considerable anxiety, conflict, and anticipatory grief. Even though Karen's problems never proved to be life threatening, the family had been subjected to high levels of "unnecessary" stress by reason of their past experiences.

An expected death in the very old may be less stressful than the dying of a child or an adult with dependents. As discussed in Chapter 1, violent deaths—such as accidents, homicides, and suicides—leave tragic scars on all those close to the experience, and are exceedingly difficult to resolve. "If-only" deaths—such as those suspected to have been caused by smoking, overeating, or drinking—evoke complicated judgmental guilt and anxiety. Persons for whom physical attractiveness or physical vigor is important may have difficulty in coping with the loss of body parts or energy.

Another important determinant in perceiving death is one's position within the extended family. The death of a child threatens the continuity of generations and the link with immortality; the death of a sibling provokes identification; and the death of a parent removes an illusion of being protected from death. Being the last surviving member of the family, who carries the family name, can cause mourning for both the "family" and the individual.

The Perception of Reality: Threats and Supports

Given a life context with its broad familial and historical features, our sense of self, and the clarity or ambiguity of the situation, will determine our depth of death awareness. As with Karen, it may be difficult to know the reality of one's physical condition, and therefore, difficult to accept or reject the threat of serious illness. Also, the treatment and prognosis of yesterday may not be accurate today, with the rapidly evolving medical advances. Uncertainty and ambiguity pose a threat to effective coping because the adaptive process is predicated on some degree of conscious awareness. Clarity of the realities, however, does not insure accurate perception.

Awareness of our own dying is a process, moving from the first symptoms and their meaning, to an acceptance of our diagnosis and prognosis (Weisman, 1974). Slowly, we accumulate the knowledge necessary to understand that our life is threatened or coming to an end. A clear perception of the reality enhances a sense of self-as-capable and in control. As the disease progresses, it is more and more likely that the person will come to the realization that life *will* end, and that "cure" denotes a comforted and "appropriate" death (Weisman, 1972).

The Fears and Anxieties of the Dying

Pain, loss of control, and isolation are dreaded components of dying. Perhaps we believe that life should end without punishment and that all our efforts to lead a good life should be rewarded by a good death. Unfortunately, suffering is part of dying, just as it is part of life. We fear both physical and emotional pain—especially that caused by the irreversible loss of bodily functioning and the deprivation of important personal relationships.

The dying fear the loss of control over their own lives—the ability to make decisions, to participate in taking care of themselves and their own business, and to have a meaningful role in the lives of others. Considering oneself (or being considered by others) a "burden" is a recognition of this loss of control which can precipitate added emotional and physical suffering. Life-long powerlessness complicates these problems. Children fear the loss of control over human relationships; losing closeness with a parent may be more painful than physical suffering.

The dying may also fear the loss of identity or a feeling that the self is merging with others or with the environment. Medication for pain may contribute to these fears since drugged states distort perception or cognition and interfere with reality testing. One of my patients demonstrated this when he decided that pain was preferable to the affects of the drugs.

There are also many practical anxieties—fears over the loss of economic and social supports, the loss of homes, belongings, pets, jobs, and so forth. Loss of body parts or surgical disfigurement is another source of anxiety, but may, if it represents relief from pain, be ambivalently welcomed. The dying also fear humiliating loss of control over bowel and bladder functions accompanied by the loss of privacy, dignity, and feelings of self worth. The frail elderly, slowly dying in institutions, speak openly of these indignities as they may wish for a merciful death (Kosberg, 1977).

GETTING ONE'S HOUSE IN ORDER

Just as nesting in the animal kingdom occurs before birth, so, too, do certain activities signify a person's anticipation of death. Anticipatory grieving, a review of one's life, making decisions and choices, planning for the future, and leaving legacies and memories comprise the work of the dying.

Anticipatory Grief

Anticipatory grief has the adaptive function of protecting the dying and the grieving from being overwhelmed when the anticipated loss actually occurs (Lindemann, 1944). The first manifestation of anticipatory grief is a strong emotional reaction, followed by a clinging response, or a desperate need to be close to meaningful others. The person may then pull away, settling into pervasive sadness, anger, or guilt. Prolonged remission of the illness, or even a "cure," can cause problems in reattachment— reconnecting the bonds loosened by the grief work. Anticipatory grief, successfully negotiated, clears the way for other purposeful activity necessary in the preparation for death.

The Life Review

Lindemann (1979) shares an account of his own preparation for dying that included a revisit to the land of his birth (Germany) for one last time. Similarly, Dr. Borg in Bergman's *Wild Strawberries* revisits through travel and fantasy the meaningful places, people, and times of his life. Erikson (1976) traces the stages of the life cycle through the reminiscences and ramblings of Dr. Borg. Clearly, the perception of the nearness of death awakens an attachment to the past. Perhaps the kindly distortions of memory in the life review can enhance the meaning and integrity of one's life. Unlike the stereotype of the elderly, reminiscing is not a sign of senility, but is associated with emotional serenity and growth (Castelnuovo-Tedesco, 1980).

Sorting through a lifetime of accumulations stored in real attics (or the attics of the mind) accomplishes the same goal. One dusts off one's prized possessions, cherishes them once again, and then makes the decision on their fate—to be shared with others, left behind as a memorial, or to be buried. The life review is a eulogy—a reverence for what one was and a time for judgment—resolving old arguments, sharing secrets, and honestly facing the reality of one's life. The more that must remain hidden, the more difficult this process. The sharing of memories can repair estrangements and lifelong broken relationships. Butler (1963) has identified the life review as also being a therapeutic technique in helping the elderly.

Making Decisions and Choices

Control comes with the right to make one's own decisions, both in daily matters and in the overall direction of one's life. The decision to die and to control the time and place of one's death is a controversial and widely debated issue. The legality of this kind of anticipatory decision-making has been questioned, but recent legislation and court decisions support the rights of the dying. Natural Death Acts, Right to Die Laws, and Death with Dignity Statutes have been commonplace since 1976.

Seriously burned patients having injuries "without precedent of survival" are given the choice of life-prolonging care or ordinary symptom relief. As discussed in Chapter 3, the question remains as to who can best make these difficult decisions: the patient, the family, or the physician. In 1981, a Massachusetts judge determined that the court, not relatives or physicians, is to decide on the continuation of supportive care in the face of seemingly irreversible dying.

Right to Live or to Die: Who Is to Decide?

Ellen Goodman

Some have called it a Right to Die case. Others have labeled it a Right to Live case. One group of advocates has called for "death with dignity." Others have responded accusingly, "euthanasia."

At the center of the latest controversy about life and death, medicine and law, is a 78-year-old Massachusetts man whose existence hangs on a court order.

On one point, everyone agrees: Earle Spring is not the man he used to be. Once a strapping outdoorsman, he is now strapped to a wheelchair.

Once a man with a keen mind, he is now called senile by many, and mentally incompetent by the courts. He is at worst, a member of the living dead; at best, a shriveled version of his former self.

For more than two years, since his physical and then mental health began to deteriorate, Earle Spring has been kept alive by spending five hours on a kidney dialysis machine three times a week. Since January of 1979, his family has pleaded to have him removed from the life support system. They believe deeply that the Earle Spring who was, would not want to live as the Earle Spring who is. They believe they are advocates for the right to die in peace. In the beginning, the courts agreed. Possible for the first time, they ruled last month in favor of withdrawing medical care from an elderly patient whose mind had deteriorated. The dialysis was stopped.

But then in a sudden intervention, an outside nurse and doctor visited Earle Spring and testified that he was alert enough to "make a weak expression of his desire to live." And so the treatments resumed.

Now, while the courts are waiting for new and more thorough evidence about Spring's mental state, the controversy rages about legal procedures: no judge ever visited Spring, no psychiatrist ever testified. And even more importantly, we are again forced to determine one person's right to die or to live.

What should the relationship be between mental health and physical treatment? Should we treat the incompetent as aggressively as the competent? Should we order heart surgery for one senile citizen; should we take another off a kidney machine? What is the mental line between a life worth saving and the living dead? Who is to decide?

Clearly, there is no absolute in this case. No right to die, no right to live. We have to take into account many social as well as medical factors. How much of the resources of a society or a family should be allotted to a member who no longer recognizes it? How many sacrifices should the healthy and vital make for the terminally or permanently ill and disabled?

I remember what my grandfather used to say: No one wants to live to be 100 until you ask the man who is 99. Well, no one, including Earle Spring, wants to live to be senile. But, once senile, he may well want to live.

Source: *Lexington* (Ky.) *Herald*, February 5, 1980.

Throughout life, at least after childhood, most of us are able to exert reasonable control over our day-to-day activities. When we are dying, others (usually with benevolent motivations) tend to take over. Nursing care is scheduled, as are visiting hours; clothing is determined by pragmatic concerns; and we eat, sleep, bathe, and eliminate at the will of others. Self-determination and sensitive care, as reflected in hospice philosophy (see Chapter 8), support the need of the dying to make decisions and choices on treatment, hospitalization, and daily care. The dying need an environment that meets their needs, protects them from dangers, and provides maximum autonomy.

Planning for the Future

The dying have many "future" concerns, especially for the care of dependents and the disposal of property. Dying parents need to actively engage in planning for the care of their children—selecting new "parents" and homes, arranging for economic needs, and preparing the children for these changes and the death of the parent. The elderly parent of a disabled and/or dependent adult child may engage in this process for years. Dying persons may also express concern for the well-being of a dependent spouse.

Pets, valued possessions, a business or life work, or a cherished belief are similarly a source of concern. Insurance must be reviewed, benefits collected, and assistance sought for unmet financial needs. One may need to plan for more adequate housing, to sell a house, to move to a nursing facility, or to find community services in order to remain in one's own home.

The dying may have to attend to spiritual business—confess sins and seek forgiveness. Plans for the funeral, burial or disposal of one's body need to be communicated to others. Mrs. B., eighty-one, showed me her "shroud," a beautiful blue negligee and slippers. She wondered if people would be shocked if she wore them at her funeral. I concluded that perhaps this was what she wanted. She had never had a chance to express herself in this way and wanted to be remembered as a beautiful person.

Leaving Legacies and Memories

Customarily, legacies are considered bequests of money and possessions, but, in a metaphorical sense, legacies can also be anything valued that perpetuates identity past death. Erikson (1959) states, "I am what remains of me when I am no more."

A person anticipating death may find it important to construct a tangible memorial—an empire, a building, or a piece of handiwork. Planting a tree or supporting a cause, perhaps anonymously, gives comfort to a dying person in looking to the future. Less tangible, but important, is the knowledge that one will continue to live in the memories of others, particularly children and grandchildren. Memories, ritually shared in the family, link the generations and give continuity, if not immortality, to one's life. Some families collect on film and tape the voices and images of members for preservation in a family "archive." In this way they share important historical information, legends, and philosophy. The image of the deceased is thus kept "alive", and the "house is put in order."

"I Pray Every Night That I May Die in My Sleep . . ."

The following letter was forwarded to the Los Angeles Times *by the anonymous author's niece. Neither woman identified herself "because we are fearful." Editors of the* Times *(and of* The Courier-Journal*) ordinarily do not accept anonymous articles for publication. They made an exception in this case because they believed that the woman's message is an exceptional one.*

Hello! Is there anyone out there who will listen to me?

How can I convince you that I am a prisoner?

For the past five years, I have not seen a park or the ocean or even just a few feet of grass.

I am an 84-year-old woman, and the only crime which I have committed is that I have an illness which is called chronic. I have severe arthritis and about five years ago I broke my hip. While I was recuperating in the hospital, I realized that I would need extra help at home. But there was no one. My son died 35 years ago, my husband, 25 years ago. I have a few nieces and nephews who come by to visit once in a while, but I couldn't ask them to take me in, and the few friends I still have are just getting by themselves. So I wound up at a convalescent hospital in the middle of Los Angeles.

All kinds of people are thrown together here. I sit and watch, day after day. As I look around this room, I see the pathetic ones (maybe the lucky ones—who knows?) who have lost their minds, and the poor souls who should be out but nobody comes to get them, and the sick ones who are in pain. We are all locked up together.

I have been keeping in touch with the world through the newspaper, my one great luxury. For the last few years I have been reading about the changes in Medicare regulations. All I can see from these improvements is that nurses spend more time writing. For, after all, how do you regulate caring?

Most of the nurses' aides who work here are from other countries. Even those who can speak English don't have much in common with us. So they hurry to get their work done as quickly as possible. There are a few caring people who work here, but there are so many of us who are needy for that kind of honest attention.

A doctor comes to see me once a month. He spends approximately three to five seconds with me and then a few more minutes writing in the chart or joking with the nurses. (My own doctor doesn't come to convalescent hospitals, so I had to take this one.) I sometimes wonder about how the nurses' aides feel when they work so hard for so little money and then see that the person who spends so little time is the one who is paid the most.

I notice that most of the physicians who come here don't even pay attention to things like whether their patient's fingernails are trimmed or whether their body is foul-smelling. Last week when the doctor came to see me, I hadn't had a bath in 10 days because the nurses' aide took too long on her coffee break. She wrote in the chart that she gave me a shower—anyway, who would check or care? I would be labeled as a complainer or losing my memory, and that would be worse.

It is now 8 o'clock. Time to be in bed. I live through each night—and it is a long night—with memories of my childhood. I lived on an apple farm in Washington.

I remember how I used to bake pies and cakes and cookies for friends and neighbors and their children. In the five years I have been here, I have had no choice—no choice of when I want to eat or what I want to eat. It has been so long since I have tasted real fruit like mangos or cherries.

As I write this, I keep wishing I were exaggerating.

These last five years feel like the last five hundred of my life.

Last year, one of the volunteers here read us a poem. It was by Robert Browning. I think it was called "Rabbi Ben Ezra." It went something like this: "Grow old along with me, the best of life is yet to be." How can I begin to tell you that growing old in America is for me an unbelievable, lonely nightmare?

I am writing this because many of you may live to be old like me, and by then it will be too late. You, too, will be stuck here and wonder why nothing is being done, and you, too, will wonder if there is any justice in life. Right now, I pray every night that I may die in my sleep and get this nightmare of what someone has called life over with, if it means living in this prison day after day.

Source: *The Louisville* (Ky.) *Courier-Journal*, October 14, 1979.

HELPING THE DYING TO COPE

As noted in the insert on the eighty-four-year-old woman, to grow old, to be lonely, to be dying is not "the best of life." A little care and concern will go a long way with persons like this. It is no wonder she prays every night to die in her sleep.

The dying are comforted as we listen to their concerns and respond simply and honestly in meeting their needs by providing resources and understanding of their situation. Helping the dying is tough, but the gentle process of communicating about death (often in silence like holding the hand of the dying) provides hope.

---

people need people
and sick people need people
and dying people
really need people

Source: JoAnn Kelley Smith. *Free Fall*. Valley Forge, Pa: Judson Press,1975.

COMMON HUMAN NEEDS

In addition to the basics needed for physical survival (air, water, food, and warmth), everyone needs human bonds and meaningful relationships to maintain psychological and social well-being. The dying experience special difficulties in meeting these needs—particularly the need for physical closeness and intimacy. Moves to institutions, hospitals, and nursing homes represent attempts to meet physical needs of dying patients, but threaten their psychological well-being. According to Kron (1976), seldom are these institutions designed to meet the social-psychological needs of the dying (the hospice, discussed in Chapter 8, being a notable exception).

The dying also have needs of the mind. Mortimer Adler encourages caregivers to understand cognitively and affectively their situation, and communicate this understanding to others. To cope with the complexity of the anger, depression, withdrawal, and pain associated with dying, requires both maturity and support. With an honest sharing of accurate information, the dying can be helped to have a clear perception of their situation—a necessity when facing so many unknowns.

Individual Assessment of Need

Every dying person has the right to care based on a deep understanding of his or her own individual needs and threats. This assessment will include attention to the physical, psychological, and social realities of the person's life—past, present, and future. The very process of doing a patient evaluation may convey the caregiver's belief in the individual's worth and uniqueness, and help to establish a therapeutic relationship.

To gain an understanding, it is important to address the following questions: What are the unmet needs and threats?, What resources are available to meet these needs and protect this person from perceived danger?, What adaptive coping mechanisms are available?, What significant life experiences color the way this person and his or her family approach death?, Do racism, sexism, and ageism threaten obtaining competent and empathetic care?, What are the patient's prior experiences with loss and mourning?, What decisions and choices have to be made?, Can the dying person make these decisions or participate in the process?, and Is the living environment supportive, familiar, and appropriate to the stage-specific needs of the person? The following case study illustrates the importance of individualized assessment of patient needs.

Mrs. D, seventy-eight, when found seriously ill with congestive heart failure, was brought to the hospital by the visiting nurse. At home was her sixty-year-old mentally retarded son, who had recently been diagnosed as having lung cancer, and her eighty-year-old husband. A cursory assessment of her circumstances identified the obvious problems: her physical condition, her son's illness and incapacity, and her husband's advanced age. Mrs. D strenuously resisted the immediate referral to social service and insisted on release from the hospital. As I visited with her, Mrs. D revealed she did not want help, no good would come from it. Tearfully, she eventually shared with me that her homemaker from the agency had died three weeks before of "overwork." She had a warm and close relationship with this person for over three years. Mrs. D said that her death was "as bad as losing a mother." I asked about her mother and learned that she had died when Mrs. D was eight, leaving her with the care of three younger children. As we talked, she grieved the loss of the homemaker, her mother, and her son. Although she was convinced she was responsible for these misfortunes (a conception common in children), she slowly recovered, accepted her need for another homemaker, and was able to return home to her family. Only by getting close to Mrs. D was it possible to know what was troubling her and provide her with what she needed—a chance to grieve her losses.

Persons like Joy Ufema, in the following insert, help to see that patients' individual needs are assessed and met. She is realistic with her patients and functions in an open awareness context. Oh, to have more Joy Ufema's in the world!

Nurse Counsels Terminally Ill

Bob Dvorchak

HARRISBURG (AP)—Joy Ufema's work requires a thick skin and a soft heart. She helps terminally ill patients die their own way.

A registered nurse at Harrisburg Hospital, she listens to their thoughts and makes sure they get the best of care, even if it means bending some rules, and protects their rights.

"I found the basic premise is there are no frail human beings. I think there's an innate quality in us that human beings can handle anything," said Miss Ufema, now in her fifth year as a death and dying nurse.

"I believe in being explicitly honest and real. If you choose not to respond to that because you can't take it, then that's your choice. I promise not to make any value judgements on how you handle it," she added.

"You definitely can choose denial. You can be angry and scream and shout. What's important is that the patient calls the shots all the way."

Joy, 35, has counseled some 400 patients. She had been in nursing for about a year when she asked her superior if she could set up a program to help the dying.

Her work was inspired by Dr. Elizabeth Kubler-Ross, a Swiss psychiatrist who has done extensive studies on death and dying. But Joy's work is unique because few hospitals have similar programs. And death is a topic generally treated as taboo.

"I'm having a great deal of difficulty understanding why we don't discuss death in our society. It's the one thing we all have in common," said Miss Ufema.

Joy pays a visit to a patient after a physician breaks the news about a terminal illness.

"I ask a patient if he feels like sharing with me what it's like to be seriously ill. And that context is that I know and he knows," Miss Ufema said.

"Dying means a loss of control over life. So if he has some control over the remainder of his life, I think it's important to finish things his way," she added.

"My greatest asset is simply being real. I'll tell a dying patient I'm uncomfortable being here. I don't want to be here, but I am. And I'm scared. I'm not coming in here with a clipboard and a lab coat. I don't wear a black cape and come in saying, 'You're dying. You're dying,'" Miss Ufema said.

"Part of it is that I have a genuine concern about their condition at this time. And part of it is also saying I have no idea what you're going through. I'm not going to tell an empathetic lie and have them say to me, 'Oh, yeah? When did you die of leukemia?'" she added.

Edward A. Miller, one of Joy's recent patients, told of his relationship with the death and dying nurse in an interview before his death last week. Miller, a 32-year-old lawyer for the state, died of lung cancer, even though the odds of a nonsmoker in his age bracket getting the disease are about one in a million.

"I'm not upset about dying. It's the breaks. You can't do anything about it. You can't blame anyone. You can't do anything to prevent it. I don't think it takes courage to die. Everybody dies," said Miller.

He was a unique patient in that he already accepted his death before meeting Joy. But his relationship with her meant a lot to him.

"Joy's intelligent. She understands what I'm going through. She's interested. Such communications are a means of building up one's own sense of worth," he added.

"There are some people I can't talk to about death. It would be too tough for them, or they would not understand. It's always nice to have another friend like Joy, someone who cares about you.

"And she does a lot of little things, like making sure the nurses are around and I'm being taken care of. If you're treated like a lump of flesh, you begin to feel like one. You can't be anything but depressed," Miller said.

"I'm very much a patient advocate. I'm very willing to get into hot water to protect a patient's rights," said Miss Ufema, who once broke hospital rules by bringing in a pair of kittens for a boy dying with leukemia.

Joy's office is a small one on the hospital's sixth floor. On the yellow walls is a poster with the words from Ecclesiastes, the biblical passage that says for everything there is a purpose—a time to live; a time to die.

Joy does have critics. Some hospital personnel call her the "Death Squad." But her program is gaining greater acceptance.

"I've had doctors hang up on me or throw charts. I've been bodily taken out of a patient's room. But that's changing. There's a better understanding," she said.

Miss Ufema disregards the dangers of developing strong emotional ties with people who only have a short time to live.

"I'm absolutely emotionally involved. I think that's why I'm effective," she said.

"There are some patients who I have just cried over. There were some emotional things in our discussions or just the whole injustice of having to die," she added.

"Some days I'm super depressed because dying is such an injustice. The rewards come from a good death. By that I mean the patient has called the shots all the way—taken control and finished it his way," Joy said.

Source: *The Centre Daily Times*, State College and Bellefonte, Pa, February 8, 1978.

Help-Seeking and Resistance

As in the case of Mrs. D, help-seeking is a relatively late step in the adaptive process because shock, disorganization, and resistance interfere with earlier efforts (Overbeck, 1977). Mechanic (1968) identifies the major determinants of help-seeking for physical illness: the symptoms must be visible and perceived as serious; they must disrupt family, work, and other social activities; they must appear frequently, persistently, and intolerable to the carrier or those close; and there must be information, knowledge, and cultural assumptions making it difficult to deny their importance. In addition, help-seeking will not occur if other needs compete with an illness response, if other possible interpretations can be assigned to the symptoms, or if resources for treatment are unavailable because of physical distance or monetary and psychological costs.

Resistance is an adaptive response aimed at maintaining autonomy and independence. Self-esteem suffers when we must admit our inability to provide for ourselves. When fearing a life-threatening illness, many resist seeking the help of others in facing the experience directly.

Initial contacts are very important, particularly when the person has been forced to seek help—as in the case of Mrs. D. The potentially helpful person must listen sensitively to the request of the client, the meaning the client attributes to the problem, and to the feelings expressed and unexpressed. Resisting clients have hidden concerns that will remain unspoken until a trusting relationship has been established. Starting where the client is, accepting the legitimacy and commonness of the feeling, and providing information helps to allay fears. If the person is overwhelmed by accumulated stress, it helps to partialize these problems and deal with "one thing at a time."

Reality resistances, such as fear of a painful procedure, can be dealt with through straightforward explanation. However, when the resistance is unconscious or less than obvious, it may be more difficult to identify the source of apprehension and respond appropriately. In life-threatened situations, confrontation or even court intervention may be necessary to save a life.

Conclusion

The diversity and complexity of individual, social, and cultural influences on the attitudes and practices surrounding the care of the dying and grieving, make it difficult to advance a prescription for effective coping with personal death. Nevertheless, those who go through a life-threatening experience are struck with the pivotal importance of sustained caring human relationships—both within the family and with the caregivers. Paradoxically, it is the release from these life-sustaining bonds that comprises the work of dying and grieving. There is sadness in the loss, but also relief in the freedom from responsibilities, concerns, and claims that accompany life.

Summary

1. An appropriate death is a complex biological, intrapsychic, interpersonal, and sociocultural adaptive process consistent with the individual and family level of development and goals for living.
2. Age, sex, race, social roles, and socioeconomic status are important determinants for the course of dying and the availability of care and resources.
3. Prior losses give unique meaning to each experience with dying, death, and grieving.
4. Pain, isolation, and loss of control are the major fears of the dying and are associated with the loss of body parts and functions, homes and jobs, meaningful relationships, privacy, dignity, and a feeling of worth.
5. Ambiguity and uncertainty are major problems faced by the dying, their families, and the caregivers.
6. Stress points in the dying process are at the times of diagnosis, hospitalization, and the increased severity of symptoms.
7. Anticipatory grief, a life review, putting one's affairs in order, leaving a legacy, and planning for the future are the essential tasks for the dying.
8. Respite care and bereavement counseling are necessary services to offer to the families of the dying.
9. A professional coping style characterized by flexibility and openness is most effective in dealing with problems of providing competent care, maintaining interdisciplinary collaboration, and meeting family demands and community concerns.

APPLICATION: SUPPORTIVE NETWORKS FOR THE DYING, THEIR FAMILIES, AND CAREGIVERS

The dying are vulnerable to inadequate and inappropriate support. If isolated, their needs will not be known; if completely surrounded with care, they may suffer from unnecessary intrusions on their privacy and independence. Doing for people that which they can do themselves results in a loss of competence or the opportunity to master new and adaptive skills, while leading to dependency and helplessness. Institutional care can frequently be faulted for encouraging such dependency.

Both formal and informal supportive networks are available to the dying. The informal system consists of family, friends, and even bosses and bartenders. In the face of death, a person may need to draw on his or her network of close personal relationships, even though there is little or no chance for reciprocity in the conventional sense. If the informal system is minimal or depleted by grief and exhaustion, a specialized or formal support network may be needed.

The formal network consists of health care professionals and hospice workers, as well as specialists in bereavement counseling, accounting, transportation, theology, and the law. Some daily services are provided by Meals on Wheels and Chore and Homemaker services. Social workers and ministers pay particular attention to the emotional and spiritual needs of the dying and their families, since their traditional roles allow for attention to these special and unusual needs. Volunteers can provide respite care and relief as families are overwhelmed with fatigue and emotional exhaustion. The professional network can similarly become depleted, but ordinarily has greater resources at its command to alleviate this stress.

In coordinating services needed by the dying, serious problems of conflicting values can arise. Some believe that specialized care for the dying should only be available for those who can pay for the services. When society adopts this orientation, many ill and dying suffer—particularly those disadvantaged by reason of race, sex, age, and socioeconomic status. Others favor universal and nondiscriminatory care for the dying, resulting in general availability of services to even those who are the least favored by society. This approach is more costly and requires a reevaluation of the method by which a society allocates its resources.

SUPPORTIVE NETWORKS FOR THE FAMILY

The family of the dying will experience some needs different from the person who is dying. The "family" of the dying consists of all those persons closely attached and significantly affected by the loss. One cannot assume that blood, marriage, or adoption assures attachment, just as one cannot ignore strong attachments formed between unrelated persons.

Families also tend to rely on the help received from their established informal and formal networks. These supporters may or may not be equipped to handle the family's special needs and concerns. As discussed in Chapter 8, hospice care provides services specifically designed to help families; but limited staff and financial resources may place restrictions on who can be helped, and for how long.

"Widow to Widow," "One Day at a Time," "Candlelighters," and "Compassionate Friends" are all groups of people who, having survived difficult and tragic experiences, attempt to reach out to others in need. These support groups (called self-help, but focused on helping others) are universally available to families of the dying and grieving. They also serve on the local, state, and national levels as active social advocates for the needs of the dying and the bereaved.

Upon the death of the patient, families may be in need of bereavement counseling. Bereavement counseling (Parkes, 1973; Glick, Weiss, and Parkes, 1974) should be initiated immediately following death and address the major physical, emotional, and social reverberations caused by the dying and grieving process. This counseling should be thought of as an extension of the care the family receives during the stressful time preceding death, for now the family may be ready to discuss and seek answers to concerns they could not face prior to the death. Counseling, at this time, becomes particularly essential if the family has been exposed to insensitive, or even unscrupulous, persons and institutions who cared for, or were involved in the burial of the deceased. Not to address these unresolved concerns leaves the family vulnerable to continuing difficulties from unexpressed anger, guilt, or ignorance.

SUPPORTIVE NETWORKS FOR CAREGIVERS

Caregivers to the dying and their families must also find support in both their professional and private worlds. In addition to adequate working conditions and compensation, the organizational setting needs to provide for reduced responsibilities, days off, changes in the nature of the work or variety of assignments, and opportunities to freely express distress without fear of criticism or censure. Training, supervision, consultation, and continuing education facilitates professional growth, while retreats, meditation areas and chapels, and "scream rooms" provide relief from emotional tensions.

In the personal world of the caregiver, a supportive family is essential. Given a life style that meets the individual's needs for physical and psychological rest, the caregiver will better be able to serve others, while finding personal satisfaction in his or her vocation.

The helper must be as good at receiving as giving. Appreciative responses, comforting words, and caring inquiries about one's well-being from the dying person, and his or her family, are important sources of support for caregivers. Years ago the mother of a dying child made me a sweater as she sat by the bedside. She was "knitting up the raveled sleeve of care," she said. Whenever I put on that sweater, I know that the dying and grieving themselves have been my greatest source of support.

Discussion Questions

1. Briefly outline and describe the five stages in the adaptive process. Give specific examples of each stage.
2. Why is individual and family assessment important in the care of the dying and grieving?

3. Maintaining control is a central concern for the dying. What conditions would enhance or threaten this ability?
4. Discuss the adaptive significance of the "life review" in the anticipatory grief work of the dying.
5. Why do those who have experienced the death of someone close need assistance? How can a person best cope or deal with the stress caused by the death of a loved one?
6. Why does someone who knows they are going to die soon go through the process of "getting their house in order?" What are the different ways of doing this?
7. What are the implications of the following statement: "We both approach and avoid an awareness of our finite destiny?"
8. Elaborate on the following quotation: "Prior losses give unique meaning to each experience with dying, death, and grieving."

Glossary

ADAPTATION: A complex biopsychosocial process precipitated by stress and characterized by a sequence of stages involving a variety of coping mechanisms with the aim of mastery or restoration of equilibrium.
ANTICIPATORY GRIEF: Grief work aimed at loosening the bonds of attachment to the dying, making loss less painful when it occurs.
BIOPSYCHOSOCIAL: A concept reflecting a synthesis of the biological, psychological, and social components of the human experience.
DENIAL: A protective coping mechanism characterized by an inability to perceive external reality.
DISBELIEF: An ability to perceive but not to affectively except external reality.
GRIEF WORK: A process occurring with loss aimed at loosening the attachment to the dead for reinvestment in the living.
RESISTANCE: An adaptive maneuver characterized by an inability or unwillingness to act with the aim of asserting or sustaining individual control, autonomy, or self-esteem.
SUPPRESSION: A more or less conscious postponement of addressing anxieties and concerns.

References

Bluebond-Langner, M. 1977. "Meanings of Death to Children," in *New Meanings of Death*, ed. by Herman Feifel. New York: McGraw-Hill.
Bowlby, John. 1980. *Loss: Sadness and Depression*. New York: Basic Books.
Butler, R. N. 1963. "The Life Review: An Interpretation of Reminiscence in the Aged." *Psychiatry*, Vol. 26:65–76.
Castelnuovo-Tedesco, P. 1980. "Reminiscence and Nostalgia: The Pleasure and Pain of Remembering," in *The Course of Life": Psychoanalytic Contributions Toward Understanding Personality Development*, ed. by S. I. Greenspan and G. H. Pollock. Adelphi, Md.: National Institute of Mental Health.

Erikson, Erik H. 1959. "Identity and the Life Cycle." *Psychological Issues,* Vol. 1, No. 1:101–164.

Erikson, Erik H. 1976. "Reflections on Dr. Borg's Life Cycle." *Daedalus,* Vol. 105, No. 2:1–28.

Erikson, Erik H. 1980. "Elements of a Psychoanalytic Theory of Psychosocial Development," in *The Course of Life: Psychoanalytic Contributions Toward Understanding Personality Development,* ed. by S. I. Greenspan and G. H. Pollock. Adelphi, Md.: National Institute of Mental Health.

Freud, Sigmund. 1915. "On Attitude Toward Death," Standard Edition, Vol. 14. London: Hogarth Press, 1957.

Glick, I. O., R. S. Weiss, and C. M. Parkes. 1974. *The First Year of Bereavement.* New York: John Wiley and Sons.

Kosberg, J. I. 1977. "Social Work with Geriatric Patients and Their Families," in *Social Work with the Dying Patient and the Family,* ed. by E. R. Pritchard, J. Collard, B. A. Orcutt, A. H. Kutscher, I. Seeland, and N. Lefkowitz. New York: Columbia University Press.

Kron, J. 1976. "Designing a Better Place to Die." *New York,* Vol. 3, No. 1:43–49.

Kubler-Ross, Elizabeth. 1969. *On Death and Dying.* New York: Macmillan.

Lindemann, Edward. 1944. "Symptomatology and Management of Acute Grief." *American Journal of Psychiatry,* Vol. 101:141–148.

Lindemann, Edward. 1979. *Beyond Grief: Studies in Crisis Intervention.* New York: Jason Aronson.

Mechanic, David. 1968. *Medical Sociology: A Selective View.* New York: The Free Press.

Overbeck, Ann. 1977. "Life Stress Antecedents to Application for Help at a Mental Health Center: A Clinical Study of Adaptation." *Smith College Studies in Social Work,* Vol. 47 (June):192–233.

Parkes, C. M. 1973. *Bereavement.* New York: International Universities Press.

Sahler, O. J. Z., ed. 1978. *The Child and Death.* St. Louis: C. V. Mosby.

Selye, H. 1956. *The Stress of Life.* New York: McGraw-Hill.

Stillion, J., and H. Wass. 1979. "Children and Death," in *Death: Current Perspectives,* 2nd ed., ed. by E. S. Shneidman. Palo Alto, Calif.: Mayfield, 1980.

Weisman, Avery D. 1972. *On Dying and Denying: A Psychiatric Study of Terminality.* New York: Behavioral Publications.

Weisman, Avery D. 1974. *The Realization of Death.* New York: Jason Aronson.

Suggested Readings

Bowlby, John. 1980. *Loss: Sadness and Depression.* New York: Basic Books.
This volume, number three in the Attachment and Loss Series, deals with biopsychosocial effects of action or threatened disruption of affectional bonds in persons of all ages.

DuBois, Paul M. 1980. *The Hospice Way of Death.* New York: Human Sciences Press.
An overview of all aspects of hospice philosophy and care from the selection of patients and staff, the goals and priorities, to physical facilities and fund raising.

Orcutt, Ben A., Elizabeth R. Pritchard, Jean Collard, Evelyn F. Cooper, Austin H. Kutscher, and Irene B. Seeland, eds. 1980. *Social Work and Thanatology.* New York: Arno Press.

An interdisciplinary collection of papers on social work practice and education in behalf of the dying and their families. Interviews and workshop proceedings are included in this volume in the Foundation of Thanatology Arno Press Continuing Series on Thanatology.

Shneidman, Edwin S., ed. 1980. *Death: Current Perspectives*, second edition. Palo Alto, Calif.: Mayfield Publishing Co.

A comprehensive, interdisciplinary compendium addressing current research findings, attitudes and feelings about dying and death.

Weisman, Avery D. 1974. *The Realization of Death*. New York: Jason Aronson.

A psychosocial multidisciplinary approach to the scientific study of death, dying, and life threatening behavior through reconstructing and synthesizing the events surrounding the terminal phase of life.

TWO

Understanding Death Attitudes

Chapter 5

A DEVELOPMENTAL APPROACH TO UNDERSTANDING DEATH ATTITUDES

I, too, am trying to find some answers.
I, too, am troubled and sad. Did you know that?
Are you surprised that I don't know all the answers
    about death?
Don't be.

Even though no one really understands it,
    death is something we must accept.
We can talk about it.
You can learn something from me.
I can learn something from you

We can help each other.
Earl A. Grollman (1970)

WHY BE CONCERNED with the development of death conceptualizations? Perhaps one could make a good case for living and dying without ever exploring it. People who have never seriously thought about it probably number in the millions. However, we are sometimes forced to wonder just how we develop our understanding of death.

A friend's sister was killed instantly when, early one morning on her way to work, she lost control of her motor scooter and crashed into a telephone pole. Her brother turned to me for help. Among the requests he made was that I explain to his sister's five-year-old son what had happened.

Since I had a boy of about the same age, I had my friend bring the youngster to our apartment where the two played happily for a while as I sorted through the issues. How would I tell him? What would I tell him?

What was he capable of understanding? Since this woman was a single parent, just how would that fact affect the feelings and future of this boy? Were there other "parent figures" available? What kinds of attachment had the boy formed with them and others? How should one handle not only the telling itself, but the funeral and other experiences that lay ahead of him?

This chapter will attempt to address some of these issues. Though most would feel a lot of compassion for a child in such circumstances, one also needs to know what the behavioral sciences have been able to discover about the way a child, an adolescent, or an adult grasps the significance of dying, death, and bereavement.

HISTORICAL BACKGROUND TO A DEVELOPMENTAL UNDERSTANDING OF DEATH CONCEPTUALIZATION

Though relatively little has been written about it, in centuries past people often looked at children simply as miniature adults. However, twentieth-century social and behavioral scientists have dispelled a good deal of ignorance and many misconceptions about the child's inner world.

As with the beginning stages of any field of study, many untried and uncharted ideas were explored. Sigmund Freud traced our conceptions of death to our earliest feelings concerning sexuality and fears of being punished for them. Alfred Adler had several brushes with death himself, and suffered seriously from a debilitating disease as a child; when he formulated his theories concerning the human psyche and its development, he attributed our need to strive and overcome to our early sensitivity to weakness and death.

Later, the ego psychologists, departing somewhat from Freud, credited the individual with a greater amount of ability in managing the stresses and problems of life. Yet, they recognized that humans raise a whole set of defenses against the idea of death. They would also point out that children, as well as adults, have the power to distort their perceptions according to inner needs. For example, people of all ages have ways of denying harsh or painful thoughts or facts. Children bereft of a father figure are able to fantasize a substitute father or protective, imaginary playmate. Adults use more subtle means, but in effect, what we "want to see or understand," is just as important as what we actually do see or understand.

Ernest Becker (1973), in his Pulitzer Prize winning book, argued that fear and denial of death are basic dynamics for everyone. He asserted that we struggle to find meaning in life through heroic efforts; or, when we discover that we cannot really be heroic, we avoid the dilemma by building elaborate systems to explain the problem away. Some even flee into neurosis or a psychotic break. Becker felt that the fear of death was a basic problem of meaning with which we all struggle. Though the subject of death was not a major concern in his writings, the Swiss developmental psychologist, Jean Piaget, was probably instrumental in nudging psychologists to employ better methods of research in the developmental approach to understanding concepts of death. Piaget was an exceptionally keen observer, both of his own children and others. He used a combination of experiments and semiclinical interviews to discover a great deal about children's thought processes. He postulated that it is not until the early teen years that we are capable of genuinely abstract thought processes. This raises questions about the ability of the younger child to adequately conceptualize death. His work with the child's awareness of time and the periodization of concrete and abstract thinking have become keystones to present-day research. (For further information of the basic ideas of Piaget, see *Piaget's Theory of Intellectual Development*, 2nd. ed., by Herbert Ginsburg and Sylvia Opper [Englewood Cliffs] N. J.: Prentice-Hall, 1979.)

Though we have said that Piaget did not study the child's concepts of death in a specific way, many things he did study hold important implications for our understanding of death awareness. His major principle, that children progress in stages of cognitive development—each qualitatively better than preceding ones—brought about discoveries that small children can grieve over the loss of something only at the point that they have realized that things (and people) are not permanent. This quality, which he called "object constancy," would have to precede any sense of loss. Piaget observed that this happens somewhere around one year to eighteen months of age. From that point, the child moves on from a rudimentary sense of how the world exists (even when not seen, heard, felt or tasted) to the ability to represent that world with language symbols.

Once in school, children begin to grasp concepts of reversibility, classification and number. Things now can be understood as both alike and different in certain aspects. They move ahead into comprehension of basic ideas like causality, time, space, and quantity. Hence, these children should be able to conceptualize that death results as a natural part of life, and not as the result of some strange force from without. All of this varies with the individual child, but generally speaking, the higher the age, the more definitely the child can portray and describe the idea of death in an accurate way. Magical thinking gradually lessens, and realism takes over. Some feel that complete freedom from magical thinking does not occur until the child is twelve to fourteen years of age.

An Englishwoman, Sylvia Anthony (1940), and a Hungarian researcher, Maria Nagy (1948), became the first significant modern-day researchers in the field of the child's conceptualizations of death. Unfortunately, neither Piaget's work nor theirs was seriously considered until the mid or late fifties. An important aspect of the research conducted by Anthony and Nagy (which is also true of the research by Piaget), was that they collected data in a manner that allowed children to speak for themselves. These research findings will be discussed more thoroughly later in the chapter.

Since the publishing of Herman Feifel's *The Meaning of Death* in 1959—including Maria Nagy's article on her studies from the 1930's in Hungary—interest and research have grown rapidly. Whether coming from a psycho-analytical, behavioristic, humanistic or other points of view, a student can now locate dozens of good articles, dissertations, and books related to a developmental approach to death attitudes and awareness.

APPLICABILITY AND SCOPE

The major implications of research for understanding death conceptions from infancy to old age will be surveyed in this chapter. It is not intended that age should be seen as the sole determiner of our death concepts because there are many other factors that influence cognitive development. Some of these factors would include the following: level of intelligence, physical and mental well-being, previous emotional reactions to various life experiences, religious background, other social and cultural forces, personal identity and self worth appraisals, and exposure to death or threats of death. Therefore, the fact that an age-based outline is followed in this chapter does not mean that these other important features should be ignored.

This chapter will discuss how psychologists are beginning to understand children's, adolescents', and adults' perception and thinking about their own deaths and the deaths of others. Several intellectual perspectives will be presented.

DEATH CONCEPTUALIZATIONS IN THE LIFE CYCLE

Infancy

It almost goes without saying that infancy is the stage of life about which we have the least possibility of direct objective reports. Some doubt whether a child under three can even conceive of death at all. Hungarian-born researcher Margaret Mahler (1975) has conducted extensive research with infants and children under three. She studied the process of how a child gradually becomes aware of its own independence from the mother, and the powerful potential for either healthy or unhealthy personality development that is involved. Mahler and her colleagues studied this interaction between babies and their mothers in a structured laboratory context for many years; however, their major conclusion—that infants are not cognizant of their separate identities nor of the possibility of death—was not published until recently (Mahler, 1975; cf. Blank and Blank, 1979; Horner, 1979). It seems as though a great deal of anxiety accompanies the process by which the child differentiates itself from the mother. Success will depend upon whether the mother feels secure in herself and allows the child to begin to venture away by crawling, creeping or walking. Verbal and nonverbal signals are read by the child to determine both the mother's feelings about the venturing, and how safe or perilous the child feels as it explores its world.

The British psychiatrist, John Bowlby (1969), has researched the effects of separation of children from their parents while in the hospital. His major emphasis has been upon the nature of the tie that exists between the infant and the mother and how separation brings about various mental and personality changes in the child. (The bonding between parents and children will be discussed in more detail in Chapter 7.)

Several writers have pointed out that the very young child usually gains some kind of experience with the death of animals, whether by killing ants on the sidewalk, coming upon a dead caterpillar, or finding a dead bird in varying stages of decay as he or she plays in the back yard (Kavanaugh, 1972; Kastenbaum, 1977a; Lonetto, 1980). Whether by identification with the animal world or by simply asking questions about why the animal no longer acts alive, the issue of being and non-being is thereby raised for the child.

Adah Maurer (1966 and 1974) has theorized that small children gradually become aware of elementary concepts of being and nonbeing through the repetitive pattern of sleeping and waking, or through experiences with presence and absence of significant people. Most probably, she affirms, the almost universally enjoyed game of "peekaboo" with children demonstrates the way the child experiences emotions when discovering appearance and reappearance of both the self and the other.

Theoretically, to the extent that infants or young children are able to grasp something concerning the significance of separation from parental figures and/or primitive concepts of being and nonbeing, they are able to grasp and react to a threat of death or abandonment and separation from significant people in their lives. Having said that, however, is to say little, since it is usually discovered much later what kind of effect this has upon a given individual. As Erik Erikson (1963) has pointed out, the infant "decides" early in life whether the universe is a warm and loving place to be, and upon that primitive but momentous subconscious conclusion is based to a large degree the ability to deal with threats and difficulties of later life. It must not be assumed, however, that the small child has no concept or grasp at all of death, nor, more importantly, that there is no need to be concerned about the effects of a given death upon their lives.

Three conclusions regarding the above research efforts to understand the child's inner world can now be mentioned. (1) Though one might not agree with this point of view, it can be recognized that in order to extrapolate from the slim research evidence now possessed about infancy, it might well be necessary for the time being to adhere to some theoretical point of view not totally acceptable. (2) The observational data concerning the world of the infant must be expanded significantly before more definite conclusions can be drawn within the parameters of any theory. (3) Regardless of one's theoretical perspective, the early experiences of the infant do have an effect upon an individual's understanding of death, views concerning the afterlife, anxiety concerning dying, and fears about separation and/or abandonment from parents.

Childhood

From what may have seemed like a guessing game, the next grouping of development—ages three to twelve—has more research evidence to build upon. Researchers have tried to determine not simply whether a child can or does *conceive* of death, but very specifically whether they conceive of it as a *permanent, final, inevitable,* and *irreversible* state. They ask the child whether death is *universal*, whether all die, and whether the child thinks he or she will die. They attempt to understand the child's time frame—is there a sense of past and future as well as present? They are also concerned with how long the child thinks the past and future might be. Other relevant questions are those that pertain to the *mobility* or *inanimateness* of the dead, as well as whether or not death itself, is *reified* as a thing or being.

It should be noted that the three-year old is just beginning to manage symbolic material through language—formulating questions as to why things are the way they are as they constantly explore and discover the surrounding world. Until this time, the outside world has existed in only a vague way for the child, since there was no effective way to represent the world (in the mind) without the aid of language or symbols.

Only gradually, however, does the child begin to move beyond a quite self-centered view of the universe, where he/she may feel personally responsible for everything that happens. Using primitive ideas concerning cause and effect, a child has the tendency to project feelings onto others or even onto inanimate objects—a trait that persists even into kindergarten age. Play and toys are the real world for the child. A great deal more about the child's thoughts and feelings can be discovered by listening and observing play than by asking questions. Drawings are also an important language medium for the child, and researchers often take advantage of this means.

Teacher of Death Mother Goose

Childhood, a famous poet once wrote, is "the kingdom where nobody dies."

A University of Minnesota psychologist would take issue with that. To illustrate his thesis, Dr. John Brantner tells this story:

> A young couple was determined to shield their children from the facts of death. They took extraordinary precautions never to mention the word, or allude to the eventual fate of all men. One day they were at a rented beach house, about ready to romp down to the ocean for a day in the sun, when the father glanced out the window and saw a dead dog in the road they would have to cross. Quickly he drew the blinds and, while his wife distracted the children, called the proper authorities and told them to come and get the carcass.
>
> Within the hour the victim of a speeding motorist had been removed and the father, peeking through the blinds, told his wife it was all right to go to the beach. The family got outside and was about to cross the road separating the beach house from the shore when the little girl looked up at her father and asked, "Daddy, what happened to the dead dog?"

Brantner believes that, by the time children are able to speak, they have some awareness of the reality of death. How do they learn about it?

One way is TV. Brantner cites a recent study which found that, on the average, a child who watches the tube for ten years will see no fewer than 13,500 violent deaths. "And the odds are great that he doesn't see a single natural death," the psychologist adds.

Another, surprising teacher of death is that nice little old lady, Mother Goose. Brantner pulls out the comprehensive Oxford Dictionary of Nursery Rhymes as evidence. Consider *The Death and Burial of Poor Cock Robin*.

> Who killed Cock Robin?
> "I," said the sparrow,
> "With my little bow and arrow,
> I killed Cock Robin."
>
> Who saw him die?
> "I," said the fly,
> "With my little eye,
> I saw him die."

And on it goes, through the funeral, grave digging, burial and final tolling of the bell.

Consider this little ditty:

There was an old woman who had three sons,
  Jerry and James and John,
Jerry was hanged, James was drowned,
  John was lost and never was found;
And there was an end of her three sons,   *
  Jerry and James and John!

Rhymes were a common conveyance of such grim news, Brantner believes, because, back when the classic children's verse came to be, death was much more of an immediate reality for those who recited them. "Until 1900," the professor said, "67 percent of everyone who died was under the age of 15. It was a common part of growing that you had young brothers and sisters who died."

Verses not only described peaceful passings. They also were not hesitant to speak of murder, drownings, hangings and other violent ends, all in light couplet. And death became the ultimate punishment.

Barnaby Bright was a sharp cur,
He always would bark if a mouse did but stir,
But now he's grown old, and can no longer bark,
He's condemned by the parson to be hanged by the clerk.

Or this one, (not likely to win accolades from "women's lib" editorialists):

Little Dicky Dilver
Had a wife of silver;
He took a stick and broke her back
And sold her to the miller;
The miller wouldn't have her
So he threw her in the river.

Death was to be mourned, the rhymes told their reciters:

Grandfa' Grig had a pig
  In a field of clover;
Piggie died, Grandfa' cried
  And all the fun was over.

Fatalism? That can be found, too, as in:

Now I lay me down to sleep,
I pray the Lord my soul to keep;
And if I die before I wake,
I pray the Lord my soul to take.

Nature's destruction of the body comes across grotesquely in this bit of verse:

On looking up, on looking down
She saw a dead man on the ground;
And from his nose unto his chin,
The worms crawled out, the worms crawled in.

Then she unto the parson said,
Shall I be so when I am dead?
O yes, O yes, the parson said,
You will be so when you are dead.

Even pitiful but benign Old Mother Hubbard recounts death, with a magical twist. The second stanza goes like this:

She went to the bakers
   To buy him some bread;
But when she came back
   The poor dog was dead.

She went to the undertaker's
   To buy him a coffin;
But when she came back
   The poor dog was laughing.

What's a child to make of that?
There's little doubt about life's brevity, however, in this well-known rhyme:

Solomon Grundy,
Born on a Monday,
Christened on Tuesday,
Married on Wednesday,
Took ill on Thursday,
Worse on Friday,
Died on Saturday,
Buried on Sunday,
This is the end
Of Solomon Grundy.

Your kids don't hear nursery verse? What about fairy tales? Again, the classics are rife with violence and death.
Remember what the giant in *Jack and the Beanstalk* repeated with lust?

Fee-fi-fo-fum,
I smell the blood of an Englishman.
Be he alive, or be he dead,
I'll grind his bones to make my bread.

Hansel and Gretel roast the witch in her own oven. Dorothy is trapped in Oz until the wicked witch of the west could be liquidated.

And Henny-Penny, the paranoid little chick who thought the sky was falling down, leads four friends, Turkey-Lurkey, Goosey-Poosey, Duckey-Daddles and Cocky-Locky, to decapitation by the fox.

Bluebeard, a misogynist turned mass murderer, began as a children's story.

Some tales have been changed. In the first version of *The Three Little Bears* there is no Goldilocks, but a little old woman who plays the intruder. Upon being discovered by the Bears she jumps out the window to an uncertain fate. The narrator speculates that she possibly broke her neck.

Before Walt Disney got hold of them, the Three Little Pigs were a morbid bunch. The wolf consumed the first two for lunch, but the third, who declined his invitations to dinner, boiled the beast and ate him for supper. *And lived happily ever after.*

Source: Richard Gibson, *The Minneapolis Star,* April 11, 1973, p. 1C.

Maria Nagy (1948) studied 378 Hungarian children ages three to ten. Her findings have been criticized but not always undermined by subsequent research. Nagy interviewed children who range across a broad spectrum intellectually and are from various religious backgrounds. She asked those from ages six to ten to draw pictures concerning death, and those seven and above to write down everything they could think of concerning death and to write comments about the pictures.

She divided the group into three subsections, each with its own peculiar way of looking at death. Children three to five years of age are grouped in stage one. The most salient feature in this age group is not seeing death as final. To them, death is reversible; it is merely a modification of aliveness. Death is gradual or temporary. Separation and abandonment are seen as equivalent to death. "Out-of-sight equals out-of-existence" for the young child.

Stage two includes children ages five to nine. She discovered her Hungarian subjects personifying death in this age group, representing death as a live person or some variation such as an angel, a skeleton, or a circus clown. (It is this element of personification that has been most difficult to replicate in studies in the United States, which may indicate cultural influences upon this group.) The child can now recognize death as final, but these subjects also tended to think that one can outmaneuver death, so that its universality is supposedly not yet acceptable to them.

Stage three, ages nine and thereafter, is the time when death is seen not only as final but inevitable and universal. "I will die. Everyone will die, as well."

Looking at the time of the research—the 1930s—and the locale—Hungary—one could surmise that many children in this sample had heard much about death from relatives and neighbors who had gone through World War I in Europe. The "miracle drugs" had not yet appeared; thus, children's deaths were much more common than in the current era. These facts, as well as cultural differences, need to be explored carefully before these research findings can be applied too freely.

Another early study of children's attitudes toward dying and death was by Sylvia Anthony (1940) in England in 1937–1939. She documents, more clearly than Nagy, the effects of war and its concomitants upon her subjects. She found that the 128 children of her study not only thought of death and spoke of it with a greater frequency than had been imagined before, but that they also associated death with deep sadness, aggression and violence. Being psychoanalytic in theoretical orientation, she speculated concerning the relevance of thoughts of punishment to death. She felt that in the child's mind thinking about death can cause it to happen to self or to others. She did discover that some children under five did not understand what the word death meant; but from seven or eight and above, every child was able to comprehend in some way what it meant to be dead, though their definitions were not always biologically nor logically correct.

A more recent researcher, Richard Lonetto (1980), asked children to draw and explain pictures portraying dead people. His study shows that earlier research is generally supported, but he is especially interested in emphasizing that drawing and talking about death is a way of managing anxiety about death for children. Children seem to put some control upon the fears they have by drawing death as a monster or a fearful personage. Death by violence such as shooting or stabbing is not thought about by children of ages three to five as frequently as death by separation, kidnaping, hiding, or some other means.

Myra Bluebond-Langer (1977) in investigating leukemic children ages three to nine in a hospital found that most of them knew not only that they were dying, but that this was a final and irreversible process. She proposes:

> All views of death—death as separation, the result of intervention by a supernatural being, and an irreversible biological process—are present in all stages in one's development.

Her research conclusion is that one needs to be much more conscious of factors other than age—one should look at factors such as life experience, life concerns, circumstances, and self-concept at the time that the child or adult is interviewed.

Such a point of view seems to undermine the developmental framework altogether. However, Bluebond-Langer still needs to demonstrate from studies of younger normal populations that, if a child does *not* have the experience of facing death in a hospital, he or she will still develop an "adult" awareness and understanding of death and of the dying process.

Nevertheless, Bluebond-Langer's concern that the various facets of a person's life be considered along with age must be taken seriously. The learning one does about anything, whether death related or not, is just as much a result of one's own personal agency and desire as it is a process of receiving passively the stimuli from around (Wenar, 1971). We are able to decide many things for ourselves, and have the inner power to either make rose gardens out of abandoned limestone quarries or mountains out of molehills. Much that is learned, therefore, depends upon one's own seeking and direction.

Much of one's socialization to death as a child may have been negative. Parents often use death as an agent of social control in curtailing a child's negative behavior. Some examples are: "I'm going to kill you;" "Get down from there before you break your neck (and die);" "The Devil will get you (and thus take you away) if you don't behave;" "You are going to catch a death of cold running around without your jacket."

Age, and its relationship to death conceptualizations, continues to maintain an important role in this description. The experiential element is powerful, but experience has a way of ordering itself along a more or less common chronological path for the majority of people in a given epoch and

Protecting the Children

The greatest zeal will not protect the normally curious child. One of many mothers who sent their children out to avoid President Kennedy's funeral tells how they stopped at a furniture store window to learn what was wrong to see at home. My own studies and numerous others reveal that death and dying are emotionally laden words for children early in life. I wonder if our efforts to spare little people a harsh reality are not our own badly disguised struggle to avoid the trauma in telling. Meanwhile, our hesitation allows time and opportunity for them to sift their own data, to learn puzzling and fearful interpretations elsewhere, while concocting weird fantasies that may affect their lifelong attitudes toward mortality.

Source: Robert Kavanaugh, *Facing Death* (Baltimore: Penguin Books, 1972), p. 128.

culture. Therefore, an age-based classification will continue, recognizing that it must serve simply as a "majority guide" and not as the prism of all truth.

Adolescence

According to Piaget and his followers, at about eleven years of age people are able to move from the use of language and ideation that is concretely oriented (that is, expresses only what the senses and other direct experiences tell them) to an abstract level of thought. This means that the adolescent can now play with "what-if" questions. Among those are ideas about the meaning of life and the possibility of death—one's own, and others'. Since the adolescent is gripped by questions such as "Who am I, really?" and "How do I fit into the scheme of things?" as well as struggling with good, evil, love, hate, belonging, and loneliness, the thought of death is particularly disturbing.

Concerning the adolescent's concept of time and futurity, Kastenbaum (1966) notes that people at this stage of life have difficulty thinking in terms of distant future in relation to their own lives. Their struggle with current features of their own lives evidently occupies such mental energy, especially the concern with their own identity and anxiety about successes during the immediate future, that thinking about what life will be like when they are age seventy, or even forty-five, is nearly impossible for them.

One research effort by Koocher et al. (1976) demonstrated that high school students experience much more anxiety, depression, and death fear than either junior high students or adults. They propose that it is the "identity crisis" of the mid-teen years that could be largely responsible for this. Robert Lifton (1973), in agreement, postulates that adolescence is the time when a sense of great potential for disintegration, separation, and instability occupies the mind and brings about greater death anxiety.

Alexander and Alderstein (1958) administered a word association test to children and adolescents and measured the galvanic skin response (GSR is an indicator for anxiety) as twenty-seven words were read, some of which were death-related. They found that children from ages five to eight and adolescents from thirteen to sixteen responded with more anxiety than children between ages nine and twelve. They hypothesize that the nine to twelve age group is in a fairly stable period of life concerning ego strength and identity, and therefore has an advantage over both the younger and the adolescent group since these latter two periods are times when less stable ego and less adequate self-concepts are more prevalent and emotional upheaval is more common.

Adah Maurer (1964) found in studying adolescents that there is a relationship between intelligence and death anxiety—the brighter the high school student, the more deeply and fearlessly that person delves into concepts concerning death and expresses them to others. Awareness of the fear of death seems to increase as ability decreases, until one reaches the retarded, where less than a fourth speak of fear in any connection. Maurer also found some relationship between self-concept and capability to manage in the face of death. The less capable the person feels, the more difficult the thought of managing overwhelming odds.

Maurer's study (1964) points out the need to identify ways in which adolescents tend to manage thoughts about death. Those ways are *shaped* by factors such as religious background, age, gender, intelligence, social skills, experience with death or serious illness (either personally or in the family), and frequency of thoughts concerning death (Fink, 1976).

While the research cited in this section does not always fit neatly together, it has been noted that whenever the individual is going through an unstable or trying period—especially when the stress has to do with basic feelings about self-worth, identity and capability—the thought of death is particularly difficult to manage. Crucial to positive outcomes is the manner in which parents, friends, peers, teachers, and other helpers enable the teen-ager to process positively the ideas of the overwhelming threats of death to self and significant others. If one were to plan a death education course to aid adolescents in coping with dying and death attitudes, it would be necessary to consider seriously how each of the influences listed above might exert itself upon the members of the class.

Learning Goes Both Ways

The most worthwhile method of teaching children about death consists in allowing them to talk freely and ask their own questions, without any adult speeches or philosophic nonanswers. They need to ramble a bit, to talk a bit crudely if they wish, to change the subject and to present unanswerable questions without being squelched. The learning goes both ways. Gradually a parent knows his child's vision of the world, his views on death, his personal worries and how seriously he regards his own questions. In such free-wheeling chats, little people will unconsciously reveal their own views and fears as distinct from those we project into their thinking and feeling.

Source: Robert Kavanaugh, *Facing Death* (Baltimore: Penguin Books, 1972), pp. 132–133.

Introduction to Adulthood

We have already observed that one of the chief problems with following a developmental scheme in the explanation of how people think, feel and integrate life's experiences is that there are so many possible combinations of factors in any one given life. In addition, the longer one lives the more complex the picture becomes as the probability of additional factors influencing a particular person increases.

Caution is needed when attempting to generalize about what is true concerning any stage of life, and especially when looking at people beyond the adolescent stage of life. The premise behind this caution is that any research findings describing a particular population, age group, or cross section of people, should not be seen as more than a description of that particular sample of people. It is to be viewed as a result of the theoretical approach of the researcher with an awareness of the limitations of present knowledge, methodologies, and conclusions. In other words, one can never say that a certain description of what *is* carries any connotations of what *must be* or what is true of anyone, anywhere outside the scope of that

---

Ecclesiastes 3:1

For everything there is a season,
and a time for every matter under the heaven,

a time to be born, and a time to die;
a time to plant, and a time to pluck up what I planted;
a time to kill, and a time to heal;
a time to break down, and a time to build up;
a time to weep, and a time to laugh;
a time to mourn, and a time to dance;
a time to cast away stones, and a time to gather stones together;
a time to embrace, and a time to refrain from embracing;
a time to seek, and a time to lose;
a time to keep, and a time to cast away;
a time to rend, and a time to sew;
a time to keep silence, and a time to speak;
a time to love, and a time to hate;
a time for war, and a time for peace.

particular sample. Watchwords are humility and tentativeness. With adult populations, there are so many possible variables to take into consideration that sweeping generalizations are often impossible.

Another implication of this attitude toward understanding adulthood is that accurate conclusions would be drawn concerning any one person at any timeframe of life, if more attention were paid to the many forces and features of a particular person's life history. Any extrapolation concerning people on a larger scale would necessarily be drawn from groups with as similar mental, social, emotional, and cultural data as could be found. The more fully we follow over a long period of time the development of the group's concepts of life, death, and the meaning they give them, the better one will be able to grasp accurately the true picture of developmental concepts.

Other limitations to studying adults' concepts of death also need to be observed. For example, no satisfactory definition of "maturity" in relation to concepts of death has yet been developed. Robert Kastenbaum, one of the most prolific writers in the field of developmental concepts of death, often mentions this shortcoming. There is no way to know when "we have arrived" in terms of a "mature" view of death.

Another limitation arises from the fact that developmental psychologists have not researched enough in the area of adulthood to draw firm conclusions about the fine nuances of change that might develop with age concerning our conceptualization of death. Freud concentrated on infancy and childhood. Erik Erikson was able to move far beyond Freud in describing theoretically how the person develops over the entire life span. Some longitudinal studies of men—fewer of women—have been published. The relationship between these studies and ways of conceiving death is seldom, if ever discussed, except in gerontological research. It seems to be assumed—probably more by default than anything else—that we only need to pay attention to the death concepts of children and the elderly. Research is not taking place in as proportionately great a scale concerning the period of young adult to later middle age as the periods of childhood and old age. The major exceptions to this rule are found in studies of mentally and terminally ill populations.

Finally, a limitation is faced in determining what *adult* actually means. Biologically, though we may stop growing any taller at a certain age, great changes continue in the human body. Psychologically, it is even more difficult to arrive at any definition of adulthood that will be generalizable to a significant percentage of the population. One must conclude that the word "developmental" takes on a more individualistic character. Therefore, one should expect that age will be less influential in explaining death conceptualizations for adult populations than other age groups already considered.

Young Adulthood

From the discussion of the development of the adolescent's intellectual understanding of death, one could expect the young adult (a person in their twenties or thirties) to have a good grasp of the universality, inevitability, and finality of death. In addition, the young adult should know, at least intellectually, that death is an entirely possible event for anyone at any moment. However, one should not expect that every adult person, unless forced to do so, would normally think of death constantly nor take it into consideration with each decision of importance. There have existed certain monastic Christian orders that practiced greeting each other daily with the words, "Remember death!" The fact, however, that one tends to recoil from such a practice is evidence that one would rather not take their advice.

It would appear that the young adult would especially reject the admonition to remember death, since at that stage, one is just entering the arena of a somewhat independent life where capabilities and skills can be tested and pride taken in positive results. Hopes, aspirations, challenges, and preparation for success in life are the focus at this age; this implies that dealing with dying or death would mean to face rage, disappointment, frustration and despair (Pattison, 1977).

Young adults struck with serious disability or life-threatening disease have demonstrated that an almost universal sense of injustice and resultant anger exist when the young man or woman is forced to "remember death." Along with all the international political issues involved, the pro-

Living with Death on Our Minds

In his book *Man's Concern with Death*, Arnold Toynbee (1968) wrote: From the moment of birth there is the constant possibility that a human being may die at any moment; and inevitably this possibility is going to become an accomplished fact sooner or later. Ideally, every human being ought to live each passing moment of his life as if the next moment were going to be his last. He ought to be able to live in the constant expectation of immediate death and to live like this, not morbidly, but serenely. Perhaps this may be too much to ask of any being.

Source: Arnold Toynbee, *Man's Concern with Death* (London: Hodder and Stoughton, 1968), p. 259.

tests against the Vietnam conflict in the 60s and 70s probably contained a good deal of repugnance to the idea of risking one's personal future at this stage of life. A walk through the wards of any major veterans' hospital would soon convince the most stubborn observer that significant physical and mental losses, and death itself seem most abhorrent when suffered by the young adult.

In a study of males between the ages of seventeen and forty-five, Levinson and his research team (1978) found that while the first major choices of life are being made, the stresses of making them are apparent. Daniel Levinson (1978) labeled the young adult stage the "novice phase" since there is a strong sense of the need to learn, practice, and train oneself in the art of reaching one's fullest potential as a person and contributor to self-fulfillment, family and society. The key word here is "potential" since the height of energy and drives are experienced at this stage of life. Achieving something worthwhile would be devastatingly contradicted by any thought of serious limitation, sickness, or death.

A study which compares four stages in the life cycle with regard to death attitudes and meaning deserves special discussion at this point. Marjorie Lowenthal, et al. (1975) evaluated 216 people grouped in four classifications: high school seniors, young newlyweds, middle-aged parents, and an older group about to retire. Each subject was asked specific questions concerning concepts and thoughts about death. Their major conclusions were:

> In the response to our questions about death, there were surprisingly few differences between the life stages or between the sexes. The circumstances under which thoughts of death were said to occur, however, did vary by stage of life. Older people thought of death mainly in connection with specific and personal circumstances, such as the death of a friend; younger people were likely to have death thoughts in response to general events such as accidents, earthquakes, or war. Young marrieds, and especially the parent group, reported thoughts about death which transcend the self—the concern being for the survivors.
>
> The frequency of thoughts of death was associated with psychiatric impairment. The complexity or depth of the death thoughts, however, was associated with a much larger array of characteristics including the following: introspection, low social involvement, and more cerebral types of behavior generally. Those with more complex thoughts were also less healthy physically, and projections of their life spans tended to be restricted (p. 229).

Again, it is evident that though age may have some influence over the way we think, individual circumstances and external forces have a more powerful effect upon an individual's thoughts about death. From the time of adolescence on, one is capable of putting perspective on what occurs both within and around. Past, as well as present and future can be utilized, and profited from, because one can draw meanings out of experiences in time. The older one grows, the more apparent it becomes that one needs to reflect on life as much as one needs to engage in it. Such a practice can provide the individual with greater life satisfaction. However, as one moves into middle adulthood, it can have both positive and negative results.

Middle-Age Adult

For the person who has lived forty or fifty years, life brings with it the advantages of experience. Promotion to supervisor, foreman, or analogous status rankings in our work or social milieu demonstrates that one gains greater political and social power during middle age. However, not everyone is promoted, and even those who are, as well as their less fortunate colleagues, become gradually aware that physical vitality has now begun to wane. The "panic" begins once we have realized that the idealized self we have so many years longed to accomplish or fulfill may never actually come to pass. Especially those whose job or self-concept depends upon youthful physical vigor suffer greatly from this recognition. No amount of jogging reverses the effects of time. No patent medicine, whether parading as a "cosmetic" or not, can undo the damage from wear and tear. The only hope is to make the best of what energies and experience remain and to focus on what one does best. Those whose strengths lie in intellectual and social skills will be less threatened since there is a cultural-social time clock that one is able to impose over the biological time clock (Neugarten, 1968). This seems to make more actual difference in the way one lives and how much satisfaction one is able to derive from life.

Similarly, Jack Riley (1968) has demonstrated that a stronger correlation exists between education and more positive views concerning death than between age and positive death views. Stated negatively, people with less education appear more often to have more negative views concerning death. One must remember, however, that a correlation between years of education and more positive views of death does not prove a *causal* connection.

The mid-life stage brings one face to face with more deaths in immediate social situations—often parents or colleagues at work. One is soon aware of getting closer to the "day of reckoning" and will need to evaluate values, meanings, and sense of self-worth in the face of finitude. One becomes increasingly conscious of thoughts of painful death, the dying process, and of ceasing to be as a person. One also becomes aware of the meaning of absence to those who depend upon us—spouse, children and others. In fact, Erik Erikson has pointed out that the middle adult stage is that of either stagnating or being "generative" (productive and nurturing for the good of the world as well as for self). Consequently, death at this point in life often carries with it some of the same sense of injustice and anger that the younger adult experiences with thoughts of death. Now, however, these thoughts are tempered with the recognition that many more forces exist which could bring death "home" to us.

So, while the mature adult needs to give up fantasies of immortality, omnipotence and grandiosity, there still needs to be a sense of accomplishment—a fulfilling of oneself and one's plans for family and personal enterprises. Consciousness of time and death, therefore, makes little difference in meaning for the middle adult. One strives to put all one's skills and experiences to the best possible use. Though one cannot, and probably does not want to return to youth again, one does want to delay death long enough to bring to life fruition and satisfaction. Neugarten (1968) calls this "a preoccupation with self-utilization."

Though the emphasis might be changing somewhat today, Neugarten (1968) pointed out that the chief benchmarks for women are usually family and children; men tend to be more attentive both to achievements outside the home and to inner biological clues concerning their physical well-being. Many women find middle adulthood the most fulfilling, however, since they are often freer to pursue some personal goals and to achieve something for themselves.

Once into the decade of the fifties, a turning point is reached in which one's finitude becomes even more evident. There tends to increase a consciousness that one no longer measures time from birth as much as one measures time until death or until the end of one's most productive years. "How many years do I have before retirement?" "How long will it be before some disability forces me to withdraw from the work place?" Focusing upon what one wants most to do before retirement or death causes one to avoid those things that are considered extraneous and/or uninteresting.

All of this is not to say that increase in age means cessation of personal growth. To the contrary, as long as there is life, growth can occur for the individual who has the will to live and the will to give of self to others. In 1974, Henry Maas and Joseph Kuypers published the results of a forty-year study that measured, among other things, the effects of aging and its implications. One of their striking conclusions was that there was no empirical support for the popular belief that the aging process is related to a massive decline in psychological functioning.

Neugarten (1968), however, points to evidence that people in their forties see the world in a more positive way than those in their sixties. Possibilities for the sixty-year-old are more likely to be faced in passive modes of coping than in active modes. She also suggests that women tend to cope increasingly in affective and expressive terms, while men at this stage will increasingly employ abstract and cognitive modes of coping.

Older Adult

According to Neugarten (1974), a changing perception of the life cycle and another meaningful division is appearing—a division between the young-old and the old-old. The young-old come from the age group composed of those between fifty-five and seventy-five; the old-old are seventy-five and over. The young-old are distinguished from the middle aged primarily by the fact of retirement. While sixty-five has been the marker of old age since the beginning of the Social Security system, age fifty-five is becoming a meaningful lower age limit for the young-old because of the lowering age of retirement. Obviously, employment and health status has a tremendous effect upon placement in either older category.

Neugarten (1974:198) pictures the young-old as possessing relatively good health, education, purchasing power, free time, and politically involved. She concludes that they are not, therefore, likely to become "the neglected, the isolated, or the expendables of the society."

Depending upon the meaning that older adults ascribe to time, persons over the age of sixty will vary in their consciousness of time and its future scarcity (Wallach and Green, 1961). Life can be compared to a train traveling through a tunnel; there is a point at which the train is leaving the tunnel rather than entering it. As older relatives and friends die, one cannot help but become aware that he or she is not immune from death. When no older generation exists, and the members of one's own generation die with increasing frequency, the awareness of the scarcity of time becomes a reality. Therefore, for the person over the age of sixty, the end of the tunnel is in sight.

What's Wrong with Being Old?
Just the Language and Life's Illusions

Della Kuhn

WASHINGTON—"Oh, you're not old" is the instinctive response if you are getting along in years and allude to the fact. It's as though you are being assured "you're not dirty."

But if you are not "old", then what are you? You are "elderly," you are "a senior citizen," you are—heaven forgive us—"mature," an honorable "older."

Has our language been robbed of a decent word? "Old" still has its uses. We are permitted old wine, old silver and china, old carpets and old furniture, to all of which age still adds value. And we can enjoy old pets, which suggests love. The ancient and honorable word has but one human use: The poor can be "old." Lacking so much else, they have at least that possession.

In his *New Dictionary of Quotations,* published when he was 62, H. L. Mencken tells us that Horace, just before he died at 57, lamented that "Waning years steal from us our pleasures one by one; they have already snatched away my jokes, my loves, my revelings and my play."

Since Mencken, life expectancy has grown considerably, chiefly among females. A crude reminder greeted a shipload of American tourists not long ago. Arriving in Manila Bay, they rated a front-page story: "Yesterday the SS Carolina docked American widows whose husbands died of heart attacks while earning the money to make their trip possible."

The idea that old people might become a serious public responsibility and an attractive market for private enterprise dawned in the '30s and burgeoned in the '60s. In the public sector, it created Social Security and Medicare; it shared in poverty programs, such as welfare and food stamps.

In the private area, it spawned national membership organizations, old-age communities, insurance schemes, small "senior citizen" privileges, countless group tours, television programs. The working sessions of a third White House Conference on Aging was held last week.

A whole literature is targeted at the "elderly," specifically at the well-heeled. One series of pamphlets is called "Action for Independent Maturity." Start with "You and Your" new retirement home. Next, "You and Your" money, "You and Your" health, "You and Your" social life—elderly gentlemen have "friends," elderly ladies "dates." Finally, "You and Your" funeral. These publications block your view of the outside world. There is only one place to look—inward. Is this what you want?

Simone de Beauvoir disposes of this question in her angry book, *The Coming of Age.* She recommends "a fairly committed, fairly justified life so that one may go on in the same path even when all illusions have vanished and one's zeal for life has died away."

To warn against an obsession with personal concerns is not to suggest that money is a bad thing. Millions of old people slide into real poverty when they "retire." Must they retire? We Americans are a working people. Leisure has not been a part of our basic culture. Can they afford to retire? Will they become a burden? What would they do?

Do I have my work? If so, I'll try and change it. What are the chances of getting another job at 60? Forced retirement, with or without pensions, legal at 70, is spreading.

Its victims find they have less money, less status, less interest in life. Taxpayers are discovering that they will have to support more and more old people who could be working. When irate stockholders rally against forced retirement, it will be good news.

Must the old be tossed into idleness and poverty so that young people can work?

"It is simply not true that there is not enough work in the United States," writes Dr. Robert N. Butler, a leading social scientist, in his excellent book, *Why Survive?* "The truth is that our need for goods and social services requires an expanded work force." Butler is for "loosening up our lives," now rigidly programmed into education for youth, work for middle life, idleness for old age. Learning, work and leisure must be available throughout life, he says. Work is, at any age, a deeply rooted and ancient source of community with the human race.

Another hold on life, perhaps even more essential to a tolerable old age, is love. But as families disperse, old people have less chance of remaining physically and emotionally involved with their own kin. And so it is perhaps lucky for the old that they need to love, even more than they need to be loved. Work and love keep alive one's affinity with the human race.

Leonard Woolf, 89, spoke for many of us: "I cannot disengage myself from the real world; I cannot completely resign myself to fate. It is in the pit of my stomach as well as in the cooler regions of my brain that I feel and think about what I see happening in the human ant-heap around me, the historical and political events that seem to me to make the difference between a good life and a bad, between civilization and barbarism."

Source: *The Louisville* (Ky.) *Courier-Journal*, December 6, 1981.

Since we live in a society where social institutions outlive the individuals who comprise them, older people and other members of society must prepare for the death of an individual who has social usefulness. There are two major ways of accomplishing this: individual disengagement and societal disengagement (see Newell, 1961 and Cumming and Henry, 1961). In the first method, the individual voluntarily gives up many of the social roles that he or she once performed. Individuals may decide to retire from their occupations in order to travel or increase time dedicated to hobbies and leisure activities. They may also encourage their children to become more independent and less reliant upon their parents. Furthermore, they may withdraw from community and civic commitments in order to give others a chance to contribute. In each of these role disengagements, individuals have lessened society's dependence upon their contributions, while preparing themselves for the ultimate form of social disengagement—death.

Kastenbaum (1969a) asserts that individual disengagement is not universal in the American society. Some people do not experience the "closing in" of time and the need to withdraw from active participation in life's activities and responsibilities. These individuals intensify their participation in order to obtain the greatest possible yield from the time remaining for them.

Society can also withdraw from individuals—there are mandatory retirement ages and children decide, in spite of their parents' wishes, to leave home to establish their own independence. Societal disengagement serves the important function of providing opportunities for new members of society, while creating a smooth transition as one person retires and another is hired. Social institutions plan for social disengagement in order that when one role occupant is replaced by another, there is continuity of performance and assurance of institutional survival.

Both individual disengagement and societal disengagement are methods by which members of society can cope, in an anticipatory manner, with death. In fact the process of living provides us with many opportunities for role disengagement. Throughout our lifetime, we take on new social roles and discard old ones. The infant gives way to the toddler, who becomes a child, and finally takes on an adult status. Symbolically, the child in us dies when we become an adult. As in A. E. Housman's (cited by Kastenbaum, 1977b:145) *To an Athlete Dying Young*, the process of living often involves experiences of self-dying before the individual dies.

> Now you will not swell the rout
> Of lads that wore their honors out,
> Runners whom renown outran
> And the name died before the man.

As we come to understand and cope with many experiences of social disengagement, we become better prepared to deal with our own death and the deaths of others.

A review of one's past, and even living in the past, can gain prominence in the older adult's mind, since this is one way of defending the self against negative feelings concerning life as it is and has been (Butler, cited by Neugarten, 1968). Erik Erikson (1963) calls this stage "Ego Integrity vs. Despair," meaning that being able to look back and value positively what has been accomplished will bring a sense of wholeness, even though the individual realizes that the amount of time left is diminishing. Such people can serve as a deposit of wisdom for younger adults and children. This may give the older man or woman "sage" a meaningful and satisfying role even when they have serious physical disabilities.

Like their younger contemporaries, the older adult will have some anxieties and concerns as they approach death. There is empirical evidence for the fact that while the older person thinks of death more often than younger adults (Kalish, 1976), they appear to have less fear and anxiety concerning death (see Leming 1979–80; Lund and Leming, 1975; Kastenbaum, 1969b; and Kalish, 1976). There are many factors that account for the lower death anxiety levels found in older persons. Kalish (cited by Atchley, 1977:182) cites the following: (1) older people see their lives as having less prospects for the future and less value; (2) older people who have exceeded a "normal life expectancy" have a sense of living on "borrowed time"; and (3) dealing with the deaths of friends can help socialize older people toward acceptance of their own death. Dumont and Foss (1972) suggest that since older people are more likely to have fulfilled their goals in life, they are less fearful of death—which for others might threaten personal achievement. For those elderly who have not attained their goals, they are more likely to have either made their goals more modest or somehow rationalized their lack of achievement. It is also possible that older people come from an age cohort which was better socialized as children to deal with death—they are more likely to come from rural backgrounds and to have had earlier encounters with deaths of siblings, family members and friends. Finally, there is evidence (Leming, 1979–80; McKenzie, 1980; Norman and Scaramelli, 1980; Kalish, 1976) that differences in death anxiety and fear appear to be more a function of religiosity than age. Older persons are more likely to be religious, which provides them with a sense of comfort as they approach death. The older person is likewise more likely to believe in an afterlife and rely on a faith in God as a coping strategy in dealing with death. Psychologically there are definite advantages to the person who deals with the "sting of death" by focusing on religious values and transcendent goals rather than simply attempting to cope with death by focusing upon the self or personal accomplishments (Norman and Scaramelli, 1980).

Death for the older person becomes a normal and expectable event. The crisis for the elderly is not so much death, but how and where the death will take place. The prospect of dying in a foreign place in a dependent and undignified state is a very distressing thought for the older person.

In a study of terminal cancer patients, Lund and Leming (1975) found that older patients had less anxiety concerning their diseases and terminal conditions than did younger persons. However, older patients tended to experience greater depression. The differences in depression may be explained by the intensity and type of support provided to younger and older terminal patients. The elderly are more likely to be separated from family and friends as they die. For them, dying may involve a fear of isolation and loneliness; while younger patients are usually more concerned about the fears: fear of pain, indignity, and dependency in the dying process, fear of leaving loved ones (especially dependents), and the fear of not accomplishing their goals (Leming, 1979–80).

CONCLUSION

Psychosocial studies of developmental concepts of death are themselves in a stage of infancy. These conclusions should, therefore, be tentative awaiting further research. However, significant progress is being made in an understanding of how children and adolescents experience loss at various stages of their development. Gains are being made in the meaning of their behaviors, words, pictures and other means of reporting these losses.

Adolescence is a particularly vulnerable period with regard to facing death. A strong sense of injustice, however, is not uncommon when one dies who has not seemed to reach the fullest potential and opportunity to experience life.

Thinking about death is powerfully influenced by experience with death or threats of death. Mental health, managing anxiety well, and meaningfulness in life are the most powerful factors discovered in relation to developmental concepts of death. Broad cultural-religious forces also enter significantly into each of these features.

Socrates on the Fear of Death

To fear death is nothing other than to think oneself wise when one is not; for it is to think one knows what one does not know. No man knows whether death may not even turn out to be the greatest of blessings for a human being; and yet people fear it as if they knew for certain that it is the greatest of evil.

People can and do manage a great deal of what happens within their minds. One gathers information and insights, helps self to cope, and gives aid to others in need. One's capacity to be an agent for self figures prominently in the discussion and is an assumption upon which this chapter was written. Children, adolescents, and adults can be helped to face both life and death more positively.

A great deal more research is needed to explore the relationships between death conceptualizations, gender-differentiation, and place within the adult life cycle. Some stereotypes are already beginning to fall concerning older men and women, but our conclusions are tentative and more empirical research is needed.

Growing older pushes one to depend more upon educational, intellectual, and social skills than upon physical prowess. Feeling that one is useful and contributes to the well-being of others, as well as having a healthy understanding of death, contributes significantly to meaningful living and dying. As Kavanaugh (1972:226) says, "I am ashamed how little I know about death and dying, but never have I enjoyed life more, dreamed more beautiful dreams each night, than when I began having courage to begin facing death."

Some pessimism can be found in older people, but disengagement from life is not necessarily a universal trait. The fear of death lessens with age, but the thought of death increases. The way time is used changes, as does the meaning one finds in life's experiences. Yet, living a happy and meaningful life is one of the best ways to develop a positive and healthy view of death."

Summary

1. Only since the 1940s has much research occurred in the area of psychological development and its implications for conceptualizing death.
2. An overall psychosocial theory acceptable to a majority of researchers is still lacking.
3. Advances in the theories of cognitive development are helpful in conceptualizing death. However, the experience with death as a child or as an adult changes the picture.
4. Because they place such emphasis upon development in the first six or seven years of life, psychoanalysts have written much about children of this age. Implications of their formulations can be drawn concerning concepts of death. However, until other research approaches can support their ideas, these implications must be held tentatively.
5. Interviews with and observations of children at play and picture drawing have been the major means of acquiring children's concepts of death. A greater variety of tests and data are available from adolescents and adults.
6. The older the person, the more complex is the task of understanding just what causes one to think about death in a particular way.
7. Mental health—or the lack of—is a crucial determinant of conceptualization and feeling about death. Vital aspects of mental health include a personal sense of identity, education, I.Q., coping strengths, experience, cultural and religious upbringing. These factors are intimately interrelated and difficult to isolate in research.
8. During adolescence the sense of personal identity is most vulnerable, and concepts and feelings of death are powerfully influenced by that vulnerability.
9. Research concerning the conceptualization of death in middle adulthood is the most difficult to find.

10. Most people are capable of thinking of death more often and more profoundly than they do, but psychological defenses sometimes prevent this from happening.

APPLICATION: EXPLAINING DEATH TO CHILDREN

After having considered a good deal of abstract theory and research about developmental concepts of death, it is now time to put some of it to work. Returning to the illustration at the beginning of the chapter, the question again appears "How will I help a child who faces death in some way?"

Beyond reading this chapter and other books which will help understand the psychothanatic stage of the child with which one is dealing, one needs to be in touch with one's own feelings and thoughts about death. Helpful in this regard would be courses on dying and death, keeping a private journal for several months with death as a major topic of inner investigation, or a thorough-going reevaluation and deepening of one's own religious or philosophical understanding of death. In order to help the child, one needs to know self enough to keep one's own concerns from getting in the way of the child's needs.

With a note of irony, Edna St. Vincent Millay (1927) calls childhood "the kingdom where nobody dies," referring to the reluctance of many adults to face the need to be open in talking to children about death. It has been noted throughout this chapter, however, that children can and do think about death and often need to talk about it. Analogous to difficulties with talking about sex with children, many adults project onto the child their own reluctance to dealing openly with death. Whenever a child asks a question about death—whether of animals, other people, or self—one should be ready to respond in a natural and matter-of-fact way to the concern raised. As Kastenbaum (1977b) suggests, do not wait or plan "one big tell-all." Parents should be good observers of the discussion and behaviors of children related to death. They should become partners in a continuing dialogue in which death is just one of the many topics that adults and children can discuss together.

Harlene Galen (1972) suggests that one capitalize on "the teachable moment" whenever it arises with children. One should encourage children to express fear, doubt, and curiosity, as well as being open to express one's own feelings concerning death. She lists four guidelines:

1. Ask yourself: "How would I treat this action, comment or question if it were not about death?" The answer would usually be, "Matter-of-factly."
2. Ask: "What is this child really seeking by this action, comment or question?" Recognize that children often act out their feelings rather than verbalizing them clearly.
3. Take care to present only basic truths about what is being asked. Total

comprehension will be achieved only gradually. Give the child time to grasp the broader implications of the subject.

4. With children younger than eleven or twelve, use concrete terms such as "died, death, buried." Abstract or metaphorical terminology such as "sleep," "passed on," "God wanted another angel," are simply confusing to the child. Euphemisms may meet the needs of adults, but can cause untold problems for children.

Ruth Formanek (1974) adds some helpful ideas when she urges teachers to explore the meanings that the child attaches to death including thoughts, associations and feelings. We should have the following concerns: "What does the child really want to know?" "Does the question represent a need for reassurance, or information about the possibility of dying, being separated from loved ones, or abandoned?"

Kastenbaum (1977b) encourages parents to remember that children are part of the family and should not be removed from the scene when the family confronts death. It may be more damaging to the child to be "protected from death" and have to deal with the imagination's construction of "what's going on" than be given the opportunity to participate in the family's response to death. A child's sense of comfort will be strengthened by the very fact that family members are available for discussion. Kastenbaum (1977b) notes that even the expression of feelings, natural to the situation (worry, sorrow, and even anger), will not harm the child but provide a basis for expressing his or her own feelings and emotions.

Formanek (1974) points out that children who are having difficulty dealing with the anxiety aroused by the subject or event of death may manifest the following behavioral changes: anger, regressive infantile attitudes and actions, aggression, hostility, withdrawal, or euphoria. However, school age children who have lost a loved one through death may manifest the following behaviors which are to be considered normal bereavement responses: preoccupation with images of the deceased, a drop in school performance, guilt, strong anger, feelings of uselessness, numbness, withdrawal, and bodily distress.

As stated before, the behaviors listed above are to be considered "normal" child responses to death and bereavement. However, if symptoms increase in intensity and continue over an extended period of time, the child may not have found a place or person with whom to vent his or her feelings about the subject or event of death. Some children may also need professional help.

In conclusion, Kavanaugh's (1972) advice deserves consideration:

The best and final answer lies in the abiding security of loving folks and family in an understanding and supportive home. In this atmosphere inordinate fears will usually recede or be outgrown. Only those few whose fears are prolonged and paralyzing will need professional therapy.

In sum, the best thing adults can *do* for children is to *be* well-adjusted, secure, and loving people. Who one *is* is basic to what one *does*. One's mental, emotional, physical and spiritual well-being undergirds all our actions in helping the child.

Discussion Questions

1. What is object consistency and explain how it is related to the cognitive development of children. Relate this concept to the subject of death and death anxiety in children.
2. Summarize Maria Nagy's conclusions concerning children's death conceptions. How does the research by Bluebond-Langer relate to Nagy's conclusions?
3. Children's experiences with death vary, such as experiences of finding a dead bird or playing games of "ring around the rosie" or "peek-a-boo." How can these experiences help children to conceptualize death? What does Adah Maurer theorize about small children and how they conceptualize death?
4. After considering *how* people fear death at different ages, *why* and *when* do people learn to fear death?
5. In what ways can children be prepared for death?
6. Should children be told of their own terminality?
7. List some of the guidelines cited in the chapter on how to talk to children about death. Do you agree or disagree with these guidelines?
8. What are some of the factors, other than age, which influence death conceptualizations? Why are these factors important in understanding the ways in which people conceptualize death?
9. Why do high school age young people and college students have a higher level of death anxiety than junior high school students?
10. Why is it that death seems much worse when it happens to a young adult rather than to a person over sixty (senior adult)?
11. Explain the concept of "disengagement" as it relates to the elderly? Is this process a universal experience among the elderly? Drawing from your own experiences with grandparents or some elderly friends, describe, if any, aspects of the disengagement theory that are applicable. In your own opinion, do you believe that the disengagement theory is applicable to the young who are dying?
12. Both death education and sex education are viewed as problems faced by contemporary American society. Can you cite any current trends that may bring death and sex education out of the "closet" (and/or institutional settings) and into the home?
13. Do you think that death conceptualizations have changed much in the past thirty years? Do you feel that death conceptualizations will change much in the next thirty years? Why or why not?
14. What are some of the limitations of the developmental approach to

the understanding of death conceptualizations? What are some of the special limitations of this approach as it is applied to people beyond the adolescent stage of life?

Glossary

AFFECT: The feelings and their expression.

BEHAVIORISTS: A school of psychology that focuses chiefly on overt behavior rather than upon inner psychological dynamics which cannot be clearly identified or measured.

EGO PSYCHOLOGISTS: A school of theorists and therapists who moved away from Freud in the direction of making more emphasis fall in therapy upon the coping strategies and strengths of the person rather than upon the more elusive dynamics of the libido and the unconscious.

PSYCHOANALYSIS: A school of theory and therapy that concentrates upon the unconscious forces behind overt behavior, dealing principally with instinctual drives and their dynamics in the individual's inner pysche; uses interplay of transference and resistance between psychoanalyst and client as principal foci.

PSYCHOTHANATIC: The psychological stage as related to the person's concept of death (from Greek words *Psyche* and *Thanatos*, soul/mind and death).

References

Alexander, Irving, and Arthur Alderstein. 1958. "Affective Responses to the Concept of Death in a Population of Children and Early Adolescents." *The Journal of Genetic Psychology*, Vol. 93:167–177.

Anthony, Silvia. 1940 and 1972. *The Discovery of Death in Childhood and After.* New York: Basic Books.

Atchley, Robert C. 1977. *The Social Forces in Later Life: An Introduction to Social Gerontology.* Belmont, Calif.: Wadsworth.

Becker, Ernest. 1973. *The Denial of Death* New York: The Free Press.

Blank, Gertrude, and Rubin Blank. 1979. *Ego Psychology II—Psychoanalytic Developmental Psychology.* New York: Columbia University Press.

Bluebond-Langer, Myra. 1977. "Meanings of Death to Children," in *New Meanings of Death,* ed. by Herman Feifel. New York: McGraw Hill.

Bowlby, John. 1969. *Attachment and Loss: Vol. I.* New York: Basic Books.

Cumming, Elaine, and William E. Henry. 1961. *Growing Old.* New York: Basic Books.

Erikson, Erik. 1950 and 1963. *Childhood and Society.* New York: Norton.

Feifel, Herman ed. 1959. *The Meaning of Death.* New York: McGraw Hill.

Fink, Roger W. 1976. "Death as Conceptualized by Adolescents," in *Dissertation Abstracts International,* Vol. 377 (6-B):3046.

Formanek, Ruth. 1974. "When Children Ask About Death." *Elementary School Journal,* Vol. 75, No. 2:92–97.

Galen, Helene. 1972. "A Matter of Life and Death." *Young Children,* Vol. 27, No. 6:351–356.

Ginsburg, Herbert, and Sylvia Opper. 1979. *Piaget's Theory of Intellectual Development,* 2d ed. Englewood Cliffs, N. J.: Prentice-Hall.

Grollman, Earl A. 1970. *Talking About Death: A Dialogue Between Parent and Child.* Boston: Beacon Press.

Horner, Althea J. 1979. *Object Relations and the Developing Ego in Therapy.* New York: Jason Aronson.

Kalish, Richard A. 1976. "Death and Dying in a Social Context," in *Handbook of Aging and Social Sciences,* ed. by Robert Binstock and Ethel Shanas. New York: Van Nostrand-Reinhold.

Kastenbaum, Robert. 1966. "On the Meaning of Time in Later Life," *The Journal of Genetic Psychology,* Vol. 109:9–25.

Kastenbaum, Robert. 1969a. "The Foreshortened Life Perspective." *Geriatrics,* Vol. 24, No. 8:126–133.

Kastenbaum, Robert. 1969b. "Death and Bereavement in Later Life," in *Death and Bereavement,* ed. by A. H. Kutscher. Springfield, Ill.: Charles C Thomas.

Kastenbaum, Robert. 1977a. "Death and Development Through the Lifespan," in *New Meanings of Death,* ed. by Herman Feifel. New York: McGraw-Hill.

Kastenbaum, Robert J. 1977b. *Death, Society, and Human Experience.* St. Louis: C. V. Mosby.

Kavanaugh, Robert E. 1972. *Facing Death.* Baltimore, Md.: Penguin Books.

Koocher, Gerald P., John E. O'Malley, Diane Foster and Janis L. Gogan. 1976. "Death Anxiety in Normal Children and Adolescents," in *Psychiatric Clinics,* Vol 9:220–229.

Leming, Michael R. 1979–80. "Religion and Death: A Test of Homans' Thesis." *Omega: The Journal of Death and Dying,* Vol. 10, No. 4:347–364.

Levinson, Daniel J., ed. 1978. *The Seasons of a Man's Life.* New York: Alfred A. Knopf.

Lifton, Robert. 1976. "The Sense of Immortality: On Death and the Continuity of Life," in *Death and Identity,* rev. ed., ed. by Robert Fulton and Robert Bendiksen. Bowie, Md.: Charles Press Publishers.

Lonetto, Richard. 1980. *Children's Conceptions of Death.* New York: Springer Publishing Co.

Lowenthal, Marjorie F., Majda Thurnher, David Chiriboga, and Associates. 1975. *Four Stages of Life.* San Francisco: Jossey-Bass Publishers.

Lund, Dale A., and Michael R. Leming. 1975. "Relationship Between Age and Fear of Death: A Study of Cancer Patients." Annual Scientific Meeting of the Gerontological Society, Louisville, Ky., October.

Maas, Henry S., and Joseph A. Kuypers. 1974. *From Thirty to Seventy.* San Francisco: Jossey-Bass.

Mahler, Margaret, Fred Pine, and Arnie Bergman. 1975. *The Psychological Birth of the Human Infant.* New York: Basic Books.

Maurer, Adah. 1964. "Adolescent Attitudes Toward Death." *The Journal of Genetic Psychology,* Vol. 105:75–90.

Maurer, Adah. 1966. "Maturation of Concepts of Death." *The British Journal of Medical Psychology,* Vol. 39:35–41.

Maurer, Adah. 1974. "Intimations of Mortality." *The Journal of Clinical Child Psychology III.* Vol. 2:14–17.

McKenzie, Sheila C. 1980. *Aging and Old Age.* Glenview, Ill: Scott, Foresman.

Millay, Edna St. Vincent. 1927. "Childhood is the Kingdom Where Nobody Dies," in *Collected Lyrics.* New York: Harper and Row, 1969, pp. 203–205.

Nagy, Maria. 1948. "The Child's Theories Concerning Death."*Journal of Genetic Psychology*, Vol. 73:3–27.

Neugarten, Bernice L., ed. 1968. *Middle Age and Aging: A Reader in Social Psychology*. Chicago: The University of Chicago Press.

Neugarten, Bernice L. 1974. "Age Groups in American Society and the Rise of the Young-Old." *Annals of the American Academy of Political and Social Science*, Vol. 415:187–198.

Newell, David S. 1961. "Social Structural Evidence for Disengagement," in *Growing Old*, ed. by Elaine Cumming and W. E. Henry. New York: Basic Books.

Norman, William H., and Thomas J. Scaramelli. 1980. *Mid-Life: Developmental and Clinical Issues*. New York: Branner/Mazel, Publishers.

Offer, Daniel, and Judith Baskin Offer. 1975. *From Teenage to Young Manhood: A Psychological Study*. New York: Basic Books.

Pattison, E. Mansell. 1977. *The Experience of Dying*. Englewood Cliffs, N. J.: Prentice-Hall.

Riley, Jack W. 1968. "Attitudes Toward Aging," in *Aging and Society (Vol. 1): An Inventory of Research Findings*, ed. by M. W. Riley et al. New York: Russell Sage Foundation.

Star, Cima. 1975. "To Write About Death, We Must Contemplate Our Own Death," in *Death and Ministry: Pastoral Care of the Dying and the Bereaved*, ed. by J. Donald Bane, Austin H. Kutscher, Robert E. Neale, and Robert B. Reeves, Jr. New York: Seabury Press.

Toynbee, Arnold, ed. 1968. *Man's Concern with Death*. London: Hodder and Stoughton.

Wallach, Michael A., and Leonard Green. 1961. "On Age and the Subjective Speed of Time," Chap. 53 in Bernice Neugarten, ed., *Middle Age and Aging: A Reader in Social Psychology*. Chicago: The University of Chicago Press.

Wenar, Charles. 1971. *Personality Development from Infancy to Adulthood*. Boston: Houghton Mifflin.

Suggested Readings

Grollman, Earl A., ed. 1967. *Explaining Death to Children*. Boston: Beacon Press.
   One of the best basic sources in this field, with chapters from several experts.
Kastenbaum, Robert, and Ruth Aisenberg. 1976. *The Psychology of Death*. New York: Springer Publishing Company.
   This volume is foundational in the area of developmental concepts of death. The reader should be forewarned that this book is somewhat technical in scope.
Le Shan, Eda. 1976. *Learning to Say Good-by: When a Parent Dies*. New York: Macmillan.
   An excellent book with a very helpful reading list for children, parents, and teachers. Aimed at a teen audience, yet helpful even for young adults and parents as a model for explaining death to teen-agers.
Wass, Hannelore, et al. eds. 1980 and 1984. *Death Education, An Annotated Resource Guide (I and II)*. Washington, D.C.: Hemisphere Publishing Corporation.
Wass, Hannelore, and Charles A. Corr, eds. 1984. *Childhood and Death*. Washington, D.C.: Hemisphere Publishing Corporation.
   Excellent resources for professionals working with children.

...FOR OF SUCH IS THE KINGDOM OF HEAVEN.

Chapter 6

RELIGION AND DEATH ATTITUDES

Religion provided me with answers to problems I didn't even know I had.

Anonymous St. Olaf College student, circa 1977

Death radically challenges *all* socially objectivated definitions of reality—of the world, of others, and of self. Death radically puts in question the taken-for-granted, "business-as-usual" attitude in which one exists in everyday life. Insofar as the knowledge of death cannot be avoided in any society, legitimations of the reality of the social *in the face of death* are decisive requirements in any society. The importance of religion in such legitimations is obvious. Religion then, maintains the socially defined reality by legitimating marginal situations in terms of an all-encompassing sacred reality.

Berger, 1969, p. 44

WHEN ONE THINKS of religion as a cultural system of meaning, an important question becomes relevant: "Why did religion come into existence?" Since this question attempts to discover the etiology of religious behavior and we have no scientific record of the first religious activity, answers to this question must be speculative in nature. They are based upon an *ex post facto* analysis of universal human needs which find fulfillment in a transcendent frame of reference. These answers are predicated upon the assumption that humans have a need for religious expression. St. Augustine has said, "Thou has made us for thyself, O God, and our hearts are restless until they find their rest in thee." This idea is also reflected in the following statement by Pascal, the physicist-philosopher: "There is a God-shaped vacuum in the heart of each man, which cannot be satisfied by any created thing but only by God, the creator, made known through Jesus Christ." However, these answers raise another more fundamental question of why humans have this need.

Death and the Origin of Religion

As discussed in Chapter 2, meanings are created and reproduced by humans. These meanings supply a base for activities and actions (behavior is in response to meanings) and provide order for the people who share a given culture. Peter Berger (1969) suggests that the human world has no order other than that created by humans. To live in a world without the order contributed by one's culture would force one to experience a meaningless existence. Sociologists refer to this condition as anomie, which literally means without order.

There are many situations in life that challenge the order upon which social life is based. Most of these situations are related to what Thomas O'Dea (1966) refers to as the three fundamental characteristics of human existence—uncertainty, powerlessness, and scarcity.

Uncertainty refers to the fact that human activity does not always lead to predictable outcomes. Even after careful planning, most people recognize that they will not be able to achieve all of their goals. Less optimistically, Murphy said the following: "Anything that can go wrong, will go wrong." The human condition is also characterized by *powerlessness*. We recognize that there are many situations in life, and events in the universe, over which humans have no control—among them are death, suffering, coercion, and natural disasters. Finally, in *scarcity*, humans experience inequality with regard to the distribution of wealth, power, prestige, and other things that make for a satisfying life. This inequality is the basis for the human experience of relative deprivation and frustration.

The three experiences of uncertainty, powerlessness, and scarcity are situations that challenge the order of everyday life, and are marginal to ordinary experiences. According to O'Dea (1966:5), these experiences "raise questions which can find an answer only in some kind of 'beyond' itself." Therefore, marginal experiences (which are characteristic of the human condition) force individuals to the realm of the transcendent in their search for meaningful answers.

Peter Berger (1969) claims that death is the marginal situation *par excellence.*

> Witnessing the death of others and anticipating his own death, the individual is strongly propelled to question the *ad hoc* cognitive and normative operating procedures of "normal" life in society. Death presents society with a formidable problem not only because of its obvious threat to the continuity of human relationships, but because it threatens the basic assumptions of order on which society rests (p. 23).
>
> Death radically puts in question the taken-for-granted, "business-as-usual" attitude in which one exists in everyday life. . . . Insofar as knowledge of death cannot be avoided in any society, legitimations of the reality of the social world *in the face of death* are decisive requirements in any society. The importance of religion in such legitimations is obvious (pp. 43–44).

It is religion (or a transcendent reference) that helps individuals remain reality-oriented when the order of everyday life is challenged. Contemplating death, we are faced with the fact that we will not be able to accomplish all our goals in life. We also realize that we are unable to extend the length of our lives and/or control the circumstances surrounding the experience and cause for our deaths. We are troubled by the fact that some must endure painful, degrading, and meaningless deaths, while others find *more* meaning and purpose in the last days of their lives than they experienced in the years preceding the "terminal period." Finally, the relative deprivation created by differential life spans raises questions that are unanswerable from a "this world" perspective.

Religious meaning systems provide answers to these problems of uncertainty, powerlessness, and scarcity created by death. O'Dea (1966:6–7) illustrates the function of religion in this regard when he makes the following statement:

> Religion, by its reference to a beyond and its beliefs concerning man's relationship to that beyond, provides a supraempirical view of a larger total reality. In the context of this reality, the disappointments and frustrations inflicted on mankind by uncertainty and impossibility, and by the institutionalized order of human society, may be seen as meaningful in some ultimate sense, and this makes acceptance of and adjustment to them possible. Moreover, by showing the norms and rules of society to be part of a larger supraempirical ethical order, ordained and sanctified by religious belief and practice, religion contributes to their enforcement when adherence to them contradicts the wishes or interests of those affected. Religion answers the problem of meaning. It sanctifies the norms of the established social order at what we have called the "breaking points," by providing a grounding for the beliefs and orientations of men in a view of reality that transcends the empirical here-and-now of daily experience. Thus not only is cognitive frustration overcome, which is involved in the problem of meaning, but the emotional adjustments to frustrations and deprivations inherent in human life and human society are facilitated.

RELIGION AS A MEANS OF PROVIDING UNDERSTANDING OF DEATH

Ten years ago, while on a field trip to a funeral home, I complimented the funeral director on the beautiful pastoral scene hanging on a wall in his establishment. He said it was a very unusual wall hanging and took it down to show me a framed velvet reverse side that could also be displayed. He then took out a box containing a cross, a crucifix, and a Star of David which could be hung on the velvet backing. The funeral director told the class that he changed the hanging as the religious affiliation of the deceased varied.

Since the time of that field trip, I have become very conscious of the way funeral homes extensively employ religious symbols in attempting to create a religious ambience. Consider the following:

1. Within the funeral home, "chapel" is the name given to the room where the funeral is held.
2. Most memorial cards have the 23rd Psalm on them.
3. The music one hears on the sound systems within most funeral homes is religious in nature.
4. Wall hangings found in most funeral homes usually have religious content.
5. Funeral homes often provide Christmas calendars (complete with Bible verses and religious scenes) for religious groups and other interested members of the community.

As discussed in the last section of this chapter, religious systems provide a means to reestablish the social order challenged by death. Our society has institutionalized the continued importance of religion by creating funeral rituals which have a religious quality about them.

There have been many attempts to explain the methods by which religion influences death meanings. Most of the discussion in this area has been strongly influenced by the theoretical writings of Malinowski, Radcliffe-Brown, and Homans.

Stated briefly, Bronislaw Malinowski held that religion functioned to relieve the anxiety caused by the crisis experiences that people encounter in their lifetimes. Religion has its origin in the crisis experience in death because it provides individuals with a means of dealing with extraordinary phenomena. Religion functions to bring about a restoration of normalcy for the individual.

Malinowski (1965:70) says:

> Every important crisis of human life implies a strong emotional upheaval, mental conflict and possible disintegration. Religion in its ethics sanctifies human life and conduct and becomes perhaps the most powerful force of social control. In its dogmatics it supplies man with strong cohesive forces.

In elaborating on his theory that religion is the "great anxiety reliever," Malinowski (1965:71) claims that "death, which of all human events is the most upsetting and disorganizing to man's calculations, is perhaps the main source of religious belief." From Malinowski's perspective, death is not only the greatest source of anxiety, it is also the primary crisis event which calls forth religious behavior. Such theorizing leads us to ask the empirical question, "Does religion provide humans with a solace in their attempts to cope with death?" From the perspective of the funeral industry, "Are attempts on the part of the funeral home to merge religious and death meanings necessary and effective in assisting persons who are bereaved?"

A. R. Radcliffe-Brown (1965) disagrees with Malinowski's contention that religion functions primarily as an anxiety reliever, and claims that religion gives people fears and anxieties from which they would otherwise be free—the fear of spirits, fear of God's judgment, fear of the devil, or of hell. From Radcliffe-Brown's perspective, we would be led to expect that the nonreligious individual would have relatively less death anxiety, and would cope better with his or her death and the deaths of others. We might also be led to the conclusion that from the point of reference of personal death anxiety, religious beliefs have dysfunctional consequences.

George Homans (1965) has attempted to resolve this problem by declaring that both Malinowski and Radcliffe-Brown are correct in their theorizing about the role of religion in death anxiety. Rather than pitting Radcliffe-Brown against Malinowski, Homans argues that Radcliffe-Brown's hypothesis is a supplement to Malinowski's theory. According to Homans (1965), Malinowski is looking at the individual, Radcliffe-Brown has a societal perspective. Malinowski is saying that the individual tends to feel anxiety on certain occasions; Radcliffe-Brown is saying that society *expects* the individual to feel anxiety on certain occasions.

If we start with a psychological frame of reference (as does Malinowski), we focus our attention on the function of religion for the individual. From this perspective, patterns of social integration are contingent upon psychological processes—what works for the individual is functional for society. Therefore, since religious actions and rituals may help some individuals provide meaning for death, and consequently dispel anomie in death-related situations, the social function of religion must be anxiety reduction. This point of view is illustrated in the following statement by Malinowski (1965:72):

> Religion in its ethics sanctifies human life and conduct and becomes perhaps the most powerful force of social control. In its dogmatics it supplies man with strong cohesive forces. It grows out of every culture, because life-long bonds of cooperation and mutual interest create sentiments, and sentiments rebel against death and dissolution. The cultural call for religion is highly derived and indirect but is finally rooted in the way in which the primary needs of man are satisfied in culture.

Turning to the perspective of A. R. Radcliffe-Brown, we find the following statement, which poses an alternative to Malinowski's reasoning (Radcliffe-Brown, 1965:81):

> I think that for certain rites it would be easy to maintain with equal plausibility an exactly contrary theory, namely, that if it were not for the existence of the rite and the beliefs associated with it the individual would feel no anxiety, and that the psychological effect of the rite is to create in the individual a sense of insecurity and danger.

In this quotation, Radcliffe-Brown argues that religion might serve to increase anxiety for the individual rather than reduce it as Malinowski would contend. Radcliffe-Brown (1965:81) begins with a societal perspective and declares that the function of religion is to create a sense of anxiety which will maintain the social structure of the society:

> Actually in our fears or anxieties, as well as in our hopes, we are conditioned by the community in which we live. And it is largely by the sharing of hopes and fears, by what I have called *common concern* in events or eventualities, that human beings are linked together in temporary or permanent associations.

Homans' treatise is that when individuals encounter death, the anxiety they experience is basically socially ascribed. Death fears can be likened to the fears of other things—snakes, electricity, communism, or whatever. These fears are learned. C. Wright Mills (1958) called these types of fears "crackpot realism." If we believe we are in a dangerous setting, we react accordingly. Religion, with its emphasis on immortality of the soul and its belief in a coming judgment, increases the level of death anxiety for individuals who follow the teachings of the religion. However, once individuals have fulfilled the religious or magical ceremonies which are required by religion, they experience a moderate amount of anxiety.

Homans brings both the perspectives of Malinowski and Radcliffe-Brown together by concluding the following:

1. Religion functions to relieve anxiety associated with death-related situations.
2. Death anxiety calls forth religious activities and rituals.
3. In order to stabilize the group of individuals who perform these rituals, group activities and beliefs provide a potential threat of anxiety in order to unite group members through a "common concern."
4. This secondary anxiety may be effectively removed through the group rituals of purification and expiation.

Summarizing the relationship between religiosity and death anxiety, we can arrive at the following theoretical model:

1. The meanings of death are socially ascribed—death per se is neither fearful nor nonfearful.
2. The meanings that are ascribed to death in a given culture are transmitted to individuals in the society through the socialization process.
3. Anxiety reduction may be accomplished through social cooperation and institutional participation.
4. Institutional cohesiveness in religious institutions is fostered by giving participants a sense of anxiety concerning death and uniting them through a common concern.
5. If the religious institutions are to remain viable, they must also provide a means for anxiety reduction.

6. Through its promise of a reward in the afterlife, and its redefinition of the negative affects of death upon the temporal life of the individual, religion diminishes the fear which it has ascribed to death and reduces anxiety definitions attributed to death by secular society.

In order to test the empirical validity of this theory, Leming (1979–80) surveyed 372 randomly selected residents in Northfield, Minnesota concerning death anxiety and religious activities, beliefs, and experiences. Subjects were divided into four groups based upon a religious commitment scale developed by Glock and Stark (1966) and Faulkner and DeJong (1966). Approximately 25 percent of the respondents were placed in each category—the first group consists of those persons who were the least religious and the fourth group contains the people who are the most religious.

Figure 6–1 gives the mean fear of death scores for each of the levels of religious commitment. It is apparent that the relationship between the variables of religiosity and death anxiety is curvilinear—persons with a moderate commitment to religion have added to the general anxiety which has been socially ascribed to death from secular sources. The person with a moderate commitment receives only the negative consequences of religion—that which Radcliffe-Brown refers to as a "common concern." These persons acquire only the anxiety, which religion is capable of producing,

FIGURE 6–1: MEAN FEAR OF DEATH SCALE SCORES BY LEVEL OF RELIGIOUS COMMITMENT

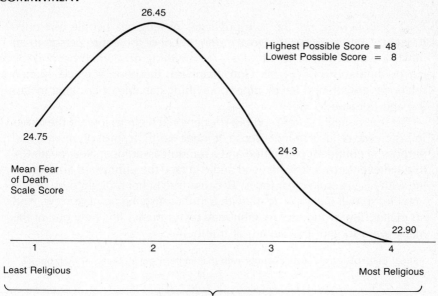

and none of the consolation. On the other hand the highly committed individual has the least anxiety concerning death. Religion, as Malinowski predicts, provides individuals with a solace when they attempt to cope with death attitudes.

In conclusion, religiosity seems to serve the dual function of "afflicting the comforted" and "comforting the afflicted." We have discovered that religion, when accompanied with a high degree of commitment, not only relieves the dread it engendered, but dispels much of the anxiety caused by the social effects of death.

TEMPORAL INTERPRETATIONS OF DEATH

Even though the funeral industry and most people in the United States tend to merge religious and death meanings, temporal interpretations of death also provide a means for protecting social order in the face of death. Temporal interpretations tend to emphasize the empirical, natural, and "this world" view of death.

Religious and Secular Orientations

Faith or belief are not the sole privileges of religious people as I once thought. Faith is simply that total commitment of the entire person to an ideal, a way of life, a set of values, to anything or anyone beyond the narrow limitations of myself: God, mankind, the poor, science, human relations, growth and development, anything capable of bringing meaning and purpose to life.

The true believer, after I sort out my personal feelings toward the tenets in his creed, reflects to me a sense of inner worth, a spirit of mission and purpose, a confident conviction and a tranquil assurance. Near death the true believer knows why he lived and can face the unfinished tasks of his life with his vision in clear focus. Because true belief brought perspective into life, so will it endow death with a more satisfying point of view. And no matter how wonderful religion may be for many, it is only one of the many ways to gain this stature of true belief.

Source: Robert E. Kavanaugh, *Facing Death* (Baltimore: Penguin Books, 1972), pp. 221, 224).

According to Vernon (1970:33), "when death is given a temporal interpretation and is seen as the loss of consciousness, self-control, and identity, the individual may conclude that he or she can avoid social isolation in
eternity by identifying him or herself with specific values, including religious ones." If we define religion as a system of beliefs and practices related to high intensity value meanings and/or meanings of the supernatural (Vernon, 1970), then it is possible for individuals with temporal
orientations to be "religious" in their outlook without affirming an afterlife. Furthermore, since any death has many consequences for the persons
on whose life it impinges, we would expect that even religious persons
would assign some temporal meanings to death.

Vernon (1970:33) has pointed out that individuals, whose interpretations
are primarily temporal, share the following beliefs and attitudes concerning the meaning of death:

1. They tend to reject or de-emphasize a belief in the afterlife.
2. They tend to believe that death is the end of the individual.
3. They tend to focus upon the needs and concerns of the survivors.
4. They tend to be present oriented for themselves, but present and future
   oriented for those who will continue after them.
5. Any belief in immortality is related to the activities and accomplishments
   of the individual during his or her lifetime—including biological offspring
   and social relationships the individual has created.

There is a strong temptation to view the person with a temporal orientation as being very different from the person who finds comfort in a religious interpretation of death. In fact both persons will attempt to restore
the order in their personal lives, and that found in society, by placing death
in the context of a "higher" order.

For the individual with religious commitments, protection from anomie
and comfort for anxiety are to be found by being in relationship with the
supernatural. For the person with a secular or temporal orientation, these
same benefits are found in becoming involved with other people, projects,
and causes. These involvements, while not pertaining to the supernatural,
still provide a frame of reference which transcends the finite individual—a
person may die but his or her concerns will continue after death.

Symbolic Immortality

As discussed in Chapter 2, symbolic immortality (Lifton and Olson, 1974)
refers to the belief that self meanings can continue after the person has
died. For the religious, symbolic immortality is often related to the concept
of soul which either returns to its preexistent state, goes to an afterlife, is

reincarnated in another body, or is united with the Cosmos. For the person whose primary orientation is temporal, symbolic immortality is achieved by being remembered by others, creating something which remains useful or of interest to others, or by being part of a cause or social movement that continues after the individual's death.

> I am assured of immortality, not by anything I do, but by not dying.
>
> *Woody Allen*

One of the reasons many parents give for deciding to have children is the need for an heir—someone to carry the family name. Research has demonstrated that in the United States families with only female children are more likely to continue having children (in hopes of producing a male offspring) than are families with only male children. For the ancient Hebrews, the cultural institution of the levirite marriage required that a relative of the deceased husband have sexual intercourse with his kinsman's widow in order to provide a male heir. If it is possible to pass on something of oneself to one's children, then children are one method employed by parents in providing symbolic immortality.

Investing oneself in relationships with others also insures that one will be remembered after death. Damon Runyon said as he was dying, "You can keep your things of bronze and stone, just give me one person who will remember me once a year." Some will argue that if we have influenced the lives of others, something of us will continue in their lives after we die. Organ donations supply a "tangible" method for providing this type of symbolic immortality. In this way, one can even insure that a part of his or her *physical self* can continue in another person.

Currently there is an increasing tendency for individuals to donate their organs and tissues upon death to the living. In many urban areas kidney foundations, eye banks, and transplant centers will supply donor cards and, when death occurs, arrange for transplants. Currently, there are over twenty-five kinds of tissues or organs used for transplantation including eye, skin, bone, tendon, bone marrow, kidney, liver, pancreas, blood vessel, lung, and heart. While some of these transplant operations are still in the areas of research, techniques are constantly improving.

Problems affecting transplantation include: 1) donor and donee tissues compatibility, 2) a chronic shortage of donors thus often producing a difficult decision in selecting among potential recipients, 3) lack of legal definition of death preventing surgeons from removing healthy organs when brain activity has stopped but the heart and lungs are still functioning, 4) lack of nationwide communications network to coordinate information, and 5) the question of who will pay for expensive transplant centers.

Jamie Fiske Story Inspired 7-Year-Old Boy to Donate Organs

Mickie Knutson and her 7-year-old son, Chad, had been watching television news reports about Jamie Fiske's liver transplant last November, and they left the boy confused.

"Chad asked me what it was, and I explained," Mickie Knutson recalled Wednesday. "He said, 'Mom, when I go to heaven I'll have a new body.'"

Then, she said, he talked about the child whose liver went to Jamie Fiske, and said: "When I die, I'd like to be able to do that."

"It hits you hard," she said. "You don't expect a 7-year-old to talk about donating his organs. But that was Chad's wish.

"And now it's come true."

Chad, his brother Trent, 4, and a 16-year-old neighbor, Carol Jo Zack, died Sunday night when a train struck the vehicle in which they were riding at a crossing south of Duluth.

On Tuesday, Chad's heart, kidneys and corneas were removed for use in five transplants.

One kidney was placed in a 33-year-old man at the University of Minnesota Hospitals, and the other was flown to New York state for use in a transplant there.

Another team of University Hospitals surgeons transplanted Chad's heart into 11-year-old Krista Larose of Bethel Tuesday morning, but she died later that night.

"It was a perfectly good heart, and the operation went very well," said Dr.R.Morton Bolman. But he said that doctors had been unable to tell before the surgery that the young girl's failing heart had caused such extensive damage to her lungs that no transplant could have worked. And with her fast-failing heart, the transplant was her only hope for survival, he said.

The corneas, which can be preserved for a long time, are expected to be used for later transplants.

Authorities said Chad and the others died instantly when the all-terrain vehicle on which the three were riding collided with an Amtrak passenger train just a quarter-mile from the boys' home in Holyoke, Minn.

Chad was rushed by ambulance 20 miles to St. Luke's Hospital in Duluth and placed on a life-support system for nearly two hours before he was pronounced "brain dead," said his father, Roy Knutson.

(Brain death means total and permanent cessation of all brain function.

It is the only way that death can be diagnosed when machines are keeping the heart and other organs working.)

The newscast concerning Jamie Fiske "came to me when we were at the hospital," Mickie Knutson said in a telephone interview.

"His only real injury was to his head. His condition was perfect for it (donating his organs). We remembered what Chad had said."

The Knutsons said they waited in the hospital through the night for a second medical opinion, and then waited for Chad's grandfather to arrive for one last look at the child. Chad's body was then flown to Minneapolis.

"We feel with all our hearts that it was God's hands which kept Chad breathing long enough to get to the hospital and fulfill Chad's physical wish," said Mickie Knutson.

"God has promised victory in all things and through Chad being able to bring life to other people, we have seen victory. He's helped five other people with his heart, his eyes and his kidneys."

"Chad would sometimes astound us by the things he'd say," said Roy Knutson. "But when we thought about it, his wish to donate his organs wasn't that surprising."

"He was in the second grade where I teach [in Wrenshall]. At a milk break, his teacher was passing around Oreo cookies and thought there'd be enough so each child would get two. When it became apparent that there weren't enough to go around, she [the teacher] said Chad's hand went immediately in the air and he said, 'I don't need a second one.'"

The Knutsons said they know the shock of the tragedy, which cost them their only two children and a neighbor they "cherished like a daughter," will linger. But they harbor no bitterness or anger, they said.

"We, as Christians, feel God has a plan for everyone," said Mickie Knutson. "We're thankful for the beautiful years he gave us with our boys and that Chad was allowed to help others.

"For us, that has been a joy."

It was one year ago this month that Jamie Fiske arrived at University Hospitals to await the donor liver she needed to survive. After Jamie's father Charles made a dramatic national appeal, the donor liver came November 5 from a Utah boy who died in a car-train accident.

In Bridgewater, Mass., yesterday, Jamie's mother, Marilyn, said in a telephone interview her daughter, now 22 months old, is "doing terrific" with no problems from the transplanted liver. And she said that Jamie's role in Chad's donation of his organs after death "means an awfully lot to us," adding:

"We can truly learn from little kids. This boy learned something at age 6 that took me much longer to learn. He is a very special boy. We can learn from him like we have learned from Jamie. And his parents are very special people."

> Funeral services for Chad and Trent Knutson were scheduled today at 10 a.m. at the Sandy Lake Baptist Church near Carlton. Services for Carol Jo Zack were set for 1 P.M. at the Barr Brothers Funeral Home in Cloquet.
>
> Those wishing to contribute to the Chad and Trent Knutson Memorial Fund to Help Life Continue On may send donations to: Transplant Assistance Fund, Box 19, Mayo Building, University of Minnesota, Minneapolis, Minn. 55455. The fund was established by the hospitals to help patients and their families meet housing, transportation and other nonmedical expenses associated with transplants.
>
> Source: Paul Levy and Lewis Cope, *Minneapolis Star and Tribune,* September 22, 1983, p. A1.

One of the reasons why people write books (especially death and dying books) is to promote their own symbolic immortality. As long as their books can be read, their influence will outlive their biological body. The same is true for television and motion picture stars. Each year the youthful Judy Garland is resurrected from the dead, as the *Wizard of Oz* is shown again on the television.

Great inventors, political leaders, and athletic "hall of famers" are also given immortality when we use their products, remember their accomplishments, and celebrate their achievements. In the case of medical practitioners and bionic inventors, not only do the living remember their accomplishments, but these efforts extend the lives of those who provide the dead with immortality.

Ozymandias

Percy Bysshe Shelley

I met a traveler from an antique land
Who said: Two vast and trunkless legs of stone
Stand in the desert. Near them, on the sand,
Half sunk, a shattered visage lies, whose frown,
And wrinkled lip, and sneer of cold command,
Tell that its sculptor well those passions read
Which yet survive, stamped on these lifeless things,
The hand that mocked them and the heart that fed;

And on the pedestal these words appear:
"My name is Ozymandias, king of kings:
Look on my works, ye Mighty, and despair!"
Nothing beside remains. Round the decay
Of that colossal wreck, boundless and bare
The lone and level sands stretch far away.

The person's finite identity is protected by the groups' permanence. Just as Standard Oil is the legacy of John D. Rockefeller, John H. Leming and Son's Insurance Agency will remain even after John H. Leming and his sons are dead (providing that the new owners feel that it is in their business interest not to change the name of the company).

The same can be said for people who give themselves to political movements and causes. Marx, Lenin, Stalin, and Mao—as leaders of communism—will be remembered by future communists, despite the efforts by present officials to accomplish the contrary. We even provide infamous immortality to villains, murders, and traitors. It seems ironical that most of us spend a lifetime working for immortality, when a single shot from the gun of John Wilkes Booth supplied him with our everlasting remembrance.

In conclusion, symbolic immortality is something that only the living can give the dead. Yet, people live with the faith that their survivors will remember them and perpetuate the meaning of their lives after they die. Like religious interpretations of death, temporal meanings enable individuals to protect themselves and their social order from death. One problem remains for those whose immortality depends upon others, "What would happen if a nuclear holocaust were to occur and there were no survivors?"

The Fading of Immortality

In quantitative terms, the twentieth century seems more death ridden than any other. Yet mass death is strangely impersonal; an eighteenth-century hanging at Tyburn probably had more immediate impact on the watching crowd than the almost incomprehensible statistics of modern war and calculated terror have today. In the last century, Byron, Shelley, Keats and a whole generation of young poets haunted by romanticism and tuberculosis could be "half in love with easeful Death," wooing it as they would woo a woman. Even before World War I, German poet Rainer Maria Rilke could still yearn for "the great death" for which a man prepares himself, rather than the "little" death for which he is unprepared.

In today's literature there are few "great deaths." Tolstoy, Thomas Mann, Conrad gave death a tragic dimension. Hemingway was among the last to try; his heroes died stoically, with style, like matadors. Nowadays, death tends to be presented as a banal accident in an indifferent universe. Much of the Theater of the Absurd ridicules both death and modern man's inability to cope with it. In Ionesco's *Amedee,* or *How to Get Rid of It,* the plot concerns a corpse that grows and grows until it floats away in the shape of a balloon—a balloon, that is, on the way to nowhere.

If there is no immortality, I shall hurl myself into the sea," wrote Tennyson. Bismarck was calmer. "Without the hope of an afterlife," he said, "this life is not even worth the effort of getting dressed in the morning." Freud called the belief that death is the door to a better life "the oldest, strongest and most insistent wish of mankind." But now death is steadily becoming more of a wall and less of a door.

For prehistoric man, everything he saw probably seemed alive; death was the unthinkable anomaly. The situation is reversed in a scientifically oriented world; amid dead matter, life seems an unaccountable, brief flash in the interstellar dark. Not that this has destroyed the power of faith to confront death. Beyond the doubts of its own "demythologers," and on a plane of thought beyond either denial or confirmation by science (Christianity still offers the hope of eternal life. Theologians are debating whether this means immortality in the sense of the survival of the soul, or resurrection, in the sense of a new creation.). Either concept is totally different from the endless treadmill of reincarnation visualized by the Eastern religions; the Christian view of eternity is not merely endless time, and it need not involve the old physical concept of heaven and hell. It does involve the survival of some essence of self, and an encounter with God. "Life after death," said theologian Karl Barth, "should not be regarded like a butterfly"—he might have said a balloon—that "flutters away above the grave and is preserved somewhere. Resurrection means not the continuation of life, but life's completion. The Christian hope is the conquest of death, not a flight into the Beyond."

The Fear of Nothingness

Admittedly, this hope so stated is more abstract than the fading pictures of sky-born glory, of hallelujah choruses and throngs of waiting loved ones. "People today could be described as more realistic about death," says one psychiatrist. "But inside I think they are more afraid. Those old religious assurances that there would be a gathering-in some day have largely been discarded, and I see examples all the time of neuroses caused by the fear of death." Harvard Theologian Krister Stendahl agrees.

"Socrates," he points out, "died in good cheer and in control, unlike the agony of Jesus with his deep human cry of desertion and loneliness. Americans tend to behave as Socrates did. But there is more of what Jesus stands for lurking in our unconsciousness."

Alone with his elemental fear of death, modern man is especially troubled by the prospect of a meaningless death and a meaningless life—the bleak offering of existentialism. "There is but one truly serious philosophical problem," wrote Albert Camus, "and that is suicide." In other words, why stay alive in a meaningless universe? The existentialist replies that man must live for the sake of living, for the things he is free to accomplish. But despite volumes of argumentation, existentialism never seems quite able to justify this conviction on the brink of a death that is only a trap door to nothingness.

There are surrogate forms of immortality: the continuity of history, the permanence of art, the biological force of sex. These can serve well enough to give life a purpose and a sense of fulfillment. But they cannot outwit death, and they are hardly satisfactory substitutes for the still persistent human hope that what happens here in three score years and ten is not the whole story.

"Timor Mortis conturbat me," wrote the fifteenth-century Scottish poet William Dunbar, and he continued:

Since for the Death remedy is none,
Best is it that we for Death dispone.

That groan may be shared by all men. And perhaps it should be, as should the Christian admonition to be ready to die at all times—counsel more applicable than ever in a day of sudden deaths. For it is only in daring to accept his death as a companion that a man may really possess his life.

Source: *Time Magazine*, November 12, 1965.

EXPERIENCES OF THE "AFTER-LIFE" BY THE CLINICALLY DEAD: IS THIS EMPIRICAL EVIDENCE FOR AFTER-LIFE BELIEFS?

In the past, one of the assumptions most people made about the field of thanatology was that the real "experts" were not among us—they were dead. With the publication of Dr. Raymond Moody's *Life After Life* (1975) many people have stepped forward to challenge this assumption.

Having been near death, or having been declared "clinically dead" by medical authorities, a number of survivors from these experiences have "returned from the dead" to tell us that they now "know" what it is like to be dead and that they possess empirical evidence to support a rational belief in the afterlife.

The description below, developed by Raymond Moody, is a composite of the many accounts by individuals who have survived the experience of being near death or being declared clinically dead. This ideal type model was constructed by interviewing more than 150 people who had these experiences. Moody reports, and other scientists (Noyes and Kletti, 1977; and Ring, 1980) support, the similarity of most of these "life after death" accounts.

Life After Life

Raymond A. Moody, Jr., M.D., Ph.D.

A man is dying and, as he reaches the point of greatest physical distress, he hears himself pronounced dead by his doctor. He begins to hear an uncomfortable noise, a loud ringing or buzzing, and at the same time feels himself moving very rapidly through a long dark tunnel. After this he suddenly finds himself outside of his own physical body, but still in the immediate physical environment, and he sees his own body from a distance, as though he is a spectator. He watches the resuscitation attempt from his unusual vantage point and is in a state of emotional upheaval.

After a while, he collects himself and becomes more accustomed to his body with very different powers from the physical body he has left behind. Soon other things begin to happen. Others come to meet and to help him. He glimpses the spirits of relatives and friends who have already died, and a loving, warm spirit of a kind he has never encountered before—a being of light—appears before him. This being asks him a question, nonverbally, to make him evaluate his life and helps him along by showing him a panoramic, instantaneous playback of the major events of his life. At some point he finds himself approaching some sort of barrier or border, apparently representing the limit between earthly life and the next life. Yet, he finds that he must go back to earth, that the time for his death has not yet come. At this point he resists, for by now he is taken up with his experiences in the afterlife and does not want to return. He is overwhelmed by intense feelings of joy, love, and peace. Despite his attitude, though, he somehow reunites with his physical body and lives.

Later he tries to tell others, but he has trouble doing so. In the first place, he can find no human words adequate to describe these unearthly episodes. He also finds that others scoff, so he stops telling other people. Still, the experience affects his life profoundly, especially his views about death and its relationship to life.

Source: Raymond A. Moody, Jr. *Life After Life: The Investigation of a Phenomenon— Survival of Bodily Death* (Boston: G. K. Hall, 1975), pp. 16–18.

Having considered this descriptive account, the following questions become relevant as we contemplate the relationship between these experiences and the other material presented in this chapter:

1. Are these experiences real, and what do they tell us about the dying process and/or being dead?
2. Can afterlife beliefs be empirically supported by these accounts?
3. How do religious beliefs affect the content of near or clinical death experiences?
4. What is the impact of near or clinical death experiences upon death anxiety?

To all of our questions, we must temper our remarks by saying that if not real, these experiences are very real to those who have experienced them. Not unlike being "in love," returning from the "dead" is an extremely subjective experience and does not lend itself to verification by others. It is difficult to doubt that the individual has experienced *something*, however, we are unable to prove, or disprove, that the person has died. All we can say scientifically is that the person claims to have had the experience of "being dead."

Returning to our analogy of being in love, all that can be known is that the person says that he or she is "in love." Whether or not the person is really in love cannot be determined empirically. From the perspective of the individual, it does not really matter, because a situation, which has been defined as real, will have very real behavioral consequences.

The same problem arises with regard to a belief in an afterlife. Scientifically, afterlife beliefs cannot be proved, or disproved, with this type of evidence. Science is based upon the principle of "intersubjectivity." This means that independent observers, with different subjective orientations, must agree that something is "true" based upon their separate investigations. Unfortunately, the opportunity to experience the afterlife (and return) is not uniformly available to all observers. Therefore, while those who have had these experiences may feel rationally justified in their beliefs, the evidence they use is not scientifically based. Science, at this point, can neither verify, nor falsify afterlife beliefs.

In responding to our last two questions, there is some scientific evidence which can provide limited answers. According to Moody (1975) and Canning (1965), the content of afterlife experiences is largely a function of the religious background, training, and beliefs of the individuals involved. Only Roman Catholics see the Virgin Mary and the host of Catholic saints, while encounters with Joseph Smith are reserved for Mormon believers. Like dreams, continuity exists between experiences in "this world" and experiences in the "afterlife." For example, personages in the afterlife are dressed in an attire that would conform to the individual's cultural customs and beliefs. Also, relatives appear to be at the same age as they were when they were last seen. In fact, there is so much continuity between this world and the "other world," that persons with afterlife experiences report few, if any, surprises. In response to this evidence, Charmaz (1980) raises the following question: "Is the consciousness reported in these near-death experiences a *reflection* of a shared myth or *evidence* for it?"

Concerning the impact of the near-death experience upon death anxiety, there is empirical evidence that fear of death is significantly reduced. However, even though the state of being dead is not distressing to them, anxiety related to the dying process is unchanged. Almost without exception, persons who have had these experiences look forward to their eventual deaths.

Finally, there is also evidence that individuals (even though their first encounters with the afterlife were initiated by suicide attempts) do not attempt to bring about an end to their lives in order to return to the "life beyond." In fact, most individuals find new reasons for living as a result of these experiences.

DEATH, ANXIETY, AND FEAR

> Lord,
> If I have to die,
> Let me die;
> But please,
> Take away this fear.
>
> *Ken Walsh (1974)*

A point made in this book a number of times is that death *per se* has no meaning other than that which people give it. If this is true, why is it that most of us believe that death is something which intrinsically engenders fear?

Anthropologists would be quick to respond that not all cultures in the world hold that death is necessarily something to be feared (see Chapter 10). However, there seems to be a large number of cultures, including our own, which attach fearful meanings to death and death-related situations. Why is it that so many people have less than positive views of death?

In the beginning of this chapter we said that death universally calls into question the order upon which most societies are based. As a marginal experience to everyday life, death not only disrupts normal patterns of interaction, but also challenges the meaningfulness of life. With the exception of those societies where death is a routine event in the lives of the people (e.g., Uganda, Cambodia, and New Guinea), death in most societies is a stressful event because it brings disorder to those whose lives it touches.

Any change in ordinary patterns of social interaction requires that the individual adjust. Most of us prefer the security of situations that are predictable, stable, and routine. The disorder created by changes in everyday life can make for a stressful situation as individuals attempt to adjust to these changes (Holmes and Rahe, 1967).

Death in the United States is also viewed as fearful because Americans have been systematically taught to fear it. Horror movies portray death, ghosts, skeletons, goblins, bogymen, and ghoulish morticians as things or people to be feared. Sesame Street tries to create for children a more positive view of monsters as children are befriended by Grover, Harry, Oscar, and Cookie Monster. With the exception of Casper, "the friendly ghost," death-related fantasy figures have not received the same positive images. Instead of providing positive images, our culture has chosen to reinforce fearful meanings of death. Cemeteries are portrayed as eerie, funerals are to be avoided, and morgues are scary places where you "wouldn't be caught dead."

One of the reasons death and dying classes incorporate field trips to hospices, funeral homes, crematories, and cemeteries is to confront negative death meanings and fantasies with first hand objective observations. The preparation room at the mortuary is a good example. If you have never been in one, think about the mental image that comes to your mind. For many, the preparation room is a place one approaches with fear and caution. Dr. Frankenstein's laboratory (complete with bats, strange lighting, body parts, and naked dead bodies) is an image that one may expect to encounter. The great disappointment for most students as they walk through the door is that they find a room that looks like a physician's examination room. "Is that all there is?" is the comment I hear most often after visiting the preparation room.

The sociologist Erving Goffman (1959) has observed that first impressions are unlikely to change and tend to dominate the meanings related to subsequent social interaction patterns and experiences. Most of us want to retain untrue fearful meanings of death, even when confronted by positive images. On a recent field trip to a funeral home, one student refused to enter the preparation room. While other students were hearing a descriptive account concerning embalming procedures, she discovered a bottle of liquid used in that process which was labeled "skin texturizer." Upon discovering this bottle the student became nauseated. Other students had a difficult time understanding her problem because they had received a positive experience.

Another reason for fearful meanings being attributed to death can be attributed to a traumatic death-related experience. Being a witness to a fatal car accident, discovering someone who has committed suicide, or attending a funeral where emotional outbursts create an uncomfortable environment for mourners can all increase death anxiety for individuals. However, such occurrences are rather uncommon for most people and do not account for the prevalence of America's preoccupation with death fears. In a survey of college students, Robert Kavanaugh (1972) found that 78 percent had yet to see a dead person up close and more that 92 percent had yet to witness a death.

In summary, death fears are not instinctive, they exist because our culture has created and perpetuated fearful meanings and ascribed them to death. They are also a function of the fact that death is a non-ordinary experience challenging the order of everyday life in society. They are a function of occasional first-hand encounters, with death being so unusual, that they become traumatic.

The Content of Death Fears

When one speaks of death fear or death anxiety, it is assumed that the concept is unidimensional and that consensus exists relative to its meaning. Such is not the case—two persons may say that they fear death, and the content of their fears may not be shared.

Death anxiety (or death fear) is a multidimensional concept and is based upon the following four foci: (1) concern with the death of self; (2) concern with the deaths of significant others; (3) concern with the process of dying; and (4) concern with the state of being dead. Elaborating upon this model, the following eight types of death anxiety emerge and can be applied to the death of self and the deaths of others: (1) fear of dependency; (2) fear of the pain in the dying process; (3) fear of the indignity in the dying process; (4) fear of the isolation, separation, and rejection that can be part of the dying process; (5) fear of leaving loved ones; (6) fear of afterlife concerns; (7) fear of the finality of death; and (8) fear of the fate of the body.

From Table 6–1 we can see that the content of fear will be influenced by whose death the individual is considering. From a personal death perspective, one may have anxiety over the affect that one's dying (or being dead) will have on others. There might also be private worries about how one might be treated by others—and even by God. From the perspective of the survivor, the individual may be concerned about the financial, emotional, and social problems related to the death of a significant other.

Since there are many factors related to the experience of death and death-related situations which can engender fear, we would expect to find differences between persons with respect to the type and intensity of death fear they experience. The social circumstance and past experiences of the individual will also have differential effects upon the type and intensity of fears the person will ascribe to death. However, with all of the potential sources for differences, it is interesting that repeated administrations of the Leming Death Fear Scale yield consistently high anxiety scores for the fears

TABLE 6–1.   The Eight Dimensions of Death Anxiety as They Relate to the Deaths of Self and Others

Self	Others
PROCESS OF DYING	
1. Fear of dependency	Fear of financial burdens
2. Fear of pain in dying process	Fear of going through the painful experience of others
3. Fear of the indignity in dying process	Fear of being unable to cope with the physical problems of others
4. Fear of loneliness, rejection, and isolation	Fear of being unable to cope emotionally with problems of others
5. Fear of leaving loved ones	Fear of losing loved ones
STATE OF BEING DEAD	
6. Afterlife concerns	Afterlife concerns
Fear of an unknown situation	Fear of the judgment of others—
Fear of divine judgment	"What are they thinking?"
Fear of the spirit world	Fear of ghosts, spirits, devils, etc.
Fear of nothingness	Fear of never seeing the person again
7. Fear of the finality of death	Fear of the end of a relationship
Fear of not being able to achieve one's goals	Guilt related to not having done enough for the deceased
Fear of the possible end of physical and symbolic identity	Fear of not seeing the person again
Fear of the end of all social relationships	Fear of losing the social relationship
	Fear of death objects
8. Fear of the fate of the body	Fear of dead bodies
Fear of body decomposition	
Fear of being buried	Fear of being in cemeteries
Fear of not being treated with respect	Fear of not knowing how to act in death-related situations

of dependency and pain related to the process of dying and relatively low anxiety scores for the fears related to the afterlife and the fate of the body. Approximately 65 percent of the more than 1000 individuals surveyed had high anxiety concerning dependency and pain where only 15 percent experienced the same level of anxiety relative to concerns about the afterlife and the fate of the body (Leming, 1979–80). Thus, it is the *process* of dying—not the *event* of death—which causes the most concern.

Religion and Death Fears Reconsidered

Returning to our discussion of the relationship between religious commitment and death fear, we might wonder how one's religious commitment affects the eight types of death fears discussed in this section. Our theoretical model and discussion in the first part of this chapter would suggest a curvilinear relationship between the two variables—those persons with moderate religious commitment experience the greatest amount of anxiety in each of the eight areas.

In attempting to empirically evaluate this relationship, Leming (1979–80) found that the theoretical model was supported with only two curvilinear trend deviations (see Table 6–2). The deviations which did exist were found among people who were the least religious for the fear of dependency in the dying process. It may be that non-religious individuals are more concerned about being self-sufficient and independent of others, and that they find dependency even more distressing than persons who are more religious. In terms of the fear of isolation, there does not seem to be a relationship between death fear and religious commitment.

Upon further investigation, Leming (1979–80) found that factors of education, age, and even religious preference did not affect the curvilinear

---

Religion and Dying

My conclusion is that religious faith of itself does little to affect man's peace near death. Worry warts are worry warts no matter their theology. It is not the substance or content of a man's creed that brings peace. It is the *firmness* and the quality of his act of believing. Firm believers, true believers, will find more peace on their deathbeds than all others, whatever the religious or secular label we place on their creed. *The believer, not the belief, brings peace.*

Source: Robert Kavanaugh, *Facing Death* (Baltimore: Penguin Books, 1972) p. 14.

TABLE 6–2.   Mean Scores for the Various Types of Death Fears by Levels of
             Religious Commitment*

| | LEVEL OF RELIGIOUS COMMITMENT | | | |
| | Least Religious | | | Most Religious |
Type of Death Fear	1	2	3	4
Fear of dependency				
in dying process	4.2**	4.1	3.85	3.75
Total Mean = 3.9				
Fear of pain	3.8	4.0	3.65	3.5
Total Mean = 3.7				
Fear of isolation	2.8	3.0	2.95	3.0*
Total Mean = 3.0				
Fear of the finality	3.05	3.25	2.8	2.75
of death				
Total Mean = 2.9				
Fear of leaving				
loved ones	3.05	3.25	2.65	2.60
Total Mean = 2.8				
Fear of the indignity				
in dying process	2.55	2.9	2.85	2.55
Total Mean = 2.75				
Fear of afterlife	2.5	2.95	2.6	2.3
Total Mean = 2.55				
Fear of the fate				
of the body	2.5	2.7	2.6	2.4
Total Mean = 2.55				
COMBINED LEMING				
DEATH FEAR SCORE	24.75	26.45	24.3	22.9
Total Mean = 24.3				

*The possible range for the subscale scores is 1 through 6, with the values of one and six indicating
low and high anxiety respectively. For the combined death fear score the potential minimum
score is 8 and the highest maximum score is 48.
**Curvilinear Trend Deviation

relationship. With the exception of the fear of isolation, persons who had
the strongest religious commitment were the least fearful with regard to
the various areas of death concern. Furthermore, in each of the eight death
fear areas it was found that the strength of commitment was the most
significant variable in explaining the relationship between religion and the
fear of death. Kavanaugh (1972:14) seems to have empirical support for his
statement: "The believer, not the belief, brings peace."

CONCLUSION

Religion is a system of beliefs and practices related to the sacred—that which is considered to be of ultimate significance. The cultural practice of religion continues because it meets basic social needs of individuals within a given society. A major function of religion, in this regard, is to explain the unexplainable.

For most "primitive," or less complex societies, events are explained by a supernatural rather than rational or empirical means. Thus, an eclipse of the sun or moon was said to be a sign that the gods had a message for humankind. These supernatural explanations were needed, in part, because there were not competing rational or scientific explanations.

Technologically and scientifically advanced societies tend to be less dependent upon supernatural explanations. Yet such explanations are still important, especially when scientific explanations are incomplete. It is not uncommon to hear a physician say, "Medical science is unable to cure this patient. It is in God's hands," or "It is a miracle that the patient has survived this illness. I cannot explain the recovery." Thus, one might suggest that religion "takes over" where science and rationality leave off. We depend less on religious or supernatural explanations than nonliterate societies, but nonetheless rely on them when knowledge is incomplete.

Religion plays a significant role in societies by helping individuals to cope with extraordinary events—especially death. Not only does religion help restore the normative order challenged by death, but strong religious commitments can enable individuals to cope better with their own dying and the deaths of their loved ones. For others, strong commitments to a temporal orientation may fulfill many of the functions provided by a religious world view.

Summary

1. Religion helps individuals when the order of everyday life is challenged by providing answers to problems of uncertainty, powerlessness, and scarcity created by death.
2. Religious systems provide a means to reestablish the social order challenged by death.
3. When one encounters death, the anxiety experienced is basically socially ascribed.
4. Religion provides individuals with a solace when they attempt to cope with death attitudes.
5. Temporal interpretations of death also provide a means for protecting the social order by emphasizing the empirical, natural, and "this worldly" view of death.

6. Symbolic immortality is evidenced through one's offspring carrying
    on the family name, by donating body organs, and by having accom-
    plishments or achievements (positive and negative) remembered by
    others.
7. Near death or "afterlife" experiences are influenced by the individu-
    al's religious background, cultural beliefs, and prior social experi-
    ences.
8. Death fears exist because cultures create and perpetuate fearful mean-
    ings and ascribe them to death.
9. Death anxiety is a multi-dimensional concept with the *process* of dying
    rather than the *event* of death causing the most concern.
10. The strength of one's religious commitment is a significant variable in
    explaining the relationship between religion and the fear of death.

APPLICATION: ASSESSING PERSONAL DEATH ANXIETY AND FEAR

This chapter and chapter 4 have discussed, at some length, the concept of
death anxiety and factors which influence it. We have suggested that death
anxiety is a multidimensional concept with at least eight areas of potential
fear for the individual as he or she contemplates the deaths of loved ones
and the death of self.

In this application section we have reproduced the Leming Fear of Death
Scale (1979–1980) which will enable you to assess your own death anxiety.
Complete the questionnaire, following the instructions provided, and then
calculate the scores for each of the eight areas of death concern and for the
total fear of death scale.

LEMING FEAR OF DEATH SCALE

Please read the following 26 statements. Decide whether or not you would
strongly agree, agree, tend to agree, tend to disagree, disagree, or strongly
disagree with each statement (SA, A, TA, TD, D, SD). Circle the appropriate number and symbol. Please give your first impression or opinion.
There are no right or wrong answers.

After you have completed this first step, you should then add the numbers under each section and divide by the number of questions in the
section to give the fear score for each area. Finally, you should add all 8
areas of death concern to give the total Leming Death Fear Score (Maximum score is 48; minimum score is 8).

KEY
SA = Strongly Agree
A = Agree
TA = Tend to Agree
TD = Tend to Disagree
D = Disagree
SD = Strongly Disagree

I.   *Fear of Dependency*

1.   I expect other people to care for me while I die.

SA   A   TA   TD   D   SD
1   2   3   4   5   6

2.   I am fearful of becoming dependent on others for my physical needs.

SA   A   TA   TD   D   SD
6   5   4   3   2   1

3.   While dying, I dread the possibility of being a financial burden.

SA   A   TA   TD   D   SD
6   5   4   3   2   1

4.   Losing my independence due to a fatal illness makes me apprehensive.

SA   A   TA   TD   D   SD
6   5   4   3   2   1

(4 Items)   _____ divided 4 = _____

II. *Fear of Pain*

5.   I fear dying a painful death.

SA   A   TA   TD   D   SD
6   5   4   3   2   1

6. I am afraid of a long slow death.

    SA A TA TD D SD
    6   5   4   3   2   1

(2 Items)   _____ divided by 2 = _____

III. *Fear of Indignity*

7. The loss of physical attractiveness that accompanies dying is distressing to me.

    SA A TA TD D SD
    6   5   4   3   2   1

8. I dread the helplessness of dying.

    SA A TA TD D SD
    6   5   4   3   2   1

(2 Items)   _____ divided by 2 = _____

IV. *Fear of Isolation/Separation/Loneliness*

9. The isolation of death does not concern me.

    SA A TA TD D SD
    1   2   3   4   5   6

10. I do not have any qualms about being alone after I die.

    SA A TA TD D SD
    1   2   3   4   5   6

11. Being separated from my loved ones at death makes me anxious.

    SA A TA TD D SD
    6   5   4   3   2   1

(3 Items)   _____ divided by 3 = _____

V. *Fear of Afterlife Concerns*

12. Not knowing what it feels like to be dead makes me uneasy.

    SA A TA TD D SD
    6   5   4   3   2   1

13. The subject of life after death troubles me.

    SA A TA TD   D SD
    6   5   4   3   2   1

14. Thoughts of punishment after death are a source of apprehension for me.

    SA A TA TD D SD
    6   5   4   3   2   1

    (3 Items)   _____ divided by 3 = _____

VI. *Fear of the Finality of Death*

15. The idea of never thinking after I die frightens me.

    SA A TA TD D SD
    6   5   4   3   2   1

16. I have misgivings about the fact that I might die before achieving my goals.

    SA A TA TD D SD
    6   5   4   3   2   1

17. I am often distressed by the way time flies so rapidly.

    SA A TA TD D SD
    6   5   4   3   2   1

18. The idea that I may die young does not bother me.

    SA A TA TD D SD
    1   2   3   4   5   6

19. The loss of my identity at death alarms me.

SA A TA TD D SD
6   5   4   3   2   1

(5 Items) _____ divided by 5 = _____

VII. *Fear of Leaving Loved Ones*

20. The effect of my death on others does not trouble me.

SA A TA TD D SD
1   2   3   4   5   6

21. I am afraid that my loved ones are emotionally unprepared to accept my death.

SA A TA TD D SD
6   5   4   3   2   1

22. It worries me to think of the financial situation of my survivors.

SA A TA TD D SD
6   5   4   3   2   1

(3 Items) _____ divided by 3 = _____

VIII. *Fear of the Fate of the Body*

23. The thought of my own body decomposing does not bother me.

SA A TA TD D SD
1   2   3   4   5   6

24. The sight of a dead body makes me uneasy.

SA A TA TD D SD
6   5   4   3   2   1

25. I am not bothered by the idea that I may be placed in a casket when I die.

SA A TA TD D SD
1   2   3   4   5   6

26.   The idea of being buried frightens me.

SA   A   TA   TD   D   SD
6   5   4   3   2   1

(4 Items)   _____ divided by 4 = _____

After you have completed this, consider the following questions:

1.   In which areas of concern did you have the most fear? In which areas of concern did you have the least fear?
2.   How did your areas of greatest anxiety compare with the subjects in the Leming (1979–80) study?
3.   What explanations can you give for why you had high and/or low anxiety scores for each of the eight areas of concern?
4.   How do you think that your religious commitments and beliefs affected your death fears?
5.   Are there any strategies which you could employ to enable you to cope better with your anxieties concerning death?

Discussion Questions

1.   How does religion function to provide a restoration of the order challenged by the event of death?
2.   What is meant by death fear or death anxiety? Why is this concept multidimensional rather than unidimensional?
3.   What types of death fears are the most salient for Americans? How might you explain why these fears are more intense than other fears?
4.   What is the relationship between religious commitment and death fear?
5.   Explain the following statement: "Religion afflicts the comforted and comforts the afflicted."
6.   Why is it that with regard to death anxiety, the believer, not the belief, brings peace?
7.   How can symbolic immortality and temporal interpretations of death provide a source of anxiety reduction for those who face death?
8.   How can organ donations provide symbolic immortality for donors and their loved ones.
9.   Do accounts of near-death experiences provide empirical evidence for afterlife beliefs? Why or why not?

Glossary

ANOMIE: A condition characterized by the relative absence or confusion of values within a group or society.
CURVILINEAR: A type of non-linear relationship between two variables where at a certain point, associated with the increasing values in the independent variable,

the relationship with the dependent variable changes. A scattergram graph of this relationship will either look like a "U" or an inverted "U."

DEATH ANXIETY: A learned emotional response to death-related phenomena which is characterized by extreme apprehension. In this chapter death anxiety is used synonymously with death fear.

DYSFUNCTIONAL: Any consequence of a social system which is judged to be a disturbance to the adjustment, stability, or integration of the group or the members of that group.

ETIOLOGY: The study of causal relationships which attempts to deliniate those factors which are responsible for a given occurrence.

INTERSUBJECTIVITY: A property of science whereby two or more scientists, studying the same phenomenon, can reach the same conclusion.

LEVIRITE MARRIAGE: The Hebrew requirement that a relative of the deceased husband must have sexual intercourse with his kinsman's widow in order to provide a male heir.

MARGINAL SITUATIONS: Unusual events or social circumstances which do not occur in normal patterns of social interaction.

RELIGION: A system of beliefs and practices related to the sacred, the supernatural, and or a set of values to which the individual is very committed.

RELIGIOSITY: The extent of interest, commitment, or participation in religious values, beliefs, and activities.

RITUALS: A set of culturally prescribed set of actions or behaviors.

SCIENCE: A body of knowledge based upon sensory evidence or empirical observations.

SYMBOLIC IMMORTALITY: The ascription of immortality to the individual by perpetuating the meaning of the person (the self).

TEMPORAL: A "here and now" or "this worldly" orientation which does not take into account the afterlife or a supernatural existence.

References

Berger, Peter L. 1969. *Sacred Canopy: Elements of a Sociological Theory of Religion.* New York: Doubleday.

Canning, Ray R. 1965. "Mormon Return-from-the-Dead Stories: Fact or Folklore?" *Utah Academy Proceedings*, Vol. 42, Pt. I.

Charmaz, Kathy. 1980. *The Social Reality of Death.* Reading, Mass.: Addison-Wesley.

Glock, Charles, and Rodney Stark. 1966. *Christian Beliefs and Anti-Semitism.* New York: Harper and Row.

Goffman, Erving. 1959. *The Presentation of Self in Everyday Life.* New York: Doubleday.

Faulkner, J., and G. T. De Jong. 1966. "Religiosity in 5-D: An Empirical Analysis. *Social Forces*, Vol. 45:246–254.

Holmes, T. H., and R. H. Rahe. 1967. "The Social Readjustment Rating Scale." *Journal of Psychosomatic Research*, Vol. 11 (August): Table 3–1, p. 213.

Homans, George C. 1965. "Anxiety and Ritual: The Theories of Malinowski and Radcliffe-Brown," in *Reader in Comparative Religion: An Anthropological Approach*, pp. 83–88., ed. by W. A. Lessa and E. Z. Vogt. New York: Harper and Row.

Kavanaugh, Robert E. 1972. *Facing Death*. Baltimore: Penguin Books.

Leming, Michael R. 1979–80. "Religion and Death: A Test of Homans' Thesis," *Omega*, Vol. 10, No. 4:347–364.

Lifton, Robert, and E. Olson. 1974. *Living and Dying*. New York: Praeger Publishers.

Malinowski, B. 1965. "The Role of Magic and Religion," in *Reader in Comparative Religion: An Anthropological Approach*, pp. 83–88., ed. by W. A. Lessa and E. Z. Vogt. New York: Harper and Row.

Mills, C. Wright. 1958. *The Causes of World War II*. New York: Simon and Schuster.

Moody, Raymond A., Jr., 1975. *Life After Life: The Investigation of a Phenomenon— Survival of Bodily Death*. Boston: G. K. Hall.

Noyes, Russell, Jr., and Ray Kletti. 1977. "Panoramic Memory." *Omega*, Vol. 8:181–193.

O'Dea, Thomas. 1966. *The Sociology of Religion*. Englewood Cliffs, N.J.: Prentice-Hall.

Radcliffe-Brown, A. R. 1965. "Taboo," in *Reader in Comparative Religion: An Anthropological Approach*, pp. 72–83., ed. by W. A. Lessa and E. Z. Vogt. New York: Harper and Row.

Ring, Kenneth. 1980. *Life at Death: A Scientific Investigation of the Near-Death Experience*. New York: Coward, McCann and Geoghegan.

Vernon, Glenn M. 1970. *Sociology of Death: An Analysis of Death-Related Behavior*. New York: Ronald Press.

Walsh, Ken. 1974. *Sometimes I Weep*. Valley Forge, Pa.: Judson Press.

Suggested Readings

Berger, Peter L. 1969. *Sacred Canopy: Elements of a Sociological Theory of Religion*. New York: Doubleday.

Excellent treatment of the role of religious world views as they relate to life crises. Death is discussed as the ultimate marginal situation to normal social functioning that calls forth religous meaning systems.

Homans, George C. 1965. "Anxiety and Ritual: The Theories of Malinowski and Radcliffe-Brown," in *Reader in Comparative Religion: An Anthropological Approach*, pp. 83–88., ed. by W. A. Lessa and E. Z. Vogt. New York: Harper and Row. and Leming, Michael R. 1979–80. "Religion and Death: A Test of Homans' Thesis," *Omega*, Vol. 10, No. 4:347–364.

Two articles that review the theoretical and empirical evidence regarding the relationship between religion and death anxiety.

Kavanaugh, Robert E. 1972. *Facing Death*. Baltimore: Penguin Books.

As a former Roman Catholic priest, Kavanaugh reflects back upon his experiences with death in the context of his religious background. He discusses the role of religion as it relates to the adjustment process to dying and death.

Moody, Raymond A. Jr. 1975. *Life After Life: The Investigation of a Phenomenon— Survival of Bodily Death*. Boston: G. K. Hall; and Ring, Kenneth, 1980. *Life at Death: A Scientific Investigation of the Near-Death Experience*. New York: Coward, McCann and Geoghegan.

Two books that describe and discuss empirical evidence relating to near-death experiences.

THREE

Coping with Dying and Death

Chapter 7

CHILDREN AND DYING

The way I see it, we die in the same order we were born. It's the
only fair way of working it!
Schulz and Hall, 1965, p. 6

THE FACTS OF DEATH are different than our best wishes and hopes, even in
today's medically advanced world. Each of us is acutely aware that some
children die. Children are forced at times to deal with the deaths of adult
relatives, siblings and close friends. As adults, we are faced with the reality
of dying children and children who are bereaved. We want to know how
we might help, or at least not increase the hurt, when death enters the lives
of children. Death challenges our sense of fairness. This is especially true,
according to the pensive child, when people die at the wrong time. The
death of children does not follow the developmental sequence of the life
cycle. One wonders, however, if the child in each of us would have still
other problems with the meaning of death if the only ones to die were our
oldest relatives and friends.

Children die today at a rate that is lower than any in the history of
humankind. In the early 1980s for instance, about twelve of every 1,000 live
newborn infants in the United States died before one year of life had
elapsed. The first month of life is the most hazardous, as the death rate in
that month is twice the rate for the remaining months of the first year.
"Congenital anomalies" lead the list of causes of death for these infants,
but many other problems are present for other babies that die.

Deaths of infants are difficult for parents, siblings and others because of
the great expectations and positive cultural meanings associated with the
birth of a child. Peppers and Knapp (1980) have estimated that as many as
one-third of all pregnancies today result in miscarriages, abortions, stillbirths and neonatal deaths. Pediatricians and maternal health-care providers are becoming interested in the bonding process between parents and
their new infant, with the result that greater parental involvement with
new borns is being encouraged, even when an infant is dying. Early reports of appreciative parents who were allowed to hold their dead child is
encouraging pediatricians and pediatric nurses to drastically change the

175

norms of patient care in their hospitals. (Moral philosophers are employed in larger hospitals in the United States to assist parents in such situations.)

The sudden infant death syndrome, also known as SIDS or crib death, is well known by the public today because of extensive federally funded research and media reports. This leading cause of death in children one month to one year of age remains a medical mystery, even as new research findings from pathological and epidemiological studies are reported almost monthly and new theories appear almost weekly. SIDS is interesting to sociologists because of the profound effect social meanings, labels, and expectations have on the health and welfare of surviving parents and siblings.

Fatal accidents are deaths we wish we could prevent because of the "human" factor. Accidents are the leading cause of death in children one month to fifteen years of age. The struggle to understand and cope with accidental childhood deaths is similar to the grief of those persons coming to terms with other forms of death of a child. The years of involvement and the sense of parental responsibility associated with nonmedical causes of death may intensify the reaction to such deaths.

Children who are dying appear to make sense of their dying just as adults do. They manage information available to them in different ways, however, depending on their cognitive maturity. When we take the time to listen to children who are dying, we discover that they often have a degree of awareness of their condition that is not easily appreciated by their parents or medical care givers. The child's awareness of dying ought to be recognized and taken into account as childhood diseases such as leukemia progress. The increasingly familiar concept of holistic health includes the child-patient, important family members, and several medical care givers. The hospice concept could be implemented in pediatric intensive care services in hospitals. Shared decision making, that includes children, does not take the burden of legal responsibility off the shoulders of adults, but widens the base of concern and understanding.

Recent research (e.g., Bowlby, 1980) confirms that adult and childhood mourning are similar, although others (e.g., A. Freud, 1943; Klein, 1944) debate this. Children who lose a close relative or friend through death are bereaved. They experience grief and express it through mourning behavior. Their individual experiences with bereavement are affected by a variety of factors such as: (1) their development level; (2) their experiences with bereavement; (3) the presence of role models; and (4) the definitions of appropriate behavior by adults. The resolution of grief in children is important, but it is not clearly understood in spite of extensive research. Helping a child who is mourning is difficult. To be a friend to a child confronted with death may mean simply being there. We may want to listen and affirm the expression of feelings and thoughts, especially when parents and other close relatives are unable to help because of their own grief.

Facing death means understanding and coping with dying in different ways. *For the child who is dying,* learning to cope means learning how to die and how to live in the time remaining. *For the medical care givers,* effective helping means honoring the person while managing the disease. *For the bereaved child,* coping with death means learning to live in a world that is very hard to understand. *For those of us concerned about death education,* our task is to increase public awareness of such a private loss as death.

This chapter on children and death is designed to familiarize the reader with some of the research and theoretical approaches to this important human experience. The experience of facing death as a dying child will be discussed in the "awareness context" of children dying from leukemia. The topic of grief in bereaved parents will be addressed. The immediate and long-term effect of childhood bereavement will be reviewed in order to understand the process of mourning and the importance of funerals, professional helpers, and friends to children.

What lies ahead in death education, in health care and illness, and in personal-social coping with death and children includes both the unique dimensions of individual experience and the broad context of the society in which we live. It is in this framework of meaning that we begin to look at some of the issues of children and death.

CHILDHOOD DEATH IN PERSPECTIVE

Each year, 17 million children in the world die (i.e., 40,000 per day), according to James Grant, Executive Director of UNICEF (1982). The last three decades have been times of gradual improvement in health conditions, particularly in the developing nations. The reduction in childhood deaths that accompanies improving economic conditions appears to be reversing as economic conditions change. Grant calls this the "silent emergency." Childhood death is a situation that most American families have been spared in recent years. Some children die in the United States, but children die to a much greater extent in other countries around the world. The reader who is putting childhood death in perspective ought to become familiar with world-wide comparisons and patterns of childhood death in the United States.

World-Wide Comparisons

North American society is not typical of the people in the world. Canada and the United States, for example, represent only 6 percent of the four-and-a-half billion people alive today. Even when we combine these two North American countries with the other more economically developed

nations, the entire group of developed countries constitutes only 25 percent of the world's population. Yet, this minority has the most favorable
life chances!

Table 7–1 helps us put our demographic world in perspective by showing the vast differences in life chances based on a few fundamental facts.
The five common statistics of the conditions of life and death in the world
include: (1) the crude birth rate (births per 1,000 population); (2) the crude
death rate (deaths per 1,000 population); (3) the infant mortality rate
(deaths of infants under one year per 1,000 live births); (4) percent of the
population under fifteen years of age; and (5) the life expectancy at birth
(estimated length of life of a newborn infant under current mortality conditions). The data are summarized in Table 7–1 not only for the entire world
population, but also for the two major categories of economic development
and the seven major geographical regions of the world.

A careful examination of Table 7–1 shows that the three-fourths of the
people in our world who live in poorer economic conditions than we are at
a distinct disadvantage in the life chances associated with birth, death and
longevity. The more economically developed countries, in contrast, tend to
have lower birth rates, lower general and infant death rates, fewer of their

TABLE 7–1.   Selected Life Chance Statistics for World Regions

Region	Crude Birth Rate[1]	Crude Death Rate[2]	Infant Mortality Rate[3]	Population Under 15 (Percent)	Life Expectancy (years)[4]
World	28	11	97	35%	62
More Developed Countries (25%)	16	9	20	24%	72
Less Developed Countries (75%)	32	12	109	39%	58
North America (6%)	16	9	13	23%	74
Latin America (8%)	32	9	75	40%	64
Europe (11%)	14	10	17	23%	72
USSR (6%)	18	10	36	26%	69
Africa (11%)	46	17	142	45%	49
Asia (57%)	29	11	102	37%	60
Oceania (1%)	21	8	51	30%	69

[1]Births per 1,000 population; [2]Deaths per 1,000 population; [3]Deaths of infants under one year per
1,000 live births; [4]Average number of years a newborn child could be expected to live if current
mortality conditions were to continue throughout his or her lifetime.

Source: Adapted from Haub, 1981b.

population under fifteen years of age, and, not surprisingly, higher life expectancy.

There is a great deal of variability in these demographic facts of life and death. This variability is particularly evident when we compare the data for the entire world with not only regions but also individual countries. Consider the following (Haub, 1981b):

1. The *crude birth rate* for the world is 28 per 1,000 live births, ranging from a low of 10 in West Germany to a high of 53 in Kenya. This birth rate in the less developed countries is twice the rate (32 vs. 16) of the more developed region.
2. The *population under fifteen* years of age in the less developed region is over 50 percent higher (39 percent vs. 24 percent) than the more economically developed region. Luxembourg has only 18 percent of its population under fifteen years of age, while Jordan has a full 52 percent. The world figure is 35 percent.
3. The world average *crude death rate* of 11 varies from 4 in places like Brunei, Costa Rica, and Fiji to 25 in Ethiopia. The death rate is one-third higher (12 vs. 9) in the less developed region of the world.
4. *Infant mortality*, in contrast, is five-and-a-half times higher (109 vs. 20) in the poorer economic region than it is in the more economically developed countries. Infant mortality rates are as low as 7 in Sweden and as high as 220 in Guinea. The world average is 97 infant deaths for every 1,000 live births.
5. We should not be surprised, therefore, that the *life expectancy* in the less developed countries is only 58 years, compared with over 70 years in the minority countries that are more economically developed. The life expectancy of a newborn child is 62 years when the entire four-and-a-half billion people of the world are considered. This ranges from an incredible low of only 39 years in Ethiopia to an "old" 76 years in Iceland.

Patterns in the United States

The quality of life we know in the United States is not common for the majority of the people in the world today. The comparisons outlined above help us to "locate" the general conditions of life and death we have come to take for granted. It is not unusual for people to conclude that what they are familiar with is typical for all others. This is not so when we compare life chance statistics world-wide.

Childhood deaths in the United States may also be examined in a comparative perspective in order to understand the variability that exists even among the fifty states. Consider the following (Haub, 1981a):

1. The *birth rate* is approximately 15 per 1,000 population in the United States. This varies from 12 in Massachusetts to 30 in Utah.
2. The *death rate* is approximately 9 per 1,000 population. There are as few as

4 deaths per 1,000 in Alaska, and as many as 11 deaths per 1,000 population in Florida.
3. *Infant mortality* averages about 14 deaths per 1,000 live births. Regional
   differences are high. Two New England states, Maine and New Hamp-
   shire, report a rate of about 10, while Mississippi is nearly 19 deaths per
   1,000 live births. The District of Columbia, with its predominantly poor
   and black population, has an infant mortality rate of 27, twice the national
   average.

The favorable circumstances of life and death in the United States have
had an interesting history of change in the twentieth century. Improved
medical technology and public health conditions have reduced the impact
of the leading causes of death in 1900, namely influenza, pneumonia, and
tuberculosis. Today we are all familiar with diseases that most often result
in death, particularly the deaths of older people—heart disease, cancer,
and stroke. The life expectancy of Americans has increased from only
forty-seven in 1900 to seventy-four in 1981. This increase in life expectancy
by over 50 percent is associated with a 50 percent decrease in the crude
death rate that was 17 in 1900 and less than 9 per 1,000 population in 1981.

The less developed condition of the United States in 1900 compares with
the less developed countries of the world today. This is most striking when
we know that the infant mortality rate in the United States in 1900 was 162
per 1,000 live births; infant deaths in 1981 were reduced to twelve per 1,000
live births. Consider also the contrast in the number of deaths of children
under fifteen and the deaths of people over sixty-five in these years. In
1900 children made up a third of the population, but they accounted for
over 50 percent of the deaths. People over sixty-five were only 4 percent of
the population, but they made up 17 percent of the deaths. Today children
under fifteen account for only 3 percent of all deaths in the United States,
while two-thirds of those who die are over sixty-five.

The dramatic reduction in infant deaths is pictured in Figure 7–1, which
illustrates the decrease in infant mortality from 1940 until 1978. The steep
decline is partly due to the logarithmic scale used for infant mortality, but
the numbers show an accurate story of prenatal and postnatal health care.

The socioeconomic conditions of life that negatively affect the majority of
nonwhite Americans have a direct impact on the continuing differential in
infant deaths. Nonwhite children continue to die at a rate that is twice the
white infant death rate. The nonwhite infant mortality rate is currently at a
level reported for white infants fifteen years earlier. The improvements in
death rates of children are welcome, but disparity between the races in the
United States remains.

Three percent of the nearly two million people in the United States who
died in 1981 were children under fifteen years of age. The deaths of these
62,160 children do not occur equally for all ages, as there is a clear pattern

FIGURE 7–1:   INFANT MORTALITY RATES BY COLOR: UNITED STATES, 1940–1978

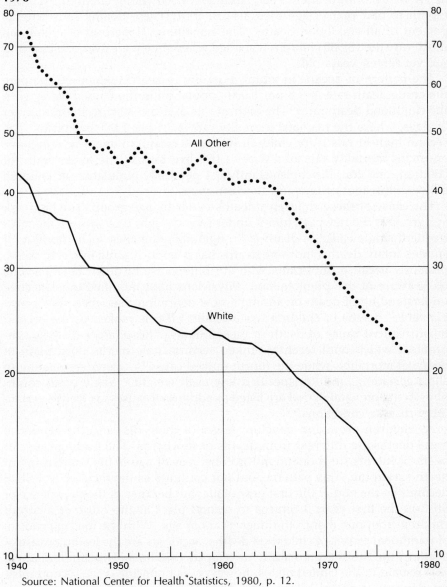

Source: National Center for Health Statistics, 1980, p. 12.

of decline of deaths with age. A full 47 percent, (i.e., 28,930 infants,) died in the first month of their lives. Another 14,300 young children from one month to one year of age died also in 1981. These deaths constitute 23 percent of all childhood deaths. The remaining 31 percent of childhood deaths are the 18,930 children who died when they were over one year and not yet fifteen years old.

The pattern of decline in infant mortality is clearest when we compare the crude death rate of 8.8 per 1,000 population in the United States with the childhood death rates. The highest rate of death is with children under 28 days, where the neonatal mortality rate is 8.1 per 1,000 live births. The second highest rate is for children from one month to one year who have an infant mortality rate of 4.0 per 1,000 live births. The lowest rate for children, and for all people, is only 0.4 per 1,000 population of children between the ages of one and fourteen years.

The cause of these children's deaths varies by age group. The high risk age group is the newborn infant under twenty-eight days, where the most frequent single cause of death is "congenital anomalies." The number of sudden infant death syndrome deaths has been increasing in recent years, primarily because physicians who attribute cause of death have become more aware of this phenomenon. Physicians have modified the collective understanding of death by adding a new definition that labels the "unexplainable" deaths of children. As a result, SIDS is ranked as the second most frequent cause of death in these infants. "Respiratory distress syndrome," which until recently ranked second, now merits third place in neonatal mortality, while the fourth ranked cause is "disorders relating to short gestation" and "unspecified low birth weight." Many other conditions in the prenatal period are listed as additional causes, as well as certain other disease conditions.

As children grow and develop, fewer of them die, and the causes of these deaths are different from deaths of newborns. The leading cause of death in infants from one month to one year of age is the sudden infant death syndrome. This pattern does not continue as the incidence of SIDS declines by the end of the first year of life; but because of the prevalence of SIDS in the first year, it returns to second place as the cause of death of children from one month to fifteen years of age. With the medical control of traditional causes of childhood deaths, accidents are the leading cause of death in the more economically developed countries. The differentials of race remain in the United States, however, as homicide is the second most frequent cause of death in non-white children, not SIDS.

FACING THE DEATH OF A CHILD

Collectively, we share definitions and symbols that label the biological facts, but in recent years we have become dependent upon medical meanings because of their usefulness in controlling many diseases. As we develop a perspective of childhood and death, we would do well to be cognizant of the human construction of medical meanings. These meanings change, as most recently demonstrated with the "new" cause of childhood death—SIDS. The death of a fetus or young child takes place in the context of medical meanings and institutional patterns of behavior, as patients and health-care providers are guided and directed by associated role expectations. These socially relevant meanings are evident when one faces the death of a fetus.

Bonding and Death of a Newborn

There are two "miracles" of childbirth. The first is the total environmental change from living in water to breathing air. The second is the emotional-social attachment of bonding, which in common-sense terms is a profound "hello!" The importance of the second miracle is evident when death occurs at the beginning of life. In human terms, "You can't say 'good-bye' until you say 'hello' " (Hartigan, 1981).

The socio-emotional phenomenon of bonding between parent and child takes place over a period of time that extends from the (presumed) planning of the pregnancy to the actual responses of the parents when they first hold their new baby. The establishment of attachment is difficult to describe with accuracy, but it appears to involve a number of elements that give meaning to the new relationships. Klaus and Kennell (1976) claim that some of the bonding variables include (1) planning the pregnancy; (2) confirmation of the pregnancy; (3) acceptance of pregnancy; (4) fetal movement where the mother perceives the fetus as separate from herself; (5) delivery; and (6) the seeing and touching of the infant that confirms the reality.

The bonding process between parent and child is similar for both parents, but important differences remain. The father, for instance, is more likely to anticipate the birth of his child in a more intellectual way. The mother-to-be, on the other hand, has the advantage of being the first to be in physical contact with the growing fetus. This is particularly evident during the spontaneous movements of quickening. The attachment of both mother and father tends to equalize later when each holds the child and makes eye-to-eye contact with a responding infant—"My child!"

Klaus and Kennell (1982) distinguish between executive and signal behaviors. Executive behaviors consist of responses such as rooting, grasping, and postural adjustment, which tend to maintain physical contact between infant and caretaker, once established. Signal behaviors, on the other hand, comprise responses such as crying and smiling, which increase proximity or establish physical contact between infant and mother. They suggest that the signal and executive behaviors act in conjunction with the reciprocal interactions just presented. One of the major advantages of the early interaction is that it helps the parents to become more quickly attuned to the individuality of their own infant and therefore to adapt their behavior to his or her needs and tempo.

Although individual infants differ in their capacity to receive and shut out stimuli, as well as in their ability to exhibit behaviors to which the environment can respond, Klaus and Kennell (1982) wonder whether some of the individual differences described in later infancy might occur partly as a result of whether the mother is permitted early or late contact. They suggest that the amazing synchronization of normal mothers and infants found at that time begins in these crucial first minutes of life.

Klaus and Kennell (1982: 83–85) present some rules or principles for which experimental data and solid evidence are scanty but that may play a significant role in this attachment.

1. *Monotropy.* Observations of nurses working in the premature nursery, discussions with the head nurse at the Matera (a large adoption home in Athens, Greece), and clinical follow-up of twin deliveries suggest another basic principle of attachment. This principle is called monotropy—mother-to-infant attachment developed and structured so that a close attachment can optimally be formed to only one person at a time.

2. *Infant-mother interaction.* During the early process of the mother's attachment to her infant, it is necessary that the infant respond to the mother by some signal, such as body or eye movements.

3. *Observing birth.* People who witness the birth process often become strongly attached to the infant.

4. *Attachment-detachment.* Another significant principle that has evolved from many clinical experiences is that the processes of attachment and detachment cannot easily occur simultaneously. It has been noted in many parents who have lost one of a twin pair that they have often found it difficult to mourn completely the baby who died and at the same time to feel attached to the survivor. The same problem is found when a mother quickly becomes pregnant after losing a neonate. Whenever feasible, it should be recommended that a new infant not be conceived until the grief is finished (six to twelve months).

5. *Early events.* Early events have long-lasting effects. Anxieties in the first day about the well-being of a baby with a temporary disorder may result in long-lasting concerns that may adversely shape the development of the child.

The attachment of parents to a child appears to have long-term consequences on the care and development of that child. Peppers and Knapp (1980) remind us that these emerging relationships take place in the context of societal roles and responsibilities. Traditional and stereotypical role expectations of oneself and others can affect identities and relationships—

not only of infant, father and mother, but also of relatives, friends and medical professionals. The process of bonding is a social process that involves our inner identities and social definitions of self.

Research on attachment behavior between parent and child has been accumulating for decades (Bowlby, 1969), but the work of Klaus and Kennell (1976) has focused the thinking of the pediatric and maternal care community by presenting a strong case for the importance of bonding in medical practice. The research and theoretical framework of bonding provide a perspective for pediatric care of infants who are critically ill and dying. The sensitivity of medical personnel to the growing relationship between parent and child allows the medical care giver to encourage attachment even as separation through death threatens.

Grief is an intense emotional experience precipitated by the loss of another, particularly through death. We express our grief with, or in spite of, others. The bereaved parents are often at a loss when trying to understand what has happened and to explain it to others. The death of a wanted child may be the first experience of intense grief for many young parents. They may prefer to grieve alone, even when they are surrounded by people who care and want to help, because so few people know what such a tragedy entails.

The stages of grief have been outlined by many (e.g., Lindemann, 1944; Kubler-Ross, 1969), but they essentially involve the shock and disorganization of realizing something is wrong—one's plans and expectations are not coming true with the new baby. All parts of one's self are torn apart in the mental and emotional confusion associated with the loss of another who is part of one's "self." Grief also includes the attempts to come to terms with the loss by learning to live without the one who has died. Parents may never totally let go emotionally and prolong their grief by maintaining what Peppers and Knapp (1980) have called "shadow grief," a chronic persistence of emotional stress in lingering sorrow and yearning. As time passes, the loss is less evident, but the grief surfaces for many at an anniversary or an unanticipated event such as meeting a mother with a newborn baby.

The Art of Consoling

As anyone knows who has ever tried, it is difficult to talk to a parent who has lost a child. Julie McGee, coordinator of the Louisville chapter of The Compassionate Friends—an organization of bereaved parents—says no one who has not lost a child can really understand how it feels.

She says bereaved parents themselves recognize how misguided were

their past efforts to console a friend or relative in the same situation. So
the organization has compiled the following list of do's and don't's:

DO

Be available, to listen, to run errands and to help with housework and
other children.

Say you are sorry about what happened to their child and about their
pain.

Allow them to express grief without holding back. Listen if they want to
talk about the child, as much and as often as they want to.

Encourage them to be patient with themselves, not to expect too much
of themselves and not to impose any "shoulds" on themselves.

Talk to them about the special endearing qualities of the child who has
died.

Give special attention to the child's brothers and sisters, at the funeral
and later.

Reassure parents about the care their child received, but be careful not
to say anything that is obviously not true.

DON'T

Avoid them because you are uncomfortable.

Say you know how they feel unless you have lost a child yourself.

Tell them they've grieved long enough and "ought to be feeling better
by now." Your guess at an appropriate timetable probably is short. Avoid
telling them, in general, what they "should" feel and do.

Change the subject when they mention their dead child.

Worry about mentioning their child's name. You won't make them
think of him or her; they probably are doing that anyway.

Try to point out some bright side. They don't want to hear, "At least
you have your other children," or, "At least you can have another child,"
or, "At least you had the child for a while."

Try to commiserate with them by saying the child's case was bungled
by the doctors or the hospital or someone else involved. They will be
plagued by guilt and feelings of inadequacy without any help from you.

Source: Joe Ward, "When Death Takes Your Child," *The Louisville* (Ky.) *Courier-Journal,*
July 27, 1980.

The deaths associated with the beginning of life are not alike in their
impact on surviving parents. Grieving differs in important ways depending on whether the loss is due to a miscarriage during pregnancy, a still-

birth, a death of a newborn infant, or sudden infant death syndrome. Hartigan (1981) and Peppers and Knapp (1980) have hypothesized about parental reactions in terms of their initial response to the death, the duration of grief, the anger and bitterness expressed, and the guilt experienced in attempting to understand the death.

The differences associated with bonding during pregnancy have an impact on the initial response of parents. The mother's response to the death of her child is very intense, regardless of cause. She has a closer relationship with the fetus throughout pregnancy and invests more of her physical and emotional self in the development and delivery of the child. The father also experiences a very intense initial response if the baby dies at full term or after, as fathers become attached in ways similar to mothers when the child is born. An important difference has been noticed in fathers' reactions to a miscarriage, as they seem to initially respond with limited intensity. Perhaps significant bonding has not yet occurred for the father (Peppers and Knapp, 1980).

The duration of intense grief may not be as long lasting for parents with a miscarriage. The grief associated with a stillbirth, death of a newborn, or SIDS is intense. It may last for a moderate length of time, but in all these cases, shadow grief may be evident for years. The anger and bitterness may also be minimal with a miscarriage, but it is very intense when a newborn dies. Stillbirths and SIDS evoke moderate, but real, anger and bitterness in parents, but this may not be felt to the same extent at newborn infant deaths. These parents, on the other hand, appear to have only a minimal amount of guilt associated with the death. The parents of children who die of SIDS appear to have the most guilt in their coping experiences, as miscarriages and stillbirths seem to evoke a moderate amount of guilt (Peppers and Knapp, 1980).

Individual differences in grief responses are common and patterns are limited in their predictive value. The struggle to adjust to the death of a fetus or child is both painful and comforting, in that the separation tears while identification with the child unites (Furman, 1978). Mother and father may experience different degrees of emotional attachment in "incongruent bonding," and they may also express their grief incongruently due to differences in male and female role expectations (Peppers and Knapp, 1980). It is no wonder that communication problems and other difficulties arise in the weeks and months that follow the death.

Davidson (1977:265) studied fifteen mothers whose fetus was born dead or whose infant died in the first twenty-four hours of life. These mothers were thwarted at three points:

(1) when trying to confirm, perceptually, whom they had lost; (2) when reaching out to others for emotional support; and (3) when trying to test their feelings against the perceptions of others. When thwarted in their process of reori-

entation they found themselves resorting to bizarre behavior in attempts to avoid chronic disorientation.

Bowie (1977) reported in diary-like format how she and her husband were isolated from their newborn son who died after many days in intensive care. She and her husband found it very difficult to obtain information and opinions about their son's condition even when direct questions were asked. Bowie (1977:11) notes "When faced with hard lay questions regarding medical decisions, the medical profession closed in its ranks." This is not a unique American experience as Giles (1970) and Cullberg (1972) report similar types of behavior from physicians in Australia and Sweden.

The medical professional is charged with healing and when all the resources of medical science do not work, the physician and nurse may react with insensitivity toward parents. Klaus and Kennell (1976:215) argue that the task for the physician and nurse is threefold:

(1) to help the parents digest the loss and make it real, (2) to ensure that normal grief reactions will begin and that both parents will go through the entire process, and (3) to meet the individual needs of specific parents.

Helping to make death real for the parents may involve allowing parents to visit their critically ill infant and to actually hold the baby even if it has died. They may also be helped by having a funeral service for the baby in the hospital, if the mother is unable to leave. Klaus and Kennell (1976) suggest that the supporting professional visit with the parents right after the death, again in two or three days, and once again three to six months later. The advantage of the third visit is that any evidence of pathological grieving might be discovered and the parents helped by referral to grief counselors. Klaus and Kennell (1976:217) note:

Helping parents through these experiences is an extremely difficult assignment, but we have been rewarded by the thanks and expressions of appreciation parents have relayed to us later.

Nurses are often faced with the long-term contact with parents in the hospital. Some pediatric and maternal care units are developing teams of nurses and other professionals who are trained and given time to work with parents whose baby is dying or has died. Smiley and Goettl (1981) are nurse practitioners who are involved in such a service. They find that the most difficult time is getting the courage to walk through the doorway into a mother's room for the first time, but once through the door it becomes easy because one is really able to see their needs. The emotional strain is great, especially when more than one death occurs in a week's time. They often find that others do not perceive their strain, and they are thankful for having at least one other professional to talk to at such a time. A dozen other nurses have been identified and trained to be part of the "Resolve Through Sharing Core Team" in their work with parents of critically ill, dying, and dead infants.

Norms of hospital life are undergoing changes as the "human" values penetrate the ideology of care. Rules that have prevented children under sixteen from visiting patients because of historical problems of communicable diseases have been eliminated or significantly revised. Hospice units are developing in hospitals so that family members are allowed even to stay overnight in a special lounge. Grief recovery groups are being made available to bereaved family members and staff. Parents of critically ill children are allowed to help care for their offspring. Pediatricians and nurses are inviting parents to touch, hold and take pictures of an infant who has died.

All of these changes, unfortunately, have not been implemented. Medical practitioners and hospital administrators may be quite traditional and slow to change established procedures. The label "tissue death" is used to describe fetal deaths and stillbirths. This type of labeling retards efforts to change patient care practices because it implies that the death has little or no effect on the parents. This implication is not true, as attachment and bonding occur between parents and a growing fetus in the womb. Loss is felt and experienced by parents whether the death is due to an abortion, a miscarriage, a stillbirth or a neonatal death. Medical practitioners would do well to provide a model of how to change from treating bereaved parents as if they have a contagious disease. It is important that people who care respond with understanding that supports and includes bereaved persons who are mourning the loss of a part of themselves and their family.

Sudden Infant Death Syndrome

The sudden infant death syndrome (SIDS) is a disease that came of age in the 1970s. It has received unusual attention from the medical community, government, and the media in recent times. SIDS is the sudden and unexpected death of a young child where no specific mechanism of death is identified in an autopsy. It is of interest to the medical and the social scientist because it is one of the leading causes of death in children.

What is the nature of this disease that has generated such medical, governmental, and media interest? The sudden infant death syndrome is "the sudden death of an infant or young child, unexpected by history, in which a thorough post-mortem fails to demonstrate an adequate cause of death" (Valdes-Dapena, 1973: 1196). The typical case of a SIDS death is putting a healthy baby to bed for the night and discovering him or her dead the following morning. There was no outcry during the night or no disturbance that would have alerted the parents. Emergency medical personnel are called and the baby is declared dead by a physician in an emergency room of a local hospital. An autopsy does not reveal any particular mechanism of death. SIDS, in effect, is a label that describes infants who die unexpectedly and suddenly from an unexplained cause.

The sudden infant death syndrome affects people in all stations of life. There are, however, some patterns. SIDS takes place usually during the first year of life, and most frequently between the second and the fourth month of age. It occurs somewhat more frequently during the winter months to males, babies born prior to a full-term pregnancy, and people living in relatively poor socio-economic conditions. When the baby's body is discovered, there appears to be no external signs of injury and the autopsy reveals no evidence of smothering. In essence, the baby seems to have died from a set of factors, none of which is medically recognized as the specific cause of death. Research continues, but the mystery remains.

Medical questions are not the only problems with SIDS. Parents, siblings, and others, such as babysitters, face serious problems of guilt. A group of sociologists at the Center for Death Education and Research at the University of Minnesota have reviewed the SIDS literature and concluded that the survivors are "victims," because SIDS is both personally traumatic and complicated with problems of social interaction.

The sociological impact of SIDS is no more easily identifiable than the medical factors. Two sociological factors that appear to shape the responses of survivors, however, are imputed deviance and anomic grief.

"Imputed deviance" occurs when emergency medical personnel fail to recognize the death as a case of SIDS. They may, in fact, define the situation and label the case as child abuse, responding to and interrogating the parents. The facts of child abuse are instructive. About 300 infants die from child abuse in the United States each year. The typical features include visible signs of injury, which might be mistaken for lividity—the settling of blood to the surface skin such as occurs frequently in the case of SIDS.

The suspicion of legal impropriety in SIDS is not the only imputation of deviance. The sudden and unexpected character of the disease, compounded with the inexplicable nature of the phenomenon, results in the moral suspicion or accusation of not having properly taken care of the baby. The public has become increasingly aware of the characteristics of SIDS, thereby reducing the uncertainty about the parents' role in child care and the death. Even more important than this, however, was the medical recognition and labeling of a syndrome whose medical mechanism is undetected. Naming does not explain the disease, but it does focus attention on the disease and not on the victims of the disease.

The second sociological factor that shapes the responses of survivors is "anomic grief," a grief that is without social support. One of the consequences of increased longevity that is common in the more economically developed countries is the reduction in personal experiences with death, grief and bereavement. The young parents whose baby dies of SIDS today have not experienced, for the most part, the death of a close relative. They are not familiar with the social and emotional aspects of grief and mourning. When a death does occur for older people, it most frequently takes place in a hospital or other institution that "helps" relatives and friends to avoid or deny the reality of death. The death of one's baby is traumatic under any conditions, but the sense of not knowing how to mourn adds to the difficulties of socially adjusting to the loss. The parents and siblings are experiencing "anomic grief"—a grief that is without the traditional supports of family, church and community.

Extensive media coverage in recent years, government research, and counseling programs have helped to educate medical personnel and the public about SIDS. Prior to 1970 very few emergency personnel were familiar with this "disease." Unfamiliarity with SIDS created an unnecessary situation of legal culpability and anxiety. The tendency to isolate bereaved SIDS parents is not unlike the isolation experienced by parents whose fetus or newborn child has died. Anomie has the effect of intensifying loss by isolating persons even while others are nearby.

FACING DEATH AS A DYING CHILD

Much has been written about the dying child in recent years by psychiatrists (e.g., Easson, 1970), psychologists (e.g., Zelligs, 1974), nurses (e.g., Gyulay, 1978), and other helping professionals. These clinicians have described their own personal experience with cases, taking as their theoretical context the developmental psychology of Anthony (1971), Nagy (1948) and others (Lonetto, 1980). They usually provide guidelines for working with dying children and their families that are very helpful in the daily work of health care professionals. These authors typically express concern about understanding how children actually experience their own dying. Few, however, have developed a method of research that clearly describes how these children make sense of their dying.

Making Sense of Dying

Awareness of dying is an elusive notion, particularly when one is trying to describe and explain the understanding of children who are dying. From birth onward each human being strives to maintain life by physiologically reacting to dying. According to Easson (1970:7):

> The feelings of inner tension aroused by this primitive but basic physiological struggle for survival seem to be fraught with the very deepest anxiety and appear to provoke the strongest feelings of tension. With good reason, these physically based, nightmarish sensations are often referred to as the "death agony."

    The fast developing infant who is dying soon responds to disease symptoms and treatment procedures. Easson (1970) claims that an infant of five or six months may obviously react to the way people treat him or her in response to the disease. Awareness of isolation and pain and the associated reactions to physicians, nurses and even family members indicate a degree of understanding that is without words but full of behavioral meaning. Easson (1970) believes that children around the age of four respond to changes in their sense of self as they are dying. Not long afterwards, between the ages of four and five, they are able to respond to the significance of the diagnosis of their condition. Between the ages five and seven the significance of the prognosis is responded to by children. By the time children are six and seven, they are quite capable of responding to changes in their social role and relationships.

    Bluebond-Langner (1978) in her anthropological study of "The Private Worlds of Dying Children" concurs. Her participant-observation study of leukemic children ages three to nine in a pediatric unit of a hospital assumes that children are able to make sense of their dying. This approach to research has a long tradition in the symbolic interaction theory of sociology. It looks to the setting, rather than to social functions or developmental readiness, to explain meaningful behavior.

    The most effective way to explain children's understanding according to Bluebond-Langner (1978:12) is by assuming the following:

1. They are willful, purposeful creatures who possess selves.
2. They interpret their behavior and act on the basis of their interpretations.
3. They interpret their own self-images.
4. They interpret the behavior of others to obtain a view of themselves, others, and objects.
5. They are capable of initiating behavior so as to affect the view others have of them and that they have of themselves.
6. They are capable of initiating behavior to affect the behavior of others toward them.
7. Any meaning that children attach to themselves, others, and objects varies with respect to the physical, social, and temporal settings in which they find themselves.
8. Children can move from one social world to another and act appropriately in each world.

    The understanding that dying children have of their prognosis cannot be easily determined by talking openly about their condition with them. An alternative method of gaining understanding of their perceptions is available by observing their behavior. Nine types of child behavior have been observed by Bluebond-Langner (1978:234):

1. Avoidance of deceased children's names and belongings.
2. Lack of interest in nondisease-related conversation and play.

3. Preoccupation with death and disease imagery in play, art, and literature.
4. Engagement of selected individuals in either disclosure conversations or disclosure speeches.
5. Anxiety about increased debilitation and about going home, but for different reasons than earlier on in the disease process.
6. Avoidance of talk about the future.
7. Concern that things be done immediately.
8. Refusal to cooperate with relatively simple, painless procedures.
9. Establishment of distance from others through displays of anger or silence.

Many of these behaviors are typical of children who are well, as children interpret and respond to others in meaningful ways. They develop a sense of self and are socialized as they interact and are constrained by the meaning imposed by parents and other significant adults. Many adults assume that children do not understand what is happening unless it is explained to them. Bluebond-Langner found that the critically ill and dying children she befriended were much more aware of their own condition than either their parents or medical caregivers chose to acknowledge.

Critically ill children are involved in a socialization process of becoming aware of factual information about their treatment and of associated meanings of self identity. At the time of diagnosis, children view themselves as well. The first stage of awareness of their condition, according to Bluebond-Langner, is in learning that " 'it' is a serious illness" and they are "seriously ill." The second stage occurs when learning the "names of drugs and side effects." The children see themselves at this stage as "seriously ill and will get better." The third stage involves "purposes of treatments and procedures" where they see themselves as "always ill and will get better." The fourth and fifth stages both involve "disease as a series of relapses and remissions," with death itself marking the final stage. In the fourth stage the children perceive themselves as "always ill and will never get better," while the fifth stage is when they understand that they are "dying" (terminally ill) (Bluebond-Langner, 1978:166–170).

Many of the children demonstrated to Bluebond-Langner that they knew and understood the seriousness of their condition. The most common way of relating to adults, however, was by "the development and maintenance of mutual pretense," an observation earlier noted by Glaser and Strauss (1965) in their study of dying adults. Mutual pretense includes the following principles (Glaser and Strauss cited by Bluebond-Langer, 1978:201–209):

1. All parties to the interaction should avoid dangerous topics.
2. Talk about dangerous topics is permissible as long as neither party breaks down.
3. All parties to the interaction should focus on safe topics and activities.
4. Props should be used to sustain the "crucial illusion."

5. When something happens, or is said that tends to expose the fiction that both parties are attempting to sustain (i.e., that the patient is not dying, is going to get better), then each must pretend that nothing has gone awry.
6. All parties to the interaction must strive to keep the interaction normal.
7. All parties must strive to keep the interaction brief.
8. When the rules become impossible to follow and the breakdown of mutual pretense appears imminent, all the individuals involved avoid or terminate the interaction.

The concept of mutual pretense is very helpful in describing the way children who are dying interact with adults. Glaser and Strauss discovered that the adults in their study tended to move toward an open awareness where patients discussed their condition with others when it was appropriate or necessary. The children in their study and the children in Bluebond-Langner's study tended to maintain mutual pretense rather than move toward openness.

Bluebond-Langner further notes that children may be able to know the truth about their condition but cannot change the rules by which the adults play. Children, on the one hand, may be close to being open and need an "open awareness context," but adults, on the other hand, are often traumatized by a child's openness and honesty. It is not easy to make sense of dying when one is a child. It is also difficult to make sense of dying when one is a parent or medical caregiver of a dying child. Children and adults have their own needs that should be respected (Bluebond-Langner, 1977:64–65).

Maintaining the balance of encouraging openness with people who can handle it and of supporting others who cannot is difficult. Making sense of dying may mean that different people make sense in different ways. One very important aid in appreciating how children experience dying is to acknowledge that in their self awareness their age is not as important as their experience with the disease and its treatment. The following extensive quotation from Bluebond-Langner (1977:54–56) highlights the important role of first hand experience.

Age and intellectual ability have not been mentioned as factors in a child's coming to know that he or she is dying. They are not significant. What is significant is the ability to integrate and synthesize information—an ability which is not age-related, but experience-related. The role of experience in developing awareness and, as we will see later, in determining forms of communicating that awareness, also explains why age and intellectual ability are not related to the speed or completeness with which the child passes through the stages. There are 3- and 4-year-olds of average intelligence who know more about their progress than very intelligent 9-year-olds. The reason for this is that the 9-year-olds may still be in their first remission, have had fewer clinic visits, and hence less experience. . . . (W)e can at least begin to see the role experience, concerns, and self-concept play in a child's coming to know that he or she is dying. . . . For example, one child on hearing the news of another child's death quickly assimilated all the information he had and came to the conclusion that he himself was dying.

TOM: Jennifer died last night. I have the same thing. Don't I?
NURSE: But they are going to give you different medicines.
TOM: What happens when they run out?
NURSE: Well, maybe they will find more before then.

Most conversations follow the same general format, regardless of what the other party to the conversation may say. The child usually opens the conversation by mentioning either an individual who has died or someone who is in danger of dying. In the next statements the child attempts to establish the cause of death by either asking a question or stating a hypothesis and assessing the other party's reaction.

SCOTT: You know Lisa.
MYRA: (Nods)
SCOTT: The one I played ball with. (Pause) How did she die?
MYRA: She was sick, sicker than you.
SCOTT: I know that. What happened?
MYRA: Her heart stopped beating.
SCOTT: (Hugged Myra and cried) I hope that never happens to me, but . . .

Having established in his own mind the cause of death, the child ends the conversation by comparing the deceased to himself.

If the child has recently discovered his or her prognosis, he or she can, when making the comparison, call attention to how he or she is different from the deceased.

BENJAMIN: Dr. Richards told me to ask you what happened to Maria. (Dr. Richards had not told him to ask other people. Later he told me that he used her name so that people would feel obligated to tell him.)
MRYA: What do you think happened to Maria?
BENJAMIN: Well, she didn't go to another hospital or home.
MRYA: She was very sick, much sicker than you are, and she died.
BENJAMIN: She had bad nose bleeds. They packed her. I had nose bleeds, but mine stopped. (Benjamin asked everyone he saw that day what happened to Maria. Later when I asked him why he asked everyone he said, "The ones who tell me are my friends. I knew Maria died. I saw the cart come for her. They told everyone to go in their rooms. I wanted to see if you were really my friend.")

If children have been aware of their prognosis for some time, they may, like Mary, talk about how they are like the deceased.

OCCUPATIONAL THERAPY STUDENT: Mary, what should I do with these? Mary? (Holding up the paper dolls that Mary and I had worked on.)
MARY: Put them in their grave, in the Kleenex box. Let me do it. Bring it over here.

(OCCUPATIONAL THERAPY STUDENT brings the Kleenex box and the dolls over to
Mary and puts them on her lap.)
MARY'S MOTHER: Well, that's the first thing you've offered to do since the doc-
tors said we could go.
MARY: I'm burying them. (Carefully arranges each doll between two sheets of
Kleenex.)

Thus, while Benjamin's speech about Maria and Mary's doll burial are both
conversations wherein the child discloses his or her awareness of the prognosis to another, Benjamin's conversation is more typical of a child who has just
become aware of his or her prognosis, whereas Mary's is more typical of a child
who has been aware for some time.

There are children who for a variety of reasons . . . feel that they cannot
speak freely about the awareness of their prognosis, even with people they
trust. Such children will not engage other people in a conversation about the
prognosis and/or with another child's death. They will simply state their
awareness and terminate the interaction. For example, one child announced,
"I'm not going to school anymore," and turned over on his side refusing to
speak to me. Another child blurted out to his brother, "I won't be here for your
birthday," and crawled under the sheet.

The difficulties in facing death as a dying child are associated with the
elaborate medical care that allows them to live considerably longer than
they would have only a few decades ago. Kidney disease treatment, for
example, now includes dialysis and transplantations (Simmons, Klein and
Simmons, 1977). Medical experimentation is conducted on children who
are ill so that the efficacy of drugs and treatment procedures are identified
(Van Eyes, 1978; Gray, 1975). Specialization in treatment means that a child
who is dying from a chronic disease, such as leukemia, can expect to confront numerous people who perform countless tasks "on" him or her,
often without a basic respect to deal with the situation honestly. The social
construction of meaning that children are bound to participate in with their
parents and others adds to the complexity of care for all concerned. The
challenge for adults is to learn how to listen well and to be available for
open conversations, even when such a topic as death is what we wish we
could postpone for a long time. This wish to postpone death in disbelief is
a denial behavior that many adults seem to prefer. (See Share, 1972, for a
discussion of the differences in the "protective" and the "open" approach
to communicate in families with dying children.)

FACING DEATH AS A SURVIVING CHILD

The adjustments of dying children are rarely considered to be expressions
of grief and mourning. In contrast, Kubler-Ross (1969) described the characteristics of dying patients as stages of adult grief. She claims that adult
patients who are dying respond with shock and denial at a fatal diagnosis.

As the reality begins to sink in, the patient feels rage and anger, often expressing it in diverse ways. The struggle to maintain life manifests itself in bargaining for survival. With the awareness of the full reality of impending death, the patient becomes depressed and withdrawn. A patient can come to acceptance of impending death, given time and the close companionship of a caring friend.

Grief is the psychological reaction to loss, particularly through death. The personal adjustment to loss involves the feeling of disruptive emotions and moods as one copes with a radically changed present and future reality. For the dying person, the inner response to a fatal diagnosis is fraught with anxiety and fear. It is also a time of redefinition of self in the light of changes in ability, mobility and social relationships. The greatest stress, however, may well be the loss of life plan—a sense of the future that is drastically changed. Perhaps the greatest difficulty of impending death is the grief associated with coming to terms with the loss of one's hopes and plans.

Mourning is the expression of grief that includes an inner and outer reality. Each of us has developed patterned ways of expressing who we are and how we relate and interact with others. The inner reality of mourning is the personal way we have developed to come to terms with personally important changes in ourselves and our world. The outer reality of mourning is the socially relevant patterns of coping that guide public behavior. Mourning a death often means that public customs of mourning are followed. It is hoped that each person who is grieving will be helped in his or her own mourning process through the public expression of concern and the affirmation of support.

Bereavement is the sociological adjustment to loss where social norms and values define expectations. The typical pattern of bereavement in American society prescribes mourning customs that principally include people who are directly related to the person who has died. In some traditions, it is limited to only the immediate relatives, while in others a wide group of relatives and friends are full participants in bereavement. The bereaved in their role are expected to grieve and mourn in ways appropriate to the family, ethnic or religious group, or community. The effectiveness or ineffectiveness of funerals in helping people cope with bereavement is dependent upon the shared definitions and the expression of thoughts, feelings and behavior.

Grief and Mourning in Children

The grief and mourning of children is becoming increasingly evident to researchers. Bowlby (1980), for example, in his comprehensive third volume of *Attachment and Loss* brings together much of the research on children in a theoretical framework that challenges the traditional Freudian assumptions while complementing the symbolic interaction theory of sociology. Bowlby's new paradigm for explaining the mourning of children takes the perspective of cognitive psychology and human information processing. His type of cognitive bias in psychology complements the social definition bias of our approach to a sociology of death. The awareness of the meanings in a person's environment and setting affects the understanding and interaction that results. For Bowlby, mourning in both adults and children involves a "defensive exclusion" of information that is available, which may be either healthy or unhealthy.

Bowlby believes that children mourn, but he takes as his frame of reference the mourning of adults. In fact, he goes into extensive detail to review the mourning of adults, including their childhood bereavement experiences, before he embarks on a review of the way children mourn. His research and clinical experience support this perspective. For more than twenty years Bowlby has been writing about childhood mourning as a reality that is very similar to adult mourning.

The evidence is building for Bowlby (1980:276) that it is possible for young children to mourn in a manner similar to healthy adults. For this to occur, the relationship between the child and his or her parents should have been a "reasonably secure relationship" before the death. The child should also have been a full participant in the awareness of what was taking place in the time during and after the death. Information should not be withheld, but rather questions should be asked and answered. The child should be part of the funeral rites. The on-going relationships with a surviving parent should be supported in a "comforting presence" with an assurance of continued relationship. When this is not possible, it should be done by a trusted substitute.

CONCLUSION

The conditions associated with children and death have changed from very common exposure to very infrequent occurrences. Death was a frequent event in the middle ages, especially when the "black death" ravaged Europe (Kastenbaum, 1972). Aries (1962) argues that the value of children was low in centuries past because infant and childhood mortality was so high (de Mause, 1974). Goldscheider (1971) notes the emergence of children as valued individuals appears to be historically correlated with the decreasing death rate that has been affecting the developed and the developing countries during the twentieth century.

For many today, the death of an elderly relative is an occasion for the barest acknowledgement of a death and most expeditious disposal of the body. Deaths in the form of miscarriages, abortions, stillbirths, and neonatal deaths share in the minimal public recognition with devalued elderly adults. Fulton (1970) argues that such "low grief" deaths are in response to minimal loss and muted grief. For the fetus and newborn it is before life has "really" begun, and for the very elderly death may come at the end of a full life or after prolonged illness and suffering. The death of a developing child, as well as the death of a young husband or wife, on the other hand, is perceived as premature and unjust. The social and emotional needs of the survivors in "high grief" deaths are acknowledged as infinitely greater.

"Improper grief" might be expressed by individuals, such as health care professionals or friends, who are expected not to mourn because they are not "the bereaved" and, therefore, are not the object of concern and social support. The public involvement and the professional cooperation that is beginning to emerge in medical care given to dying people and their families can be expected to continue. Health-care professionals are responding to new directions in holistic health by acknowledging their own humanity even as they practice their profession. Resistance by certain professionals and others in authority should not deter dying patients and family members from asserting their concerns and expressing their needs.

Summary

1. Children die today at a rate lower than any time in history, but nearly 50 percent of children who die in the United States die in the first month of life.
2. Parents suffering the death of a fetus or newborn grieve differently depending upon the quality of bonding with the child, the type of death, and their role experiences in bereavement.
3. The sudden infant death syndrome, a leading case of death in young children, received governmental attention in the 1970s.
4. Children who are dying from chronic diseases, such as leukemia, have an understanding of their condition that is more dependent on the stage of their illness and involvement in institutional care than on the child's developmental age.
5. Bereaved children grieve and mourn in ways that are similar to adults, but they tend to express a wide range of extreme mourning behaviors.
6. Childhood bereavement appears to be traumatic for most children, with some having grief symptoms years later.
7. Research on dying children and childhood bereavement is fraught with difficulties that often yield conflicting conclusions when numerous studies are compared.

APPLICATION: PARENTAL INVOLVEMENT WITH PROFESSIONAL HELPERS IN PERINATAL DEATHS

The death of a fetus or newborn infant is stressful not only for parents and siblings, but also for all people who are involved with the child. Increas-

ingly, parents are being included in the direct care of their critically ill child
until the time of death and following. Familiarity with the types of procedures and decisions that parents may face at the death of their child is
essential. Most bereaved parents will learn about hospital procedures and
how to share in decision-making only when they are faced with such a
situation.

The nursing procedures are fairly clear, and they instruct the nurse to
respond in ways that can help in the socio-emotional adjustments. The
nurse notifies a nursing/social worker counselor at the time of admission
concerning the fetal death or infant trauma. Even baptism is offered by
some hospitals where it may be done by anyone in the absence of a chaplain. The pastoral care department of a hospital is notified as is the communications department so that accurate information is available to others.

In the case of stillbirths, fetal deaths and infant deaths, the parents may
be given the option to see and hold their infant, to learn the baby's sex, to
make a decision regarding autopsy, and to decide on funeral arrangements. The medical staff explains to the parents what the parents can expect the baby to look like. Furman (1978) is of the opinion that the age of
siblings is the major factor in determining their involvement in these settings. Furman (1978:217) notes:

> Adolescents should decide for themselves. Elementary grade children are
> helped by attending a service but not helped by seeing a malformed dead
> body. Children under school age are particularly not helped by seeing their
> dead brother or sister, but they are sometimes helped by being in the company
> of the parents at the time of the funeral.

The extent of individual involvement depends upon the preference of individual family members.

The nurses' responsibility includes attaching identification bands to
wrist and ankle, measuring the weight, length and head circumference,
taking footprints and possibly a handprint, and completing standard
forms. These forms might include a fetal death certificate, an authorization
for autopsy, and a record of the death for the receptionist. Medical photographs may be taken by the medical photographer of a full front and back
view, as well as close-ups of any abnormalities. These are used by physicians to describe the infant's medical condition. The nurse is also encouraged to take nonmedical photographs that include the infant in a blanket,
unclothed, a close-up of the face, and the parents holding the child if they
so desire. These pictures are given to the counselor and later to the parents
when they are interested.

The dead infant is wrapped in a blanket, labeled, and taken to the
morgue. In the case of a fetus the body is sent to pathology with a surgical
pathology lab slip. The physician may request that the placenta be in-

cluded in the case of spontaneous abortions or fetal deaths. Genetic studies may also be requested which might include a cord blood sample, a placenta sample, fresh tissue such as gonadal tissue or connective tissue around the kidneys, skin sample, and a complete genetic study that is sent to the state laboratory. The nurse then completes a checklist for assisting parents experiencing perinatal deaths, and she or he may, if procedure calls for it, place an identifier by the name tag at the entrance to the mother's room.

Hospitals with a special program to help the survivors of fetal and infant deaths provide nursing, medical, social work, and/or pastoral counselors who may assist the surviving parents and siblings. Time is taken to explain and help in the following matters: (1) autopsies and hospital procedures after death; (2) funeral or cremation options (arrangements for the disposition of the body are required in most states if the fetus was at least twenty weeks); (3) the nature and expression of grief and mourning; (4) coping with the reactions of friends and relatives; (5) other children in dealing with the death of their brother or sister; and (6) decisions regarding another pregnancy. Monthly meetings of bereaved parents can be established to provide a setting for sharing and learning about grief. These experiences of sharing with other parents allow for reality-based comparisons and for active support of other parents whose loss is also great.

This list of hospital procedures is by no means complete, but it does present an outline of what parents of spontaneous abortion, stillbirth, fetal death, or neonatal death may encounter. The attitudes and responses of physicians, nurses and others may vary greatly. At times, the helpers are in need of socio-emotional support along with parents and siblings. Many hospitals, on the other hand, have not dealt with the special needs of families experiencing perinatal deaths. While these practices are becoming more common around the country, one should not be surprised if a nurse or physician appears stunned at the request of a parent to spend some time with the body of his or her child. We can only hope that the "human" values of medical care will prevail over "bureaucratic" values as the welfare of the whole person is taken into account in the medical arena. This can be accomplished most effectively if parents are provided with accurate information, encouraged to ask questions, given plenty of time to make decisions, and given opportunities to share their experience in parental bereavement with others.

Discussion Questions

1. Approximately one-third of all pregnancies in America result in miscarriages, abortions, stillbirths, and neonatal deaths. How have American medical institutions traditionally dealt with these deaths? What are the unique problems that parents experience with regard to the usual treatment of these types of deaths? What are some positive

procedures that are being tried to meet the needs of parents who have experienced these types of losses?

2. Are adult and childhood experiences of bereavement similar or different? Give evidence to support your answer.

3. What conclusions can you reach concerning infant deaths in America relative to other countries, especially developing nations? What factors affect infant mortality?

4. Davidson says that mothers experience three basic problems when they have lost a child within twenty-four hours of birth. What are these problems? Klaus and Kennell suggest three practical solutions to the problems that physicians and nurses can facilitate. What are these solutions? Elaborate upon your answer giving examples when possible.

5. What is sudden infant death syndrome (SIDS)? How many children are claimed by SIDS each year? What are some of the unique problems faced by parents who have lost a child to SIDS?

6. What are the conclusions Bluebond-Langner reaches relative to the understanding children have of their terminal conditions? What are the five stages she suggests the children go through as they become aware of their terminality? Do you agree with these stages?

7. What is the function of "mutual pretense" as these children deal with their diseases? Why do they use this strategy instead of open discussion of their disease?

8. Does childhood bereavement invariably lead to pathology in later life? How do bereavement experiences and divorce experiences compare in pathological behaviors in later life? Cite specific examples to support your arguments.

9. Sociologists tend to emphasize role loss and adaptation in explaining children's behaviors related to a bereavement experience. Explain this approach and discuss its utility in explaining pathological and normal behavior of children who have had a parent die.

10. Explain how suggestions related to medical procedures involved in perinatal deaths might better help parents cope with the death of their child.

Glossary

ANOMIC GRIEF: A term to describe the experience of grief, especially in young bereaved parents, where mourning customs are unclear due to an inappropriate death and the absence of prior bereavement experience; typical in a society that has attempted to minimize the impact of death through medical control of disease and social control of those who deal with the dying and the dead.

BONDING: The socio-emotional attachment between a parent and a child that develops during pregnancy and after delivery. Bonding is affected by role definitions, and provides a framework to health-care professionals for guiding parents in their mourning of a dying or dead child.

CHILDHOOD BEREAVEMENT: The temporary role of children who are adjusting to the death of one or both parents. Bereavement is a social process of mourning where personal expressions of grief are socially defined and responded to by others in ways that may exclude a grieving child.

DEATH AGONY: The tendency for *all* humans to physiologically struggle for life, and the consequential tension and anxiety. (Many have been observed dying a quiet death with minimal agony, however.)

IMPUTED DEVIANCE: The labeling of a person as morally or legally accountable for an action or a failure to act. A special problem for survivors of SIDS deaths because of the absence of medical explanations and the tendency to fix blame when such an unexpected tragedy occurs.

MUTUAL PRETENSE: The term to describe one of the four types of "awareness contexts" that shape the interaction between patients and their medical caregivers and family members. Mutual pretense is extremely common among children who are dying, as observed by Bluebond-Langner in her study of leukemic children from ages three to nine.

SHADOW GRIEF: The chronic sorrow and lingering yearning at the loss through death of a person of great socio-emotional importance. Peppers and Knapp use the term to describe the long-term mourning of parents who experience the death of their fetus or infant.

SUDDEN INFANT DEATH SYNDROME: Also known as SIDS and Crib Death. The sudden unexpected death of a child where autopsy does not reveal a single cause of death. SIDS is the leading cause of death in children age one month to one year, and second only to fatal accidents as a cause of death of children under fifteen.

References

Anthony, Sylvia. 1971. *The Discovery of Death in Childhood and After*. New York: Basic Books.

Aries, Philippe. 1962. *Centuries of Childhood: A Social History of Family Life*. New York: Alfred A. Knopf.

Bluebond-Langner, Myra. 1977. "Meanings of Death to Children," in *New Meanings of Death*, pp. 47–66, ed. by Herman Feifel. New York: McGraw-Hill.

Bluebond-Langner, Myra. 1978. *The Private Worlds of Dying Children*. Princeton, N.J.: Princeton University.

Bowie, Wende K. 1977. "Story of a First Born." *Omega*, Vol. 8, No.1:1–17.

Bowlby, John. 1960. "Grief and Mourning in Infancy and Early Childhood." *The Psychoanalytic Study of the Child*, Vol. 15:9–52.

Bowlby, John. 1969. *Attachment and Loss*, Volume I: *Attachment*. New York: Basic Books.

Bowlby, John. 1973. *Attachment and Loss*, Volume II: *Separation, Anxiety and Anger*. New York: Basic Books.

Bowlby, John. 1980. *Attachment and Loss*, Volume III: *Loss, Sadness and Depression*. New York: Basic Books.

Cullberg, J., and S. Karger. 1972. "Psychosomatic Medicine in Obstetrics and Gynecology," 3rd International Congress, Basel, Switzerland.

Davidson, Glen W. 1977. "Death of the Wished-for Child: A Case Study." *Death Education*, Vol. 1, No. 3:265–275.

deMause, Lloyd. 1974. "The Evolution of Childhood," in *The History of Childhood*. New York: Harper and Row.

Easson, William M. 1970. *The Dying Child: The Management of the Child or Adolescent Who is Dying*. Springfield, Ill: Charles C Thomas.

Freud, Anna, and D.T. Burlingham. 1943. "The Shock of Separation," in *War and Children*. New York: Medical War Books.

Fulton, Robert. 1970. "Death, Grief and Social Recuperation." *Omega*, Vol. 1, No.1:23–28.

Furman, Erna P. 1978. "The Death of a Newborn: Care of the Parents." *Birth and the Family Journal*, Vol. 5, No. 4:214–218.

Furman, Erna P. 1974. *A Child's Parent Dies: Studies in Childhood Bereavement*. New Haven, Conn.: Yale University Press.

Giles, P.F.H. 1970. "Reactions of Women to Perinatal Death." *Australian and New Zealand Journal of Obstetrics and Gynecology*, Vol. 10, No. 4:207–210.

Glaser, Barney G., and Anselm L. Strauss. 1965. *Awareness of Dying*. Chicago: Aldine.

Goldscheider, Calvin. 1971. *Population, Modernization and Social Structure*. Boston: Little, Brown.

Grant, James. 1982. Interview on "All Things Considered," National Public Radio, February 1, 1982.

Gray, Bradford H. 1975. *Human Subjects in Medical Experimentation*. New York: Wiley.

Gyulay, Jo-Eileen. 1978. *The Dying Child*. New York: McGraw-Hill.

Hartigan, J. Michael. 1981. "Maternal-Infant Bonding: Differences in Bonding/Grieving Response to Neonatal Death, Stillborn and Miscarriage."Session III of "Resolve Through Sharing Core Team Training Program" at La Crosse Lutheran Hospital, La Crosse, Wisconsin, September 15.

Haub, Carl. 1981a. "The United States Population Data Sheet of the Population Reference Bureau, Inc." Washington, D.C.: Population Reference Bureau.

Haub, Carl. 1981b. "1981 World Population Data Sheet of the Population Reference Bureau, Inc." Washington, D.C.: Population Reference Bureau.

Kastenbaum, Robert. 1972. "The Kingdom Where Nobody Dies." *Saturday Review of Science*, Vol. 5:33–38.

Klaus, Marshall H., and John H. Kennell. 1976. *Maternal-Infant Bonding: The Impact of Early Separation or Loss on Family Development*. St. Louis: C.V. Mosby.

Klaus, Marshall H., and John H. Kennell. 1982. *Parent-Infant Bonding*, 2nd ed. St. Louis: C. V. Mosby.

Klein, M. 1944. "A Contribution to the Theory of Anxiety and Guilt." *International Journal of Psychiatry*. Vol. 23:114–123.

Kubler-Ross, Elisabeth. 1969. *On Death and Dying*. New York: Macmillan.

Lindemann, Erich. 1944. "Symptomatology and Management of Acute Grief." *American Journal of Psychiatry*, Vol. 101:141–148.

Lonetto, Richard. 1980. *Children's Conceptions of Death*. New York: Springer.

Nagy, Marie. 1948. "The Child's Theories Concerning Death." *Journal of Genetic Psychology*, Vol. 73, 3–27.

Peppers, Larry G., and Ronald J. Knapp. 1980. *Motherhood and Mourning: Perinatal Death.* New York: Praeger.

Schulz, Charles, and Kenneth F. Hall. 1965. *Two-by-fours: A Sort Of Serious Book About Children.* Anderson, Ind: Warner.

Simmons, Roberta G., Susan D. Klein, and Richard L. Simmons. 1977. *Gift of Life: The Social and Psychological Impact of Organ Transplantation.* New York: Wiley.

Share, Lynda. 1972. "Family Communication in the Crisis of a Child's Fatal Illness: A Literature Review and Analysis." *Omega,* Vol. 3, No. 3:187–201.

Smiley, Carolyn, and Kathy Goettl. 1981. "Resolve Through Sharing Core Team Training Program." Paper presented at La Cross Lutheran Hospital, Wisc., September 8, 10, and November 3.

Valdas-Dapena, Maria A. 1973. "Sudden, Unexpected and Unexplained Death in Infancy: A Status Report—1973." *New England Journal of Medicine,* Vol. 289, No. 22:1195–1197.

van Eys, Jan, ed. 1978. *Research on Children: Medical Imperatives, Ethical Quandries and Legal Constraints.* Baltimore: University Park.

Zelligs, Rose. 1974. *Children's Experience with Death.* Springfield, Ill: Charles C Thomas.

Suggested Readings

Bluebond-Langner, Myra. 1978. *The Private Worlds of Dying Children.* Princeton, N.J.: Princeton University Press.
   A participant observation study by an anthropologist interested in how dying children construct and control the meaning of dying.

Borg, Susan, and Judith Lasker. 1981. *When Pregnancy Fails: Families Coping With Miscarriage, Stillbirth, and Infant Death.* Boston: Beacon Press.
   A readable discussion of social-psychological issues surrounding the death of a newborn child by a sociologist and an architect, both of whom experienced the death of their first child. A helpful discussion of the parent's experience, personal networks, public issues and decisions parents face, including resource groups throughout the country and an extensive bibliography.

Bowlby, John. 1980. *Attachment and Loss.* Vol. III: *Loss, Sadness and Depression.* New York: Basic Books.
   A thorough review of research literature concerning the impact of death on the immediate and subsequent lives of children. A refreshing psychiatric discussion that incorporates information theory with biological processes in the brain to present Bowlby's analysis of the process of mourning in children.

Furman, Erna. 1974. *A Child's Parent Dies: Studies in Childhood Bereavement.* New Haven: Yale University Press
   A study by child analysts associated with the Cleveland Center for Research in Child Development of twenty-three children who lost a parent through death. An in-depth discussion of ten children's experiences with bereavement complements the review of research literature and the concern for understanding both internal and external forces in the struggle to resolve grief.

Lonetto, Richard. 1980. *Children's Conception of Death.* New York: Springer Press.
   A developmental psychology overview of children's beliefs about death that in-

cludes a summary of research and children's drawings that show conceptions of death at various ages. A brief discussion of how children's experiences with death affects their understanding of death, as well as recommendations on how to talk to children about death.

Peppers, Larry G., and Ronald J. Knapp. 1980. *Motherhood and Mourning: Perinatal Death.* New York: Praeger Press.

A brief sociological assessment of the problem of perinatal death, maternal grief, problems in relationships, funeral arrangements, the subsequent pregnancy, and support groups. Includes an interesting discussion of "shadow grief" and the role of the community in coping with perinatal deaths.

Chapter 8

THE HOSPICE APPROACH: AN ALTERNATIVE TO INSTITUTIONAL DEATH

Does dying frighten you? Frequent responses to this question are the following:

"I am afraid of the pain."

"I do not want to be alone when I am dying."

"I am afraid of a long protracted period of suffering."

"I do not want to die in a hospital. Let me die at home."

"I am not afraid for myself but I am worried about the effect of my death upon those I love."

You will note that most of these fears relate to the *process* of dying, and this chapter concerns questions related to that process. The hospice movement has developed because of concern over these and other issues.

In medieval times the word *hospice* referred to a way station for travelers. The word hospice is rooted in the Latin word *hospitium* meaning hospitality, inn or lodging. It is also derived from the word *hospes* which means host or guest. Sandol Stoddard (1978) describes some of the early hospices in her book *The Hospice Movement.* Probably the most famous hospice in the world is the Hospice of Great Saint Bernard in the Alps. This hospice trains dogs to rescue travelers lost on the Alpine slopes. With the passing of time, the word hospice encompassed houses maintained for the sick as well as the traveler.

A pivotal role in the development of the modern hospice movement was played by St. Christopher's Hospice in London, England, opened in 1967. St. Christopher's was founded by Dr. Cicely Saunders who began her career as a nurse and subsequently became a social worker. It was not until Dr. Saunders later became a physician, however, that she was able to influence the course of health care for people dying of a terminal illness. Dr. Saunders' achievements were recognized by Queen Elizabeth II in 1981 when she granted her the status of dame.

DEVELOPMENT OF A HOSPICE

The first modern hospice program in the United States was the Connecticut Hospice. Much of this chapter will describe the Connecticut Hospice in order to give an idea of how a hospice program can be set up. The origin of the program was directly related to that of St. Christopher's in London. In 1963 Dr. Cicely Saunders was invited to lecture in New Haven at the Yale University School of Medicine. Contacts between Dr. Saunders and personnel from the Yale Nursing and Medical Schools were frequent over the next several years. Local leaders from various disciplines became involved in the development of a hospice in Connecticut. Their planning resulted in the establishment in 1971 of Hospice Incorporated (later changed to The Connecticut Hospice).

The original intent of the planning group was to build an inpatient facility similar to St. Christopher's. Funding proved to be a problem, and the group decided to inaugurate its home care program in 1974. The National Cancer Institute provided funds for a three-year demonstration project to test the viability of home care. An inpatient facility was eventually built with the help of both federal and state funds and opened in 1980.

Since that beginning, the number of hospice programs throughout the United States has increased considerably; every state is now represented on the list. The National Hospice Organization (NHO) was formed in 1978 to provide for coordination of hospice activity, and especially to assure that high quality standards of care would always be demonstrated by any program calling itself a hospice. The NHO has been instrumental in working toward the development of an accreditation procedure.

Meanwhile, The Connecticut Hospice, with the help of a foundation grant, organized the Connecticut Hospice Institute for Education, Training, and Research, Incorporated—a separate corporation. The Institute offered special help to health care leaders desiring to improve the quality of care to the terminally ill and their families. In 1981 the Institute was merged with its founder and continues its educational work as a department of The Connecticut Hospice.

THE NATURE OF THE CONTEMPORARY HOSPICE

The hospice is a specialized health care program that serves patients with illnesses such as cancer during the last days of their lives. Its primary goals are to enable patients to find real quality of life before they die, and to enable families of patients to receive supportive help during the traumatic period of the illness and the bereavement period. In the hospice the *patient-family* is the unit of care.

The hospice is not primarily a counseling service. Basically it is a medical program with physician direction and nurse coordination. Hospice leaders have discovered that patients cannot achieve quality of life unless physical pain and symptoms such as nausea, vomiting, dizziness, constipation, and shortness of breath are under control. A major emphasis of hospice, therefore, is pain and symptom management.

Medical care is often based upon a "P.R.N." (Latin for *pro re nata*) approach, which means that medication is given "as the situation demands." In practice, this means that often a person must first hurt and ask for relief before the pain can be stopped. This procedure is responsible for much suffering among the terminally ill. Hospice physicians believe that a patient should not hurt at all. Regular medication is, therefore, given in advance before the pain begins. The aim is to erase the memory of the pain that has been experienced and to deal with the fear of pain in the future. Dosages are standardized to the needs of the patient. The aim is to control the pain and other symptoms without sedating the patient. Every symptom is treated as a separate illness, for only when each symptom is under control can a patient begin to find fullness and quality of life.

The hospice concept includes both home care and inpatient care. Ideally, hospice care represents a continuum which includes both forms of care when each is necessary. The major emphasis in the movement is upon home care. The Connecticut Hospice learned in its early years of operation that the percentage of patients dying in their own homes increased from approximately 50 percent to 75 percent before inpatient services were available.

Inpatient care usually becomes necessary for one of three reasons. The first is that in order to bring the patient's pain and symptoms under control, a stay of a few days in an inpatient facility is necessary or helpful. The second is that the family taking care of the patient at home may become exhausted and need a few days rest while the patient is cared for elsewhere. The third reason is that home care is inappropriate at a given stage of the illness because of the patient's condition or the situation at home. It is hoped that upon admission to an inpatient facility, patients will be able to move back and forth from home care to inpatient care at various stages of the illness.

The Hospice Team

Hospice care is provided by an interdisciplinary team. Each discipline has something to contribute to the whole; all disciplines work together, each in its own area of expertise.

The interdisciplinary team includes several layers or levels of care. At the

center of the team is the patient and his or her family. The hospice movement emphasizes the need for people to make their own decisions with the
supportive help of health care professionals and other trained persons. A
vital part of the process is the patient's own physician; it is hoped that this
professional will continue to be in charge of the care of the patient and
write medical orders when necessary.

The next layer of the team includes the hospice professional caregiving
staff. This consists first of physicians. Hospice medical care must be directed by a qualified physician. Nurses comprise the next category. Registered nurses are responsible for coordinating the patient's care. Licensed
practical nurses and nursing aids are also included—especially in inpatient
settings.

The hospice social worker constitutes an important part of the team. The
social worker spends considerable time working with families, enabling
family members to communicate with each other. While family members
may be aware that the patient is dying, they may never have discussed it
with each other or with the patient. There may be other social problems
needing attention such as alcoholism and marriage problems. The social
worker also spends considerable time in working with the children or
grandchildren of patients. All too often in modern society children have
been shielded from participation in events centering on the death of a
family member.

Pastoral care is a basic part of the team. A larger hospice may employ a
chaplain. Chaplains' duties include direct pastoral care to patients and
their families, counsel to other members of the caregiving team on spiritual
issues, and efforts to involve clergy of the community in the care of their
own people. In smaller hospice programs all of the care may be provided
by local clergy who work closely with the hospice staff.

Arts are increasingly recognized as an important component of hospice
care. The Connecticut Hospice pioneered in the development of an arts
program which considers the arts as a means of helping patients find a
meaningful fulfillment to their life during their last days. A grant made it
possible for artists in such areas as metalwork, drama, dance, and gardening to work with patients interested in that means of expression.

Financial counseling is a significant aspect of the hospice team. Patients
and families have often exhausted their financial resources at the time of
care. Attention is needed to forms of third-party reimbursement, such as
those provided by Medicare or private insurance companies, and to possible other programs for which the patient may be eligible.

Trained volunteers also comprise an essential part of the team. No hospice can exist for long without a strong volunteer component. Some volunteers are health care professionals such as physicians or nurses. Others are
nonprofessionals who are deeply interested in the needs of patients and
families. Some volunteers work in patient care tasks such as providing

transportation, sitting with a patient to free family members to get out of the house for awhile or carrying equipment. Listening is essential to all volunteers as well as paid staff members. What is most needed are training programs which require commitment over a long period of time.

The next layer of the hospice team involves a variety of health care professionals or other key leaders in the community whose help may be called upon during the illness. A psychiatrist or psychologist may be needed to provide expert counseling help. Nurses, home health aides, and homemakers employed by public health nursing agencies, such as visiting nurse associations, may be needed to provide special continuing health care or to share in the process of providing patient care. Physical or occupational therapists may be needed to work with the patient. The services of a lawyer may be required to help the patient settle personal affairs.

Within the community at large, there are a number of influences at work which either assist with patient care or help to make it possible. The patient-family support system is a most significant factor. Elements of the system may include numerous close or distant relatives, friends, neighbors, members of local churches and other civic groups.

Hospice programs are dependent upon a high degree of community interest and support. Bringing this about requires a planned program of public information.

The concept of hospice must be sold to the community. Specific activities require not only the obvious financial support (especially while the hospice program is developing), but a willingness to testify before regulatory agencies relative to the granting of approval to begin offering services to the people of the area.

Bereavement Care

Since the family is the unit of care, the responsibility of the caregiving organization cannot arbitrarily stop when the patient dies. Hospice programs offer continuing bereavement follow-up to members of the patient's family for as long as may be appropriate. Some hospices have a bereavement team, consisting primarily of volunteers, which follows up on all the families after the patient dies or on those family members for whom there is felt to be a major risk of serious problems developing later.

The bereavement team of the Connecticut Hospice illustrates this continued follow-up. The team consists of a number of persons who have previously served as volunteers within the organization. A considerable amount of time was spent by the team studying grief and how they might best aid people in the grieving process.

When the members of the interdisciplinary team feel that bereavement follow-up would be helpful to a family, a referral is made to the team. Usually this takes place after the death of a patient. The team has found that many family members appreciate and need the opportunity to tell the story of the patient's illness to someone who has not previously heard. Occasionally, a bereavement team member enters the picture while the patient is still alive.

Once the referral has been made, the team works out a care plan for the family and a team member accepts the family as his or her own responsibility . The objective of bereavement care is to encourage the family to carry on its grieving process in an open and helpful manner. Here, too, as in other aspects of hospice care, considerable importance is given to the art of listening. Family members need someone willing to listen while they discuss their feelings. Bereavement team support may last for a year or more, although the team tries to encourage family members to stand on their own feet as soon as possible.

Persons Served by the Hospice

Hospice care knows no age restrictions, though one-half to two-thirds of the patients tend to be persons over sixty years of age. Most hospices provide care for patients suffering from any illness with a time-limited prognosis. The largest percentage of hospice patients have cancer.

Eligibility criteria include a diagnosis of a terminal illness, a prognosis of six months or less, and consent and cooperation of the patient's own physician. Home care is often more viable when there is a relative (or friend) who can serve as a primary care person in the home and assume responsibility for caring for the patient when the latter is unable to provide care for himself or herself. Inpatient care usually requires that help is needed with pain or symptom control.

A Very Special Kind of Caring

Dorothy Storck

David is sitting cross-legged on his bed in his striped pajamas as the three of us came into the room—his mother, Toviah Freedman who is his family counselor, and I.

It is dim because David's medication is making his eyes water and the light bothers him. But there is nothing of gloom in the room.

Four brightly colored balloons hang over David's head, suspended by a string from the ceiling. On each one is printed: "Get Well."

There is little chance that David will get well.

David is 24 and for a year now he has known that he has leukemia. A bone marrow transplant operation could buy him some time, if he survives it. Without it he will almost certainly die within months. In April his disease went into remission and they sent him to Johns Hopkins hospital in Baltimore for the bone marrow transplant. Before the specialists could begin the grueling procedure, his condition changed. He came out of remission. They sent him back to Philadelphia.

"Hi, Mom," David says cheerfully. "Hi, Toviah," to the palliative care counselor who has been like a member of his family for a year. And "Hi" to me, the stranger he allows briefly into his life to ask questions about his dying.

He holds out his hand. We have not met before. His grip is strong. He smiles and makes apologies for the twilight of the room. I am nervous; he is not. David has put behind him in this year the inconsequential worries of social intercourse. His mother, a small, dark-haired woman with lovely eyes, waves a paper bag at him.

"Apple strudel," she says, and he applauds. She puts it on a table.

In the last year David has been in and out of the seventh floor oncology (cancer) unit at the Hospital of the University of Pennsylvania several times. He was forced, finally, to give up his job as a medical orderly in a small New Jersey hospital. He keeps his apartment while he waits for a remission that may not come.

He has some pain while he waits. He says he has reached a point in his mind where he can control much of it. The drugs help with the rest. The specially trained team that is caring for him will give him whatever pain-killing drugs he needs, at any time, 24 hours of the day or night. He is on palliative care for the terminally ill. He is in hospice.

David is one of 42 patients who are now in this care program at HUP. All but six of them are living at home. They will continue to do this as long as they are able.

"Palliative care" means patient comfort, not only of a physical kind. It includes emotional care for the dying, and for their families. It is an offshoot of the hospice movement that began in England.

"Our job is to make the patient's remaining life as pleasant as it can be," says Dr. Barrie Cassiieth, the psychologist who started the hospice program at HUP a year ago. "Hospitals are geared to treat disease. There comes a point where you can't do that any longer. Then you treat the patient. . . . The family is part of that."

A trained counselor, a member of the team, visits both the patient and the family regularly. He or she is there whenever needed, night or day. He will help with whatever problems come up, whether it's as simple as the transfer of a car title from the patient to his wife, or as complicated as the transfer of guilt from the sick to the well. There is bereavement counseling for family members after the death.

"When we were in Maryland," David's mother is saying, "and we found out the operation was cancelled, I was sitting in that motel room that night and I couldn't stop crying. I needed to call someone, but I couldn't call anyone who didn't understand. I called Toviah."

David nods, remembering.

"I used to be hostile, angry," he says. "I'd say terrible things to my mom. . . It was difficult to face up to reality, to say, 'Look, Mom, we'll have to make plans about when I die.' It was hard enough to accept it myself. . . Then I saw my relationship changing with my friends, my brother, my parents. I was losing contact."

There is silence for a moment in the room. Not grief, but a fullness.

"My husband and I, we were feeling cut off," David's mother says after a while. "I had to reach out and say, 'Hey, if you don't want to talk, OK. But don't ignore us.' It was a risk."

"We were trying to protect each other," David says softly. "I was trying to be the strong one."

His mother looks at him. The understanding between them is a long, shimmering cord. "So was I," David's mother says.

Source: *The Philadelphia Inquirer*, October 1981.

Special Aspects of Home Care

One of the questions frequently raised by family members is what to do if an emergency develops in the middle of the night or on a holiday. Many health care professionals do not make house calls, but hospice people do. Home care for hospice patients is made viable by the fact that a physician and a nurse are on call twenty-four hours a day, seven days a week, to make house calls when needed. This gives patients and families confidence that they can manage at home.

Community physicians continue to be involved in the care of their patients, and usually remain primary, while the patient is on home care. Such community involvement relates the hospice program to the area in which it is located and tends to give hospice care greater visibility than is sometimes true of health care programs.

In inpatient care the patient's own physician turns over the care of the patient to a hospice physician but must be willing to resume care if the patient is able to return home. Whereas traditional medical care in recent years has tended to concentrate care in specialized hospitals or in nursing homes, hospice care returns the focus to the family.

Special Aspects of Inpatient Care

The family remains the unit of care within the inpatient hospice facility. This means that there must be space for a large number of family members to congregate.

Hospice inpatient care requires a homelike environment—the aim is to make the facility as much like a home away from home as is possible. Patients are encouraged to bring with them favorite possessions such as pictures, a favorite chair, or plants.

No arbitrary visiting restrictions are placed on those wishing to see hospice patients. One may visit at any time of day or night. Visitors of any age, including young children, are not restricted in their visitation. Furthermore, family pets, such as dogs or cats, may come as well.

The inpatient facility of The Connecticut Hospice in Branford illustrates the above principles. There is a family room that is off limits to staff and solely provided for the comfort of family members. Kitchens, containing a refrigerator, a microwave oven, a stove and a sink, are available for use by families. Washing machines are maintained for their use. Large living rooms with fireplaces are also available. Ten four-bedded rooms for patients help to develop social support systems among family groups. There are also four single bedrooms. A commons room and chapel are used not only for religious services but for presentations by various kinds of artists. Spacious corridors next to patient rooms contain plants and areas for family gatherings. Beds may be moved around as desired—on a nice day these beds are often outside on patios. A beauty parlor, operated by volunteers, is available for helping patients feel better about themselves. There is a preschool for three- and four-year-old children of staff, volunteers, and people in the community. When patients die, they are taken to a viewing room available for the use of family members.

Hospice care places considerable emphasis on the tastiness, attractiveness, and nutritional value of food prepared for patients. The Connecticut Hospice employs a gourmet chef with training in Paris to supervise its food preparation.

Models of Hospice Care

There are several models of hospice care. A *freestanding hospice* is entirely independent. It works closely with other components of the health care system, but employs its own staff and raises its own funds. The Connecticut Hospice is a forty-four-bed freestanding inpatient facility and home care program. The second model is a *hospital-based hospice* that provides a unit for inpatient care within its physical plant. It provides for home care through the hospital's own home care department by arrangements made with a local public health nursing agency or by its own staff employed for that purpose. Bellin Hospital in Green Bay, Wisconsin and Bethesda Hospital in St. Paul, Minnesota are two examples of hospitals that have developed such hospice programs. The third model is the *nursing home based hospice* that also provides inpatient care when needed and arranges for home care in various ways.

Hospice planning groups exist in virtually every major, and many smaller, cities across the United States (DuBois, 1980). They are in various stages ranging from discussion groups of interested citizens to developed programs like The Connecticut Hospice.

DuBois (1980) describes several hospice programs. Calvary Hospital is classified as a chronic disease hospital with one-third of all deaths from cancer in New York City occurring there. Patients are admitted with a minimum of three weeks of life remaining and a maximum of around six weeks. Daily care at Calvary costs half that of a well-known acute care hospital for cancer patients nearby, but is approximately the same cost as some other less renowned nearby hospitals not focusing on dying patients. One primary physician is assigned to each patient. A well-organized recreation program includes trips for patients to nearby special events such as operas and plays. While the patients sleep in two constant care units with twenty-four beds, day rooms are provided for patient use.

Hospice-type features are found at St. Luke's Hospital in Manhattan, notes DuBois (1980). The program began in 1975 with a special hospice team working with five to ten patients scattered throughout the hospital. Patients are told they are hospice patients. They receive special privileges and extra attention from hospice staff (coordinator, two half-time nurses, half-time physician, half-time social worker, and additional assistance from chaplains and volunteers). Special privileges include extra visitors outside normal visiting hours, visits by children and even pets, and an apartment to enable visitors to stay overnight. Alcoholic beverages are allowed as determined by the primary physician.

HOSPICE ISSUES

Some have called the development of hospices a "people's movement." Hospices have originated in local communities as the result of the desire of health care professionals and civic leaders to provide better care. If the existing health care programs in the community had been meeting the needs of the dying and supporting their families throughout the period of the illness and bereavement, hospices would not have been necessary. Many hospice leaders have seen their role as eventually working themselves out of a job as the principles of hospice care are absorbed by the health care system. At any rate, hospices pose a number of critical issues for health care in America. We will now examine those issues.

Quality of Life

The hospice movement demonstrates that every human being has an inherent right to live as fully and completely as possible up to the moment of death. Some traditional health care, emphasizing the curing of the patient at any cost, has ignored that right.

Many physicians have been trained to emphasize restoring the patient to health. Accordingly, many patients are subjected to a series of operations designed to prolong life, even though a cure is sometimes impossible as in the case of a rapidly progressing cancer. Most hospice patients have had some surgery, chemotherapy, or radiation treatments. Some continue these even while they are hospice patients because of the pain relieving nature of the treatments (radiation may reduce the size of a tumor, and therefore reduce the discomfort). There comes a point, however, if quality of life is a goal, that one should refuse further surgery, seek ease of pain without curing, and attempt to live qualitatively rather than quantitatively.

Because of the emphasis upon quality of life, hospices pay attention to many different facets of pain reduction. Usually when people refer to pain, they are thinking of physical pain. Hospice medical professionals have spent considerable time in developing a variety of methods of pain control that subdue, not only what the patient describes as pain, but also the symptoms related to the illness.

Much of this emphasis upon pain control has developed despite the practice by some professionals of sedating patients in pain. Quality of life cannot be achieved if the patient is "knocked out." An effort is made to find the point at which the pain is managed, but before sedation occurs. This has necessitated some considerable retraining of health care leaders toward this end.

Hospice people also emphasize social, psychological, financial, and spiritual pain. Terminally ill patients experience the abandonment that comes when friends and acquaintances stop visiting them because of an inability to cope with issues of death, lack of knowledge about what to say or do, or simply lack of awareness of what the patients are experiencing. Financial pain is experienced by those seeking to pay off a huge hospital or medical bill. Finally, there is a spiritual pain which people experience. "Why did God do this to me?" is a question frequently asked. The movement therefore challenges the medical community and the health care system to make the meeting of these needs a major priority.

None of the social, psychological, financial, or spiritual needs of patients (or their families) can be met until all health care professionals are comfortable with discussing questions of death. If a physician, for example, is afraid of death, or chooses to ignore it, it will be difficult for him or her to enable the patient to deal with the issues involved.

Likewise the hospice movement emphasizes the importance of the environment in which quality of life can be experienced. The term "environment" refers to the home setting where provisions are made for the patient's needs. Much of the architecture, decor and furnishings of the buildings in general has been provided for the convenience of staff rather than the patients.

A critical question is "What constitutes quality of life?" What do people most want to accomplish before they die? What do they most want to do? When a patient in an Arizona hospice was asked that question, she said that she had always wanted to take a helicopter ride. That she did! Like this patient, almost everyone has "unfinished business" in life. Some may wish to renew relationships with friends or family members. Others may desire to put their own affairs in order, to write their memoirs, to plant a garden, to watch the sunset.

Kavanaugh (1972) tells the story of Elaine who, in her last months of life, studied for her real estate license examination, passed the test, and with the help of her husband sold two houses. Thus, at age thirty-seven, Elaine found her first job while dying.

The Patient-Family as the Unit of Care

Traditional health care has concentrated on the patient and ignored the family. Perhaps many health care workers would, if given an opportunity to state their opinions confidentially, say that they would prefer family members to stay away. Traditional ratios of physicians, nurses, social workers or chaplains to those needing care have been based upon an assumption that only the patients need attention. Hospice staff, to be sure, are not given the responsibility to meet physical needs of family members, but they do have tremendous concern for the social, psychological and spiritual needs of the family.

Hospices challenge the health care system to provide for an adequate number of professional staff members in ratio to patients. The Connecticut Public Health Code, in its regulations for hospice licensure, stipulates that at all hours of the day or night there must be at least one registered nurse for every six patients and at least one nursing staff member (licensed practical nurse or nurse's aide and a registered nurse) for every three patients.

Family care, however, involves much more than numbers of staff. It requires that health care workers know how to cope with fears, worries, tears and turmoil of family members, when to speak, when not to speak, and what to say. It requires that they take time to listen, to determine how they may be most helpful.

Hospice care is costly care because of the number of staff people involved. It challenges society as a whole to give priority to such care because of the right of the dying to quality of life. A harried nurse in a traditional hospital setting, trying to meet the needs of perhaps a floor of patients at night, is not being granted the time required to sit with a dying patient for whom night is especially fearful, and then to be of assistance to husbands, wives or children struggling with grief at that time.

The interdisciplinary team supports the staff person within each discipline by enabling resources of the entire team to come into play in meeting family needs. For example, if a nurse on the night shift is asked questions relating to spiritual care, she or he may wish to give an answer at the time the question is asked, but she or he will also have the resources of the chaplain in determining the best methods to meet patient needs. In hospice care the patient-family unit is involved in decision-making. This poses crucial questions to caregivers who may be accustomed to making decisions and having everyone go along with what they have decided.

The Costs of Care

No prospective hospice patient may be turned away because of lack of money. Some of the cost of hospice care is covered by third party reimbursements. Under certain circumstances Medicare covers the costs of some hospice services for those who are eligible. Medicaid pays the cost of care for those who are eligible. Some Blue Cross programs are underwriting care for their subscribers. The General Electric Company was the first major employer in the United States to provide a hospice benefit for its employees; Westinghouse and RCA also provide such coverage. Major medical insurance policies, provided through insurance companies and offered to employees as part of a benefit package, also underwrite coverage in some instances.

Thus far, however, the problem has been that provisions are not made for all hospice services. This is true because the laws and regulations governing programs such as Medicare were written on the assumption that the patient was the unit of care and that she or he would recover.

Hospice leaders have been active in working for wider coverage under Medicare. A major need has been data regarding cost effectiveness. In 1981 the Health Care Finance Administration started a demonstration through twenty-six hospice programs to secure cost effectiveness data in return for waivers of some of the restrictions then governing third party payment. This led to partial Medicare payment for hospice expenses in November of 1983.

Hospice leaders hope to make it possible for any person of any age suffering from a terminal illness to be eligible for Medicare payments for the costs of hospice care. They are also firm in their conviction that such care saves considerable money in the long run. Many patients currently hospitalized would not need hospitalization if home care services were available for patients and families. A basic societal question is whether as Americans we believe enough in quality of life for the dying to be willing to make it possible.

Though hospice care requires a higher ratio of staff to patients than that usually provided in health care programs, the cost is nonetheless lower than other forms of care. Because the majority of hospice patients are able to remain at home for much if not all of the illness, the costs of patient home care, when compared with any forms of inpatient care, are proportionately low. Because of the level of services provided, hospice inpatient care will normally be higher than that provided in a nursing home, but should be lower than inpatient care in a general hospital setting where patients must bear their proportionate share of the costs of expensive diagnostic and treatment equipment which are not needed in a hospice program.

The Training of Professionals

Most physicians, nurses, social workers and clergy were trained in their respective fields of work without special attention to the needs of the dying. If Americans are to be assured of adequate care at the time of death, health care professionals must be provided with continuing education opportunities.

Throughout the country many seminars and workshops have been conducted in recent years in the principles of hospice care. Mention has been made of the Hospice Institute; its objective has been not only to train leaders in the specifics of hospice care but to provide health care workers with the knowledge and skills to do a better job in their own settings regardless of whether there is a hospice program or not.

Health care decision-makers need to be encouraged to invest the time and money required for their staffs to better cope with the terminally ill and their families. Likewise, the curricula of schools of medicine, nursing, social work and theology need to be revised in order to provide specialized training along the lines outlined in this chapter.

Public Attitudes

The hospice movement began at a time when public consciousness of dying and death issues had reached an all-time high. The movement afforded an opportunity to do something tangible for other people. Many individuals took advantage of the opportunity by volunteering to play an active role. At the same time increasing public awareness of dying and death gave rise to considerable hospice publicity in the media. This helped to provide public support when hearings were held by regulatory agencies relative to the granting of approval for hospice services.

Public attitudes toward care of the terminally ill and their families will play an increasingly important role in the future. These attitudes will help to determine whether health care professionals will in fact broaden the scope of care to encompass the family and strengthen their skills in dealing with dying patients. Patients and families are, after all, consumers. In this age of consumer awareness it is becoming increasingly evident that those who purchase services can control to some extent the type of services available for purchase. Health care professionals are increasingly responsive to desires of their clients. The most important factors causing caregivers to seek improvement of skills will be the desires of those they serve. At the same time, especially in areas of competition among hospitals, consumer awareness will play an important part in encouraging such institutions to humanize the care they give.

Many physicians, nurses, social workers, clergy, and other personnel at hospitals and nursing homes have heard about hospice care and have taken the initiative to secure specialized training. When any people's movement arises, an immediate question is whether it will become institutionalized to such an extent that the original spirit will be lost as it adjusts to the reality of regulation, control, and payments of costs. The hospice movement will soon be at that juncture. There is every cause for encouragement that one of two things will happen. Hospices will be organized to provide the specialized care or the health care system itself will change to incorporate many of the concerns of hospices. The end result should be an improvement in medical care.

Evaluation of Hospice Programs

While evaluations of hospice programs have not flooded the literature, some studies have taken a look at the hospice approach. In an inhouse evaluation of the Connecticut Hospice, Lack and Buckingham (1978) reported less depression, anxiety, and hostility among terminally ill patients receiving home care as compared to others without these services. In addition, it was found that the overall social adjustment of family members was improved—individuals were better able to express thoughts and feelings with less distress.

Parkes (1978) reports that only 8 percent of those who died at St. Christopher's Hospice in London suffered unrelieved pain; this compares with 20 percent who died in hospitals and 28 percent who died at home. Hinton (1979), in comparing the attitudes of terminally ill patients at a British hospice to those at hospital wards, noted that hospice patients appeared least depressed and anxious while preferring the more open type of communication environment available to them.

A prominent figure in the thanatology movement, Robert Kastenbaum (1981), notes that while these evaluations of hospice programs are encouraging, methodological flaws and limitations existed that were difficult to avoid under the circumstances. He notes three limitations to such evaluations: (1) High quality research is difficult to conduct in such settings where the sensitivities of so many people must be considered. (2) Techniques for effective research into care of the terminally ill are at an infant stage of development. (3) Research and evaluation priorities generally fall way down on the list—improved care is the primary objective.

While Kastenbaum notes that many emerging reports on hospice are emphasizing the relative cost of hospice care as compared with traditional hospitalization, he hopes that the question of cost does not gain undue prominence. He is concerned that financial issues may warp our expectations and affect our ability to concentrate on the caring process itself.

It is the conclusion of C.E. Crowther (1980) that the United States is not ready for the hospice. He notes that it is not a question of training or funding, but more of a problem of being unable or unwilling to change our attitudes toward what constitutes proper care for a dying patient.

Crowther cites hospice development committee problems as power struggles, personal conflicts, and different opinions on the best approach to take. The biggest stumbling block, however, seems to be attitudinal. He notes that the medical community must be convinced that current methods of treating the terminally ill must be changed. The dying cannot be treated in the same way as those who can expect to be cured. With this attitude change, then the sort of care the hospice offers can be provided in the United States, notes Crowther. Physicians must learn the difference in the hospice goal of "care" and the traditional goal of "cure." The care concept admits that the patient is dying. Medical personnel must put their knowledge and efforts into relief of distressing symptoms and into human understanding.

Other reservations concerning the hospice movement are cited below from *Science* (Vol 193, July 1976). Some American doctors are cautious about the hospice idea. John C. Hisserich of the Cancer Center at the University of Southern California is eager to see the idea tried, but he warns that no scientific evaluation has been made of hospice care and that evidence of success is largely anecdotal. He also believes that hospice enthusiasts sometimes exhibit "a certain zealotry about the thing that may be necessary but that has the effect of turning off physicians who might otherwise be interested. . . ."

Perhaps the most serious reservations about efforts to sprout hospices in America come from Mel Krant, director of cancer programs at the new University of Massachusetts School of Medicine in Worcester. "My first reaction," he says, "is it's going to fail as an American idea. It will get into operation, but its intent will fail." The reason, he feels, is that hospices will simply add to the excessive fragmentation, overspecialization, and discontinuity in American medicine. A hospice will be the incarnation of yet another specialty—care of the dying—and will become "another discontinuous phenomenon" when what is needed is integration. Krant has high regard for the English hospices, but he fears that without the spirit of voluntarism and community feeling that exists in England, and without leaders as "utterly devoted" as Cicely Saunders, hospices will turn out looking like nursing homes. He also thinks hospices would help relieve hospitals and physicians of their true responsibilities, which should include more community involvement. Krant thinks it better that Americans develop their own indigenous models for incorporating hospice concepts.

CONCLUSION

As the American way of life has changed from a primary group orientation to a more secondary impersonalized style, so has dying shifted from the home to the hospital or nursing home setting—away from kin and friends to a bureaucratized setting. The birth of the hospice movement in the United States might be considered a countermovement away from this trend. As we seek out primary group relations in our secondary-oriented society, we seek to die in the setting of a familiar home rather than in the sterile environment of a hospital. Perhaps we are evidencing a return to a concern for each other—a dignity to dying may be on the horizon.

Hospice is a return to showing care and compassion. It is a revival of neighbors helping neighbors—a concept so often lost in our urbanized society. Hospice is professionals literally going the extra mile and coming to one's home when needed—medical personnel actually making house calls! Hospice encourages "children under fourteen" to be present with the terminally ill person rather than making them wait in the hospital lobby. Hospice is a grass roots movement springing up in small communities, as well as larger urban settings, to provide better health care. Hospice sounds almost too good to be true.

With Medicare now covering some hospice expenses and with rigid government requirements for approval of hospice programs, will hospice programs be able to continue with its concern for clients as human beings? It is to be hoped that hospice programs will not be strangled by the bureaucracy that financially assists patients, giving them little choice from dying in traditional hospital and nursing home settings.

APPLICATION: PERSONAL EXPERIENCE IN HOSPICE
TREATMENT

The Last Days of Mary Ball

Judy Sklar Rasminsky

It was in May 1978 that 30-year-old Mary Ball, a vivacious practical nurse, learned she was probably going to die. That month she had undergone four operations: the diagnosis was widespread cancer. Unprepared, panic-stricken, Mary became deeply depressed. The fact that her mother had died of cancer when Mary was 16 magnified her dread. Then one day her mother-in-law yelled at her, "You're not trying!" Mary realized that she wanted to make the most of her remaining time with her 32-year-old husband, Karl, and their two children.

Through 17 months of chemotherapy, she and Karl leaned on each other. Their hopes soared when Mary regained enough weight and strength to return to work. Then in 1980, there was more surgery, followed by more chemotherapy. The prognosis was not good. This is the story of Mary Ball's dying—and of how a remarkable program helped to ease her last four months with grace and dignity.

November 12, 1980. In bed in their trim little house in rural Northford, Conn., Mary and Karl cling together, crying. Earlier that day they have learned from Mary's doctor, Bruce Lundberg, that cancer has spread throughout her bones. No treatment will make her well. Dr. Lundberg has suggested a different kind of help—The Connecticut Hospice, a Branford-based team that, since 1974, has cared for more that 1800 dying patients and their families.

November 13, 1980. A hospice nurse telephones to ask if she can visit that night. Mary and Karl say no. Mary has just had radiation treatment for her pain, and she is tired. Besides, they are uncertain, apprehensive. What are they getting into? They must know more before they involve the children, Karl, Jr., 15, and Matthew, 6.

November 17, 1980. The hospice nurse calls again. The Balls take the outstretched hand. Home-care nurse Florence Larson arrives. Forthright, lively and gray-haired, she has been a nurse for over 30 years. She tells them that the hospice team can assist with pain management, nursing care, household help, money problems, counseling for the children: "We will support you in whatever *you* want to do to make Mary's life as happy and normal as possible."

Mary would like to remain with her family as long as she can. Winter is the slack time for a painting contractor, and Karl will stay home to care for her. Florence says she will visit regularly. The hospice team will be available day or night, seven days a week.

Mary has one urgent question: Can her pain be controlled? Dr. Lundberg has suggested morphine, but she is scared of it. Florence gently explains that morphine is an excellent painkiller and the correct dose "won't bomb you out."

"Who will pay for all these services?" Karl asks. "Your insurance," Florence answers. "But you'll never see a bill. We'll handle the paper work."

When Florence leaves 90 minutes later, the Balls feel as if a weight has been lifted from their shoulders. But they do not want counseling for the children. "I want to deal with them in my own way," says Karl. Leery of interference in their lives, they ask Florence to come just once every two weeks.

November 24, 1980. Mary visits Dr. Lundberg. Her pain persists, and having mulled over Florence's explanation, she is willing to try morphine. Dr. Lundberg prescribes a dose to be taken orally every four hours.

November 27, 1980. Karl's brother and sister-in-law are at the house for Thanksgiving Day. Suddenly, Mary's pain becomes unbearable. Anxious not to spoil the holiday, she takes more morphine and huddles on the sofa in the den trying to hide her agony. Karl telephones Florence. She calls Dr. Lundberg, who doubles the dose of liquid morphine and prescribes a booster shot. Florence picks up the medicine at the hospice in-patient building. About an hour after Karl's call she is giving Mary a shot of morphine. A half-hour later, Mary's torment over, Florence leaves and the party goes on.

December 11, 1980. Dr. Lundberg and Mary discuss the prospect of more chemotherapy. They conclude that the risks outweigh the potential benefits at this stage. To Florence Mary says, "I don't want to feel sick. I want to use the time I have left to enjoy and be part of my family." Florence says, "I think that's up to you and your doctor, and I support you in that decision."

Christmas 1980. Mary makes three shopping trips to buy the family's presents. She tires easily, so Karl pushes her up and down the store aisles in a wheelchair that Florence had ordered. She attends a church pageant Matt is in and supervises the trimming of their tree. In good spirits, Mary refuses a visit from Florence.

December 31, 1980. Mary is constipated. Florence comes to her aid. Natural fruit juices finally do the trick. "Florence is my security blanket," says Mary. "It's a relief just to hear her voice." Florence always seems to have time for a chat, a cup of coffee, a back rub for Mary.

January 2, 1981. Unable to keep her liquid morphine down, Mary needs a booster shot. Noreen Peccini, another member of the hospice home-care team, teaches Karl to give the injections to relieve him of the helplessness he hates. "Five years ago I couldn't even show him an I.V. bottle," grins Mary. "Now he does everything."

January 22, 1981. Mary is in greater pain, and Dr. Lundberg increases her morphine. She is eating less and sleeping more, but she is awake when the boys come home from school. Reserved and self-sufficient like his father, Karl, Jr., says little when he comes in to see her. Matt, ebullient and gregarious like his mother, hops into bed for a cuddle. Karl, Jr., still brings home top marks and plays football after school; Matt still asks Mary's permission to have friends over and she still reminds him to change his clothes. "We just take one day at a time," Karl says. "I answer the kids' questions and try to tell them things at the right time. I told Karl, Jr., that his mother might have to go into the hospice in-patient facility, and he is aware of the eventuality and that is enough."

January 28, 1981. At 6:30 p.m., Florence receives a call from a terrified Karl: Mary's face is puffed up like a balloon. When Florence arrives at seven, Mary is so scared she has vomited. Florence establishes that the swelling isn't life-threatening. While she is alone with Florence, Mary's eyes fill with tears. "I am getting so discouraged," she says. "Sometimes I hate to tell Karl how much I hurt, because he goes crazy—not that crying is crazy—wishing he could do more for me." Florence sits with her a long time, talking quietly.

January 29, 1981. Hospice physician Will Norton visits to check on Mary's swelling. He notices her bed sores and orders a hospital bed with an automatic inflating and deflating mattress to relieve the pressure on her back. The bed, delivered the next day, makes Mary "at least 100 percent more comfortable."

February 10, 1981. Mary wakes up disoriented. For a moment she doesn't even recognize Karl. After he moves her about in the bed and gives her some apple juice, she is herself again. But she is no longer able to walk to the bathroom alone, and Karl wakes every three hours to give her her morphine and turn her in bed.

February 28, 1981. Mary's pain is increasing, her breathing is shallow, her pulse rapid. At times she is confused. "I'm taking a turn for the worse," she tells Karl.

March 2, 1981. Mary is worse. Her dying is down to a matter of days. She is relieved and ready, but suddenly desperately afraid of becoming a burden. Should she go to the in-patient facility? Florence consults with Karl, who assures Mary he can handle the situation. To take some of the pressure off Karl during the day, Florence arranges for eight-hour-a-day help.

Evening. Mary perks up when Charles Rodrigues, their minister, comes in. "You know, Charles, I'm dying," she says. "and I'm not frightened." Karl is immensely comforted to hear this.

March 3, 1981. On behalf of the children of the church, a boy presents Mary with a card and a dozen roses. As Karl arranges the flowers in the kitchen, Matt asks for one. Later he gives his mother the rose and a card. On it he has drawn himself with arms spread wide, the way he did when he was very small, saying, "I love you, Mom, this much."

March 5, 1981. Mary's pain is excruciating. Karl calls the hospice for the go-ahead to give Mary a shot of morphine. Later Florence offers to stop by, but Karl says, "Gee, Florence, I don't think you need to. Everything is fine." Florence doesn't insist. "Mary is dying, and they're handling it," she says.

March 8, 1981. Mary has a 105-degree fever and is often delirious. Her family—sister, brother, father, aunt—come to say good-by.

March 9, 1981. Karl is worried that the children might be frightened by their mother's dying at home. He considers moving Mary to the hospice building. Yet he believes she still wishes to stay at home. Mary is in a dreamlike state, unresponsive; but, while Karl is talking with hospice nurse Ruth Mulhern, she becomes alert. The time has come for her to go into the hospice, she says. She thanks Karl for all he has done for her and tells him she loves him.

That afternoon, Florence helps to settle Mary into her new surroundings—a cheerful, plant-filled room at the hospice building.

March 10, 1981. Evening. Mary is in a dream world, but when Florence touches her she responds, "Florence, I'm so glad to see you." It is so like Mary to be thinking positively. Then she drifts away, and as Florence and Mary's aunt stand at her bedside, she quietly stops breathing.

Karl is walking out of his front door when the phone rings. The boys are already on the way to the car to go to the hospice. He calls them back and sits them down on the living room couch. As he puts an arm around each, he tells them that their mother has just died. Crying, he says, "Except for her love, you two are the greatest gift your mother ever gave me."

March 13, 1981. At Mary's wake, flowers overflow the room. Karl, Jr., stands beside his father. When Florence approaches, the shy, quiet boy, who never reaches out to people, embraces her.

March 24, 1982. Florence visits Karl. The boys have gone back to school. He is preparing to return to work. Karl's father, who came from Florida for Mary's funeral, will stay as long as he is needed. Florence tells Karl the hospice has volunteers trained to help families with their grieving. He declines more help, but thanks her for everything. "Without your assistance we couldn't have lived Mary's last months the way we wanted to," he says. Back at the hospice, Florence has a sense of completion.

She shrugs off her colleagues' praise. "We're here to guide, not take over," she says. "From the day I walked in, I was amazed at the way Mary and Karl related to each other and to me. They never drained me; they gave. I always left there a little wiser."

Source: *Reader's Digest*, Vol. 119 (October 1981): 178–184.

Summary

1. Hospice is a specialized health care program that serves patients with illnesses such as cancer during the last days of their lives.
2. Hospice care includes both home care and inpatient care.
3. The hospice interdisciplinary team includes the patient, family, physician, nurse, social worker, chaplain, trained volunteer, psychologist, physical therapist, and lawyer.
4. A homelike environment is provided for hospice inpatient care.
5. The first hospice program in the United States was the Connecticut Hospice modeled after St. Christopher's in London.
6. The hospice movement demonstrates that every human being has an inherent right to live as fully and completely as possible up to the moment of death.
7. Hospice people emphasize physical, social, psychological and spiritual pain.
8. Much of the cost of hospice care is covered by third party reimbursements, but no prospective hospice patient is turned away because of lack of money.

Discussion Questions

1. What is hospice care? How does it differ from the treatment given by most acute care hospitals? Identify the major functions of a hospice program.
2. Trace the history of the hospice movement in the United States.
3. Discuss issues related to the family as a unit of care in hospice programs. How do hospices try to achieve quality of life for each of the "patients" they serve? How does the interdisciplinary hospice team concept help accomplish this?
4. What are some of the special aspects of inpatient and home care in hospice programs? What are some of the advantages of each of these approaches?
5. What, in your opinion, are the negative aspects of hospice care? How would you suggest they be rectified?

6. Do you feel that bereavement care should be offered to the families of the terminally ill even after their loved one has died? Justify your answer in terms of medical, emotional, and financial considerations.
7. If you were terminally ill, would you consider entering a hospice? Explain your answer referring to specific reasons such as cost, family burden, and imminent death.

Glossary

BEREAVEMENT TEAM: Made up primarily of volunteers who follow up on families after the patient dies.
HOSPICE: A specialized health care program that serves patients with illnesses such as cancer during the last days of their lives.
INPATIENT CARE: When one's illness requires institutionalized help, for example, in a hospice facility.

References

Crowther, C. Edward. 1980. "The Stalled Hospice Movement." *The New Physician*, pp. 26–28.
DuBois, P. M. 1980. *The Hospice Way of Death*. New York: Human Sciences Press.
Hinton, J. 1979. "Comparison of Places and Policies for Terminal Care. *Lancer*, pp. 29–32.
Kavanaugh, Robert E. 1972. *Facing Death*. Baltimore: Penguin Books, Inc.
Kastenbaum, Robert J. 1981. *Death, Society, and Human Experience*, 2d ed. St. Louis: C. V. Mosby.
Lack, S. A., and R. Buckingham. 1978. *First American Hospice: Three Years of Care*. New Haven: Hospice, Inc.
Parkes, C. M. 1978. "Home or Hospital? Terminal Care as Seen by Surviving Spouses." *Journal of the Royal College of General Practice*. Vol. 28: 19–30.
Stoddard, Sandol. 1978. *The Hospice Movement: A Better Way of Caring for the Dying*. New York: Vintage Books.

Suggested Readings

Death Education, Vol. 2, Nos. 1 and 2, 1978.
   Special issues on the hospice movement that cover six models of hospice care as found in the United States, England, and Canada.
DuBois, Paul M. 1980. *The Hospice Way of Death*. New York: Human Sciences Press.
   An overview of the hospice movement highlighting case studies of three hospices as well as the federal government's involvement.
Koff, Theodore H. 1980. *Hospice: A Caring Community*. Cambridge, Mass.: Winthrop Publishers.
   Delineates the practical and theoretical principles of the hospice and provides information on the administrative, developmental and personal elements of hospice care.

Lamberton, Robert 1973. *Care of the Dying*. London: Priory Press, Ltd. and Saunders, Cicely, 1959. *Care of the Dying*. London: Macmillan.
    Two early influential works that explain the hospice philosophy and care for dying patients and their families.
Stoddard, Sandol. 1978. *The Hospice Movement: A Better Way of Caring for the Dying*. New York: Vintage.
    A vivid description of the workings of the hospice program emphasizing how the patients and their families begin to help others.

FOUR

Understanding Bereavement

Chapter 9

CROSS-CULTURAL PATTERNS OF BEREAVEMENT BEHAVIOR

> There is no group, however primitive at the one extreme or civilized at the other, which left freely to itself and within its means, does not dispose of the bodies of its members with ceremony. So true is this universal fact of ceremonial funeralization that it seems reasonable to conclude that it flows out of human nature.
>
> *Habenstein and Lamers (1963)*

AT THE MOMENT OF DEATH, survivors in some societies remain rather calm, others cry, while others slash their bodies. Some societies prefer to dispose of the corpse by burial in the ground, others place the corpse in a tree, some leave it alone for the animals to remove, and others burn the body. Within hours after burial, some cultures dictate that close relatives of the deceased remove the body, scrape the meat off the bones and distribute the bones to the next of kin as keepsakes. While some societies officially mourn for months, others complete the ritual within hours. Family involvement in preparation of the corpse for the funeral ritual exists in many societies while others call professional morticians to handle the job. While they surely vary, all societies, nonetheless, seem to have some social mechanism for managing death-related emotions and reconstructing family interaction patterns modified by death. These customs are passed down from generation to generation and are an integral part of a society's way of coping with a major event like death.

The entire web of human social interrelations is founded on many invisible and indirect meanings that we bestow on various individuals (Cuzzort and King, 1980:55). While we cannot actually see a mourner or a mortician, we can observe those who occupy such statuses. Until we are informed that they occupy such statuses (and are expected to behave accordingly), however, we cannot respond in an appropriate way. The cultural anthropologist is concerned as a scientist with the meanings that different events have for different societies. A true understanding of various rituals and activities results from an "immersion" in the culture. While the anthropologist cannot determine what is in the mind of the person acting, he or she can observe similar events over time and come to some understanding of the behavior within that context.

Cuzzort and King (1980) note that though social forces may be hidden, they are real. They are real because they are real in their effects. They also stress that social behavior is subject to interpretation. Often it is difficult to interpret our observations.

In explaining differences among three cultures, the anthropologist Ruth Benedict (1934) cites a myth contributed to the Digger Indians: "God gave to every people a cup, a cup of clay, and from this cup they drank their life. . . . They all dipped in the water, but their cups were different." Perhaps only God knows why people do what they do is one way to explain this myth. Marvin Harris (1974:4) notes that human life is not merely random or capricious. He says we do not expect dreamers to explain their dreams, nor should we expect lifestylers to explain their lifestyles. Through careful observation over time, we can come to a better understanding of why people do what they do.

This chapter will present various bereavement patterns and discuss the functions of such activities. While some examples cited may appear bizarre to the reader, bereavement rituals in our culture may also appear strange to persons from other cultures.

All animals eventually die, but we humans are unique in that we conceptualize and anticipate death. Students in classes on dying and death are sometimes asked to write their obituary—anticipate how they will be remembered by others. In so doing they must state how they died, how old they were at the time of death, and describe the plans made for final disposition of their body. Some students have difficulty with such an assignment since they do not want to state a "time of death." Some students die "heroically" while rescuing others from a burning building—a reflection of their perception of how they wish to be remembered after death. These "deaths" are reflections upon the culture in which the individuals were socialized.

All societies establish cultural patterns of behavior to assist individuals in coping with death. These ritualized behaviors follow norms whereby the survivors are provided with "blueprints" or "scripts" to follow in making sense of the situation before them and enabling them to respond in "appropriate" ways.

Why should a student of dying and death become familiar with the death customs of other cultures? We are too often ethnocentric and tend to judge others by standards existing in our own culture. Just because another society's customs differ from our own does not mean they are wrong. It is our belief that one can better understand death in American culture by being aware of the death customs of other societies. It is often surprising to some to discover that the similarities are often greater than the differences when comparing different death-related customs. As you read this chapter and study the death rituals of other groups, please note the many parallels that exist between our death customs and those of others.

Becoming familiar with cross-cultural death customs should aid in better understanding the American concept of death. To blame a supernatural being, a physician, or someone else for one's death is functional in both literate and nonliterate societies. It serves as an "explanation" for the death and a scapegoat to relieve one's guilt feelings. While some nonliterate groups might attribute a death to the ghost of a deceased ancestor, a literate group might "blame" medical personnel. Nonetheless, explanations for death are sought.

The concept of soul and immortality is found in most societies. For many, a belief in a soul concept explains what happens in sleep and after death. For some, the belief in souls explains how the supernatural world becomes populated (Tylor, 1873). Much of the ritual performed at death is related to the soul and an appeasement of the beings in the spiritual world. This spiritual dimension of death plays a significant role in the social structure of societies that hold such beliefs.

Souls of the dead become ghosts for many groups. Ghosts may take up residence. After a short period of wandering, however, or frequenting the graves or places their human owners visited during life, ghosts may cease to exist. Some have conversations with the ghost and make offerings to them. This is sometimes referred to as the "cult of the dead" (Taylor, 1980). These ghosts are not worshipped but simply maintain a relationship with a spirit that acts as a guide and protector and confers power. To have a guardian spirit is a positive thing in societies where this is believed.

This chapter will address many of the above issues using examples of customs selected from many cultural groups. In no way are these various cultures representative of all. The purpose of citing several groups is to illustrate both the similarities and differences found in a cross-cultural study of death attitudes and rituals.

ATTITUDES TOWARD DEATH

How is death viewed in different cultures? For some, death is a continuation of life, simply in a different form. Death may be accepted by some as a natural part of life—the "final stage of growth" as Elizabeth Kubler-Ross calls it. For others death is the end of everything, and therefore, something to be feared.

The Kanuri of Nigeria (Cohen, 1967) believe that as pregnancy marks the potential beginning of life, so death marks its end. They have a quiet accepting attitude toward death. Death is unpleasant, but it is always there. Death and funerals are much more closely noted and accepted than in the United States where, according to Cohen, the entire subject is considered repugnant. Death for the Tiwi of Australia (Hart and Pilling, 1960) is the natural phenomenon around which they have woven their most elaborate web of ritual.

In Nigeria the Igbo (Uchendu, 1965) believe that death is important for joining the ancestors. Without death, there would be no population increase in the ancestral households and thus no change in social status for the living Igbo. The lineage system is continued among the dead. Thus the world of the "dead" is a world full of activities.

The view of death and aging among the Ulithi of Micronesia (Lessa, 1966) is that old age is dreaded not so much because people do not want to die but because they do not want to live to be senile dependents. Sickness is not dreaded so much in old age for it can always be cured by death. Death comes to the aged Ulithi ordinarily as the result of natural causes; death comes to younger people because of sorcery, taboo violations, or the hostility of spirits or ghosts.

The Ulithi are not morbid or defeated by death, according to Lessa (1966). Their rituals afford them some victories and their mythology provides a hope for a happy life in another realm. Though their gods are somewhat distant, they assure that the world has an enduring structure and their ancestral ghosts stand by to give more immediate aid when merited. Thus after expressing their bereavement, rather than retreating, they spring back into their normal work and enjoyment of life.

For the Lugbara of Uganda (Middleton, 1965) when people die, they cease to be "people of the world outside" and become "people who have died" or "people in the earth." Death marks the beginning of an elaborate rite of passage as a dead man has relations with both living and dead kin.

Death for the Cheyenne of the Great Plains (Hoebel, 1960) was clearly a traumatic experience for the surviving relatives even though a happy destination awaited the dead. Each individual was highly valued since the population was small. Like the Cheyenne, the Mardudjara aborigines of Australia (Tonkinson, 1978) view death as almost always a traumatic experience for the bereaved. Death evokes strong passions of grief (often involving anger and resentment) and disrupts the network of kin ties and social interaction—sometimes resulting in important consequences for intergroup relationships.

For the Dunsun of North Borneo, few events focus more on the beliefs and acts concerned with the non-natural world than the death of a family member. According to Williams (1965:39):

> Death is considered a topic most difficult to discuss, conceive, or deal with in any sense. Everyone is afraid of death and fears to talk about it. Yet we must

prepare for it because it causes great changes in things. But how can we do that, for death is such a terrible event?

As the Abkhasians (Benet, 1974) see it, their bereavement system is rational but death is, by its very nature, irrational and unjust. The one occasion when outbursts of feeling are permitted is at a funeral. At such times, one is permitted to rage and express grief by wailing and scratching at one's flesh. However, even the expression of sorrow must be done according to specific rules. Benet notes a saying among the Abkhasians, "A man who can't cry will break his head open with his fists."

The Navaho Indians (Habenstein and Lamers, 1963) have no belief in a glorious immortality for the soul. They hold death to mean only the end of everything good. Similarly, the Semai of Malaya (Dentan, 1968) talk about life after death, but most admit they do not believe in it.

For some then, death is the avenue by which one is united with the ancestors. Death is the link between the living and dead kin. This is not true for all, however, as some do not believe in immortality. Though death tends to be feared, it must be prepared for since it "causes great changes." In summary as Williams (1965) notes, death is viewed in most societies as a "terrible event."

CUSTOMS FOR THE DYING JUST PRIOR TO DEATH

Some social groups have specific norms just prior to the death of a person. For example, the Magars of Nepal (Hitchcock, 1966) purify a dying man by giving him water that has been touched with gold.

Among the Huron of the Iroquois tribe (Trigger, 1969), a dying man was often shown the clothing in which he was to be buried—even frequently being dressed for burial before he died. A man about to die often gave a farewell feast for friends and relatives. If able, he sang his war song to show he did not dread death.

Among the Ulithi in Micronesia, if the dying person has taught any of the sacred professions or arts to others, he must be visited by his living pupils during his last moments of life (Lessa, 1966). They come into his room and recite formal requests for the ghost of the dying person to help them after the death in the exercise of his work.

Among the Dunsun of North Borneo (Williams, 1965), relatives come to witness the death. The dying person is propped up and held from behind. When the body grows cold, the social fact of death is recognized by announcing "he exists no more" or "someone has gone far away."

The Salish Indians of the Northwest United States (Habenstein and Lamers, 1963) leave the dying person alone with an aged man who neither receives pay nor is expected to have any special qualifications for the task.

One near death must confess his misdeeds to this person. The confession is to prevent the ghost from roaming the places in life frequented by the dying person.

The Ik of Uganda (Turnbull, 1972) place the dying person in the fetal position since death for them represents a "celestial rebirth." Therefore, it is important that the body be placed in the fetal position before rigor mortis sets in.

It is significant in many societies, including the United States, that one be with the dying person at the time of death. So often we hear, "If only I had gotten there a few minutes earlier. . . ." A visit prior to death allows one to say goodbye and "let go," as discussed in Chapter 2. It is a time to "recite" for the last time.

Having a cultural framework that prescribes proper behavior at the time of death provides an established order and perhaps gives comfort to the bereaved. These behavioral norms give survivors something to do during the dying process and immediately thereafter, and therefore facilitate the coping abilities of the bereaved.

Mourning Rituals

Taylor (1980:198) defines ritual as "the symbolic affirmation of values by means of culturally standardized utterances and actions." A "ceremony" is a given complex of rituals associated with a specific occasion. People in all societies are inclined to symbolize culturally defined feelings in conventional ways. Ritual behavior is an effective means of expressing or reinforcing important sentiments. Mourning to express solidarity and clapping the hands to show approval have ritual significance.

Rituals differ from other behavior (Rappaport, 1974) in that they are formal—stylized, repetitive, and stereotyped. They are performed in special (often sacred) places and occur at set times. Rituals include liturgical orders—words and actions set forth previously by someone.

Anthropologists distinguish between rites of passage and calendrical rites. Rites of passage occur when individuals or groups move from one status to another—baptisms, initiation rites, graduation exercises, and funerals, for example. Calendrical rites are associated with events that occur within a society—annually, seasonally, etc. Christmas, Thanksgiving, and Memorial Day are examples of calendrical rites.

Functions of rituals include validation and reinforcement of values, reassurance and feelings of security in the face of psychological disturbances, reinforcement of group ties, aiding status change by acquainting persons with their new roles, relief of psychological tensions, and restabilizing patterns of interaction disturbed by a crisis (Taylor, 1980). Ritual can also have negative functions by causing tensions.

Effie Bendann (1930) in her well-documented study entitled *Death Cus-*

toms: *An Analytical Study of Burial Rites* notes that the expression of emotions ranges from complete abstinence to amplified wailing. She notes that after a death the aborigines of Australia and Melanesia indulge in the most exaggerated forms of weeping and wailing; they display other manifestations of emotional excitement seemingly because of grief for the departed. However, at the end of a certain designated time period, they cease with metronomic precision and the would-be mourners indulge in laughter and other forms of amusement.

The Kalinga in the Philippines (Dozier, 1967) strictly observe mourning and food taboos. A year after the death, a ceremony of celebration is given which ends the mourning period.

Among the Dinka of the Sudan (Deng, 1972), the women in mourning cut their leather skirts, leave them unoiled and dry. They also cover their bodies with dirt and ashes for as long as a year. Survivors of the deceased are viewed as impure and spiritually dangerous; therefore, they are expected to avoid interaction with others. A Turkish custom (Pierce, 1964) requires those who mourn to be constantly teased and thinking of things other than death "lest they lose their minds completely."

In Uganda the Lugbara (Middleton, 1965) women have special cries of mourning. The lineage sisters who touch the corpse are unclean. Other kin respond by shaving their heads. This shaving of heads is also found with widows among the Swazi in Africa (Kuper, 1963). Widows remain "in darkness" for three years before they are given the duty of continuing the lineage for the deceased through the levirate. Mourning imposed on the husband is less conspicuous and shorter than on the wife.

As soon as the soul leaves the body, the Kapauku Papuans of West New Guinea (Pospisil, 1963) require the relatives of the deceased to give a formal expression of their grief. They weep, eat ashes, cut off their fingers, tear their garments and net carrying bags, and smear their faces and bodies with mud, ashes or yellow clay. A loud sing-song lamentation follows.

In writing about the Cheyenne Indian customs, Hoebel (1960) states that mourning falls most heavily on the women. Female relatives cut off their long hair and gash their foreheads as the blood flows. If the dead one was killed by enemies, they slash their legs until caked with dried blood. A widow would sometimes isolate herself in the brush for up to a year. Mourning gives the women their own masochistic outlet. Taking death somewhat calmer, Cheyenne men simply let down their hair in mourning and do not bother to lacerate or isolate themselves.

Among the Tiwi of North Australia (Hart and Pilling, 1960), a death immediately divided the whole tribe into two groups. A small group of relatives automatically became mourners in a state of strict taboo; others did not have to observe such a posture. The mourners could scarcely do any work as their time was spent weeping, wailing, and gashing their heads with stone axes. Nonmourners were asked to carry out the mourners' everyday tasks; thus, the mourners became obligated to the nonmourners.

The widow and other closely related females among the Mardudjara aborigines in Australia (Tonkinson, 1978) usually cut their hair and remain anointed with red ochre throughout the period of mourning. Later they return to the grave, remove and clean the bones of the deceased, rub them on their bodies, and carry the skull to the widow who rubs it against her body.

For the Barabaig in Tanzania (Klima, 1970) funeral activities last for eight or nine months. On the final day, a black ox is tossed to the ground near the burial monument and suffocated. An elderly woman is selected to skin and carve up the carcass.

The Kanuri of Nigeria (Cohen, 1967) mourn officially for forty days by saying special prayers and remaining close to home. During the ceremony men remain impassive, quietly *saying* their beads and praying softly to themselves. Women come in groups, walking slowly in single file, wailing and crying.

Among the Dakota Indians (Habenstein and Lamers, 1963), loud wailing and bitter complaints were responses to death announcements. This behavior was usually followed by the tearing off of garments and body mutilation. Forms of mutilation included chopping a joint from a finger, running knives along the thighs and forearms, and gashing limbs until covered with blood. Women would gash their shoulders and breasts. Many would cut off their hair at the shoulder or the tip of the ear and refuse to comb it (normally pride is taken in the hair). Chief mourners among the men painted their faces black and refused to wash themselves until they killed an enemy or gave a feast in honor of the dead relative.

From his studies of Trobriand Islanders, Malinowski (1929) reports that when a man dies, his wife is not set free by the event. Custom forces her to play the burdensome role of chief mourner and make "an ostentatious, dramatic, and extremely onerous display of grief for her husband." This behavior begins at the moment of his demise and continues for several months or even years. For the widower, the same applies but to a lesser degree. At death the widow utters the first piercing shriek to which the other women immediately respond. The hut is full of mourners with tears flowing from their eyes, mucus running from their noses, and all the liquids of grief carefully displayed and smeared over their bodies.

Abkhasians—The Long-Living People

Over 125,000 native Abkhasians live mostly in rural areas on the coast of the Black Sea in Abkhasia, a country about half the size of New Jersey. These people do not have a phrase for "old people" —those over 100 years of age are called "long-living people." Most of the aged work regularly performing light household tasks, working in the orchards and gardens and caring for the animals.

While a large percent of Abkhasians live a very long time, they also seem to be in fairly good health in their "old age." Close to 40 percent of the aged men (over 90) and 30 percent of aged women have good vision— do not need glasses for any sort of work. Nearly half have "reasonably good hearing." Most have their own teeth. Their posture is unusually erect.

Why do these people live so long? First, they have no retirement status but simply decrease their expected work load as they grow older. Second, they do not set deadlines for themselves, thus, no sense of urgency is accepted in emergencies. Third, overeating is considered dangerous; fat people are regarded as sick. When eating, they take small bites and chew slowly. This insures proper digestion. Leftovers are not eaten. Milk and vegetables make up 74 percent of their diet. The aged average 1900 calories per day — 500 less than the U.S. National Academy of Science recommends for those over 55. They do not use refined sugars; they drink water and honey before retiring in the evening. A fermented milk (like buttermilk) with a high food value and useful for intestinal disorders is drunk. They eat a lot of fruit. Meat is eaten only once or twice per week. They usually cook without salt or spices. A dry red wine not fortified with sugar and with a low alcohol content is drunk. Few of them smoke, and they do not drink coffee or tea. Their main meal is at lunch (between 2 and 3 p.m.), and their supper is light. Between meals they eat fruit or drink a glass of fermented milk. They have a relaxed mood at mealtimes and eat slowly. Fourth, stress is avoided by reducing competition. Fifth, they exercise daily. Sixth, their behavior is fairly uniform and predictable. Seventh and last, moderation is practiced in everything they do.

Much of the above is advice we have often heard but failed to put into practice. Perhaps we should adhere to some of the Abkhasians' practices. Who knows, we might even live longer—if that is a goal to be sought.

Source: Adapted from Sula Benet, *Abkhasians: The Long-Living People of the Caucasus.* New York: Holt, Rinehart and Winston, 1974.

Among the Abkhasians (Benet, 1974), the spouse, parent, or child of the deceased may not show grief at all, but everyone else cries, yells, and scratches cheeks and forehead. The women in particular may scratch their cheeks until the blood flows. Close relatives must wear black for forty days.

For some, mourning rituals are not so physically harmful. Among the Magars of Nepal (Hitchcock, 1966), close relatives segregate themselves for thirteen days. On the thirteenth day a Brahman places cow urine and offerings on a fire in order to remove pollution from family members.

Among the Tausug of the Philippines (Kiefer, 1972), there is no public expression of grief on the part of kinsmen and friends when death occurs. There may be some crying, but it is thought better not to do so. Burial usually takes place the afternoon following the day of death. Likewise, the Tewa Indians in Arizona (Dozier, 1966) practice no formal ceremonial wailing at the time of death, and the body is interred as quickly as possible. Sympathy is considered useless by the Semai of Malaya (Dentan, 1968), and mourners who break down and cry are ignored.

For the Ulithi in Micronesia (Lessa, 1966) the whole village observes a ten-day period of respect when a member dies. No one may laugh, shout, dance, wash too freely, or put on adornments. For close relatives, no sexual relations are allowed for "five lunar months." Furthermore, they are not allowed to enter the sacred garden or eat of food grown in it, nor may they enter the man's house. Men and women must also cut off all their hair.

In the United States some funeral directors have noted that occasionally individuals "carry on to the point of fainting" but catch themselves before completely "passing out" and hitting the floor. If such behavior is "expected" within the subculture, some will comply. However, a more stoic approach appears to be normative in the United States.

The "brave and stoic" response of Jacqueline Kennedy when President John F. Kennedy was shot in Dallas in 1963 was praised by the media—"She took it so well, never shedding a tear." Perhaps we Americans should not emulate such an extreme model. Males in particular tend to avoid any emotional display such as crying over a death. "Macho men" do not cry. However, we agree with Rosie Greer when he sings, "It's All Right to Cry." It's all right for girls, boys, women *and* men to cry.

One could argue that people cry at the time of a death because they are sad. Perhaps it is not as simple as that. Radcliffe-Brown (1964) notes two types of weeping. There is reciprocal ritual weeping that is "to affirm the existence of a social bond between two or more persons." It is an occasion for affirming social ties. Although participants may not actually feel these sentiments that bind them, participation in various rites will strengthen whatever positive feelings they do have. The second type of ceremonial weeping, where one cries over the remains of a significant other, expresses the continued sentiment of attachment despite the severing of this social bond.

Huntington and Metcalf (1979) note that the anthropologist Radcliffe-Brown was greatly influenced by the French sociologist Emile Durkheim. However, Durkheim must face the same difficulty that Radcliffe-Brown put aside, according to Huntington and Metcalf. One cannot assume that people actually feel the sorrow they express nor claim that ritual expression results from inner emotions. However, for these rites to fulfill their manifest social function, the acted sentiments must become real to the actors. While Radcliffe-Brown claimed that those participating in ceremonial weeping come to feel emotion which is not sorrow but togetherness, Durkheim (1954) argued that the emotions developed are feelings of sorrow and anger and are made stronger by participation in the burial rite. What Durkheim finds significant is the way that other members of society feel moral pressure to put their behavior in harmony with the feelings of the truly bereaved. Even if one feels no direct sorrow, weeping and suffering may result. Thus, to say that one weeps because of sadness may be too simplistic.

In conclusion, cross-cultural studies of bereavement reveal that mourning rituals tend to last for a set period of time—it may be a matter of days or months, but the time seems to be prescribed by the culture. We also discovered that a sexual double standard for mourning rituals seems to prevail among many of the cultures cited. While in many cases women are expected to react more by expressing extremely sorrowful emotions and by mutilating their bodies, cultural expectations for men are not nearly so exaggerated. Likewise in the United States, women are "expected" to display more of their emotions than men.

HANDLING THE CORPSE

As discussed in Chapter 11, when death occurs in the United States a professional is generally called to prepare the body for final disposition. When a mortuary is called, the body is taken away and not seen again until "prepared for viewing." The kin and friends normally play no significant role in handling the corpse. Compared with other societies, the United States is unique in the level of professional specialization relative to the preparation of the corpse and the actual disposal of the body. In contrast to the practices found in the United States, the cultures discussed in this section encourage families and friends to become very involved in corpse preparation.

For the Bornu of Nigeria (Cohen, 1967), when a death occurs family members and friends are required to wash the body, wrap it in a white cloth, place it on a bier, and take it to the burial ground. The Semai in Malaya (Dentan, 1968) have the housemates bathe the corpse and sprinkle it with perfume or sweet-smelling herbs to mask the odor of decay. It is then wrapped in swaddling.

At death the Mapuche Indians of Chile (Faron, 1968) lay the body out on a bier in the house after it has been washed and dressed in the deceased's best clothes. The kin then place the body in a pine coffin. Sometimes the body is smoked.

The Cheyenne Indians (Hoebel, 1960) dressed the body in its finest clothing and wrapped it in a number of robes. It was then referred to as the "burial bundle" and placed in a tree upon a scaffold, or covered over with rocks on the ground.

On the afternoon of a death the in-law relatives of the dead among the Kapauku Papuans of West New Guinea (Pospisil, 1963) usually bind the corpse by its arms and legs to a pole and carry it in a procession to the place of burial. The Qemant of Ethiopia (Gamst, 1969) wash the corpse. They close the eyes and mouth so that the face will have a "natural" appearance. The body is then placed on its back with the face up. Hands are tied to the front of the thighs with thumbs tied together. Big toes are also tied together. The corpse is then wrapped completely in a piece of white cloth and covered with a mat of woven grass.

Among a group in South Thailand (Fraser, 1966), the body is held and bathed using water specifically purified with herbs and clay. The corpse is then rinsed and dried, and all orifices are plugged with cotton.

The Tausug in the Phillippines (Kiefer, 1972) believe that the body is both physically and ritually polluting. They believe the corpse must be thoroughly cleansed by religious officials before interment. This is accomplished by a series of bathings in ritually prepared water. After defecation is removed from the anus and all body orifices cleaned and plugged with cotton, the body is dressed in a loosely fitting white shroud.

In the French West Indies (Horowitz, 1967) when an adult dies, the neighbors wash the body with rum, seal the orifices with small pieces of lime and force a liter or more of strong rum down the throat as a temporary preservative. The body is then dressed and laid out on a bed.

Jewish Group Buries Its Own

When a Jewish congregation here first began the practice of offering simple, inexpensive burials for its dead, some members were upset. But they now increasingly condone it.

Back in 1977, some people had felt it was barbaric when the body of a devout member, Al Sudit, 75, was lowered into his grave in a plain wooden box, with mourners themselves shoveling on the dirt.

But recently, when another respected member, Morris Weiner, 81, was given the same sort of elemental funeral, relatives say they neither sensed nor heard any criticism.

Rabbi Arnold M. Goodman, spiritual leader of Adath Jeshurun Congregation, says volunteers of its society to honor the dead—Chevra Kevod Hamet—now handle about half the funerals of members.

Goodman, recently elected president of the Rabbinical Assembly, representing the nation's 1,200 Conservative rabbis, regards his congregation as a pioneer in setting up a model for traditional, simplified funerals.

He says congregations in Highland Park, Ill., Portland, Ore., and Washington, D.C., have adapted the method for their own use. But some other rabbis remain dubious.

The Chevra was formed in 1976 after Goodman, in a sermon, dealt with the impact of American values upon the funeral practices of Jewry. He suggested a committee study the requirements of the Halacha, or Jewish law, for responding to death.

Months of study convinced committee members that a simple wood coffin should be used, the body should be washed in a ritual process called tahara and, because dust is to return to dust as quickly as possible, there should be no formaldehyde in the veins, no nails on the coffin.

The society decided to offer traditional funerals free to Adath Jeshurun members. The congregation provided seed money. Memorial donations and voluntary contributions from the bereaved are accepted.

Here's how the Chevra functions:

A congregation member signs a revokable agreement, asking for the Chevra's service when needed.

When death occurs, chaverim (friends) call on the family, aid in writing the obituary, explain death benefits, aid in other ways and remain available for help.

Chevra Kadisha (sacred society), people of the same sex as the deceased and usually five in number, wash the body at the mortuary while saying prayers. The body is dressed in a shroud sewn by Chevra members and placed in a wooden coffin.

Shomrin (guards) watch over the body, in blocks of two hours, until burial.

The coffin with rope handles is light enough to be borne by pallbearers, including women. Spurning mechanical contrivances, the pallbearers lower the coffin into the grave. Chaverim, the rabbi and cantor shovel in dirt. Family members may participate.

Judaism historically insists that the greatest commandment is to take personal involvement in burying the dead, Goodman says, but affluence enables people to pay surrogates to do it.

Goodman says a funeral costs the Chevra less than $500. A comparable no-frills funeral handled by professionals would cost about $1,500, says Elliot Pinck, a local funeral home director.

Source: Associated Press story in the *Rocky Mountain News* (Denver, Col.), June 25, 1982.

Zinacantecos of Mexico (Vogt, 1970) cover the face of the deceased. The corpse is then bathed and dressed by an older person and placed in a pine coffin with the head placed to the west. At the cemetery the coffin is set down while the grave is being dug. About every half hour, the deceased is given a drink of water to relieve thirst.

For the Dunsun of North Borneo (Williams, 1965), the face of the deceased is bathed at death, the hair is combed, and the best clothes are put on the body. The Yoruba of Nigeria (Bascom, 1969) bathe the corpse in soap and water, shave the head, and put clothes on backwards so the soul will know its way back to earth when time comes for it to be reborn. The Ulithi in Micronesia (Lessa, 1966) wash the corpse, cover it with tumeric (a tuberous plant), and decorate it with flower garlands around the head and hands.

The Konyak Nagar in India (Furer-Haimendorf, 1969) place the corpse on a bier. Six days after the funeral, the head of the corpse is wrenched from the body. The skull is cleaned by removing the remains of the decomposing brain. Then the skull is placed in an urn that has been hollowed from a block of sandstone. For three years the skull is given portions of food and beer whenever the kinsmen celebrate a feast. Other bones gradually fall to the ground as the bamboo platform disintegrates. Jungle growth soon covers the remains. The skull is important since it contained a portion of a dead person's soul.

The body is placed on its right side with hands under the head "as in a sleeping position," among the Dinka of the Sudan (Deng, 1972). They wash and anoint the body with oil, then lay it out facing east where the sun rises and life begins.

The Tiwi of Australia (Hart and Pilling, 1960) wrap the body in bark. Tewa Indians in Arizona (Dozier, 1966) bury a woman in her wedding outfit and wrap a man in a blanket for burial. The Barabaig of Tanzania (Klima, 1970) require the sons and wives to anoint the head with butter. Among the Dakota Indians (Habenstein and Lamers, 1963), women were assigned the task of preparing the body for burial by painting the face red, sometimes even before death.

For the Trobriand Islanders (Malinowski, 1929) the remains of the man are continually handled throughout the death ritual. His body is exhumed twice and cut up. Some of the bones are peeled out of the carcass, handled and given to different individuals. Regarding bone removal upon exhumation of the body, Malinowski (1929: 155–6) says, "I have seen the jawbone of a man with whom I had spoken a few days before dangling from the neck of his widow." The sons of the deceased are expected to suck some of the decaying matter when they are cleaning the bones. Speaking with pride they will say, "I have sucked the radius bone of my father." Prior to burial, the Trobriand Islanders wash the corpse and anoint and cover it with ornaments. Then the bodily openings are filled with coconut husk fiber, the legs are tied together, and the arms are bound to the sides. The corpse is fondled by stroking the skin with caressing hands, pressing valuable objects against the chest and abdomen, and moving the limbs slightly and agitating the head. The body is made to move and twist with slow and ghastly gestures to the rhythm of incessant wailing.

From the customs of groups cited above regarding corpse handling, it seems important that the body be cleaned prior to final disposition. Various steps are also taken to assure a tolerable odor. A reverence for the body seems common in most societies. As in the United States, it is important that the deceased look "good" to the mourners. Limited efforts are made by some groups for short-term preservation of the body prior to burial. Others go so far as to keep parts of the body for ornamental and serviceable purposes.

While in the United States the body is not exhumed to take various parts of the body home, some individuals have been known to keep the cremains (remains from cremation) in a vase in the home or carry them around in their purse. Some people in the United States take photographs of the deceased or collect important reminders of the deceased to be placed in a scrapbook or album. According to Tatelbaum (1980), keepsakes like photographs, clippings, and stories about the deceased can provide a satisfying memorial later on. She says we often fear we will not be able to remember the deceased distinctly enough, so we desire a "piece" of the person we loved—something solid and real.

BURIAL RITES

As noted in Chapter 6, Bronislaw Malinowski (1948) stressed the roles of religion and magic as means of reducing anxiety and fears; however, A. R. Radcliffe-Brown (1965) argued for a different interpretation. He suggested that rites may contribute to anxiety and insecurity. These are simply different explanations for the same rites. For one raised within the cultural tradition of a particular society, performance of the rite does relieve anxiety—it is the socially approved means of doing so, notes Kottak (1982). On the other hand, anxiety may result *because* the rite exists. A common stress may be produced by participation in the rite, thus enhancing the social solidarity of the participants.

While expressions of mourning vary with societies, different burial rites tend to be widespread among cultures. Types of final disposition of the body, place of disposal, importance of the status of the deceased, and depth of burial are examined in this section.

The Kalingas in the Philipines (Dozier, 1967) bury adults in six-feet deep and three-feet wide graves. The wealthy are buried in concrete tombs. Pierce (1964), in writing of a Turkish village, states that the grave is an uneven rectangular hole three feet deep. The body is removed from the wooden casket and lowered into the hole. The Mardudjara aborigines of Australia (Tonkinson, 1978) dig a rectangular hole about three feet deep, line the bottom with leafy bushes and small logs, then place the body inside.

For the Semai of Malaya (Dentan, 1968) the grave is dug some two to three feet deep. The body is placed in an east-west direction with the head in the west "where the sun dies." The Dunsun of North Borneo (Williams, 1965) bury the corpse in an earthenware jar that is two feet at the mouth, three feet at the midsection and between four and six feet high.

The grave for the Lugbara of Uganda (Middleton, 1965) is not important as such and is soon forgotten. An adult man is buried inside his first wife's hut in the center of the floor. The grave is from four to six feet deep. The corpse is placed with legs straight and the right hand under the head. Elders and very senior women are buried outside the huts "because they are big" and thus feared.

Yoruba of Nigeria (Bascom, 1969) dig the grave in the room of the deceased. Some dirt is saved for creditors who claim debts owed by the deceased. If debts are not common knowledge, creditors are made to eat dirt while taking an oath that debts are legitimate.

At death the Huron (Trigger, 1969) would put the body in a crouching position and bury it after waiting three days. The Tiwi of Australia (Hart and Pilling, 1960) bury the corpse within twenty-four hours of death by digging a hole near the camp where the death had occurred and place the body in it. Seldom is the body carried any distance for burial. Normally, one is buried within a hundred yards of where death has occurred.

The Swazi of Africa (Kuper, 1963) bury the woman on the outskirts of her husband's home. For the Qemant of Ethiopia (Gamst, 1969) burial is usually on the same day of death. The body is buried in a shallow grave, placed on its right side with the soles of the feet facing toward the east. The corpse is now "facing east"—the direction faced when praying. In South Thailand, Fraser (1966) notes that one is buried in a coffin in a shallow grave in the village burial ground.

Among the Kapauku Papuans of West New Guinea (Pospisil, 1963), burial customs are determined by the deceased's status and cause of the death. The simplest burial of all is given to a drowned man. The corpse is laid flat on the bank of the river, a protective fence is erected around it, and the body abandoned to the elements. Very young children and individuals who were not particularly liked and were considered unimportant during their lives are completely interred. Children, women, and old people who were considered unimportant, but were loved, are tied with vines into a squatting position and are semi-interred with the head above ground. A dome-shaped structure of branches and soil is then constructed to protect the head. A window is left open in the dome in front of the face of the deceased to induce its soul to become a guardian spirit for the surviving relatives.

Pospisil (1963) continues by saying an adult man who was loved and respected receives a respectable tree burial. Tied in a squatting position, the corpse is placed in a tree house with a small window in front. Corpses of important individuals, of whom their relatives are afraid, and of women who died in childbirth, require a special type of burial. The bodies are placed in the squatting position on a special raised scaffold constructed in the house where death occurred. The house is then sealed and abandoned.

According to Pospisil (1963), the Kapauku Papuans give the most elaborate burial to a rich headman. A special hut is built on high stilts. The body is tied in a squatting position and a pointed pole driven through the rectum, abdomen, chest cavity and neck with its pointed end supporting the base of the skull. Then the body is placed in the dead house with the face appearing in the front window of the structure. The cadaver is pierced several times with arrows in order to allow the body fluids to drain away. Years later, the skull of the respected man may be cleaned and awarded a second honor of being placed on a pole that is driven into the ground near the house of the surviving relatives.

Not everyone among the Barabaig of Tanzania (Klima, 1970) is entitled to a burial. A council of neighborhood men decide the method by which the body will be disposed. At death, most women and all children are placed out in the surrounding bush where they are consumed by the hyena. Only certain male and female elders will receive a burial.

While the corpse remains unburied in its hut, deliberations on the possibility of a burial may last a week. If the decision is favorable, a hole five feet deep is dug in the cattle coral of the deceased's homestead. A black ox is sacrificed and the skin is used as a shroud for the body. Then, the corpse is placed in a sitting position with the head protruding through the opening in the shroud. The body is placed facing east and the hole is filled with dirt. A mound made of mud, cow dung, and four-feet-high poles is built over the grave. Layers are added over time producing a cone-shaped mound some twelve feet high, eight feet wide at the base and three feet wide at the top.

If a Yanomamo Indian in Venezuela or Brazil dies in an epidemic (Chagnon, 1983), the body is placed on a tree platform and allowed to decay. After several months, an old man is appointed to strip the remaining decayed flesh from the bones. These remaining bones are then cremated.

Under normal circumstances, the body of a deceased Yanomamo is placed on a pyre of logs, covered with additional wood and allowed to burn until nothing but the large bones are left. After the coals are cool enough to handle, the relatives sift the ashes meticulously with shallow, loosely woven baskets, collecting every bit of bone they can find. The bones are crushed into a black powder by a young man. The ashes, mixed with boiled plantain soup, are eaten during a feast. Prior to a raid to seek revenge from a previous killing, the raiders eat the ashes of their slain kinsmen to put them in the appropriate state of rage for killing the enemy. This "endocannibalism" is the supreme form of displaying friendship and solidarity for the Yanomamo.

Yanomamo—The Fierce People

Approximately 12,000 Yanomamo Indians live in Venezuela and Brazil in South America. They live in villages ranging in size from 40 to 250 inhabitants. The Yanomamo are horticulturalists and grow 85 percent of their food. For delicacies they occasionally enjoy caterpillars, roasted spiders, and armadillos.

The Yanomamo are very aggressive and fierce persons. They live in a state of chronic warfare and believe it is the "nature of men to fight." Because they define themselves as fierce, they act accordingly. The "fierceness" of the Yanomamo is exemplified by their gruesome methods of infanticide and abortion; their planned raiding parties where the men are killed and women raped and brought back as wives in some cases; their "games" of chest pounding, side slapping, club pounding and ax fights played at village feasts; their chopping with machetes the heads of their wives and sometimes cutting off an ear to "show their love"; and 24 percent of adult males dying in warfare.

Women are not held in very high esteem among the Yanomamo. While men do the heavier ground-breaking duties in the gardens with their dibbles (digging sticks), the women perform the bulk of garden work. Men almost daily get high on hallucinogenic drugs shot into their nostrils in a powdery form. Though side effects of this drug are vomiting, runny nose, and watery eyes, the men have contact with the deceased ancestors while on the drug. They lie in their hammocks while the women till the gardens. Husbands frequently beat their wives. Brothers will trade their sisters to other groups of brothers for wives for themselves.

In the United States we are very competitive and aggressive. Indeed, a characteristic of middle-class Americans is aggression. We have a reputation of high crime and violence rates and of being very competitive economically. While not like the Yanomamo, the United States would fall closer to the Yanomamo on a continuum with aggressive behavior at one end and passive behavior at the other.

Source: Adapted from Napoleon A. Chagnon, *Yanomamo: The Fierce People*, 3rd ed. New York: Holt, Rinehart and Winston, 1983.

In order to avoid the ritual of a funeral the Ik of Uganda (Turnbull, 1972) would hastily stick the deceased in the ground to avoid any fuss. Since they are at a near starvation level of existence and since a ritual feast is supposed to occur at death, they are quick to dispose of the body due to their having no surplus with which to give a feast. A funeral was said to be a nuisance to everyone and "made everyone upset with all the crying and wailing."

For the Abkhasians near the Black Sea (Benet, 1974), one must be buried "as soon as possible" after death. The neighbors build the coffin, dig the grave, prepare and serve food for the guests, and contribute to the funeral expenses. Women are buried ten centimeters deeper than men.

Thus, in death as in life, one's social status affects how one is treated. Whether one is buried or left to the elements is often determined by sex, age, socioeconomic status, and cause of death. Where one's remains are placed varies with cultures, but it is largely determined by the social status of the deceased. If one is buried underground, even the depth of burial may vary by one's social position.

Burying the deceased in an east-west direction is noted in several societies cited above. The same is practiced in the United States. Several years ago, an 86-year old woman called me requesting an appointment to discuss cremation. I went to the nursing home where she resided and learned of her desire to be buried on the family plot with her parents. However, the only space available was at their "feet" in a north-south direction. She was told that burial could only be in an east-west direction in that cemetery—thus, her desire to learn about cremation. Direction of placement is not important with cremation!

FUNCTIONS OF BURIAL RITES

The term "function" refers to the extent to which some part or process of a social system contributes to the maintenance of that system. Function means the extent to which a given activity promotes or interferes with the maintenance of a system (Cuzzort and King, 1980:172). Merton (1957) distinguishes between two forms of social function. "Manifest functions" are objective consequences for the person, subgroup or social system that contribute to its adjustment and were so intended. "Latent functions" are consequences that contribute to adjustment but were not so intended. Manifest functions are the official explanations of a given action; latent functions are the sociological explanations.

Why have a ceremony following the death of a significant other? Why not leave all corpses to the elements? Obviously, an event like a funeral must have some positive consequences for the survivors of the deceased. The following customs selected from various cultures around the world illustrate such positive functions.

For the Mapuche Indians of Chile (Faron, 1968), the ritual of the dead is to maintain ancestral spirits. Among the Qemant of Ethiopia (Gamst, 1969) death requires two observances. The first is to usher the deceased out of human society; the second is to send the soul to the other world.

Japanese (Norbeck, 1965) funerals are a mixture of joy and sadness. Commemorative services for the dead hold more joy than sadness as women work hard to feed and care for the guests. A funeral—referred to as "Grandchildren's New Year"—is fun even for the small children, because it is a wholly pleasurable time of good food and play with other children. Likewise, for the Yoruba of Nigeria (Bascom, 1969) funerals bring relatives and friends together in a mood that is festive rather than mournful.

The idea that it is the duty of the widow and relatives to show grief and perform all the funeral services emphasizes the strength and permanence of marriage bonds as viewed by the traditions of the Trobriand Islanders (Malinowski, 1929). Horowitz (1967) notes that since Radcliffe-Brown and Malinowski, the main social significance for death rituals has been the reaffirmation of group structure and social cohesiveness of the individuals suffering loss.

According to Williams (1981), funerals among the lower class in Pittsburgh, Pennsylvania tend to be rites of intensification and solidarity. Petty squabbles and large feuds are put aside for the funeral ceremony and the rituals which follow. A middle-class funeral is designed to establish, validate and reinforce social status.

Since appeasement of the deceased's spirits is a manifest function of burial rituals, what are some of the practices involved in this appeasement? When one dies among the Swazi in Africa (Kuper, 1963), both flesh and spirit must be correctly treated to safeguard the living from attacks from beings in the spirit world. In the Philippines, the Kalinga (Dozier, 1967) have a wake and offer sacrifices to honor the spirit of the deceased and ask that misfortune and illness not be brought to the living.

In Southwestern Nigeria the Yoruba (Bascom, 1969) have a man with a live chicken precede the carrier of the corpse. He plucks out feathers along the trail so the soul of the deceased can follow them back to town. When they reach the town gate, the chicken is killed by striking its head against the ground and left there. If a coffin is not used, the blood and feathers of a chicken are placed in the grave so that others will not die. Another chicken is also killed and its blood put in the grave so that the soul of the deceased will not bother the surviving relatives.

Many of the funeral rituals are to insure that the deceased will be reborn again. For the Dunsun of North Borneo (Williams, 1965) animals are killed to accompany the deceased on the trip to the land of the dead. The Ulithi in Micronesia (Lessa, 1966) place a loincloth and turmeric (a gingerlike plant) in the right arm of the deceased so that gifts can be presented to the custodian at the entrance of the other world. Chickens are used by the Zinacantecos of Mexico (Vogt, 1970). A chicken head is put in a bowl of broth beside the head of the corpse. The chicken allegedly leads the "inner soul" of the deceased. A black dog carries the "soul" across the river, and tortillas compensate the dog.

The Washo Indians of California and Nevada (Downs, 1966) feared and avoided the spirits of the dead. They made sure the dead person's spirit would not return by burning or abandoning the home and by burning or burying the clothing and personal property. A taboo existed for using the name of the deceased. Child-raising practices were also affected by beliefs in ghosts. Parents avoided striking or spanking a child for fear of angering some dead relative.

In the United States some Appalachians build soul houses (Gaines, 1981). These little houses were placed directly over the grave. They were meant to provide added protection for the deceased from evil spirits, wild animals, grave robbers, and other unwelcome visitors. Some soul houses are rock piles, others are box-shaped concrete slabs, while others have rooftop structures. The most elaborate of the soul houses are miniature homes with actual tin roofs and gutters, drainpipes, carpets, furniture, and various objects dear to the deceased.

Thus, burial rituals serve the functions of maintaining relations with ancestral spirits, reaffirming social solidarity, and restoring group structures dismembered by the death. Whereas maintaining relations with ancestral spirits is a manifest function of burial rites, the other social benefits appear to be latent functions. Burial rituals provide individuals with the opportunity of paying respect to the deceased while showing concern for those who are bereaved. As noted above, funerals are family reunions—bringing together the kin network under amicable circumstances. Thus, funerals not only reaffirm group structure, but enhance social cohesiveness.

CONCLUSION

As discussed in Chapter 2, dying is more than a biological process. One does not die in a vacuum but in a social milieu. An act of dying has an influence on others because it is a shared social experience. The sharing mechanism is death-related meanings composed of symbols.

Since death meanings are socially constructed, patterns of "correct" or "incorrect" behavior related to dying and death will largely be determined within the social setting in which it occurs. Death-related behavior of the dying person and of those relating to him or her is in response to meaning, relative to the audience and the situation. As noted, death-related behavior is shared, symboled, and situated.

Since death generally disrupts established interaction networks, shared "scripts" aid in providing socially acceptable behavior for the bereaved. Such "scripts" are essential because they prevent societal breakdowns while providing social continuity. Burial rituals are important in assuring social cohesion at the time of family dismemberment through death. Since death is a family crisis (see Dickinson and Fritz, 1981), appropriate networks for coping must be culturally well grounded.

Death-related meanings are socially created and transmitted. Through participant observation, small children learn from others how to respond to death. If children are sheltered from such situations, their socialization will be thwarted. As noted in this chapter, family involvement plays an important role in most societies as individuals prepare for death, as they prepare the corpse for final disposition, and in funeral rituals which follow. Therefore, whether death rituals involved killing a chicken, scraping the meat from the bones of the corpse, crying quietly, wailing loudly, mutilating one's own body, and/or burying or burning the corpse, all bereavement behavior has three interconnected characteristics—it is shared, symboled, and situated.

Summary

1. Customs for caring for the dying prior to death assist both the dying individual and the survivors in coping with the impending death.
2. Death for some is viewed as the end, while for others it is viewed as a continuation of life in a different form.
3. While mourning rituals tend to be commonplace with different cultures, the prescribed behavior is effected by the social status and sex of the individuals involved.
4. Some social groups mourn for a few hours after death while others mourn for months or years.
5. The depth of burial often varies by the sex and socioeconomic status of the deceased.
6. Burial rituals serve the functions of appeasing the ancestral spirits and the soul of the deceased, bringing the kin together, reinforcing social status, and restoring the social structure of the group.
7. In most societies, the body of the deceased is cleaned and prepared for burial. Some groups even keep parts of the body—like a bone—for ornamental or special purposes.

APPLICATION: A LOCAL STUDY OF CROSS-CULTURAL PATTERNS OF BEREAVEMENT BEHAVIOR

This chapter has presented numerous examples of bereavement patterns of various cultures. While some may have appeared bizarre to you, others probably reminded you of familiar customs. With limited funding at most colleges and universities today, a field trip to various countries to "check out" some of the death practices cited here would be out of the question; however, there are very likely sources of information (other than the library) nearer than you might think.

Take advantage of the situation on your campus of the wealth of information to be gained from international students. While most of us enjoy talking about ourselves, we especially like it if someone is showing enough interest to ask us questions about ourselves! Interview students on your campus from selected countries regarding their death customs. (If you have a limited number of students from other countries on your campus, you might want to interview students who differ from you in their ethnic backgrounds—e.g., blacks, Jews, Mexican-Americans, and Native Americans.) While such an exercise will not only enhance your firsthand knowledge of other cultures, it will give you an "excuse" to become acquainted with other individuals.

You might wish to construct an interview schedule to follow in talking to these students. Not only should you inquire about their own death customs, but obtain their impressions of such customs in the United States. Remember, while you may have had strong reactions to some examples of death behavior cited in this chapter, international students in the United States may likewise respond to some of our death practices.

Briefly explain to the student your desire to learn about death behavior in different cultures. Then from your interview schedule ask open-ended questions regarding some of the topics in this chapter. Make notes on the interview schedule as the respondent answers the questions.

After you have interviewed several students, note if differences in responses varied by sex and by regions of the world. While your sample of students may not be large enough to draw conclusive evidence, you may be able to see some patterns of similarity in their responses. Especially look for patterns in their views of death customs in the United States.

Compare your findings with those in this chapter. Do you conclude that cross-cultural patterns of death customs are basically more similar to each other or different from each other?

Discussion Questions

1. Why is it important to learn about bereavement patterns in other cultures?
2. Cite as many death custom similarities between other cultures and the United States as you can. Cite death custom differences between other cultures and the United States.
3. What is your own concept of "soul"? How is your concept of soul similar to and different from some other cultures' soul concept? How does a concept of "soul" relate to death?
4. Discuss any United States customs for the dying just prior to death with which you are familiar. How do these customs compare to those cited in this chapter?

5. Describe mourning rituals commonly found in the United States. Mourning rituals may differ by region of the country or ethnicity. Discuss these differences.
6. It is suggested that an explanation of crying at the time of death may be rather complex. Discuss the "why" of crying over a death.
7. While in the United States a professional generally prepares the corpse for final disposition, this is not universally true. Discuss the importance of the family being involved in preparing the body for final disposition.
8. Observe the layout of a cemetery near you. Are the graves in an east-west direction as is indicated in this chapter? How is religion related to this idea of direction in burial both among Americans and other groups cited here?
9. In death as in life sexual discrimination occurs. Discuss with a local funeral home director the differences in funerals for males and females. Do you notice discrepancies in grave markings (e.g., size of stone, epitaphs) between males and females?
10. Unlike many societies where squatting occurs, in the United States we basically give birth and bury in a horizontal position. Why do you suppose the United States has a "laid-back" approach from the womb to the tomb? Can you cite advantages and disadvantages to horizontal burials?
11. What are some of the functions of burial rites noted in this chapter?

Glossary

BIER: A framework upon which the corpse and/or coffin is placed for viewing and/or carrying.

CADAVER: A dead human or animal body usually intended for dissection.

ETHNOCENTRISM: (Culture-centeredness) Judging the cultural customs of another culture in terms of one's own cultural standards.

EXHUME: To remove a corpse from its place of burial.

INTERMENT: The act of depositing a corpse in a grave or tomb.

LATENT FUNCTION: Consequences of behavior that were not intended (e.g., a funeral brings the family together usually in an amiable way).

LEVIRATE: A marriage rule whereby a widow marries her deceased husband's brother.

LINEAGE: A group of relatives who trace their descent unilineally from a common ancestor.

MANIFEST FUNCTION: Consequences of behavior which are intended and overt (e.g., going to a funeral to pay respects to the deceased).

PYRE: A combustible pile (usually of wood) for burning a corpse at a funeral rite.

RITES OF PASSAGE: Ceremonies centering around transitions in life from one status to another (e.g., baptism, marriage ceremony, and the funeral).

References

Bascom, William. 1969. *The Yoruba of Southwestern Nigeria*. New York: Holt, Rinehart and Winston.

Bendann, Effie. 1930. *Death Customs: An Analytical Study of Burial Rites*. New York: Alfred A. Knopf.

Benedict, Ruth. 1934. *Patterns of Culture*. Boston: Houghton Mifflin.

Benet, Sula. 1974. *Abkhasians: The Long-Living People of Caucasus*. New York: Holt, Rinehart and Winston.

Chagnon, Napoleon A. 1983. *Yanomamo: The Fierce People*. 3d ed. New York: Holt, Rinehart and Winston.

Cohen, Ronald. 1967. *The Kanuri of Bornu*. New York: Holt, Rinehart and Winston.

Cuzzort, Ray P. and Edith W. King. 1980. *Twentieth Century Social Thought*. 3d ed. New York: Holt, Rinehart and Winston.

Deng, Francis M. 1972. *The Dinka of the Sudan*. New York: Holt, Rinehart and Winston.

Dentan, Robert K. 1968. *The Semai: A Non-Violent People of Malaya*. New York: Holt, Rinehart and Winston.

Dickinson, George E., and Judy L. Fritz. 1981. "Death in the Family." *Journal of Family Issues* Volume 2 (September):379–384.

Downs, James F. 1966. *The Two Worlds of the Washo: An Indian Tribe of California and Nevada*. New York: Holt, Rinehart and Winston.

Dozier, Edward P. 1966. *Hano: A Tewa Indian Community in Arizona*. New York: Holt, Rinehart and Winston.

Dozier, Edward P. 1967. *The Kalinga of Northern Luzon, Philippines*. New York: Holt, Rinehart and Winston.

Durkheim, Emile. 1954. *The Elementary Forms of the Religious Life*. New York: The Free Press.

Faron, Lovis C. 1968. *The Mapuche Indians of Chile*. New York: Holt, Rinehart and Winston.

Fraser, Thomas M. Jr. 1966. *Fishermen of South Thailand: The Malay Villagers*. New York: Holt, Rinehart and Winston.

Furer-Haimendorf, Christoph Von. 1969. *The Konyak Nagar: An Indian Frontier Tribe*. New York: Holt, Rinehart and Winston.

Gaines, Judith. 1981. "Appalachia Comes Alive in Studying Tombstones." *Louisville* (Ky.) *Courier-Journal*, November 1, p. 5.

Gamst, Frederick C. 1969. *The Qemant: A Pagan-Hebraic Peasantry of Ethiopia*. New York: Holt Rinehart and Winston.

Habenstein, Robert W., and William M. Lamers. 1963. *Funeral Customs the World Over*. Milwaukee: Bulfin Printers, Inc.

Harris, Marvin. 1974. *Cows, Pigs, Wars and Witches*. New York: Vintage Books.

Hart, C.W.M., and Arnold R. Pilling. 1960. *The Tiwi of North Australia*. New York: Holt, Rinehart and Winston.

Hitchcock, John T. 1966. *The Magars of Manyan Hill*. New York: Holt, Rinehart and Winston.

Hoebel, E. Adamson. 1960. *The Cheyennes: Indians of the Great Plains*. New York: Holt, Rinehart and Winston.

Horowitz, Michael M. 1967. *Morne-Paysan: Peasant Village in Martinique*. New York: Holt, Rinehart and Winston.

Huntington, Richard and Peter Metcalf. 1979. *Celebrations of Death*. Cambridge, Eng.: Cambridge University Press.

Kiefer, Thomas M. 1972. *The Tausug: Violence and Law in a Philippine Moslem Society*. New York: Holt, Rinehart and Winston.

Kottak, Conrad Phillip. 1982. *Cultural Anthropology* 3d ed. New York: Random House.

Klima, George J. 1970. *The Barabaig: East African Cattle-Herders*. New York: Holt, Rinehart and Winston.

Kuper, Hilda. 1963. *The Swazi: A South African Kingdom*. New York: Holt, Rinehart and Winston.

Lessa, William A. 1966. *Ulithi: A Micronesian Design for Living*. New York: Holt, Rinehart and Winston.

Malinowski, Bronislaw. 1929. *The Sexual Life of Savages*. New York: Harcourt, Brace and World.

Malinowski, Bronislaw. 1948. *Magic, Science and Religion, and Other Essays*. Boston: Beacon Press.

Merton, Robert K. 1957. *Social Theory and Social Structure, Revised Edition*. New York: The Free Press.

Middleton, John. 1965. *The Lugbara of Uganda*. New York: Holt, Rinehart and Winston.

Norbeck, Edward. 1965. *Changing Japan*. New York: Holt, Rinehart and Winston.

Pierce, Joe E. 1964. *Life in a Turkish Village*. New York: Holt, Rinehart and Winston.

Pospisil, Leopold. 1963. *The Kapauku Papuans of West New Guinea*. New York: Holt, Rinehart and Winston.

Radcliffe-Brown, A. R. 1964. *The Andaman Islanders*. New York: The Free Press.

Radcliffe-Brown, A. R. 1965. *Structure and Function in Primitive Society*. New York: The Free Press.

Rappaport, Roy A. 1974. "Obvious Aspects of Ritual." *Cambridge Anthropology*. Vol. 2, pp. 2–60.

Tatelbaum, Judy. 1980. *The Courage to Grieve*. New York: Lippincott and Crowell, Publishers.

Taylor, Robert B. 1980. *Cultural Ways* 3d ed. Boston: Allyn and Bacon, Inc.

Tonkinson, Robert. 1978. *The Mardudjara Aborigines*. New York: Holt, Rinehart and Winston.

Trigger, Bruce G. 1969. *The Huron: Farmers of the North*. New York: Holt, Rinehart and Winston.

Turnbull, Colin M. 1972. *The Mountain People*. New York: Simon and Schuster.

Tylor, E. B. 1873. *Primitive Culture: Researches into the Development of Mythology, Philosophy, Religion, Language, Art and Custom* 2d ed. Vol. 2. London: John Murray.

Uchendu, Victor C. 1965. *The Igbo of Southeast Nigeria*. New York: Holt, Rinehart and Winston.

Vogt, Evon Z. 1970. *The Zinacantecos of Mexico: A Modern Maya Way of Life*. New York: Holt, Rinehart and Winston.

Williams, Melvin D. 1981. *On the Street Where I Lived*. New York: Holt, Rinehart and Winston.

Williams, Thomas R. 1965. *The Dunsun: A North Borneo Society.* New York: Holt, Rinehart and Winston.

Suggested Readings

Bendann, Effie. 1930. *Death Customs: An Analytical Study of Burial Rites.* New York: Alfred A. Knopf.
    A thorough anthropological analysis of death customs—including an analysis of burial rites, causes of death, attitudes toward the corpse, mourning, and beliefs in the afterlife.
Habenstein, Robert W. and William M. Lamers. 1963. *Funeral Customs the World Over.* Milwaukee: Bulfin Printers, Inc.
    A review of the cultures of the world especially significant to assist in a cross-cultural study of the various practices of funeralization in all cultures, including those of Eastern and Western origins.
Huntington, Richard, and Peter Metcalf. 1979. *Celebrations of Death: The Anthropology of Mortuary Ritual.* New York: Cambridge University Press.
    An excellent anthropological analysis of dying and death.
Kalish, Richard A. 1980. *Death and Dying: Views from Many Cultures.* Farmingdale, N.Y.: Baywood Publishing Co.
    A discussion of death customs among groups in such areas as Finland, New Guinea, India, Melanesia, and the United States.
Stannard, David E. 1977. *The Puritan Way of Death.* New York: Oxford University Press.
    A portrayal of death in the Western tradition including discussions of death, childhood, and burial.

Chapter 10

THE HISTORY OF BEREAVEMENT AND BURIAL PRACTICES IN AMERICAN CULTURE

As long as the cemetery is being filled with a fresh stream of the recently dead, it stays symbolically a live and vital emblem, telling the living of the meaning of life and death.

W. Lloyd Warner, The Living and the Dead

THIS CHAPTER TRACES the development of bereavement practices in America from the Puritans to the present. As death bereaves family members, friends, and more distant relatives, the survivors generally follow established rituals to care for the corpse, to reaffirm the solidarity of important groups, to create a new status for the dead person, and to comfort each other in such a way that they can eventually resume their roles in society. These established rituals were established in time, and come to us from the past. Therefore, we need an historical explanation to fully understand them.

We deal with historical explanations every day, but we seldom consider what constitutes an historical explanation. Historians mainly determine chronology and context in order to demonstrate causation and coincidence in human affairs. We begin with chronology in order to determine the order in which events or processes occurred. This in itself has a certain explanatory value; for example, it is useful to know that discovery of the germ theory of disease preceded the widespread use of embalming in America. Too often, however, history begins and ends with chronology, and students are stuck with memorizing names and dates. History also explores the context of events to help explain them. For example, it is easier to understand the development of the funeral parlor if we see it in the context of developments in the domestic parlor.

Sometimes, historians can use chronology and context to determine causation. Knowing, for example that rural cemeteries preceded the public parks movement in America, we might conclude that cemetery reforms caused the parks movement. More frequently, however, chronology and context allow us only to identify coincidences (events or processes that occurred during the same period of time). Especially in social and cultural history, this chronicle of coincidences is crucial because people think analogically as much as they think logically. They do not isolate problems or ideas when they are faced with them; instead their whole range of prior experience affects their decision. In evaluating embalming, for example, few people treated the preservation of the corpse as a discrete issue. Instead, it coincided with other issues like the importance of appearances in a consumer culture, the sanitary movement, the germ theory of disease, the privacy of the home, a stress on the "natural," a respect for surgery and surgeons, and the need to delay many funerals for distant relatives to return home.

Historians, who use chronology and context to determine causation and coincidence, inevitably find complexity. "There is" says Charles Rosenberg (1966:162), "an aesthetic of complexity in history."

In viewing the history of bereavement, it is assumed that bereavement is but one part of a social construction of reality that changes through time. Bereavement practices are virtually inseparable from prescriptions for dying and descriptions of death, just as the whole American way of death is inseparable from the American way of life. Therefore, this chapter explains how changes in the American way of life brought changes in the American way of death and bereavement. It traces the historical roots of our bereavement practices so that we can begin to trace the routes of future change.

LIVING DEATH, 1600–1830

The Reformed Tradition

Between 1600 and 1830, death was a living part of the American experience. Most people in this primarily agricultural period were well acquainted with death. In New England towns, for example, if people escaped death in their own homes, they still heard the toll of the funeral bell, encountered the funeral procession winding through the streets, or saw the stark "memento mori" of the graveyard. Even more, death was highlighted by the intellectual and emotional framework of the Reformed Tradition.

The Reformed Tradition was the one part of the Protestant Reformation that most influenced colonial Americans. Although most colonists followed the beliefs of the Reformers, the New England Puritans made the most convincing synthesis of their ideas and attitudes. In their view, a sovereign God ruled over an earth inhabited by depraved people. God displayed his sovereignty in "special providences" in which He intervened in the natural or social world. One such providence was death.

Because of original sin and their own sinfulness, Puritans knew they deserved death and damnation. They also celebrated, however, the fact that God freely elected a select few for salvation. Therefore, they approached death with an amazing ambivalence. They believed that "the last Enemy was Death; and God had made that a friend too" (Sewall, 1973:1,599). Death was an enemy because of the pain, because it was a punishment for sin, because it was a possible prelude to everlasting hellfire, and because it meant separation from loved ones. Death was a friend, however, because it ended the pain and the earthly pilgrimage of the deceased, because it could serve as a "sanctified affliction" (Geddes, 1981:31)—either confirming a saint's faith or converting a sinner—and because it might open the gates to Heaven. Indeed, it was both a friendly enemy and a fearful friend.

Unlike modern thanatologists, the Puritans encouraged each other to fear death. They increasingly used that strong human emotion to rouse people from their psychological and spiritual security. Puritans knew *that* they would die, but not *when* they would die, or if they were among the elect. Therefore, they admonished themselves and each other to be constantly prepared for death. "It will do you no hurt. You will Dy not One Minute the sooner for it," argued Cotton Mather, "and being fit to Dy, you will be the more Fit to Live" (Geddes, 1981:64–65). Over and over again, they prayed, "Lord, help me to redeem the time!" Like modern thanatologists, they felt an awareness of death could improve the quality of their lives, and that they had a role to play in the work of God's redemption. Indeed, for them, dying, death and bereavement were opportunities to glorify God by demonstrating human dependence on divine providence.

The deathbed was the final place of preparation. Dying Puritans received visitors who wanted to help provide "a lift towards heaven." Unlike Catholics, who relied on the sacramental rite of extreme unction, the Puritans focused on the state of the dying person's soul and mind. They prayed together, read the Bible, and urged active acceptance of the will of God.

In the same way, "the funeral was another opportunity for the bereaved to turn affliction into spiritual growth through resignation to, and joyful acceptance of, the will of God" (Geddes, 1981:104). Most Puritan deaths occurred at home. The family sent out for midwife-nurses to care for the corpse, ordered a coffin, and notified friends and relatives not already present. Puritans considered the corpse a mere shell of the soul. They simply washed it, wrapped it in a shroud, and placed it in the coffin. They embalmed bodies only to transport them to other towns for burial, or to prevent an offensive stench in hot weather.

Friends and relatives visited the home to console and congratulate the bereaved. They brought gifts of food to allow the survivors to mourn and to prepare the funeral. In this way, as in their own participation in the funeral, they reaffirmed the solidarity of the covenanted community. The funeral itself usually took place within a few days of death, and it followed the simple guidelines of the 1644 Westminister Confession: "When any person departeth this life, let the dead body, upon the day of Buriall, be decently attended from the house to the place appointed for publique Buriall, and there immediately interred, without any ceremony" (Geddes, 1981:110–124).

Pallbearers, ministers, and civil officials were commonly invited to a funeral with a gift of gloves. Wealthier families might also bestow scarves and/or memorial rings, and give gloves to anyone who marched in the procession. These items were the common symbols of mourning in colonial society, but more elaborate mourning apparel was also available. The tolling of the town bell announced the onset of a funeral, and participants gathered at the home for prayer and the procession.

Puritans prayed not for the soul of the deceased but for the comfort and instruction of the living. They believed that judgement occurred at death and that the dead were beyond human aid, so they prayed to reaffirm their faith and to glorify their God. For example, upon the death of his two-year-old daughter, Samuel Sewall had his surviving children read passages from the Bible. John read Ecclesiastes 3 on the acceptance of the seasons of life, Elizabeth read Revelation 22 on the theme of hope, Hannah read Psalm 38 on the mercy of God, and young Samuel asked for God's comfort in Psalm 102 (Sewell, 1973:1,364). In addition to prayers, Puritans might also read an elegy, which generally depicted the dead person as a saint freed from the world and entering eternal bliss. Such elegies confirmed the new, separate status of the deceased, helping to bring grief under control, and provided a good example for structuring life after bereavement. Sometimes a copy of the elegy was pinned to the coffin or hearse for the funeral procession (Geddes, 1981:130–131).

The mourners walked from the home to the graveyard, where the men of the family, or the sexton, had opened a grave. They carried the coffin on a bier, covered with a black cloth "pall"—both of which were the property of the town instead of the church, as was the custom in England. During the procession, mourners were supposed to "apply themselves to mediations and conferences suitable to the occasion." At the gravesite, the pallbearers lowered the coffin into the earth, and the grave was refilled (Geddes, 1981:111,133–135).

After the burial, the mourners returned home where they shared food, drink, prayers, and comforting words. The family thanked the pallbearers and participants, and sometimes gave additional presents. They might also request the minister to deliver a funeral sermon, which would occur not on the day of burial, but at the next regular meeting of the congregation. Sometimes families had such sermons and/or the elegies published and distributed to friends as "memento mori." At a later date, the family might also erect a marker over the grave to proclaim the imminence of death or God's promise of salvation. Such markers near the much-frequented meetinghouse were another way of maintaining the vitality of death in early American culture (Geddes, 1981:139–140; Ludwig, 1966).

The Puritan funeral was the primary social institution for channeling the grief of survivors. It provided for the disposition of the body and the acknowledgement of the absence of the deceased. It drew the community together for mutual comfort, and it allowed mourners to honor the dead, to express their sorrow at separation, and to demonstrate their acceptance of God's will. After the funeral, Puritans expected mourners to return to their calling and to resume their life's work. They did not approve elaborate or extended mourning of the sort that became customary in the nineteenth century because it undermined the cheerful resignation to God's will that was essential to the Puritan experience.

Reforming the Reformed Tradition

In 1802, Nathaniel Emmons delivered a magnificent funeral sermon called "Death without Order." In it, he reviewed the Puritan orthodoxy about death, observing that "in relation to God, death is perfectly regular; but this regularity he has seen proper to conceal from the view of men." Emmons saw the uncertainty of death as a demonstration of God's sovereignty and human dependence and as a way of teaching people "the importance and propriety of being constantly prepared for it." He, however, also saw that, despite the fact of death's disorder, multitudes of Americans had resolved "to observe order in preparing to meet it" (Emmons, 1842:3,29–38). Between the 1730s and the 1830s, such orderly Americans were influenced by the Enlightenment, the American Revolution, Unitarianism, and Evangelicalism, and all of these were influenced by an underlying market revolution. These movements slowly but surely reformed the Reformed Tradition, and gave Americans an eclectic tradition from which to fashion new beliefs and behavior about dying, death, and bereavement.

The Enlightenment replaced the Puritans' providential God with a First Cause who designed the universe to operate by orderly and observable natural laws, and it replaced depraved dependent Puritans with Enlightened, rational people. Enlightened people, therefore, viewed death not as a time of judgment, but as a natural occurrence. They looked for a serene and stoic death, and a simple, emotionally controlled funeral. Because Enlightened ideas were exchanged almost entirely among the educated classes of the Eastern seaboard, they had little immediate impact on American bereavement practices. In conjuction with the social forces of the American Revolution, however, the Enlightenment eventually affected American society.

In most areas of America, a basically Puritan Way of Death persisted until the nineteenth century, especially in rural areas where religion remained the focus of life. The increasing specialization and commercialization of life, however, eventually shaped death customs too. During the eighteenth century, economic, geographic, and population growth began to produce cities, social stratification and diversity, political dissent, and cultural controversy. Anxiety over the ideology of opportunistic individualism that produced many of these internal conflicts combined with extended imperial control to produce a Revolution that reinforced Enlightenment ideas of rationality and activity. The Revolution "acted as an inspirational model of men's power to alter their own lives, to think new thoughts, to act on the best ideas of mankind, to liberate themselves from the dead weight of the past" (Gross, 1976:191). As a newly independent people pursued life, liberty and happiness, they no longer depended on God's will; instead they made their own plans—plans which did not include death as a fact of life.

In religious developments, both Unitarianism and Evangelicalism accepted the enhanced view of human nature and human agency. The Unitarian gospel of "capitalism, theism, liberalism, and optimism" appealed especially to the commercial and professional classes of Boston—America's cultural capital in the nineteenth century (Howe, 1970:21). The Unitarians, however, were influential far beyond their numbers. Many people in other denominations accepted their progressive optimism—which derived from conceptions of a beneficent God. Unitarians were viewed by others as being basically good people whose lives were the best evidence of their religiosity, and they were admired for their rational approach to religion. Almost all Americans accepted the mid-nineteenth century rural cemetery reform that began in Brahmin Boston.

Outside of Boston, more Americans were affected by revivalistic evangelicalism than by Unitarianism. The Second Great Awakening of American Evangelicalism began in the 1790s as a response to the Enlightenment, and grew throughout the nineteenth century. Evangelicals stressed the Bible, a conversion experience, and a Christian life (and death). They preached God's persuasiveness more than His arbitrary power, His moral government rather than the ideas of predestination and election, and willful sinfulness more than innate depravity. Therefore, although evangelicals generally approached death from a Puritan position, they believed that God offered salvation, and people could take it if they willed. Consequently, evangelicalism offered assurance to the saved, even as it heightened the anxiety of the unregenerate. With the idealization of home and family, this could account for the abundant literature on the death of children as parents agonized over an ailing child "hoping all the while that death would terminate its sufferings, and fearing that something worse would be the result." After 1850, however, the romanticization of childhood overcame ideas of infant damnation, provided more assurance to worried parents, and tipped the delicate balance of evangelical belief from anxiety to assurance. By that time, however, evangelicalism had begun to be affected by sentimentalism, scientific naturalism, and liberal theology, as well as the social and institutional developments of the dying of death.

THE DYING OF DEATH, 1830–1945

Separate Spheres: The Rise of the Middle Class

Between 1830 and 1945, the ideas and institutions with which Americans approached death changed in a process that an English author of 1899 called "The Dying of Death." This process brought "the practical disappearance of the thought of death as an influence bearing upon practical life" ("The Dying of Death," 1899:364–365) and the tactical appearance of funeral institutions designed to keep death out of sight and out of mind.

Both ideas and institutions were the product of a new American middle-class, a group of people trying to distinguish themselves from the European aristocracy and from the American common people. Alexis de Tocqueville saw the middle-class as "an innumerable multitude of men almost alike, who, without being exactly rich or poor, possess sufficient property to desire the maintenance of order;" (Tocqueville, 1945:2,145) contemporary historians see them as substantial property owners, professionals, businessmen and merchants, shopkeepers and skilled artisans, commercial farmers, and their families. They possessed property, but their property (and the hope of increasing it) also possessed them, intensifying their fear of death. For the acquisitive member of the middle-class, "the recollection of death is a constant spur.... Besides the good things that he possesses, he every instant fancies a thousand others that death will prevent him from trying if he does not try them soon." Therefore, the middle-class wanted death *with* order.

One strategy for achieving death with order was the ideology of separate spheres. In the course of the nineteenth century, middle-class people separated management from labor, men's work from the home, and women's work from men's. They also tried to separate death from life, both intellectually and institutionally. Increasingly, specialists (either medical or clerical or academic) revised ideas of death, while other specialists segregated the funeral from the home, and the cemetery from the city.

Both separation and specialization were strategies of control, an increasingly important idea in Victorian society. Nineteenth century Americans worked for self-control, social control, and control over nature. They saw self-control as the key to character, and sexual control as the key to marriage. In separating their homes from their shops, they tried to control both spheres of their lives. The home would be a controlled environment for reproduction and socialization, while the workplace would be a controlled environment for increased production and time-discipline. Schools served as a transition from one controlled environment to another, while asylums provided controlled environments for societal deviants. Science and technology attempted to make the whole continent a controlled environment. Therefore, it should not surprise us that the same class that practiced birth control should also devise forms of death control (Rosenberg, 1973:137; Howe, 1970:304; Hale, 1971:25).

Intellectual Influences

In the process of the dying of death, the three most important intellectual influences were Romanticism and sentimentalism, scientific naturalism, and liberal religion. Romanticism was an intellectual response to the rationality and uniformity of the Enlightenment. Romantics discarded the Enlightenment idea of God as First Cause of a mechanistic universe operating according to predictable natural cycles. Instead, they emphasized the emotional and intuitive communion with the Oversoul (or Cosmos) in a mysteriously organic nature. Asher B. Durand depicted the essential correspondence of God, nature, and humanity in his painting *Kindred Spirits* (1849). It shows painter Thomas Cole and poet William Cullen Bryant in a beautiful natural setting, kindred to each other, to nature, and to the spirit that informed them all.

Such Romantic naturalism converted death from an untimely, unnatural event into a natural, conclusive communion with nature. In Romantic poetry such as Bryant's "Thanatopsis" or "A Forest Hymn," death was swallowed up in the teeming life of the landscape. Such soothing conceptions of natural death encouraged people to accept their demise. At the same time, such Romantic ideas influenced the institution of rural cemeteries, which institutionalized Romantic naturalism, even as they provided the consolations of Mother Nature to mourners.

The Romantic emphasis on emotions led to simple sentimentalism, which was "part of the self-evasion of a society committed to laissez-faire industrial expansion and disturbed by its consequences." As Americans began to experience the hard-headed rationalism of the industrial revolution, they began to create counterpoints to the "railroad principle" of American life. These counterpoints included the conventions of romantic love, the cult of true womanhood, the idealization of childhood, the home as "haven in a heartless world," residential suburbs, and an "emotional revolution" that bound family members with ties of intimacy. Domestic intimacy heightened the sense of loss upon the death of a "loved one," and required public outlets for the expression of private grief (Douglas, 1977:12–13, 200–226).

For most of the nineteenth century, the main outlet for the grief of sentimentalism was the mourning ritual, including the funeral, but also extending beyond it. This ritual differed markedly from the simple Puritan rite as mourners immersed themselves in grief to become, through their expressive (and often excessive) emotions, the central feature of the ritual. It allowed many members of the middle-class (especially the women, who were supposed to be creatures of the "heart") to indulge in grief as "therapeutic self indulgence." Like other forms of sentimentality, the sentimental mourning ritual counterpointed "the real world" because it forced all mourners to consider the power of personal connections in their lives. It turned people from life to death, from the practical to the ceremonial, from the ordinary to the extraordinary, and from the banal to the beautiful (Taylor, 1980:39–48).

Belief in the beauty of death and the funeral was new to the nineteenth century as the middle-class used its aesthetic awareness to beautify corpses, door badges, caskets, casket backdrops, hearses, horses, funeral music, cemeteries, monuments, mourning costume, and death itself. In the process, they made death so artistic that it almost became artificial, and therefore, less fearful. At the same time, concerned with an etiquette of proper social relations, people used the beauty of the funeral to preserve appearances among their middle-class peers. Finally, the middle-class called for "taste" and "refinement" in funerals as mourning rituals served to distinguish them from the common folk (Farrell, 1980:110–111).

Especially around the mid 1800s, the tastefully refined middle-class funeral was a dark and formal affair. After death, which still generally occurred in the home, the family either cleaned and dressed the deceased, or, if possible, hired an undertaker to care for the corpse. If they had secured an undertaker, he would place a black badge over the doorbell or door knocker to indicate the presence of mourning and to isolate the intimate family from the unwanted intrusions of everyday life. The family would also close window shades and drapes. Sometimes they draped black crepe over pictures, mirrors, and other places throughout the house (Habenstein and Lamers, 1962:389–444).

By the time of the funeral, family members had swathed themselves in black mourning garb that symbolized the intimacy of relationship to the deceased and the depth of grief. After the funeral, custom encouraged the continued expression of grief, as widows were expected to spend a year in "deep" mourning, and a year in "second" mourning. For the first year, a bereaved woman wore dull black clothes, matched by appropriately sombre accessories. In the second year, she gradually lightened her appearance by using a variety of materials in somewhat varying colors. Widowers and children were supposed to follow a similar regimen, but in practice, women bore the burden of nineteenth century mourning. Social contact and correspondence followed similar rules with widened social participation or narrowed black borders on stationery as indicators of different stages of mourning.

The funeral ceremony itself reflected and affected the sombre atmosphere in which it occurred. In the mid 1800s, people were invited to funerals with hand-delivered printed cards. By the end of the century, the obituary began to serve as a funeral notice, and the telephone allowed people to deliver their own invitations without leaving the house of mourning. Once invited, people generally came to the house, offered condolences to the bereaved family, viewed the corpse, and sat in chairs arranged in the parlor by the undertaker. Sometimes, however, the funeral took place in church, in which case people would process from the home to the church. In either place, services were generally extended affairs in which ministers counterbalanced fears of death, decay, and damnation with hopes of regeneration and resurrection. Funerals might include music and hymns, but the central feature of the ceremony was the sermon which combined an elegy with exhortations for repentance and renewal. This gloomy funeral was not, however, the only type of sentimental funeral. As the nineteenth century proceeded, a more hopeful sentimentality entered funeral services as middle-class religious liberalism began to domesticate death (Habenstein and Lamers, 1962:389–444; Stannard, 1980:26; Hillerman, 1980:101).

As noted on the modern day obituary of H. P. Murphy, the highlights of his life are recalled. Unlike many obituaries today, a personal touch is found here. The importance and pride of family are stressed—a sort of continuation of life through his children. It is more than the facts of Mr. Murphy's life; that which made him "special" to others is noted. As was true in the mid 1800s, the obituary today is a way of informing the public of this vital statistic—death—and of the forthcoming event of final disposition—burial or whatever.

Henry P. Murphy, Was an Institution in Dorchester, at 86

Dorchester lost one of its institutions Friday. Henry P. (Harry) Murphy died in Carney Hospital, Dorchester, after a short illness. He was 86.

Although he was born in Charlestown before the turn of the century and took his early education in that closely knit section of the city before serving in the US Navy during World War 1, it was as a citizen of St. Mark's Parish in Dorchester that Harry Murphy made his mark.

His job as an attendance supervisor for the Boston School Department brought him into contact with people of all ages and backgrounds. His face was a familiar one to many families as he went about his business in the days when playing hookey from school was considered a serious sin.

He retired 16 years ago, but his interest—and pride—in the world around him, specifically his family, his Somoset street neighborhoods (spell that Ward 16), and St. Mark's Parish, never waned.

His devotion to his late wife, Mary (Livingston), who died in 1975 after a long illness at home, and his constant attention to the affairs of his active family were the stuff of Harry Murphy's life.

His oldest son, Paul, served for many years as a state representative from Ward 16 before being named presiding justice at West Roxbury District Court. To have a son reach such peaks of accomplishment was the ultimate reward for a father like Harry Murphy.

Add to that the fact that his only daughter, Mary, proved her mettle in the groves of academe and beyond before moving to Connecticut with her husband, Len Manchuck, and raising a family; that his son, Albert, made his way to a responsible position in the probation section of Roxbury District Court; that his son, Joseph, worked and studied enough to gain appointment as vice-principal of Boston Technical High School; and that his youngest, James, has become a successful educator in Stoughton, and you know that Harry Murphy, husband, father, and citizen, was a successful man.

A funeral Mass for Mr. Murphy will be said Wednesday at 10 A.M. in St. Mark's Church, Dorchester.

Mr. Murphy was a charter member of the Bunker Hill American Legion Post and a member of the Bunker Hill Council of the Knights of Columbus. He was a 50-year member of St. Mark's Holy Name Society.

He leaves his daughter, Mary V. Manchuck of Stamford, Conn.; four sons, Joseph A. of Scituate, James J. of Brockton, Albert J. and Judge Paul Murphy, presiding justice of West Roxbury District Court, both of Dorchester; a sister Gertrude FitzGerald of Quincy; 14 grandchildren and two great-grandchildren.

Burial will be in Mount Benedict Cemetery, West Roxbury.

Source: *Boston* (Mass.) *Sunday Globe*, June 21, 1981, p. 39.

After the funeral, the procession continued to the cemetery, which was, as we shall see, beautified in order to belie the presence of death. There, the body was interred, and people returned home, not like the Puritans to resume their life's work, but like Victorians to extend their expressions of emotional grief. Mourning garb was one symbol of such sorrow, but mourning portraits and consolation literature were other ways to prolong the period of lamentation.

In the early nineteenth century, embroidered or painted mourning pictures flourished as a form of memorialization. These pictures often showed stylized graveyard scenes including such standard features as the weeping willow, the gravestone and epitaph of the deceased, the mourners, and a memento mori. These remained popular until the 1830s when printed memorials with spaces for names and dates came into vogue. During the middle third of the century, posthumous mourning portraiture also flourished depicting the deceased with conventional symbols of mortality like the broken shaft or roses held with blooms downward. These paintings were drawn from the corpse, and they expressed "the desire for the restoration of the dead through art." All of these forms of mourning art provided icons for the bereaved to contemplate as a part of the extended mourning ritual (Lloyd, 1980:71–89).

Consolation literature allowed people to share their grief without sharing it with people they knew. It showed mourners that they were not alone in the house of sorrow, and it showed them the emotional and moral benefits of their heartache. Consolation literature included obituary poems and memoirs, mourner's manuals, prayer guidebooks, hymns, and books about heaven. Such writings inflated the importance of dying and the dead by every possible means; they sponsored elaborate methods of burial and commemoration, communication with the next world, and microscopic viewings of a sentimentalized afterlife. Books like *Agnes and the Key of Her Little Coffin* (1857) or *Stepping Heavenward* (1869) or *The Empty Crib: The Memorial of Little Georgie* (1873) all featured and championed the ideal of "the sensitized mourner" (Douglas, 1977:240–249).

To the modern mind, these sentimental expressions of grief may seem forced, overdone, or even false. Such attitudes, however, tell more about us than about our Victorian ancestors. "Nineteenth century Americans mourned well" because they gave themselves symbols, rituals, and time in which to work out their feelings. We do not understand this because of important intervening historical forces, one of which was scientific naturalism.

If sentimentality was one way of controlling the hard fact of death, scientific naturalism was another. Although it systemized the hard-headed rationalism that sentimentalism tried to smother, scientific naturalism contributed to the dying of death, as the middle-class used the "laws" of science like they used the "customs" of etiquette to legitimize their cultural values.

"What strikes the historian," writes Burton J. Bledstein (1976:55), "is the totality of the mid-Victorian impulse to contain the life experiences of the individual from life to death by isolating them as science." Another instance of the ideology of separate spheres, the rise of science in the last half of the nineteenth century allowed Americans to invoke authority for "those scientific plausibilities which fitted most conveniently into their social needs and presuppositions" (Biedstein, 1976:55). An integral part of the social construction of reality, science isolated the mystery of death as "a matter of fact," and interpreted that fact in order to reduce the impact of death on practical life.

Scientific naturalists insisted first that death was "natural, a product of natural causes, the same as any other natural phenomenon, and that these causes are bound to the fixed, and as we believe beneficient, laws of the universe" (Johnson, 1896:77). Their insistence on the "natural" quality of death complemented the natural death of Romanticism, but the scientific fact of death eliminated providential intervention and the possibility of death as punishment.

Consequently, scientific naturalists insisted that death was painless, and that all people could eventually attain an "easy" natural death at an advanced age. Pain, which (like fear) was an important part of the Puritan world, lost its cultural relevance in the nineteenth century. With the discovery of ether in the 1840s and the coining of the word "painkiller" in the 1850s, Americans applied physical and mental anaesthetics to kill the pain of death ("Pain, Life, and Death"). Magazine articles constantly stressed "the modern belief that the process [of dying] is easy," as easy and "as painless as falling asleep" ("The Fear of Death," 1912:21). In so doing, they eliminated a major reason for people to think seriously about death.

Other scientific and medical innovations persuaded many Americans that death might be postponed or prevented. Even before the demographic transition, they began to treat death as an occurrence of old age, an idea which encouraged people to postpone or preempt preparation for death. In addition, some prominent medical researchers asserted that even old age was a curable congenital disease, and asked "Why Not Live Forever?" Indeed, when Elie Metchnikoff, the head of the Pasteur Institute in Paris, claimed that cultured milk products could combat the "autointoxication" of old age, Americans immediately began to buy yogurt and buttermilk. Especially between 1900 and 1920, the prestige of science convinced many Americans that individual physical immortality might be imminent (Farrell, 1980:60–61).

Other scientific naturalists admitted individual mortality, but promoted a species immortality whereby "we are immortal if we but form a sturdy link in the great chain of life." Influenced by Darwin's idea of natural selection, these scientists viewed death as "an inevitable corollary to the advancement of the species" (Hutchinson, 1893:637). Therefore, they advised Americans not to take death personally, but to accept it as part of human progress. This species perspective did not prevent individuals from dying, but it did turn their attention from death and the deceased to survivors and posterity. As we shall see, this species perspective of death and immortality was institutionalized in "life" insurance.

By itself, scientific naturalism had almost no impact on American bereavement practices. In conjunction with religious liberalism and the culture of professionalism, however, scientific naturalism did affect changes in funeral service.

Religious liberals tried to reconcile new scientific knowledge with traditional religious interpretations of death. Between 1850 and 1930, liberals like Henry Ward Beecher and Phillips Brooks enunciated "the attitudes and values of a new urban middle-class" (Clark, 1978:3). They combined scientific naturalism, higher Biblical criticism, Romantic idealism, and sentimentality in order to show the place of evolution in God's plan, the place of death in evolution, and the progress of life through death to an exalted immortality. In addition, changing ideas of death and immortality brought them into the arena of funeral reform.

Henry Ward Beecher was the most popular and influential of liberal clergymen. His pulpit at the Plymouth Congregational Church of Brooklyn Heights gave him opportunities for public speaking and publication, and he became a "symbol for a middle-class America" (Clark, 1978). He rejected the evangelicalism of his youth, and preached instead a gospel of divine immanence, natural law, and human hope. He accepted scientific naturalism, and wrote an article for the first issue of the *Popular Science Monthly*. He believed that God acted primarily in the world through natural laws, and that people responded naturally to God by electing their own salvation. Eventually, he even rejected the doctrine of everlasting punishment in hell.

Beecher viewed death as the first step up toward heaven, as God's call to "Come home!" "I would not, for the world, bring up a child to have that horror of death which hung over my own childhood," claimed Beecher, because "the thought of death was to me awful beyond description" (Beecher, 1859:194–195). Instead, he wanted people to see that "a funeral is the nearest place to heaven," and that sorrow was inappropriate. He suggested:

> When friends have gone out from us joyously, we should go with them to the grave, not singing mournful psalms, but scattering flowers. Christians are wrong to walk in black, and sprinkle the ground with tears, at the very time when they should walk in white, and illumine the way by smiles and radiant hope. The disciples found angels at the grave of Him they loved; and we should always find them too, but that our eyes are too full of tears for seeing (Beecher, 1858:189).

At his own funeral in 1887, Beecher's family reversed the somber formality of the Victorian funeral by making sure that "no emblem of parting or sorrow was there, but the symbols of love, and faith, and hope, the glad tokens of eternal reward, such as befitted his life, his death, and his fame" (Handford, 1887:47–49). On a practical, pastoral level, other ministers counseled people to follow Beecher's example. They celebrated death as a passage to eternal life, not as a moment of judgment. They tried to soothe survivors instead of promoting self-examination or preparation for death. They worked with funeral directors to effect funeral reforms. In 1913, Lyman Abbott recalled the achievements of liberal funeral reform:

> We have done much to Christianize our farewells to those who have gone before us into the next stages of life. We no longer darken the rooms that now more than ever need the light and warmth of the sun; we no longer close the windows as if to shut out Nature at the moment when we are about to give back to Mother Earth all that was mortal in the earthly career now finished; we no longer shroud the house in black, we make it sweet with flowers; for the hymns of grief we are fast substituting the hymns of victory; for words charged with a sense of loss we listen to words that hold wide the door of hope and faith; and on the memorials which we place where they lie who have vanished from our sight we no longer carve the skull and crossbones, the hourglass and the scythe—we recall some trait or quality or achievement that survives the body and commemorates the spirit.

Such changes, thought Abbott, helped people "to think of life as one and indivisible, of immortality as our possession, here and now, of death as normal change in an eternal process of growth" ("There Are No Dead," 1913:979–980).

By defining death as part of evolutionary progress propelled by an immanent and merciful God, liberals allowed bereaved Americans to approach death optimistically. This new definition of death derived from ideas of Romanticism, scientific naturalism, and religious liberalism. Together with the institutional innovations of cemetery superintendents, life insurance agents, and funeral directors, these ideas caused the dying of death in America.

Institutional Influences

Like religious liberalism, cemetery reform derived from Romantic naturalism, middle-class family sentimentality, and scientific concerns. In 1895, a writer in *American Gardening* wrote that "the modern garden cemetery like the modern religious impulse seeks to assuage the cheerlessness and the sternness of life and to substitute the free and gracious charity of One who came to rob death of its hideousness" ("Extracts," 1895:108). By the 1830s, many physicians had begun to worry about the possible health hazards of city graveyards. By the same time, commercial development had raised the price of land on which graveyards were located, and Romantic ideas of landscape architecture had begun to affect the aesthetically-oriented members of the middle class. Also, space limitations of city graveyards pre-

vented the possibility of family plots, and many of the burial places had
become overcrowded, unkempt, and unsightly.

The solution to these problems was the rural cemetery, a landscaped
garden in a suburban setting. In 1831, Mount Auburn Cemetery was
founded four miles west of Boston, and its success stimulated the spread of
such cemeteries all over the country. In rural cemeteries, family plots aver-
aging 300 square feet were nestled among trees and shrubs upon the slopes
of soft hills, or on the shores of little lakes. Paths curled throughout the
grounds, passing lots enclosed by stone coping or wrought iron fences and
surmounted by a monument of some sort. Such cemeteries were invented
to bury bodies and to ease the grief of survivors; to bring people into communion with God, with Nature, and with deceased family and friends, and
to teach them important lessons of life; to surround bereavement with
beauty and to divert the attention of survivors from death to the setting of
burial; and to display "taste" and "refinement" and to reinforce the class
stratification of the status quo (Rotundo, 1973:231–42; Bender 1973:196–
211; French, 1975:69–91).

The founders of Mount Auburn were liberal Unitarian reformers, progressive professionals and businessmen who considered the cemetery in
the context of social developments of their day. They equated the family
with the garden, and imagined both as a counterpoint to a society of accu-
mulation. In the same way that upper middle class families moved to suburbs where curved roads and greenery contrasted the grid-block plan of
the cities and offered space to raise a family, they moved from the "cities of
the dead" to rural cemeteries that offered space to "plant" a family.

During this period of "the discovery of the asylum," social deviants were
located in restorative rural settings that would rehabilitate people away
from the contaminating influence of urban life. Like insane asylums, or-
phanages, and penitentiaries, many of these reformers saw the cemetery
as an "asylum" from urban ills. In the cemetery, "the weary and worn
citizen" was also rehabilitated. Cleveland (1847:13–14,26) noted:

> Ever since he entered these greenwood shades, he has sensibly been getting
> farther and farther from strife, from business, and care.... A short half-hour
> ago, he was in the midst of a discordant Babel; he was one of the hurrying,
> jostling crowd; he was encompassed by the whirl and fever of artificial life.
> Now he stands alone in Nature's inner court—in her silent, solemn sanctuary.
> Her holiest influences are all around him.

The rehabilitation of the rural cemetery paralleled the philosophy of education found in the common school. Like the new compulsory schools,
rural cemeteries responded to middle-class fears of mobilization of the
masses in the Age of Jackson. Educational reformers like Horace Mann
both reflected and affected cemetery proponents in their belief that "senti-

ment is the great conservative principle of society," and that "instincts of patriotism, local attachment, family affection, human sympathy, reverence for truth, age, valor, and wisdom...constitute the latent force of civil society" (Tuckerman, 1856:338–342).

Like these other reforms of antebellum society, rural cemeteries "took the public mind by storm." Cities and towns throughout the United States established rural cemeteries, and people flocked to visit them. In New York, Baltimore, and Philadelphia, Andrew Jackson Downing estimated that over 30,000 people a year toured the rural cemeteries. Consequently, he wondered whether they might not also visit landscaped gardens without graves. In articles like "Public Cemeteries and Public Gardens" and "The New York Park," Downing (1921:28–40, 374) advanced the idea that would eventuate in New York's Central Park and in a new direction for cemetery development.

The new direction was the lawn-park cemetery emphasizing a new aesthetic, efficiency, and the absence of death. By the end of the century, members of the Association of American Cemetery Superintendents routinely wrote in journals like *Park and Cemetery* that "a cemetery should be a beautiful park. While there are still some who say 'a cemetery should be a cemetery,' . . . the great majority have come to believe in the idea of beauty" (Simonds, 1919:59). This new aesthetic emphasized the open meadows of the beautiful style over the irregular hill-and-dale outcroppings of the picturesque style and the irregular outcroppings of obelisks and monuments in the unregulated rural cemetery. This aesthetic coincided with considerations of efficiency as the uncluttered landscape required less upkeep than the enclosures and elaborate monuments of the rural cemetery. Finally, this aesthetic buried death beneath the beauty of the design. Andrew Jackson Downing (1921:59) had said that "the development of the beautiful is the end and aim of all other fine arts. . . . And we attain it by the removal or concealment of everything uncouth or discordant." The cemetery superintendents practiced what Downing preached. "Today cemetery making is an art," said one superintendent in 1910, "and gradually all things that suggest death, sorrow, or pain are being eliminated" (Hare, 1910:41).

Cemetery superintendents eliminated suggestions of death by banning lot enclosures and grave mounds, and by encouraging fewer gravestones and fewer inscriptions. They banned lot enclosures (fencing or stone coping) because they broke up the unified landscape, blocked the path of the lawn mower, and signified a "selfish and exclusive" possessive individualism. Grave mounds also obstructed the view and the lawn mower, but they reminded people of death. Without them, a cemetery lot would evoke "none of the grewsomeness [sic] which is invariably associated with cemetery lots....No 1 grave mounds are used, so save the headstones, *there is nothing to suggest the presence of Death*" (Smith, 1910:539).

Forest Lawn

Song by Tom Paxton

Oh, lay me down in Forest Lawn in a silver casket,
Put golden flowers over my head in a silver basket.
Let the drum and bugle corps blow taps while cannons roar,
Let sixteen liveried employees pass out souvenirs from the funeral store.
I want to go simply when I go, and they'll give me a simple fun'ral there, I
    know.
With a casket lined in fleece,
And fireworks spelling out "rest in peace."
Oh, take me when I'm gone to Forest Lawn.

Oh, lay me down in Forest Lawn—they understand there.
They have a heavenly choir and a military band there.
Just put me in their care, and I'll find my comfort there, with sixteen
    planes in last salute, dropping a cross in a parachute.
I want to go simply when I go, they'll give me a simple fun'ral there, I
    know.
With a hundred strolling strings.
And topless dancers in golden wings,
Oh, take me when I'm gone to Forest Lawn.

Oh come, come, come, come,
Come to the church in the wildwood,
Kindly leave a contribution in the pail.
Be as simple and as trusting as a child would
And we'll sell you a church in the dale.

To find a simple resting place is my desire,
To lay me down with a smiling face comes a little bit higher.
My likeness done in brass will stand in plastic grass,
And weights and hidden springs will tip its hat to the mourners filing past.
I want to go simply when I go.
And they'll give me a simple fun'ral there, I know.
I'll sleep beneath the sand, with piped in tapes of Billy Graham.
Oh, take me when I'm gone to Forest Lawn.
Rock of Ages, cleft for me, for a slightly higher fee.
Oh, take me when I'm gone to Forest Lawn.

Some superintendents did not want to save the headstones either, proposing instead "a cemetery where there is no monument, only landscape" (AACS, 1889:59). Most superintendents favored sunken stones at the site of the grave. Howard Evarts Weed (1912:94), author of the influential *Modern Park Cemeteries*, argued that "with the headstones showing above the surface we have the old graveyard scene, but buried in the ground they do not appear in the landscape picture and we then have a park-like effect." Some superintendents zoned the cemetery to permit monuments only on large "monument lots." This allowed the superintendent, like a realtor, to charge premium prices for such lots and for prime locations for corner lots or hillside or lakeside property. This social stratification of the cemetery allowed for the social mobility of the dead, as ambitious dead people moved to better "neighborhoods" as their survivors saw fit. Where they could not ban or limit the number of monuments, superintendents tried to make them as unobtrusive as possible, preferring horizontal monuments to the earlier upright markers, and preferring sorted inexpressive inscriptions to the poetic epitaphs of earlier times. They wanted to replace the memento mori (remembrance) of earlier stones with "forgetfulness" as they buried death with the dead (Farrell, 1980:122–127).

Grave Remarks
or
I'll Write My Own Epitaph Before I Leave, Thank You

Epitaphs are footnotes chiseled on tombstones.

They are parting shots taken at or by the deceased. They can be patriotic, poetic, profound or pathetic. They can be wise, witty or just weird. They can glorify, be grievous or gruesome.

Few of them have summed up a person's attitude toward life as well as one found in a Georgia cemetery:

I told you I was sick!

Perhaps the most famous epitaph is one credited to W.C. Fields, written for himself:

On the whole I'd rather be in Philadelphia.

But Fields' epitaph was not used and his tombstone in Glendale, California, contains only his vital statistics.

Here are some others.

Epitaph from Kilmurry Churchyard, Ireland:
> This stone was raised to Sarah Ford.
> Not Sarah's virtues to record,
> For they're well known to all the town,
> No Lord, it was raised to keep her down.

From Streatham Churchyard. England:

Here lies Elizabeth, my wife for 47 years, and this is the first damn thing she ever did to oblige me.

Epitaph on one of three tombstones in a family burial plot in Niagara Falls, Ontario:
> Here I lie between two of the best women in the world:
> my wives. But I have requested
> my relatives to tip me a little toward Tille.

In a Falkirk, England, cemetery:
> At rest beneath this slab of stone
> Lies stingy Jimmy Wyatt;
> He died one morning just at ten,
> And saved a dinner by it.

Here's one from Boot Hill, Dodge City, Kansas, that reflects a popular epitaph theme:
> Here lies the body of Mannie,
> They put him here to stay;
> He lived the life of Riley
> While Riley was away.

From Burlington Churchyard, Mass.:
> Sacred to the memory of Anthony Drake
> Who died for peace and quietness sake,
> His wife was constantly scolding and scoffin',
> So he sought repose in a twelve-dollar coffin.

Railroad conductor Charles B. Gunn's tombstone in Colorado Springs, Colo., contains these words:
Papa—Did you wind your watch?

And in a Moultrie, Ga., cemetery:
> Here lies the father of twenty-nine
> He would have had more but he didn't have time.

From Burlington, Mass., again:
> Here lies the body of Susan Lowder
> Who burst while drinking Seidlitz powder;
> Called from the world to her heavenly rest
> She should have waited til it effervesced.

On a hanged, sheep-stealer from Bletchley, Bucks, England:
> Here lies the body of Thomas Kemp

Who lived by wool and died by hemp.
Abraham Newland, a lonely London Banker, who wrote his own epitaph:

> Beneath this stone old Abraham lies;
> Nobody laughs, and nobody cries.
> Where he has gone, and how he fares,
> Nobody knows and nobody cares.

In a Thurmont, Md., cemetery:

> Here lies an atheist—All dressed up
> and no place to go.

And in a Stowe, Vt., cemetery:

> I was somebody. Who is no business of yours.

An infant's epitaph in a Plymouth, Mass., cemetery:

> Since I have been so quickly done for
> I wonder what I was begun for.

In a Uniontown, Pa., cemetery:

> Here lies the body of Jonathan Blake;
> Stepped on the gas instead of the brake.

Written by a widow on her adulterous husband's tomb—stone in an
Atlanta, Ga. cemetery:

> Gone. But not forgiven.

Similarly, a Middlesex, England, widow put this on the gravestone of
her wandering husband:

> At last I know where he is at night!

An "old maid's" epitaph in Scranton, Pa.:

> No hits, no runs, no heirs.

At Cripple Creek, Colo., an epitaph to a man who died by accident:

> Within this grave there lies poor Andy;
> Bit by a snake no whiskey handy.

Another one from Cripple Creek:

> Here lies the bones of a man named Zeke,
> Second-fastest draw in Cripple Creek.

Near Atlanta, Ga., a cemetery hosts this unique epitaph:

> Due to lack of ground in this cemetery,
> two bodies are buried in this one plot.
> One of them was a politician, the other
> was an honest man.

An English epitaph over the grave of Sir John Strange, a lawyer:

> Here lies an honest lawyer, and that is Strange.

Epitaph to Joseph Crump, a musician:

> Once ruddy, and plump
> But now a pale lump
> Beneath this save hump
> Lies honest Joe Crump

What, tho' by Death's thump
He's laid on his rump
Yet up he shall jump
When he hears the last triumph.
   An 1890 epitaph of Arthur C. Hormans of Cleveland, Ohio, puts things
in startling clear perspective:
Once again I wasn't. Then I was.
Now I ain't again.

Source: Epitaphs selected from David Wallechinsky and Irving Wallace *The People's Alma-nac*, Garden City, N.Y.: Doubleday and Company, 1975, pp. 1312–1320 and *Lexington* (Ky.) *Herald*, September 21, 1979, p. D-5.

Superintendents tried to structure cemetery services "to mitigate the harshness and cruelty of death and its attendant details and ceremonies" (Seavoy, 1906:448) and to provide a sort of grief therapy for bereaved individuals. They encouraged private, family funerals, and they tried to remove or conceal the uncouth and discordant aspects of interment. They carted the dirt away from the grave, or they hid it beneath cloth, flowers, or evergreens. They lined the grave with cloth to make it look like a little room. They suggested changes in religious services, and they escorted mourners away from the grave before filling it in order to avoid the finality of death. In all of these services, "everything that tends to remove the gloomy thoughts is done....The friends cannot but leave the sacred spot with better, nobler thoughts, freed from the gloom and terror that otherwise would possess them" (Hay, 1900:46).

A second institutional innovation, life insurance, tried to exorcise the anxiety and financial insecurity that would otherwise possess people contemplating death. Established about the same time as rural cemeteries, life insurance flourished after 1850. In 1850, forty-eight companies held policies valued at $97 million; by 1920, 335 companies recorded 65 million policies worth $40 billion. Life insurance contributed to "the practical disappearance of the thought of death as an influence bearing upon practical life," and thus, it contributed to the dying of death (U.S. Bureau of the Census, 1975:1050–59).

Life insurance emerged from the same historical context as rural cemeteries and funeral reform; it assumed the uniformity and continuity of death as a natural occurrence. Life insurance depended on the science of statistics and on a species perspective of death and immortality that focused attention, not on the life of the individual policyholder, but on the lives of beneficiaries. Like the rural cemetery, life insurance was praised for its educational benefits as it taught lessons of self-reliance, forethought, thrift, discipline, and (very) delayed gratification. For these reasons, clergymen like Henry Ward Beecher endorsed the system of life insurance, responding to critics that in effect, God helps those who help themselves. Also, life insurance accentuated the importance of the family, as did Romantic sentimentalism and the family plot of the rural cemetery. Finally, life insurance provided families with money to pay for elaborate funerals, a fact that affected both the development of funeral service and of the history of bereavement.

Like burial service, funeral service also changed between 1850 and 1920. Because "the growing wealth and prosperity of our country has caused people to demand something more in accordance with their surroundings" (Benjamin, 1882:3), and because funeral directors cultivated a "steadily advancing appreciation of the aesthetics of society" (Funeral Directors, 1883:3), the new funeral would be, like the 19th century cemetery, a work of art. As cemetery superintendents used their art to hide the uncouth and discordant aspects of death, so did funeral directors use "the varied improvements in (their) art to conceal much that is forbidding in (their) calling" (NFDA, 1882:5). As cemetery superintendents institutionalized "the modern religious impulse" to "assuage the cheerlessness and sternness of life," the funeral director worked to "adopt some philosophy or some new customs and ideals that will make death less of a tragedy" ("The Ideas of a Plain Country Woman," 1913:42).

The demand for a new funeral service came from the American middle class, but it was created and supplied by casket manufacturers and funeral directors. The National Funeral Directors Association was founded in 1882 in Rochester, New York, the home of the Stein Casket Manufacturing Company. The association's official journal was *The Casket*, founded and funded for several years by the Stein Company. As this suggests, the first widespread innovation in funeral service was the casket, a stylish container for the corpse. Before 1850, most Americans were laid to rest in a coffin, a six-sided box that was constructed to order by the local cabinetmaker. By 1927 "the old wedge-shaped coffin [was] obsolete. A great variety of styles and grades of caskets [were] available in the trade, ranging from a cheap, cloth-covered pine box to the expensive cast-bronze sarcophagus" (Gebhart, 1927:8). The rectangular shape of the new caskets complemented the artwork in concealing the uncouth corpse. In applying for a casket patent in 1849, A.C. Barstow explained:

> The burial cases formerly used were adapted in shape nearly to the form of the human body, that is they tapered from the shoulders to the head, and from the shoulders to the feet. Presently, in order to obviate in some degree the disagreeable sensations produced by a coffin on many minds, the casket, or square form has been adopted (Habenstein and Lamers, 1962:270, 251–310).

The adoption of the word "casket" also accelerated the dying of death, as the word had previously denoted a container for something precious, like jewels.

Accepting the associated idea of the preciousness of the body, Americans decided that a dead-looking corpse looked out of place in an elaborate silk-lined casket. Rather than remove the casket, they decided to stylize the body. Originally a way of preserving bodies for shipment home from Civil War battlefields or western cities, embalming soon became a way of preserving appearances. Responding to the germ theory of disease and the public health movement, funeral directors attempted to gain professional status by emphasizing the disinfectant qualities of embalming. Most funeral directors, however, wanted simply "to retain and improve the complexion" so that the corpse would look "as natural as though [it] were alive" (Hohenschuh, 1921:82,88). To do this, they began to cosmetize the corpse, and to clothe and position the body naturally. They replaced the traditional shroud with street clothes, and they tried "to lay out the body so that there will be as little suggestion of death as possible." By 1920, they succeeded so well that a Boston undertaker supposedly advertised (Dowd, 1921:53):

> For composing the features, 1$
> For giving the features a look of quiet resignation, $2.
> For giving the features the appearance of Christian hope and contentment, $5

Bereavement practices were affected by the change from coffin to casket and by the "restorative art" of the embalmer; they were also changed by the movement of the funeral from the domestic parlor to the funeral parlor. As they began banishing death from their homes to hospitals, they started moving the funeral from the family parlor to a specialized funeral parlor. After the Civil War, middle class Americans began to exclude the formal parlor from their homes and to replace it with a "living room." At the same time, funeral directors wanted full control of the corpse and the funeral. The ease and efficiency of directing funerals in a funeral home made them more profitable. In spite of all these benefits, however, the transition to the funeral parlor was a slow process, extending well into the twentieth century (Farrell, 1980:172–177).

Both in the domestic parlor and in the funeral parlor, the procedure of the turn-of-the-century funeral changed. In conjunction with the reform forces of religious liberalism, funeral directors began to redirect funerals to be shorter, more secular, and more soothing. They shortened the service by trying to revise the long sermon with its exhortations of repentance and renewal. Although some clerics resisted, funeral directors wanted the sermon redirected from theology to psychology, from preaching to grief therapy, and from the state of survivors' souls to the state of their emotions, The funeral director took care of all the details of the funeral and performed as much as a stage manager as a mortician. "Really it is much the same," wrote one director, "I work for effect—for consoling and soothing" ("The Man Nobody Envies: An Account of the Experiences of an Undertaker," 1914:68–71).

After 1880, funeral directors used their arts and "the culture of professionalism" to effect a massive change in the American way of bereavement. Professionalism was part of the middle class strategy of specialization. It required education in an area of expertise and an ethic or service, and it provided autonomy and income for its practitioners. The American undertaker sought professional status because it would help him to become "enough of an *authority* to convince his clients, without offense, that there are better methods than are prescribed by custom" (Hohenschuh, 1921:9). Etiquette books reinforced this culture of professionalism by advising readers that "the arrangements for the funeral are usually left to the undertaker, who best knows how to proceed" (Wells, 1887:303). To the middle-class people who feared death anyway, this established a situation in which the public passively accepted changes in funeral service suggested by funeral directors (Hohenschuh, 1921:9; Wells, 1887:303).

Indeed, restraint and passivity became the watchwords of twentieth century bereavement. If the funeral director was a stage manager, then the family was the audience, responding to the drama in prescribed ways in the hopes of achieving a catharsis of death. Instead of the expressive grief of the sentimental funeral, the family was expected to contain and control their emotions and to meet death stoically. At the turn of the century, some religious liberals saw grief as lack of faith in the imminence of immortality. Others reacted to the central place of the mourners in the mournful Victorian funeral, and charged that "over-much grief would seem mere selfishness" (Mayo, 1916:6). Over and over again, writers proclaimed that "the deepest grief is the quiet kind" (Sargent, 1888:51). An 1890's etiquette book suggested that "we can better show our affection to the dead by fulfilling our duties to the living, than by giving ourselves up to uncontrolled grief" (Pike and Armstrong, 1980:125). Portraying grief as a selfish ploy to stop the ongoing business of life, these reformers called for controlled and private grief. In the long run, they predicted the modern practice of grief therapy in which grief is seen as a disorder by people who still want death with order (Mayo, 1916:6; Sargent, 1888:51; Pike and Armstrong, 1980:125).

The decline of mourning wear, which occurred after World War I, is accounted for here. This explains why Americans ceased to express their grief symbolically because extended grief offended others who preferred to live for life. In concealing mourning, Americans reversed the nineteenth century tradition that *required* good mourning. Like cemetery superintendents and funeral directors, Americans in general began to conceal the uncouth and discordant emotion of grief. Thus, modern grief isolates the mourners and forces them to discover their own private mourning ritual. It dictates the appearance of control and the dying of death (Hillerman, 1980:104–105; Oxley, 1887:608–14).

The Display of the Dead

Truly, we need to do away with some of the false ideas of Death which are shown in so many gruesome ways at funerals, and strive to give the young a different and truer idea of what the passing away of a soul means. The awfulness of some funerals is nothing short of criminal, especially as it affects the minds of the young. If there is work cut out for the minister of today, it is the enlightenment of his people on the subject of death and the funeral. But the minister must, first of all, imbibe a wholesome lesson of self-restraint for himself, and abolish the fulsome and tiresome eulogy which is the bane of so many funerals. He must learn for himself, and teach to his people, the beauty and solemnity of the brief service as prescribed by his church and attempt nothing more, and he must also relentlessly oppose the tendency which exists to turn the modern funeral, especially in the country, into a picnic. The present outpouring of a heterogeneous mass of folk from every point of the countryside is a farce that cannot be too soon abolished. A funeral is essentially a time for the meeting of the family and relatives and the closest friends, and the fewer the number of outsiders present the better. Nor is there anything quite so barbarous as the present custom at so many funerals of "viewing the remains" by a motley collection of folk, many of whom never even knew the dead in life, or, if they did, never thought enough of him to come and see him. The vulgar curiosity that prompts "a last look" at a loved one cannot be too severely denounced. Only second to it is the pretentious line of vehicles that "escorts the remains to the grave" and the mental calibre of a community that bases the popularity of a man on the number of carriages that follow him to the grave!

If there is a crying need of the gospel of simplicity it is in connection with funerals. It seems inconceivable that Death should be made the occasion for display, and yet this is true of scores of funerals. The flowers, including those fearful conceptions of the ignorant florist, such as "Gates Ajar"; the quality of casket and even of the raiment of the dead, the "crowd" at the "obsequies," the number of carriages in the "cortege"— oh, oh, "what fools these mortals be," to say naught of the wicked and wanton waste of much-needed money. It is difficult to conceive that a national love of display should have become so deep-rooted as to lead to the very edge of the grave!

Source: *Ladies Home Journal,* September 1903.

These modern bereavement practices proceeded from a simple desire to make death as painless for survivors as for the deceased. It came from a widespread cultural attempt "not to mention trouble or grief or sickness or sin, but to treat them as if they do not exist, and speak only of the sweet and pleasant things of life" ("Ideas of a Plain Country Woman", 1913:42). This dying of death came from the desire of the middle-class for control— of self, society and the environment. It ended exactly where Alexis de Tocqueville (1945:2,4) predicted:

> As they perceive that they succeed in resolving without resistance all the little difficulties their practical life presents, [the Americans] readily conclude that everything in the world can be explained, and that nothing in it transcends the limits of the understanding. Thus they fall to denying what they cannot comprehend.

Denying and disguising death, middle-class Americans achieved, on the surface at least, the dying of death.

THE RESURRECTION OF DEATH, 1945 TO THE PRESENT

Although Americans sought a death sentence for death, the Judge granted only life imprisonment. Consequently, although death had disappeared from the streets, Americans worried that this hardened killer might escape. After World War II, some Americans suggested instead that death had been rehabilitated, and like nineteenth-century "resurrectionists," they began to resurrect death. Presently Americans are deciding between the dying of death and "living with dying."

The Atomic Age

On August 6, 1945, the United States dropped a single atomic bomb on the Japanese city of Hiroshima. It exploded in the air, with a heat flash that inflamed clothing within a half-mile radius and trees up to a mile and a half. The shock wave followed soon after, rupturing internal organs. Finally, the blast blew bodies at 500–1000 miles per hour through the flaming rubble-filled air. The bomb destroyed everything within 8000 feet, killed at least 70,000 people, and destroyed or damaged 98 percent of Hiroshima's buildings. The effects of atomic radiation have disfigured or killed thousands more, and the whole world bears the psychological scars of the blast.

President Truman announced the explosion:

> It is an atomic bomb. It is a harnessing of the basic power of the universe. . . .
> What has been done is the greatest achievement of organized science in history.

One of the scientists, Albert Einstein, responded "Ach! The world is not ready for it." Within a year, Einstein argued that "the unleashed power of the atom has changed everything save our modes of thinking, and we thus drift toward unparalleled catastrophe."

The atomic bomb and the arms race did, however, begin to change our mode of thinking. For the first time, it was possible to imagine that the human race might destroy itself. This apocalyptic possibility reminded many people of the fragility of life and the uncertainty of existence—ideas that the Puritans could surely appreciate. The threat of the bomb has taken the traditional future away from young people. Twenty-eight percent of high school seniors in 1975–1978 believed that "nuclear or biological annihilation will probably be the fate of all mankind in my lifetime." "For the first time in six centuries (since the great European plagues)," says Edwin Shneidman, "a generation has been born and raised in a thanatological context, concerned with the imminent possibility of the death of the person, the death of humanity, the death of the universe, and, by necessary extension, the death of God" (Shneidman, 1973:189). Some of these people have expressed their concern in protest and reform, and others have repressed concern and participated in the culture of narcissism—a sort of cultural hedonism that derives from a sense of helplessness (Lasch, 1978).

The threat of the end of the world had taken away some of the traditional consolations of the dying and bereaved, including three cultural conceptions of immortality, biosocial—(immortality through reproduction), natural—(immortality through the continuity of Nature), and creative—(immortality through creative endeavors). It has forced people to abandon faith in the future, or to place their faith fully in spiritual immortality, a choice that is difficult in a secular society (Fulton and Gottesman, 1981).

Thanatology

The "thanatological context" of the postwar world has led some people to examine our reservation as a culture to discuss the death which faces us. In 1955, Geoffrey Gorer published "The Pornography of Death" in which he showed that death was the taboo topic of modern civilization. In 1959, Herman Feifel edited *The Meaning of Death,* an interdisciplinary attempt to restore death to cultural consciousness. In 1963 Jessica Mitford blasted "the American way of death" in her book of the same title. Elisabeth Kubler-Ross's *On Death and Dying* in 1969 advised Americans that they can play a significant role in the lives of the dying. Most of these people have promoted the Puritan position, "Life is not comprehended truly or lived fully unless the idea of death is grappled with honestly" (Feifel, 1959).

As they effected this fluidity in American funeral practices, many thanatologists have realized the creative possibilities of the past. They have learned that the American way of death and bereavement has deep intellectual, institutional, and emotional roots in American culture, and they know that our way of death will be hard to change. In a country that conspires to cover up unpleasantness, it will be difficult (if not impossible) to make Americans confront the mysterious reality of death. At the same time, by showing the social *construction* of reality, history teaches us that rituals of dying and bereavement *do change* when people act. It offers hope that Americans can free themselves from the restrictions of the past by recognizing their history and by adapting rituals from the past to meet their human needs. Indeed, in more ways than one, it helps us "to redeem the time."

CONCLUSION

This historical approach to death has taken the reader full circle from living death, to the dying of death, to the resurrection of death. This change of attitude has taken place over a 400-year period. One of the real assets of history is its ability to demonstrate causation and coincidence in human affairs by determining chronology and context.

In this chapter the reader has been exposed to bereavement and burial practices in the United States from the early beginnings of European settlement. While European influences were obviously present in this development, a "breaking away" from the European aristocracy is evidenced by middle-class Americans in the 1830s. Certainly various "isms" played significant roles in the shaping of American bereavement and burial practices. An historical perspective blends the various influences upon the development of American death customs as we know them today.

With the developing of cemeteries, building of funeral homes, and the establishing of life insurance companies, certain needs of Americans have been fulfilled. Security comes from the shear orderliness and structure of these "institutions." One should know what to "expect" from these services and, through paying, turns the responsibility over to the professionals. We Americans differ significantly from nonliterate societies where such functions are completed within the kin network. However, paying someone else to perform a service fits middle-class Americans' specialization and division of labor.

It is important that the consumer stay well informed about burial practices and insurance in our society through staying abreast of various funeral home regulations and different life insurance offerings. It is also significant with the threat of nuclear war that the public be well-informed and actively involved in seeking peace and avoiding such a war. Perhaps this recent "resurrection of death" in an atomic age will be history behind us and not continue into the future.

APPLICATION: BEREAVEMENT NOSTALGIA

"At a Country Funeral" by Wendell Berry presents a contemporary reflection on bereavement customs of the past. The author illustrates many of the major perspectives presented in this chapter—especially the "dying of death" in contemporary American mourning rituals.

Now the old ways that have brought us
farther than we remember sink out of sight
as under the treading of many strangers
ignorant of landmarks. Only once in a while
they are cast clear again upon the mind
as at a country funeral where, amid the soft
lights and hothouse flowers, the expensive
solemnity of experts, notes of a polite musician,
persist the usages of old neighborhood.
Friends and kinsmen come and stand and speak,
knowing the extremity they have come to,
one of their own bearing to the earth the last
of his light, his darkness the sun's definitive mark.
They stand and think as they stood and thought
when even the gods were different.
And the organ music, though decorous
as for somebody else's grief, has its source
in the outcry of pain and hope in log churches,
and on naked hillsides by the open grave,
eastward in mountain passes, in tidelands,
and across the sea. How long a time?
Rock of Ages, cleft for me, let me hide my
self in Thee. They came, once in time,
in simple loyalty to their dead, and returned
to the world. The fields and the work
remained to be returned to. Now the entrance
of one of the old ones into the Rock
too often means a lifework perished from the land
without inheritor, and the field goes wild
and the house sits and stares. Or it passes
at cash value into the hands of strangers.
Now the old dead wait in the open coffin
for the blood kin to gather, come home
for one last time, to hear old men
whose tongues bear an essential topography
speak memories doomed to die.
But our memory of ourselves, hard earned,

is one of the land's seeds, as a seed
is the memory of the life of its kind in its place,
to pass on into life the knowledge
of what has died. What we owe the future is not a
new start, for we can only begin
with what has happened. We owe the future
the past, the long knowledge
that is the potency of time to come.
That makes of a man's grave a rich furrow.
The community of knowing in common is the seed
of our life in this place. There is not only
no better possibility, there is no
other, except for chaos and darkness,
the terrible ground of the only possible
new start. And so as the old die and the young
depart, where shall a man go who keeps
the memories of the dead, except home
again, as one would go back after a burial,
faithful to the fields, lest the dead die
a second and more final death.

Summary

1. Historians mainly determine chronology and context in order to demonstrate causation and coincidence in human affairs.
2. Rural Americans between 1600 and 1930 were well acquainted with death as it was commonplace.
3. The Reformed Tradition of the Protestant Reformation stressed that death and damnation were deserved; however, God elected a select few for salvation. Thus, death was approached with ambivalence.
4. Death was feared by the Puritans. Following death, they prayed not for the soul of the deceased but for the comfort and instruction of the living. The funeral was the main social institution for channeling the grief of Puritan survivors.
5. The Enlightenment replaced depraved dependent Puritans with rational people who viewed death as a natural occurrence rather than a time of judgment. Unitarianism and evangelicalism accepted this view of human nature.
6. Between 1830 and 1945, as a middle-class America emerged, "the dying of death" occurred as funeral institutions designed to keep death out of sight and mind appeared.
7. Important intellectual influences on "the dying of death" were romanticism, sentimentalism, scientific naturalism, and liberal religion.
8. At the middle of the nineteenth century, the rural cemetery evolved—

a landscaped garden in a suburban setting. Life insurance was established at this time to remove anxiety and financial insecurity.
9. Death was resurrected after 1945 with the ushering in of the atomic age.

Discussion Questions

1. Describe and discuss the Puritan view of death. Describe the procedures and atmosphere surrounding the typical Puritan funeral.
2. How did the Enlightenment affect the Reformed Tradition of funerals and view of death?
3. Discuss its influences of the following on the "Dying of Death": Romanticism and Sentimentalism, scientific naturalism, and liberal theology.
4. What are the influences of the following occupations upon the "Dying of Death": life insurance agents, cemetery superintendents, and funeral directors.
5. Describe and explain the reforms that have taken place over the years in the construction and maintenance of the cemetery.
6. What effect has the dropping of the atom bomb had on American death conceptions?
7. Describe the changes that have taken place with regard to the role of the family in funeralization.

Glossary

ELEGY: A song or poem expressing sorrow especially for one who is dead.
EPITAPH: An inscription, often on a tombstone, in memory of a deceased person.
OBITUARY: Notice of a death, usually with a brief biography.
RITUAL: A behavioral form prescribed by custom or law, often associated with religion.
SEXTON: A church custodian charged with the upkeep of the church and parish buildings and grounds.
SOCIALIZATION: The learning process through which an individual is taught to be accepted in his or her society.
SOCIAL STRATIFICATION: A ranking of social status (position) in groups (e.g., upper, middle, and lower classes are basically distinguished in the United States' social class system, while India's stratification is a caste system).

References

AACS. 1889. Vol. 3, p.59.
Beecher, Henry Ward. 1858. Life Thoughts. Boston: Phillips, Sampson.
Beecher, Henry Ward. 1859. Notes from Plymouth Pulpit. New York: Derby and Jackson.
Beecher, Henry Ward. 1866. Royal Truths. Boston: Tichnor and Fields.

Bender, Thomas. 1973. "The 'Rural Cemetery' Movement." *New England Quarterly*, Vol. 47 (June):196–211.

Benjamin, Charles L. 1882. "Essay" *The Casket*, Vol. 7 (February):2.

Bledstein, Burton J. 1976. *The Culture of Professionalism: The Middle Class and the Development of Higher Education in America*. New York: Norton.

Clark, Jr., Clifford E. 1978. *Henry Ward Beecher: Spokesman for a Middle-Class America*. Urbana: University of Illinois Press.

Cleaveland, Nehemiah. 1847. *Green-Wood Illustrated*. New York: R. Martin.

Douglas, Ann. 1977. *The Feminization of American Culture*. New York: Alfred A. Knopf.

Dowd, Quincy L. 1921. *Funeral Management and Costs: A World-Survey of Burial and Cremation*. Chicago: University of Chicago Press.

Downing, Andrew Jackson. 1921. *Landscape Gardening*, 10th ed. New York: Wiley.

"The Dying of Death". 1899. *Review of Reviews*, Vol. 20 (September):364–365.

Emmons, Nathaniel. 1842. "Death Without Order" in *The Works of Nathaniel Emmons*, ed. by Jacob Ide, Vol. 3. Boston: Crocker & Brewster, pp. 29–38.

"Extracts." 1895. *Park and Cemetery*, Vol. 5 (August):108.

Farrell, James J. 1980. *Inventing the American Way of Death, 1830–1920*. Philadelphia: Temple University Press.

"The Fear of Death." 1912. *Harper's Weekly*, Vol. 56 (October 5):21.

Feifel, Herman, ed. 1959. *The Meaning of Death*. New York: McGraw-Hill.

French, Stanley. 1975. "The Establishment of Mount Auburn and the 'Rural Cemetery Movement'" in *Death in America*, ed. by David Stannard. Philadelphia: University of Pennsylvania Press, pp. 69–91.

Fulton, Robert, and David J. Gottesman. 1981. "Loss, Social Change and the Prospect of Mourning." Unpublished Paper.

"Funeral Directors." *The Casket*, Vol. 8 (June 1883).

Gebhart, John C. 1927. *The Reasons for Present-Day Funeral Costs*. Unpublished.

Geddes, Gordon. 1981. *Welcome Joy: Death in Puritan New England*. Ann Arbor: University of Michigan Press.

Gross, Robert A. 1976. *The Minutemen and Their World*. New York: Hill and Wang.

Habenstein, Robert W, and William M. Lamers. 1955. "The Pattern of Late 19th Century Funerals."*The History of American Funeral Directing*, pp. 389–444. Milwaukee: Bulfin Printers.

Hale, Nathan G. 1971. *The Origin and Foundations of the Psychoanalytic Movement in the United States, 1876–1918*. New York: Oxford University Press.

Handford, Thomas W., ed. 1887. *Beecher: Christian Philosopher, Pulpit Orator, Patriot and Philanthropist*, pp. 47–49. Chicago: Donahue, Henneberry.

Hare, Sidney J. 1910. "The Cemetery Beautiful." *AACS* Vol. 24:41.

Hay, Mrs. E.E. 1900. "Influence of Our Surroundings." *AACS*, Vol. 14:46.

Hillerman, Barbara. 1980. "Chrysallis of Gloom: Nineteenth Century Mourning Costume," in *A Time to Mourn: Expressions of Grief in Nineteenth Century America*, p 101, ed. by Martha V. Pike and Janice Gray Armstrong. Stony Brook, N.Y.: The Museums at Stony Brook.

Hohenschuh, W.P. *The Modern Funeral: Its Management*. Chicago: Trade Periodical Company.

Howe, Daniel Walker. 1970. *The Unitarian Conscience: Harvard University Press, 1805–1861*. Cambridge: Harvard University Press.

Hutchinson, Woods. 1893. "Death as a Factor in Progress." *North American Review*, Vol. 156 (May):637.

"The Ideas of a Plain Country Woman." 1913. *Ladies Home Journal*, Vol. 30 (April):44.

Johnson, J.B. 1896. "A More Rational View of Death." *Proceedings of the Association of American Cemetery Superintendents. AACS*, Vol. 10:77.

Lasch, Christopher. 1978. *The Culture of Narcissism: American Life in an Age of Diminishing Expectations*. New York: Norton.

Lloyd, Phoebe. 1980. "Posthumous Mourning Portraiture," in *A Time to Mourn: Expressions of Grief in Nineteenth Century America*, ed. by Martha V. Pike and Janice Gray Armstrong. Stony Brook, N.Y.: The Museums at Stony Brook.

Ludwig, Allen.1966. *Graven Images: New England Stonecarving and its Symbols*. Middletown, Conn.: Wesleyan University Press.

"The Man Nobody Envies: An Account of the Experiences of an Undertaker," 1914. *American Magazine*, Vol. 77 (June):68–71.

Mayo, Wyndham R. 1916. "Address." *AACS*, Vol. 2:51.

Oxley, J. MacDonald. 1887. "The Reproach of Mourning." *Forum*, Vol. 2 (February):608–614.

"Pain, Life, and Death." 1914. *Littell's Living Age*, Vol. 281 (May 9):370.

Pike, Martha V., and Janice Gray Armstrong, ed. 1980. *A Time to Mourn: Expressions of Grief in Nineteenth Century America*. Stony Brook, N.Y.: The Museums at Stony Brook.

Proceedings of the National Convention at Rochester, N.Y. and the Reported Constitution and By-Laws. 1982. Rochester, N.Y.: A.H. Nirdlinger.

Rosenberg, Charles. 1966. "Science and American Social Thought." *Science and Society in the U.S.*, ed. by David Van Tassel and Michael Hall. Homewood, Ill.: Dorsey Press.

Rosenberg, Charles E. 1973. "Sexuality, Class, and Role in Nineteenth Century America." *American Quarterly*, Vol. 25 (May):137.

Rotundo, Barbara. 1973. "The Rural Cemetery Movement." *Essex Institute Historical Collections*, Vol. 109 (July): 231–242.

Sargent, A.H. 1888. "Country Cemeteries." *AACS*. Vol. 2:51.

Seavoy, Mr. 1906. "Twentieth Century Methods." *Park and Cemetery*, Vol. 15 (February):488.

Sewall, Samuel. 1973. *The Diary of Samuel Sewall*, ed. by M. Halsey Thomas. 2 vol. New York: Farrar, Straus and Giroux.

Shneidman, Edwin. 1973. "Megadeath: Children of the Nuclear Family." *Deaths of Man*. Baltimore: Penguin Books.

Simonds, O.C. 1919. "Review of Progress in Cemetery Design and Development with Suggestions for the Future." *AACS*, Vol. 24:41.

Smith, Bayley. 1910. "An Outdoor Room on a Cemetery Lot." *Country Life in America*, Vol. 17 (March):539.

Stannard, David E. 1980. "Where All Our Steps Are Tending: Death in the American Context." *A Time to Mourn: Expressions of Grief in Nineteenth Century America*, p. 26., ed. by Martha V. Pike and Janice Gray Armstrong. Stony Brook, N.Y.: The Museums at Stony Brook.

Taylor, Lawrence. 1980. "Symbolic Death: An Anthropological View of Mourning Ritual in the Nineteenth Century."*A Time to Mourn: Expressions of Grief in Nine-*

teenth Century America, pp. 39–48, ed. by Martha V. Pike and Janice Gray Armstrong. Stony Brook, N.Y.: The Museums at Stony Brook.

"There Are No Dead." 1913. *Outlook,* Vol. 104 (August 30):979–980.

Tocqueville, Alexis de. 1945. *Democracy in America.* New York: Vintage Books.

Tuckerman, Henry. 1856. "The Law of Burial and the Sentiment of Death." *Christian Examiner,* Vol. 61 (November):338–342.

U.S. Bureau of the Census. 1975. *Historical Statistics of the United States, Colonial Times to 1970,* pp. 1050–59. Washington, D.C.: Department of Commerce, Bureau of the Census,

Wells, Richard A. 1887. *Decorum: A Practical Treatise on Etiquette and Dress of the Best American Society.* Springfield, Mass.: King, Richardson.

Suggested Readings

Farrell, James. 1980. *Inventing the American Way of Death, 1830–1920.* Philadelphia: Temple University Press.

Examines the transformation from the Puritan Way of Death to the American Way of Death. Includes intellectual and institutional changes, and concludes with a case study of how such changes affected a single county.

Geddes, Gordon. 1981. *Welcome Joy: Death in Puritan New England.* Ann Arbor: U.M.I. Research Press.

Good descriptive study, rich in detail. Particularly good on the Puritan funeral and bereavement.

Habenstein, Robert, and William Lamers. 1962. *The History of American Funeral Directing.* Milwaukee: Bulfin Printers.

Prepared for the National Funeral Directors Association, this detailed study is a good history of the development of the profession.

Jackson, Charles O., ed. 1977. *Passing: the Vision of Death in America.* Westport, Conn.: Greenwood Press.

A collection of classic essays on death in America, a few of which have been superseded by more recent work in the area.

Pike, Martha, and Janice Gray Armstrong. 1980. *A Time to Mourn: Expressions of Grief in Nineteenth Century America.* Stony Brook, N.Y.: The Museums at Stony Brook.

A beautifully illustrated collection of excellent essays, a must for anyone who wants to see and feel the grief of nineteenth century America.

Stannard, David, ed. 1975. *Death in America.* Philadelphia: University of Pennsylvania Press.

The December 1974 special issue of *American Quarterly,* with an added essay on the cemetery as a cultural institution by Stanley French.

Chapter 11

THE FUNERAL: EXPRESSION OF CONTEMPORARY AMERICAN BEREAVEMENT

You must express your grief at the loss of a loved one and then
you must go on. The eyes of the dead must be gently closed and
the eyes of the living must be gently opened.
Jan Brugler, Indian Lake (Ohio) High School Student

MOST ANTHROPOLOGISTS AGREE that there has been no civilization discovered and studied that has not in some form given evidence of a funeralization process. This process varies greatly from culture to culture, but the basic elements of the recognition of the death—a rite or ritual and the final disposition of the body—have their counterparts in every culture. As concluded in Chapter 9, funeral rituals allow individuals of every culture to maintain relations with ancestors, while uniting family members, reinforcing social status, fostering group cohesiveness, and restoring the social structure of the society.

SOCIAL AND CULTURAL ROOTS OF AMERICAN FUNERALIZATION

The process of final disposition of the body in the contemporary American culture should be studied within its cultural and historical context. As we discovered in Chapter 9, it is wrong to believe that funeralization is either unique to western culture, or has been invented or created by it. To bury the dead is a common social practice, and the methods to accomplish this, and the meanings associated with it are culturally determined.

This process requires a functionary to be associated with it. The functionary may be a professional, a tradesperson, a religious leader, a servant, or even a member of the family. The functionary in each society is closely associated with the folkways and mores of the culture and its philosophical approach to life and death.

Scripture reveals in the 50th Chapter of Genesis (Verse 2) that physicians embalmed the body of Jacob, the father of Joseph. This is followed by a detailed description of the funeral and burial. The historian Herodotus records embalming preparation as early as circa 484 B.C. These are but two documents in addition to archeological discoveries of earlier cultures that give evidence of the disposition of the dead.

It is often stated that Egypt had a secret process for the preservation of the dead. However, the Egyptian embalming process is fully described in several resources. There is perhaps no ancient culture that provides more evidence of its burial procedures than the great number of Egyptian mummies available for observation and study.

The Egyptians believed that the soul made a journey following death. According to their beliefs, this journey took approximately 3000 years followed by the soul's returning to the body it had left. This required the preservation of the body so that the soul, upon its return, would have a final destination or home. In addition to the embalming procedures, the Egyptians attempted to exclude air and moisture from the body by the liberal use of wrappings, oils, and gums. They also practiced elaborate encasement and burial of the remains. Such attempts at body preservation were obviously effective as evidenced by the many specimens still in existence today.

In many cultures the religious beliefs of the people influence their funeral and burial practices. Such was the case on the European continent during the period of the feudal estates. Each landholder or lord was responsible for the people who worked for him and were members of the lord's extended family. These lords had a chaplain or religious person as a part of their staff, and they became responsible for the care and burial of the dead.

In the structure of the church, priests were assigned to certain duties during specified hours. It is suggested that our use of the word sexton today comes from the practice of assigning the priest in charge of the sixth hour (in Latin *sex*) with the burial of the dead and the supervision of the churchyard or cemetery.

As western civilization developed and progressed, there is evidence that many of the functionaries were anatomists, doctors, or artists. Each wanted to preserve the human body to further his own professional interest and offered to do so in return for the availability of the body for study and research. Still in existence today are anatomical plates that daVinci drew from his observations of human specimens.

With the advent of the discovery of the circulatory system of the body, circa 1600, and the possibility of diffusion of preserving chemicals through that system, more sophisticated methods of embalming the body were developed. Dr. Hunter of England and Dr. Gannal of France, independently of each other, furthered the process in the early 1600s. In France, this coincided with the advent of the bubonic plague. During this period of time, extensive attempts were made to preserve the bodies of the dead to protect the health of those who survived the plague.

Historically, through a considerable period of time, the pattern of mortuary behavior in any society is subject to change, although basic death beliefs remain fundamentally unchanged. The roots of American funeral behavior extend back in a direct line several thousand years to early Judaeo-Christian beliefs as to the nature of God, man, and the hereafter, and, in turn, these beliefs and practices were influenced to some extent by even earlier beliefs and practices.

Source: Habenstein and Lamers, 1962

Early American Funeral Practices

During the colonization of America, there is early evidence of the care and burial of the dead. There is, however, no evidence of any attempt at body preservation, even though the body was bathed and dressed prior to burial. This was usually done by nurses, midwives, or members of the family. It was not until the time of the Civil War that embalming was promoted as a means of temporary preservation of the body for return to the soldier's home. Some reports credit this practice to a military doctor by the name of Thomas Holmes. It was not until the late 1800s and early 1900s that states began to promote the practice of embalming for the protection of the public's health. With the advent of the practice of embalming, laws were soon passed to regulate both the practice and the practitioner.

The current practitioner of this profession evolved from the craftsmen or cabinetmaker (who built the casket as part of his trade) and the livery owner (who provided the special vehicles needed at the time of the funeral—particularly the hearse and special buggies for the family). As the public came to expect the services associated with the casket and transportation, persons began to specialize in providing these services, and the funeral functionary of today evolved as a provider of these services.

With the development of contemporary funeral practices over the past eighty years, it is interesting to observe the kind of facilities evolving to provide these services. It was not customary to hold funerals in the church in Colonial America. The Puritans gave little importance to the funeral and seemed only to demand proper and reverent disposition of the dead by burial. Almost without exception, death occurred in the home. It was, therefore, expected that the dead would be bathed, dressed, put in a casket, and laid out (viewed) in the home. The funeral rite was either in the home or at the grave site. When the first practitioners began to specialize in the burial of the dead, they continued to use the home for this purpose. They often would acquire a large house in the community and convert it to use as a "funeral home." It should be noted that the word "home" was associated with this facility and today is still the most commonly used term to describe funeral facilities.

Casket Colors, Costs Concern Mortician

Boston—Casket styles haven't changed much over the years but "doom and gloom" colors have given way to more lively shades, say morticians gathered for the start of the five-day National Funeral Directors Association.

"We use mostly pastel colors now. Blue is used traditionally because it is the favorite color of women. Pink rates second. Men still like the coppertone and brown caskets," said Edward J. Keohane, president of the Massachusetts Funeral Directors Association.

Keohane, of the Keohane Funeral Home in Quincy, Mass., said the switch from "doom and gloom" colors will be discussed at workshops starting today, along with topics such as the increasing desire of clients for nontraditional funerals and the concern of families for "greater personalization of services."

"They want to get involved in the funeral services," he said. "We find this a very healthy attitude."

"One depressing thought: inflation will follow you to your grave," Keohane said.

Partly because of inflation, a service including casket that cost $983 in 1971 would cost $1,809 in 1980, Keohane said.

"Even the net margin of profit per funeral before taxes has dropped to 5.9 percent, or about $120," he said.

Mergers of funeral homes also are being considered to offset the sizable overhead for real estate, equipment, hearses, and limousines, according to Richard Myers of Ogden, Utah, president of the national association.

Keohane said many funeral directors are fighting federal efforts to impose national standards in the field. He said states already protect consumers.

"We are grateful that we do have avenues that families can go to if there is a disagreement," he said. "They can go to the Massachusetts Funeral Directors Association and, if it is not resolved, they can go to the state Board of Embalming and Funeral Directing that has authority to fine or withdraw a license."

Other convention topics include coping with on-the-job stress, how to work with the news media, and the growing number of women caretakers.

Source: *Lexington* (Ky.) *Herald,* October 26, 1981.

It was only natural that with specialization, special facilities would be developed for the funeral ceremony. The influence of the family and the church is readily seen in that most facilities try to provide both a home-like atmosphere for the gathering of the community and a chapel-like atmosphere for the funeral service. If the family chooses not to use a church for the funeral service, the funeral home provides a similar setting. Approximately 50 percent of the funerals today are held in churches, and the remaining 50 percent are held in funeral homes or cemetery chapels. The Department of Commerce of the United States Government estimates that approximately 22,000 funeral homes serve the families of the approximately 1.9 million annual deaths.

The Decline of Mourning

A decade ago, Anthropologist Geoffrey Gorer wrote a much reprinted article on "the pornography of death." Gorer's point, also made by German Theologian Helmuth Thielicke, is that death is coming to have the same position in modern life and literature that sex had in Victorian times. Some support for the theory is provided by the popular movie *The Loved One,* which turns death into a slapstick dirty joke.

Is grief going underground? People want briefer funeral services, says Dr. Quentin Hand, an ordained Methodist minister who teaches at the theological school of Georgia's Emory University. "No one wants a eulogy any more—they often ask me not to even mention Mother or Father." Even those much scolded death-denyers, the undertakers, seem to sense that something is missing. Dean Robert Lehr of the Gupton Jones College of Mortuary Science in Dallas says that whereas students used to study only embalming, they now go in heavily for "grief psychology and grief counseling." Explains Lehr: "There are only 16 quarter hours in embalming now and 76 in other areas. We're in a transition period."

The outward signs of mourning—veils and widows weeds, black hat and armbands, crepe-hung doorways—are going the way of the hearse pulled by plumed horses. There is almost no social censure against re-marrying a few months after bereavement in what one psychiatrist calls "the Elizabeth Taylorish way" (referring to her statement six months after husband Mike Todd was killed in a plane crash: "Mike is dead now, and I am alive"). Many psychologists who have no quarrel with the life-must-continue attitude are dubious about the decline in expression of grief. Psychology Professor Harry W. Martin of Texas Southwestern Medical School deplores the "slick, smooth operation of easing the corpse out, but saying no to weeping and wailing and expressing grief and loneliness. What effect does this have on us psychologically? It may mean that we have to mourn covertly, by subterfuge—perhaps in various degrees of depression, perhaps in mad flights of activity, perhaps in booze." In his latest book, *Death, Grief and Mourning,* Anthropologist Gorer warns that abandonment of the traditional forms of mourning results in "callous-ness, irrational preoccupation with and fear of death, and vandalism."

Whether or not such conclusions are justified, the take-it-in-stride atti-tude can make things difficult. Gorer cites his brother's widow, a New Englander, whose emotional reticence, combined with that of her British friends, led her to eschew any outward signs of mourning. As a result, "she let herself be, almost literally, eaten up with grief, sinking into a deep and long-lasting depression." Many a widow invited to a party "to take her mind off things" has embarrassed herself and her hostess by a flood of tears at the height of the festivities. On occasion, Gorer himself "refused invitations to cocktail parties, explaining that I was mourning; people responded to this statement with shocked embarrassment, as if I had voiced some appalling obscenity."

Funerals seem ever harder to get to in a high-pressure, commuterized way of life. But the social repression of grief goes against the experience of the human race. Mourning is one of the traditional "rites of passage" through which families and tribes can rid themselves of their dead and return to normal living. Black funeral parades, Greek klama (ritual weep-ing), Irish wakes—each in their own way fulfill this function. Orthodox Jewish families are supposed to "sit *shivah*"; for seven days after the burial they stay home, wearing some symbol of a "shredded garment," such as a piece of torn cloth, and keeping an unkempt appearance. Friends bring food as a symbol of the inability of the bereaved to concern themselves with practical affairs. For eleven months sons are enjoined to say the prayers for the dead in the synagogue twice a day.

By no means all observers agree that the decline of such demanding customs is a bad thing. The old rituals, while a comfort and release for some, could be a burden to others. And grief expressed in private can be more meaningful than the external forms. London Psychiatrist Dr. David Stafford-Clark thinks that the new attitude toward death should be considered in the context of "the way the whole structure of life has changed since World War II, particularly the very different attitude toward the future which has arisen. It is a much more expectant attitude—an uncertain one, but not necessarily a more negative one."

Source: *Time Magazine*, November 12, 1965.

THE CONTEMPORARY AMERICAN FUNERAL

Most people use the words death, grief, and bereavement synonymously. This can lead to difficulty in communication. The words are closely interrelated, but each has a specific content or meaning. As discussed in Chapter 1, death is that point in time when life ceases to exist. *Death* is an event. It can be marked to a certain day, hour, and minute. *Grief* is an emotion, a very powerful emotion. It is triggered or stimulated by death. Although, as noted in Chapter 6, one can have "anticipatory grief" prior to the death of a significant other, grief is an emotional response to death. *Bereavement* is the state of having lost a significant other to death. Alternative processes— such as denial, avoidance, and defiance—have been shown by psychologists and psychiatrists to be only aberrations of the grief process and, as such, are not viable means of grief resolution.

The ultimate method of final disposition of the body should be determined by the persons in grief. Those charged with these decisions will be guided by their personal values and by the norms of the culture in which they live.

With approximately 70 percent of American deaths occurring in hospitals or institutions for the care of the sick and infirm, the contemporary process of body disposition begins at the time of death when the body is removed from the institutional setting. Most frequently the body is taken to a funeral home. There, the body is bathed, embalmed, and dressed. It is then placed in a casket selected by the family. Typically, arrangements are made for the ceremony, assuming a ceremony is to follow. The funeral director, in consultation with the family, will determine the type, time, place, and day of the ceremony. In most instances, this will be a public rite or ceremony with a religious content (Pine, 1971). The procedure described above is followed in approximately 75 percent of funerals. There are, obviously, alternatives to this procedure that will be examined later in this chapter.

Following this ceremony, final disposition of the body is made by either burial (85 percent), cremation (10 percent), or entombment (5 percent). (These percentages are approximate national averages and will vary by geographical region.) This bereavement process will then be followed by a period of postfuneral adjustment for the family. While it certainly will vary with individual cases, Lindemann (1944) indicates that this period will last from ninety to 190 days. Davidson (1975) suggests that total resolution of the grief process will take from eighteen to twenty-four months. The grief process will likely last at least one year since the bereaved have to experience every anniversary, holiday, and special event once without the person who dies. Both Davidson and Lindemann agree that grief is never completely resolved, but will remain with the individual throughout his or her lifetime. One does not "get over" a death but, with time, learns to live with it.

HOW THE FUNERAL MEETS THE NEEDS OF THE BEREAVED

Irion (1956) has described the following needs of the bereaved: the need for reality, the need for expression of grief, the need for social support, and the need to place the death in a context of meaning. For Irion, the funeral is an experience of significant personal value insofar as it meets the religious, social, and psychological needs of the mourners. Each of these dimensions is necessary for returning bereaved individuals to everyday living and, in the process, resolving their grief.

The *psychological* focus of the funeral is based on the fact that grief is an emotion. Jackson (1963) has indicated that grief is the other side of the coin of love. He contends that if a person has never loved the deceased—had an emotional investment of some type and degree—he or she will not grieve upon death. Evidence of this can easily be demonstrated by the number of deaths that we hear, see, or read about daily that do not have an impact on us unless we have some kind of emotional involvement with those deceased persons. We can read of seventy-eight deaths in a plane crash and not grieve over any of them unless we personally knew one or more of the individuals killed. Exceptions to the above might include the situation when a celebrity or public figure dies and people experience a sense of grief even though there has never been any personal contact.

In his original work on the symptomology of grief, Lindemann (1944) stressed this concept of grief and its importance as a step in the resolution of grief. He defines how the emotion of grief must support the reality and finality of death. As long as the finality of death is avoided, Lindemann (1944) believes grief resolution is impeded. For this reason, he strongly recommends that the bereaved persons view the dead. When the living confront the dead, all of the intellectualization and avoidance techniques break down. When we can say, "He or she is dead, I am alive, and from this day forward my life will be forever different," we have broken through the devices of denial and avoidance, and have accepted the reality of death. It is only at this point that we can begin to withdraw the emotional capital which we have invested in the deceased and seek to create new relationships with the living.

On the other hand, viewing the corpse can be very traumatic for some. Most people are not accustomed to seeing a significant other stretched out with eyes closed and a cold body. Indeed, for some this "scene" may remain in their memories for a lifetime. Thus, they remember the cold corpse, not the warm, responding person. Whether or not to view the body is not a cut and dry issue. Many factors should be taken into account when this decision is made.

The power of the emotion of grief has been the subject of much study in the last fifteen years. The death of a spouse or a child can be one of the most stressful experiences a person can experience (Holmes and Rahe, 1967).

Grief resolution is especially important for family members, but others are affected also—the neighbors, the business community in some instances, the religious community in most instances, the health care community, and the circle of friends and associates (many of whom may be unknown to the family). All of these groups of people will grieve to some extent the death of their relationship with the deceased. Thus, many people are affected by the death. Each of the persons affected will seek not only a means of expressing their grief over the death but also a network of support to help them cope with their grief.

Sociologically, the funeral is a social event which brings the chief mourners and the members of society into a confrontation with death. The funeral becomes a vehicle which can bring persons of all walks of life and degrees of relationship to the deceased, together in one place, for expression and support. It is for this reason that in our contemporary culture the funeral becomes an occasion to which no one is invited but all may come. This was not always the case, and some cultures make the funeral ceremony an "invitation only" experience. It is perhaps for this reason that private funerals (restricted only to the family or a special list of persons) have all but disappeared in our culture. (The only possible exception to this statement are the funerals for celebrities—where participation for the general public is limited to media coverage.)

At a time when emotions are strong, it is important that human interaction and social support become a high priority. A funeral can provide this atmosphere. To grieve alone can be devastating because it becomes necessary for that lone person to absorb all of the feelings into his or herself. It has often been said that "joy shared is joy increased"; surely grief shared will be grief diminished. People need each other at times when they have intense emotional experiences.

A funeral is in essence a one-time kind of "support group" that assembles to undergird and support those grieving persons. A funeral provides a conducive social environment for mourning. We may either go to the funeral home to visit with the bereaved or for the purpose of working through our own feelings of grief. Most of us have had the experience of finding it difficult for the first time to discuss the death with a member of the family. We seek the proper atmosphere, time, or place. It is during the funeral, the wake, the shiva, or the visitation with the bereaved where we are provided the opportunity to express our condolences and sympathy comfortably.

Anger and guilt are often deeply felt at the time of death and will surface in words and actions. They are permitted within the funeral atmosphere as honest and candid expressions of grief, when at other times, they might bring criticism and reprimand. The funeral atmosphere says in essence "You are okay, I am okay; we have some strong feelings, and now is the time to express and share them for the benefit of all." Silence, talking, touching, feeling, and all means of sharing can be expressed without the fear of it being inappropriate.

The third function of the funeral is to provide a *theological or philosophical* perspective to facilitate grieving and provide a context of meaning in which to place one of life's most significant experiences. For the majority of Americans, the funeral is a religious rite or ceremony (Pine, 1971). For those who do not possess a religious creed or orientation, death will find definition or expression in the context of the values which the deceased and the grievers find important. Theologically or philosophically, the funeral functions as an attempt to bring meaning to the death and life of the deceased individual. For the religiously oriented person, it will perhaps contain a belief or understanding of an afterlife. For others, it may be seen only as an end of biological life and the beginning of symbolic immortality caused by the effects of one's life on the lives of others. The funeral should be planned in order to give meaning to whichever value context is significant for the bereaved.

"Why?" is one of the most often asked questions at the moment of death or upon being told that someone we know has died. Though it cannot provide the final answer to this question, the funeral can place death within a context of meaning that is significant to those who mourn. If it is religious in context, the theology, creed, and articles of faith confessed by the mourners will give them comfort and assurance as to the meaning of death. Others who have developed a personally meaningful philosophy of life and death will seek to place the death in that philosophical context.

Cultural expectations require that we typically dispose of the dead with ceremony and dignity. The funeral can ascribe importance to the remains of the dead.

THE AMERICAN PRACTICE OF FUNERAL SERVICE

Education and Licensure

It was indicated earlier in this chapter that with the evolution of the funeral there likewise has been an evolution of a funeral functionary. Our contemporary American culture refers to that functionary as a funeral director. One hundred years ago this functionary was a "layer out of the dead." It was often a member of the family who physically and emotionally could perform the necessary tasks of bathing the body, closing the eyes and mouth, and dressing the body. It was not unusual for a midwife or other person who provided nursing-like services in the community to be called upon to assist the family. Early advertisements indicate that nurses did offer services as "layers out of the dead."

The advent of the cabinetmaker and livery person has been discussed, and, as indicated, out of this transition evolved the funeral director. As early as the 1890s, the various states began to enact legislation to protect the public's health by licensing persons as embalmers.The early licenses directed their attention to the embalming process, and it was not until the decades of the 1920s and 1930s that licensing agencies began to regulate the other aspects of the funeral and the operation of funeral homes. The rationale for this licensure was based upon the felt need to protect the public, primarily in the financial area. However, regulations also addressed themselves to the conduct of the funeral where the cause of death was due to a contagious disease. Another issue of public health protection was the transportation of the dead from the place of death to the location of final disposition. Public health authorities claim that the regulation of the treatment of the dead has significantly contributed to the advanced standard of health this country enjoys.

Based on these concepts, the licensing agencies most often charged with responsibility of regulating the funeral industry have been the various state boards of health. In some states, special boards were established for the regulation and enforcement procedures.

Licensure in the various states includes three basic licenses, and it has been reserved to the individual states as to what kinds of licenses they will require. A license as an embalmer permits a person to legally remove the dead from the place of death and prepare the body through the process of embalming for viewing and funeralization. All states require persons who function in this regard to be licensed. A license to practice as a funeral director permits the holder to arrange the legal details of the funeral, including the preparation of the death certificate and counseling with the family to arrange, plan, and implement the kind of funeral desired for the deceased. A third license is one that permits the licensee to practice mortuary science—defined as all-inclusive and covers the practices of both embalming and funeral directing.

A few states have a license for a funeral director—a license that may be held by only one person in each firm, usually the owner or manager—and serves to give the licensing agency control over all of the practitioners within that firm as well as the conduct of the firm. A greater number of states have created a funeral home license or permit that is required to be issued to each funeral home and would permit the state to close the funeral home by the withdrawal of the license without taking action against the licensees employed by that firm. In addition to every state requiring embalmers to be licensed, forty-five states and the District of Columbia require practitioners to be licensed as funeral directors. The exact number of states requiring funeral home licenses or permits is hard to determine inasmuch as some are required by law, some by regulation, and some by local ordinance. Approximately one-half of the states have some requirement that governs the operation of a funeral home.

The qualifications for licensure deal basically with age, citizenship, and specifically with education. As of 1984, all states require a high school education. In addition, thirty-four states require one calendar year of professional preparation, and nine states require only nine months. Seven states require one academic year of college in addition to the professional preparation, and twenty-one states require two academic years of college in addition to the professional preparation. Following the academic training, and in some instances before academic training is begun, all states require an internship or apprenticeship period. This varies from six months to three years. The variance is directly related to the amount of college and professional training required. Upon the completion of academic and internship or apprenticeship requirements, all states require applicants for licensure to successfully pass a qualifying examination prior to the issuance of the license to practice.

Approximately 1 percent of the licensees in the United States are women. However, in the last decade, the number of women entering colleges of funeral service education and becoming licensed has greatly increased.

As of 1982, eight states require or mandate continuing education to renew the license to practice. There is also an Academy of Professional Funeral Service Practice that provides a voluntary program of continuing education.

> Clarence Darrow, discussing an ancestor reported to have been an undertaker, said: "One could imagine a more pleasant means of livelihood, but, almost any trade is bearable if the customers are sure."

The Role of the Funeral Director

Rabbi Earl Grollman (1972) described the role of the funeral director as that of a caretaker, caregiver and gatekeeper. He indicates that the etymology of the word "undertaker" is based upon the activities of the early undertaker who "undertook" to do those things for people at the time of death that were crucial in meeting their bereavement needs. It is obvious that in the process of taking care of people, supportive care would be given to those persons they served. The funeral director, from the perspective of the community, was viewed as a secular gatekeeper between the living and the dead.

Brantner (1973), elaborating upon the caregiver role, has emphasized that the funeral director is a crisis intervenor. Support for this idea can be documented in the vast amount of literature dealing with the counseling role of the crisis intervenors who are not clinical practitioners by training, but are those professionals to whom the public turns in the crisis of death.

The funeral director will serve the family by determining their needs and responding to them (Raether and Slater, 1974). This will include, but not be limited to, the funeral (or its alternative) that together they will plan and implement. As a licensee of the state, the funeral director will handle the details requiring the death to be properly recorded and filing permits for transportation and final disposition of the body.

The funeral director will serve as a liaison with other professionals working with the family—medical personnel, clergy, lawyers, cemetery personnel, and when necessary, law enforcement officials.

Body Preparation

While the Egyptian process of embalming required seventy days to perform, today body preparation is completed within a period of a few hours and is more effective and acceptable. Body preparation may be as simple as bathing the body, closing the eyes and mouth, and dressing it for final disposition. This procedure, infrequently selected, is utilized by families who wish direct disposition. Later on in this chapter we will discuss direct disposition where this procedure may be an acceptable and a logical choice.

Nationally, it is estimated that four out of five bodies are embalmed before final disposition. Embalming, by definition, is the replacement of normal body fluids with preserving chemicals.This process is accomplished by using the vascular system of the body to both remove the body fluids and perfuse the body with preserving chemicals. The arterial system is used to introduce the chemicals into the body, and the venous system is used to remove the body fluids. This intravascular exchange is accomplished by using an embalming machine. The machine can best be described as an "artificial heart" outside of the body, which produces the pressure necessary to accomplish the exchange of fluids. This, together with procedures to remove the contents of the hollow viscera from the body organs, constitutes the embalming procedure.

In addition to the embalming procedure and the thorough bathing of the body, cosmetic procedures are used to restore a normal color to the face and hands. When death occurs, the pigments of the skin, which give the body its normal tone and color, no longer function. It is for this reason that creams, liquids, and/or sprays are used to restore color.

The question is often asked, "Why embalm or cosmetize the dead body?"—the assumption being that if one of the needs of the family is the reality of death, then why not leave that body in its most deathlike appearance? Those who have seen a person die (especially if the dying process was painful, prolonged, and emaciating) know that the condition of many bodies at the time of death is very repulsive. Many people cannot accept this condition. It is for this reason that contemporary funeral directors embalm and cosmetize the body.

Another reason for embalming is based on the mobility of citizens. Viewing, which is practiced in over 75 percent of the funerals today, often requires more than a bathing and dressing of the body. Due to the time involved, embalming is necessary to accomplish a temporary preservation of the body to permit the gathering of the family which may take as long as two or three days. If the body were to remain unembalmed for this length of time, the distasteful effects of decomposition would create a significant problem for grievers.

Though arguments have been presented favoring embalming, it may not always be necessary or desired. Embalming is not required in all states. In some states, for instance, if the body is disposed of within a certain time period (for example, 24 hours), is not transported on a common carrier or across state lines, or the person did not die of a contagious disease, embalming is not required. If a body is to be cremated and no public viewing is held, certainly embalming would not be necessary. Many consumers just assume that embalming should or must occur.

A frequently asked question is, "If a body is embalmed, how long will it last?" There is no simple answer to this question. It is for that reason that contemporary funeral directors talk in terms of "temporary preservation."

Most families are interested in a preservation that will permit them to view the body, have a visitation, and allow the body to be present for the funeral. Beyond that, they are not concerned with the lasting effects of embalming.

Final Disposition

Earlier in this chapter we indicated three forms of final disposition and their approximated percentage of utilization. Earth burial is by far the most widely used. Almost without exception, earth burial is accomplished within established cemeteries. In some instances, earth burial can be made outside of a cemetery if the landowner where the interment is to be made, and the health officer of jurisdiction, grant their permission. By law, cemeteries have the right to establish reasonable rules and regulations to be observed by those who arrange for burial in them. A person does not purchase property within a cemetery, but rather purchases the "right to interment" in a specific location within that cemetery. Most cemeteries will require that the casket be placed in some kind of outer receptacle or burial vault. The cemetery will also control how the grave can be marked with monuments or grave markers.

Cremation is the next most common method of final disposition. Until very recently, almost all crematories were located within cemeteries. With the increase of cremation as an option for final disposition, some funeral homes have now installed crematories. Cremation is accomplished by the use of either extreme heat or direct flame. In either instance, the actual process of reducing the casket (or alternative container) and the body to "ashes" takes approximately two hours. After the cremation, the residue of cremated remains is collected, put in a container and disposed of according to the wishes of the family. The cremains may be buried in the earth, scattered in an appropriate or significant place, or placed in a niche in a columbarium—a special room in a cemetery—or in some churches where cremated remains may be placed and memorialized.

Irion (1968) discusses cremation in great depth as to its historical, psychological, and theological perspectives. His book on the subject is worthwhile reading for anyone interested in the subject or who for personal reasons might want to consider cremation as a means of final disposition.

Entombment is the least practiced of final disposition options. It consists of placing the body (contained within a casket) in a special building designed for this purpose. There are large buildings, called mausoleums, constructed within cemeteries and offered by the cemetery as an alternative to earth burial or cremation. In some instances, families may purchase the right to interment in a cemetery, and on the designated space build a private or family mausoleum that will hold as few as one or two bodies or as many as twelve to sixteen. Both types of mausoleums must be specifically constructed and designed in such a way as to provide lasting disposition for the body. Most states and/or cemeteries regulate the specifications and construction of the mausoleum.

President Roosevelt left detailed instructions for his funeral and burial, should he die while President. He directed that the funeral service be simple, that the casket be plain and of wood, that there be no embalming of the body or sealing of the casket and that his grave have no lining.

These instructions were found in a private safe days after his burial, too late to be considered. Consequently, Franklin D. Roosevelt's remains were embalmed, sealed in a copper coffin and placed in a cement vault.

Source: *Consumer Survival Kit: The Last Rights: Funerals*. Owings Mills, Maryland.

Alternatives to the Funeral

People often ask if there are alternatives to the conventional, traditional or typical funeral. There are primarily three alternatives to the funeral— immediate disposition of the body of the deceased, the bequest of the deceased to a medical institution for anatomical study and research, and the memorial service. Each of these alternatives is defined and discussed below.

Immediate disposition is that procedure where the deceased is removed from the place of death. Proper certificates are filed and permits received so the body can be disposed of by cremation or earth burial without any ceremony. In these instances, the family is not present, usually does not view the deceased after death, and is not concerned with any further type of memorialization. It is immediate in that it is accomplished as quickly after death as is possible. It is in this situation where the body will not likely be embalmed, and the only preparation will consist of bathing and washing the body.

Body bequest programs have become more well known in the last three decades and permit the deceased (prior to their death) or the family (after the death) to donate the body to a medical institution. A Compendium on Body Donation (NFDA, 1981) indicates that, when the family desires, 75 percent of the donee institutions permit a funeral to be held prior to the delivery of the body to the institution for study or research. Some medical schools will pay the cost of transporting the body to the medical school while others will not. With regard to expenses, this is the least expensive way of disposition of the body, especially if a memorial service is conducted without the body present. The Compendium also indicates that in almost every instance the family may request that either the residue of the

Father Keeps Son's Memory Alive With Corpse in Home

A. P. Louisville, Ky.—William Sneed's son died November 8 of injuries suffered in an auto accident. He won't be buried. Instead, Sneed said, the body will remain in a casket with a clear plastic top in a room off the family kitchen.

"There are three especially painful moments one goes through at the death of a loved one," Sneed said. "The first is at the news of the death, the second when you see the body in the casket at the funeral home, and the third and most difficult is when you have to turn away from the grave site and know you'll never see that person again. We simply decided not to go through that last step."

Sneed obtained a burial permit naming himself custodian of the body of his son, William B. Sneed III, 29. The permit names the place of entombment as the Sneed Family Mausoleum—the room off the kitchen.

There is no law in Louisville that requires burial below ground. Sneed said the decision to keep the body of his son at home really began eight years ago.

"At first, it was like a joke, just between the three of us (himself, his daughter and his son)," he said. "But after talking about it for a while, it got serious. We decided then—I don't remember how long ago it was—that whichever one of us was the first to go, the other two would take care of everything like this."

Sneed said he plans to remodel the interior of his home to accommodate a small chapel at the rear, and the body will be placed there.

Source: *Minneapolis Tribune*, November 20, 1975.

body or the cremated remains be returned when it is of no further benefit to the donee. In those instances where the family does not desire to have the body or the cremated remains returned, the donee institution will arrange for cremation and/or earth burial—oftentimes with an appropriate ceremony. People who are considering donating their bodies should be aware of the fact that at the time of death the donee institution may not have the need of a body. If this does happen the family will have to find another institution or make other arrangements for the disposition of the body.

To some this may not be seen as an alternate to the funeral if a ceremony is held prior to the delivery of the bequested body or after the study is complete; but inasmuch as the procedure is different from the most common methods, it may be considered as an alternative. Approximately 7000 such donations are made each year out of 1,900,000 deaths.

The memorial service is defined as a service without the body present. It is true that every funeral is a memorial service—inasmuch as it is in memory of someone—but a memorial service, by our definition, is an alternative to the typical funeral. It may be conducted on the day of the death, within two or three days of the death, or sometimes as much as weeks or months following the death.The content of the service places little or no emphasis on the death. Instead, it often is a service of acclamation of philosophical concepts. These services may be religious or nonreligious in content. It is obvious that this type of service can meet the needs of some of the bereaved.

There are organizations for consumers called memorial societies. Such an example is the one in Ithaca, New York. The by-laws of this particular nonprofit and nonsectarian organization establish the following as purposes of their society:

1. To promote the dignity, simplicity, and spiritual values of funeral rites and memorial services.
2. To facilitate simple disposal of deceased persons at reasonable costs, but with adequate allowances to funeral directors for high quality services.
3. To increase the opportunity for each person to determine the type of funeral or memorial service he or she desires.
4. To aid its members and promote their interests in achieving the forgoing.

Thus, such a memorial society would help educate comsumers regarding death prior to the actual death of a significant other and present options for final disposition of the body. Likewise, many funeral directors today serve as valuable resource persons by sharing information regarding death with various community groups.

POST-DEATH COSTS AND EXPENSES RELATED TO FUNERALS AND FINAL DISPOSITION

In a recent survey (Pine, 1982) of funeral costs covering 125,819 deaths reported by 945 funeral homes in all parts of the United States, it was determined that the average funeral cost (including children's services, welfare adult, and partial adult services) was $1,845. If children's services, welfare adult, and partial adult services are excluded, the bill for the average adult funeral was $2,138. Each of these figures is exclusive of outer receptacles (vaults), cash advances, and cemetery expenses. According to death statistics released in 1982 by the National Center for Health Statistics of the Department of Health and Human Services, funerals cost the most in the North Central states and are cheapest in the West where cremation is increasingly popular. States with the highest averages have large rural populations where they tend to choose the more traditional and costly funeral services that include visiting hours, limousines, and other extras, according to one funeral director.

Charges made by a funeral home ordinarily involve the services of the professional staff, the use of the funeral home facilities and equipment, transportation, and the casket or other alternate container. In addition, most funeral homes provide burial vaults or other types of outer enclosures for the casket and ancillary items that may be purchased from the funeral director—clothing, register books, acknowledgment cards, and crucifixes or crosses.

The other major cost which the family will incur at the time of the funeral will be the cemetery charges—either for the purchase of cemetery property for the right to interment therein, or a mausoleum space, or an urn for the cremated remains, and in some instances, a space in a columbarium in which to memorialize the urn. Most families will also select, in one form or another, a monument or marker to identify the grave or other place of final disposition.

A final category of expenses incurred by the family is money which is sometimes advanced by the funeral home at the request of, and as an accommodation to, the family. Such cash advances might include, but are not limited to, the following: charges for opening and closing the grave, crematory costs, honoraria for clergy and musicians, obituary notices, flowers, and transportation costs in addition to the transportation ordinarily furnished by the funeral home.

There have traditionally been three ways a funeral home could present its charges for services and merchandise as selected by the family. The first is the *unit method*. In this procedure, all of the costs involved with the funeral home providing the services (including the staff, the facilities, the automative equipment, and the casket) are included in a single charge. In making a selection under this procedure, the family looks at a "bottom line" figure to which only other charges paid by the funeral home (a vault, additional burial merchandise, cash advances, etc.) might be added.

A second method of presentation is referred to as the *bi-unit or tri-unit* pricing system. In this method, the bi-unit procedure is to make separate charges for professional services and the casket. In a tri-unit procedure, separate charges are made for professional services, the use of facilities, and the casket selected. This enables a family to understand the charges for the three basic components which make up funeral costs.

A third and final method of presenting costs is referred to as either *functional, multi-unit, or itemization*. There is an interchange of the use of these terms. However, they usually refer to the same basic procedure. In this method of pricing, each and every item of service, facility, and transportation is shown as a separate item together with its related cost. When this method is used, there is usually a minimum of eight to ten items listed, and the family decides in each instance whether or not that item will become a part of the funeral service which they are arranging. As of May 1, 1984, funeral homes are required by law to offer funeral statements and costs to the family in the form of itemization.

A major advantage of itemization is the opportunity to provide family members great flexibility in arranging a funeral and the ability to control costs. It is felt that the family should have the freedom to decline those items of service or facility which they do not want, and a proper allowance should be made for such items that are not used. For example, one may ask to see "the pine box"—usually a cloth covered wood casket or a pressed wood container. These caskets are the least expensive functional devices and may or may not be in the display room. If the body is to be transported a great distance to the gravesite or creamatorium, perhaps the funeral director's van or station wagon could be used rather than the expensive hearse. If one looks carefully at the itemized services it makes it possible to obtain the most adequate services at the best price—which is the greatest advantage of the process of itemization.

In Pine's (1981) survey of funeral costs, of the 945 funeral homes surveyed, 373 firms practiced unit pricing, 133 practiced bi-unit pricing, 136 practiced tri-unit pricing, and 303 of the firms practiced functional, itemization or multi-unit pricing. This variation throughout the United States would imply that no single method dominates funeral practice and that probably the funeral home and the community it serves are in the best position to determine the method by which funeral costs are presented.

Want a Budget Casket for $75? Richard Jongordon Has One at America's Only Coffin Supermarket.

Richard Jongordon is out to beat the high cost of dying. "America is the only country where people make a strong effort to avoid the concept of death," says the 52-year-old director of the Neptune Society of Northern California, an organization dedicated to bringing the cost of funerals back down to earth.

Jongordon has opened the nation's first retail coffin store, sandwiched between a Mexican restaurant and an apartment house in San Francisco's Mission District. "We're geared for modesty and simplicity," he says. In the Early American Coffin Company's unpretentious showroom, potential buyers can browse among the five casket models that range from a $75 "army-style" pine box to a $245 top-of-the-line redwood.

"Buying your coffin in advance means that your family can avoid heavy expenses and tough decisions during a bad time," says Jongordon. He learned the hard way 20 years ago, when the unexpected death of his wife left him with two young children and a burial bill that took four years to pay off.

At the showroom, salesmen suggest alternative uses for the hard-to-hide coffins. Unsqueamish customers have turned the products into coffee tables, wine cabinets, clocks, even spice chests. Although they sell only 50 coffins a month, Jongordon's master carpenter can make coffins to order in four hours, and he expects to sell more than 100 coffins monthly by the end of this year.

"All we're advocating is a return to the basics of our forefathers," Jongordon says. "Simplicity was the practice in early America, before morticians ever existed. We're simply providing an alternative to the high cost of dying." Conventional funeral arrangements can easily run $5,000 to $10,000.

This coffin vendor puts his money where his mouth is. Asked how he would like to be ushered into the hereafter, Jongordon points to the $75 pine box. "That will be perfectly adequate," he says.

Source: *Us*, February 2, 1982.

CONCLUSION

Grief is the emotional working through of a significant loss. This chapter has indicated that the funeral is a part of the grief process in contemporary America.

In our discussion, we have described funerals and their alternatives within a cultural and historical perspective. In the United States an evolutionary, and not a revolutionary, process has occurred. Americans did not invent the funeral nor the funeral functionary. However, contemporary Americans have found an expression for their bereavement.

APPLICATION: CHILDREN SHOULD NOT BE DENIED ATTENDANCE AT FUNERALS

For children, as well as their adult counterparts, the funeral ceremony can be an experience of value and significance. At a very early age, children are interested in any type of family reunion, party, or celebration. To be excluded from the funeral may create questions and doubts in the mind of the child as to why they are not permitted to be a part of an important family activity.

Another consideration in denying the child an opportunity to participate in post-death activities is to determine what goes through the child's mind when such participation is denied. Children deal with other difficult situations in life, and when denied this opportunity, many will fantasize. Research suggests that these fantasies may be negative, destructive, and at times more traumatic than the situation from which the child is excluded.

Children should not be excluded from activities prior to the funeral service. They should be permitted to attend the visitation, wake or shiva. (In some situations it would be wise to permit children to confront the deceased prior to the public visitation.) It is obvious that children should not be forced into this type of confrontation, but by the same token, children who are curious and desirous of being involved, should not be denied the opportunity.

The child will react at his or her own emotional level, and the questions asked will usually be asked at his or her level of comprehension. It is important that those who answer these questions follow two rules—never lie to the child, and do not overanswer the child's question.

At the time of the funeral, there are two concerns that parents have concerning their children's behavior at funerals. The first is that they are worried that the child will have difficulty observing the grief of others—particularly if the child has never seen an adult loved one cry. The second concern is that parents themselves become confused when the child's emotional reactions may be different from their own. If the child is told of a death and responds by saying "Oh, can I go out and play?" the parent may interpret this as denial or a suppressed negative reaction to the death. Such a reaction can increase emotional concern on the part of the parent. However, if the child's response is viewed as only a first reaction, and the child is provided with loving, caring, and supportive attention, the child will ordinarily progress into an emotional resolution of the death.

The final reasons for involving children in postdeath activities are related to the strength and support that they give other grievers. They often provide positive evidence to the fact that life goes on. In other instances, having been an important part of the life of the deceased, their presence is symbolic testimony to the "immortality" of the deceased. Furthermore, it is not at all unusual for a child to change the atmosphere surrounding bereavement from one of depression and sadness to one of laughter, verbalization, and celebration. Many times the child does this through normal childlike behavior without any understanding of the kind of contribution being made.

Summary

1. To understand the contemporary funeralization process as it is found in the United States, one must understand its cultural and historical context.
2. Embalming, a process as old as 484 B.C., was introduced in France and England in the 1600s, and to the United States during the Civil War. Presently four out of five American bodies are embalmed.
3. The contemporary role of funeral director has evolved from the occupations of cabinetmaker and livery owner.
4. Presently there are approximately 22,000 funeral homes in the United States which serve the families of the approximately 1.9 million annual deaths.
5. Within the contemporary funeralization process, final disposition of the body is made by either burial (85 percent), cremation (10 percent), or entombment (5 percent). (These percentages are approximate national averages.)
6. The funeral is designed to meet the psychological, sociological, and theological or philosophical needs of bereaved persons.
7. A person does not purchase property within a cemetery, but rather purchases the "right to interment" in a specific location within that cemetery.
8. There are alternatives to funerals including: immediate disposition, body donation, and memorial services.
9. Funeral bills have traditionally been presented to customers utilizing the following pricing systems: unit pricing, bi- or tri-unit pricing, and itemization. The latter is mandated by law as of May 1, 1984.
10. Children should not be excluded from participating in funerals. To do so might have adverse effects on the child's emotional well-being and impede his or her bereavement.

Discussion Questions

1. Describe how the funeralization process can assist in coping with grief and facilitate the bereavement process.
2. Distinguish between grief, bereavement, and funeralization.
3. Describe and compare each of the following processes: burial, cremation, and entombment.
4. Based on Irion's concept of psychological needs of the bereaved, explain how funeralization can be related to the meeting of each of these needs.
5. Discuss the factors which affect postdeath costs and the expenses related to funerals and final disposition.

6. Discuss the psychological, sociological, and theological-philosophical aspects of the funeralization process. How do each of these aspects facilitate the resolution of grief?
7. What would you include in your own obituary if you were to write it?
8. What would be your choice of final disposition of your body? Why would you choose this method and what effects might this choice have upon your survivors (if any)?

Glossary

CREMATION: The reduction of human remains by means of heat or direct flame. The cremated remains are called "cremains" or "ashes" and weigh between six and eight pounds. "Ashes" is a very poor description of the cremated remains because they look more like crushed rock or pumas.
CREMATORY: An establishment in which cremation takes place.
CRYPT: A concrete chamber in a mausoleum into which a casket is placed.
COLUMBARIUM: A building or wall for above-ground accommodation of cremated remains.
DISPOSITION: Final placement or disposal of a dead person.
EMBALMING: A process which temporarily preserves the deceased by means of displacing body fluids with preserving chemicals.
ENTOMBMENT: Opening and closing of a crypt, including the placement and sealing of a casket within.
FUNERALIZATION: A process involving activities, rites, and rituals associated with the final disposition of the deceased's body.
ITEMIZATION: A method of pricing a funeral in which every item of service, facility, and transportation is listed with its related cost.
MAUSOLEUM: A building or wall for above-ground accommodation of a casket.
MEMORIAL SOCIETY: A group of people joined together to obtain dignity, simplicity, and economy in funeral arrangements through advanced planning.
NICHE: A chamber in a columbarium into which an urn is placed.
URN: A container for cremated remains.
VAULT OR GRAVE LINER: A concrete or metal container into which a casket or urn is placed for ground burial. Its function is to prevent the ground from settling.

References

Brantner, John P. 1973. "Crisis Intervenor." Paper presented at the Ninth Annual Funeral Service Management Seminar, National Funeral Directors Association, Scottsdale, Ariz. (January).
Davidson, Glen W. 1975. *Living with Dying*. Minneapolis: Augsburg Publishing House.
Grollman, Earl A. 1972. Commencement Address, Department of Mortuary Science, University of Minnesota, Minneapolis, Minn. (May).
Habenstein, Robert W., and William M. Lamers. 1962. *The History of American Funeral Directing*. Milwaukee: Bulfin Printers.

Holmes, Thomas H., and R. H. Rahe. 1967. "The Social Readjustment Rating Scale." *Journal of Psychosomatic Research*. Vol. 11:213–218.

Irion, Paul E. 1956. *The Funeral: An Experience of Value*. Milwaukee: National Funeral Directors Association.

Irion, Paul E. 1968. *Cremation*. Philadelphia: Fortress Press.

Jackson, Edgar N. 1963. *For the Living*. Des Moines, Iowa: Channel Press.

Johnson, Edward C. 1944. "A History of the Art and Science of Embalming." *Casket and Sunnyside*.

Lindemann, Erich. 1944. "Symptomatology and Management of Acute Grief." *American Journal of Psychiatry*. Vol. 101 (September):141–148.

National Funeral Directors Association. 1981. "Body Donation: A Compendium of Facts Compiled as an Interprofessional Source Book." Produced by the College of Health Sciences (University of Minnesota) and the National Funeral Directors Association.

Pine, Vanderlyn R. 1971. *Findings of the Professional Census*. Milwaukee: National Funeral Directors Association (June).

Pine, Vanderlyn R. 1982. *A Statistical Abstract of Funeral Service Facts and Figures of the United States* (1982 Edition). Milwaukee: National Funeral Directors Association.

Raether, H. C., and R. C. Slater. 1974. *Facing Death as an Experience of Life*. Milwaukee: National Funeral Directors Association.

Suggested Readings

Consumers Union. 1977. *Funerals: Consumers' Last Rights*. Mount Vernon, New York: Consumers Union.

   A report by Consumers Union on conventional funerals, burials, and alternatives including cremation, direct burial and body donation.

Habenstein, Robert W., and William M. Lamers. 1962. *The History of American Funeral Directing*. Milwaukee: Bulfin Printers, Inc.

   An excellent source for the study, review, and analysis of the history of funeral directing in the American culture from its introduction in Colonial times to present.

Habenstein, Robert W., and William M. Lamers. 1963. *Funeral Customs the World Over*. Milwaukee: Bulfin Printers, Inc.

   A review of the cultures of the world especially significant to assist in a cross-cultural study of the various practices of funeralization in all cultures, including those of Eastern and Western origins.

Irion, Paul E. 1954. *The Funeral and the Mourners*. Nashville, Tenn.: Abingdon Press.

Irion, Paul E. 1956. *The Funeral: An Experience of Value*. Milwaukee: National Funeral Directors Association.

Irion, Paul E. 1966. *The Funeral—Vestige or Value?* Nashville: Abingdon Press.

Irion, Paul E. 1968. *Cremation*. Philadelphia: Fortress Press.

Irion, Paul E. 1971. *Humanistic Funeral Service*. Baltimore: Waverly Press.

   This series of books gives the serious student an excellent background in the whole area of grief and bereavement as well as its relationship to the funeral.

Jackson, Edgar N. 1957. *Understanding Grief*. Nashville, Tenn.: Abingdon Press.

   A basic reference to understanding human grief. The book has served as the primary reference for students in seminaries, colleges of funeral service education, and the health related fields more than any other text on the subject. The book deals with grief—its roots, dynamics and treatment.

Maryland Center for Public Broadcasting. 1977. *The Last Rights: Funerals.* Owings Mills: Maryland Center for Public Broadcasting.
   A detailed report describing funerals, burials, and alternatives including memorial societies, cremations, and organ donations. Issues of cost and specific steps to be considered in burying the dead are discussed. Outstanding resource for lay persons.

Pine, Vanderlyn R. 1975. *Caretaker of the Dead.* New York: Irvington Publishers.
   An excellent source to discover the ways in which a society views death and cares for its dead. It is written from both a funeral director's and a sociologist's analytical perspective. Pine is not only a licensed funeral service practitioner but also a professor of sociology at New Paltz University in New York.

Chapter 12

EPILOGUE

The mass is ended, go in peace.

IF AT THE CONCLUSION of the funeral service grief work were finished, the process of reintegration of the bereaved into society would be completed. The funeral service and the final disposition of the dead only mark the end of public mourning; however, private mourning continues for some time.

THE BEREAVEMENT ROLE

In earlier chapters we discussed bereavement behavior within an historical and cross-cultural perspective. We have given a general description of the norms and cultural patterns that prescribe proper conduct for the bereaved within American society. When these bereavement norms are applied to particular persons occupying statuses within a group or social situation, we are concerned with bereavement roles.

In discussing the adaptation to the crisis and stressful situation of becoming ill, Talcott Parsons (1951:426–437) describes the "sick role" as being composed of two rights and two obligations. The first right is for the sick person to be exempted from "normal" social responsibilities. The extent to which one is exempted is contingent upon the nature and severity of the illness. The second right is to be taken care of and to become dependent upon others as one attempts to return to normal social functioning. In exchange for these rights, the sick person must express a desire to "want to get better" and must seek technically competent help.

Robson (1977) suggests that behavior related to the death of a significant other (spouse, parent, etc.) is quite similar to illness behavior patterns. At the onset of death, the bereaved are exempted from their normal social responsibilities. Depending upon the nature and the degree of relationship with the diseased, the bereaved are awarded time away from employment in much the same way as they are given sick leaves—spouses and children may be given a week while close friends and relatives may only be given time to attend the funeral.

327

The bereaved are also allowed to become dependent upon others for social and emotional support and for assistance with tasks related to the requirements of normal daily living. In offering this type of support, neighbors and friends call on survivors with gifts of food, flowers, and other expressions of sympathy. This custom lead Kavanaugh's (1972) brother to ask if "dead people ate meatloaf and chocolate cake?"

In exchange for these privileges created by the death of a loved one, those adopting the bereavement role are not only required to seek technically competent help from funeral directors and clergy members, but are expected to return as soon as possible to normal social responsibilities. The bereavement role is considered a temporary role, and it is imperative that all role occupants do whatever necessary to relinquish the role within a reasonable period of time. Time extensions are usually granted to spouse and children, but there is a general American value judgment that normal grieving should be completed by the first anniversary of the death.

American folk wisdom would contend that "time heals"—with the intensity of the grief experienced diminishing over time. However, a more accurate picture of mourning would point out that the time intervals between intense experiences of grief increase with the passing of time, that it is not abnormal to experience periods of mourning for losses that occurred many years before. What is abnormal behavior, from the perspective of the American bereavement role, is the preoccupation with the death of the loved one and refusing to make attempts to return normal social functioning. Examples of deviant behavior of this type would include the following:

1. Malingering in the bereavement role and memorializing the deceased by refusing to dispose of articles of clothing, personal effects, and living as if one expected the dead to reappear.
2. Rejecting attempts from others who offer social and emotional support, refusing to seek professional counseling, and taking up permanent residence in "Pity City."
3. Rejecting public funeral rituals and requesting that the funeral functionaries merely pick up the body and dispose of it through cremation without any public acknowledgment of the death which has occurred.

Behaviors such as these are usually sanctioned by others through social avoidance, ostracism, and criticism. As a consequence, most people are not only encouraged but forced to move through the grieving process.

The Grieving Process

The grieving process, like the dying process, is essentially a series of behaviors and attitudes related to coping with the stressful situation of changing the status of a relationship. As discussed in Chapters 3 and 4,

The Loss of a Significant Person

The loss of a significant person can be one of life's most devastating experiences. Yet, every human relationship is destined to end in loss. Loss is the price paid for relationships that insure survival and participation in the human experience.

The death of a loved one is, of course, the ultimate loss. Death is final and complete. But many little deaths are suffered by all of us along the way. Divorce, desertion, separation, abortion, stillbirth, and rejection mean losses of significant people. Jobs, military service, travel, and geographic moves also take us away from important others. So does placing the aged, mentally retarded, emotionally ill, criminal and delinquent, and putting dependent and neglected children up for adoption or foster care. Further, illness, accidents, and aging can change a loved one so drastically that the person we once knew is gone.

From infancy on our lives are bound up with those of others. We are social beings whose very existence depends on attachment to others. The loss of such an attachment can feel like a threat to life itself. That is not to say that all close ties are ties of love. Love and hate are closely interwoven, and every relationship has some of both. Ambivalence is the essence of every relationship. Whether the relationship is weighted toward positive or negative feelings, however, it has to end. No matter how much we love someone we cannot keep that person alive forever or at our side forever. So loved ones die or go away, and those who are more hated than loved do also, and sometimes we get rid of those whom we do not love in other ways. Such losses bring their own kind of pain because we have had a say in them.

Source: Bertha G. Simos, *A Time to Grieve: Loss as a Universal Human Experience* (New York: Family Service Association of America, 1979), pp. 10 and 11.

many have attempted to understand coping as a series of universal, mutually exclusive and linear stages. However, since most will acknowledge that not all people will progress through the stages in the same manner, it might be more appropriate to list a number of coping strategies that people employ as they attempt to resolve the pain caused by the loss of a personally significant relationship.

Robert Kavanaugh (1972) identifies the following seven behaviors and feelings as part of the coping process: shock and denial, disorganization, volatile emotions, guilt, loss and loneliness, relief, and reestablishment. It is not difficult to see similarities between these behaviors and Kubler-Ross' five stages of the dying process.

As one moves toward reestablishment of a life without the deceased, it is obvious that the process involves extensive adjustment and time, especially if the relationship was meaningful. It is likely that one may have feelings of loneliness, guilt, and disorganization at the same time and that just when one may experience a sense of relief, something will happen to trigger a denial of the death which has occurred.

What facilitates bereavement and adjustment is to fully experience each of these feelings relating to the coping process as normal and realize that it is hope (holding the person together in fantasy at first) which will provide the survivor with the promise of a new life filled with order, purpose, and meaning.

ASSISTING THE BEREAVED

In his book *Bereavement: Studies of Grief in Adult Life*, Parkes (1972:161) notes that the funeral often precedes the "peak of the pangs" of grief that tends to be reached in the second week of bereavement. The "face" put on for the funeral can no longer be maintained and a need exists for the bereaved to be freed to grieve. The most valued person at this time is the one who makes few demands on the bereaved, quietly completes household tasks, and accepts the bereaved person's vented anguish and anger—some of which may be directed against the helper. It is important to recognize that the bereaved person has a painful and difficult task to perform which cannot be avoided or rushed.

Parkes (1972:162) observes that it is often reassuring to the bereaved person when others show they are not afraid to express feelings of sadness. Such expressions make the bereaved person feel understood and reduce a sense of isolation. How one grieves will vary. The important thing is for feelings to emerge into consciousness. How they appear on the surface may be of secondary importance.

It is not uncommon for one approaching a newly bereaved person to be unsure as to how to react. Parkes (1972:163) suggests that while a conventional expression of sympathy can probably not be avoided, pity is the last thing the bereaved person wants. Pity makes one into an object; the bereaved person somehow becomes pitiful. Pity puts the bereaved person at a distance from and in an inferior position to the intended comforter. Parkes maintains it is best to get conventional verbal expressions of sympathy over as soon as possible and to speak from the heart or not at all. There is not *a* proper thing to say at this time; a trite formula serves only to widen the gap between the two persons.

The encounter between the bereaved and the visitor may not seem satisfactory since the helper cannot bring back the deceased and the bereaved person cannot gratify the helper by seeming helped (Parkes, 1972:163). Bereaved people do, however, appreciate the visits and expressions of sympathy paid by others. These tributes to the dead confirm to the mourner the belief that the deceased is worth all the pain. The bereaved are also reassured that they are not alone and feel less insecure.

While many bereaved people are frightened and surprised by the intensity of their emotions, reassurance that they are not going mad and that this is a perfectly natural behavior can be an important contribution of the helper (Parkes, 1972:164–5). On the other hand, absence of grief in a situation where expected, excessive guilt feelings or anger, or lasting physical symptoms should be taken as signs that all is not going well. These persons may require special help, and the caregiver should not hesitate to advise the bereaved to get additional help if the caregiver is uncertain about the course of events.

PRACTICAL ISSUES: WILLS AND LIFE INSURANCE

Among other things, this book has concerned itself with preparation for dying and death—our own and that of others significant to us. Most of our discussion has dealt with intellectual and emotional preparation. It is also important to briefly mention some financial considerations as one prepares for death.

Wills

In a society dominated as it is by legal institutions, it is imperative to have a properly drawn will. Yet only 24 percent of all Americans have prepared for their deaths in this manner (Shepherd, 1975:131).

Each state makes key specific provisions for the settling of an estate when one dies intestate—without a will. Often these provisions work to the disadvantage of the survivors. A well-executed will can reduce the expense and aggravation resulting from court-appointed administrators, can save thousands of dollars in taxes, and can apportion assets according to the desires of the dying under the guidance of someone they trust (Shepherd, 1975).

When an individual dies, someone must be legally responsible for settling the estate, paying debts and taxes, and dividing up assets among the heirs. With a will, an executor is named—usually a spouse (providing that the individual was married). Signed copies of wills should not be kept exclusively in a safety deposit box. Since many states require that the box should be sealed, it is a good idea to have copies in the possession of the designated executor, members of one's family, one's lawyer, and/or in one's personal papers.

Wills are not just for the rich. They can be drawn rather inexpensively with a simple one being executed by most attorneys for approximately $100. More complex estate planning is also available through lawyers who specialize in this area.

What's Fair Is Fair

Even where a will or the law of intestacy calls for equal division of a bequest among a group of beneficiaries and the beneficiaries accept the principle of equal division, conflict may occur. Some possessions are indivisible but desirable to more than one person, such as a prized antique clock. Problems may arise in the attempt to divide valuables equally. Under what circumstances can a treasured rocking chair and a family Bible be divided equally between two or more family members?

If all beneficiaries want fair treatment and a will attempts fair treatment, conflict may occur because beneficiaries have different perceptions of what is fair. Fairness can mean that something is divided equally, but fairness also takes into account various principles of deservingness or right; a division of an estate can be fair without being equal. Because fairness can be determined on many different bases, there may be many competing interpretations on what is fair. The following list, derived from the work of Sussman et al. (1970) and from interviews carried out during our research, indicates some of the competing principles for determining if the outcome in inheritance is fair.

1. Long residence in a house confers some right to it.
2. Last name identity with the deceased confers some rights to the property of the deceased.
3. Blood relationship confers some rights.
4. High frequency of contact with the deceased confers some rights.
5. Material support of the deceased confers some rights.
6. Coresidence with the deceased confers some rights.
7. Having given the deceased a thing confers rights to its return.
8. Need arising from relative poverty, handicap, minorhood, orphan status, or infirmity confers rights.
9. Contribution in building the deceased's estate increases rights.
10. Kinship closeness confers rights.

11. Previous perceived underinheritance increases rights.
12. Overinheritance reduces rights.
13. Hostile relationship with the deceased reduces rights.
14. Congenial relationship increases rights.

In addition to people having discrepant interpretations of what is equal or what is fair, there will be instances where equality and fairness may be competing principles. Some individuals will believe that the estate should be divided equally, while other individuals will believe that it should be divided on the basis of what is fair, though fairness may be perceived differently by different persons.

Because there are so many possible interpretations of what is fair or what is equal and because people often seek fairness or equality, a dispute may not be resolved easily. Disputes over inheritance may be one of the major reasons for adult siblings to break off relationships with each other. In some cases the inheritance dispute may be the final battle between competitive siblings, and in that sense it resembles the "last straw" reported in breakups in other close relationships (Hill, Rubin, and Peplau, 1976; Nevaldine, 1978).

Source: Sandra L. Titus, Paul C. Rosenblatt, and Roxanne M. Anderson, "Family Conflict Over Inheritance of Property." *The Family Coordinator,* July 1979, pp. 337–338.

Life Insurance

The amount of life insurance needed is directly related to the number of dependents one has. For example, if an individual was the sole provider in a family consisting of a spouse and three small children, he or she would have a greater need for life insurance than a single person with no dependents. Life insurance is to protect one's dependents and to give the insured person a feeling of security knowing they are covered in the event of death. If the sole provider were to die, those four dependents would need some immediate source of revenue to tie them over until other financial arrangements could be made. At the time of grief, the added burden of the loss of income is not needed.

Term life insurance tends to have the lowest premiums for the greatest amount of coverage. Whole life and universal life insurance provide coverage and the opportunity to build cash assets. Group insurance plans can be less expensive than individual plans. It is advisable to shop around and compare the benefits of the different life insurance programs. The premiums vary considerably for the same coverage. Be aware of high-powered salespersons who may try to sell coverage which is not needed. Become informed about life insurance by talking with knowledgeable consumers or by reading consumer magazines before purchasing any insurance. Comparison shopping will pay off.

THE NEED FOR DEATH EDUCATION

As noted earlier, most individuals today in the United States die "offstage" away from the center of the arena (the home), in the rather institutional setting of a hospital or nursing home. Removing death from kin and friends has made the event a taboo, not-to-be-seen or talked about, experience. Since death is inevitable—at present a 100 percent chance of our dying, with the probability of change unlikely—learning skills and attitudes related to death should definitely be useful. Certainly death education should prove as helpful, if not more so, as many other subjects we learn in school.

In a study of thirty-four institutions selected from the AAHE Directory of Institutions offering specialization in Undergraduate and Graduate Professional Programs in Health Education, Tandy and Sexton (1983) discovered that 61 percent offered one or more undergraduate or graduate classes in death education. The responsibility for teaching these classes was shared largely by health educators, psychologists and sociologists. However, death education should not be limited to adults, but should be a vital aspect of the child's socialization process. Death education on one's deathbed is no better than sex education the day of the wedding.

Learning to express ourselves—sadness or happiness—as children, would perhaps loosen our inhibitions as adults. To discourage, or even punish, children for expressing grief through crying does not allow the individual to cope with the loss and then go on with life. In an unpublished study by Dickinson in 1979 and 1980, college students' responses to their first experiences with death revealed that crying was deemed unacceptable for some and, in a few cases, physical punishment resulted from the child's crying. For some, they were "scared," "frightened," and "upset" at seeing their parents cry. It was the first time many had seen their fathers cry. Crying in front of others in expressing one's grief should be as natural as laughing in front of others.

Whether a professional such as a nurse, physician, social worker, clergyperson, or mortician who frequently deals with death, death education does not only prepare one to deal with one's own mortality but makes one more aware, and hopefully more sensitive to the needs of others. Our society does not have a very good record in medical and theology schools in offering courses on dying, death, and bereavement, despite the fact that physicians and clergy are among the first to be involved with dying and death.

While some instruction on dying and death occurs in the medical school curriculum, much is indirect and impersonal and does not allow time for the student to work through personal feelings about death (Barton, 1972). A possible approach to changing attitudes of practitioners might be to convince medical schools to focus on the social-psychological aspects of dying and death as part of their curricula (Schultz and Anderman, 1976). Since a physician is often the professional present as death approaches, it seems only appropriate that death education be incorporated into the required offerings of medical schools. Such exposure can help the medical student work through individual attitudes toward dying and death in order to be more sensitive to the needs of patients. In the end, both physician and patient would benefit.

What the Doctor Orders Is Sometimes Just What the Patient Needs

Brillat-Savarin attended his 93-year-old great-aunt when she was dying. "She had kept all her faculties and one would not have noticed her state but for her smaller appetite and her feeble voice. 'Are you there, nephew?' 'Yes aunt, I am at your service and I think it would be a good idea if you had some of this lovely old wine.' 'Give it to me, my friend, liquids always go down.' "I made her swallow half a glass of my best wine. She perked up immediately and turning her once beautiful eyes toward me, she said, 'Thank you for this last favor. If you ever get to my age you will see that death becomes as necessary as sleep.' These were her last words and half an hour later she was asleep forever."

Source: Brillat-Savarin, "Meditation XXVI, de la mort," cited by Ivan Illich, *Medical Nemesis: The Expropriation of Health*, New York: Pantheon Books, 1976.

Kalish and Dunn (1976) noted from their survey of theology schools that the majority do not offer courses on dying, death, and bereavement. When these courses were offered the seminaries were responding to student demands for such a course. It should be noted, however, that schools not offering a thanatology course justified their decision by saying that some death-related materials were covered in the courses on pastoral counseling. Even family sociologists in writing about crises in the family have included little about death. *The* crisis in the family seems to be divorce which will occur in *some* families, but death will occur in *all* families. It is our argument—perhaps somewhat biased—that everyone could benefit from death education.

Death education should not only prove useful in coping with dying and death situations (our own as well as others), but can actually improve the quality of our living. As Elizabeth Kubler-Ross notes, relating to the dying does not depress her but makes her appreciate each day of life and thankful each morning she awakes for the potential of another day. Learning more about dying and death should make one strive to make each day count in a positive way. It tends to make one "look for the good in others and dwell on it," as Alex Haley suggests, rather than always bad-mouthing and criticizing others.

Rather than wait until after the individual dies to make positive statements *after life*, why not tell those significant others in our lives *while they are alive* what they mean to us. If you cannot verbalize this face-to-face, drop that special person a note and simply tell him or her what you think of him or her. As Kavanaugh (1972) says, "It doesn't have to be a poem since most of us are not poets." Make it plain and simple, but do it! Hopefully, an awareness of the importance of something like this will be a result of death education.

CONCLUSION

It is our hope that this book has helped you in understanding and coping with dying, death, and bereavement; and that in doing this you will be able to assist others in doing the same. Furthermore, it has been our ultimate objective that this understanding will facilitate a more meaningful experience of life. Just as one cannot fully appreciate a beautiful day without experiencing its opposite, so too the richness of life is enhanced by the knowledge of its finitude.

APPLICATION: RESOURCES FOR BEREAVED PERSONS

In reading this book you have acquired many resources to assist you in facing your own death and the deaths of others. Rabbi Earl A. Grollman (1976), in his book *Talking About Death: A Dialogue Between Parent and Child*, provides the following annotated list of organizations and groups which are additional resources for bereaved persons. It is our opinion that your utilization of these resources will greatly compliment what you have gained from reading this book.

ORGANIZATIONS

American Association of Retired Persons
1909 K Street, N.W.
Washington, D.C. 20049

An excellent division for widowed persons is "Action for Independent Maturity" in Morris County, New Jersey; Tulsa, Oklahoma; Atlanta, Georgia; and Washington, D.C. The association publishes a helpful brochure, *On Being Alone.*

The American National Red Cross
National Headquarters
Washington, D.C. 20006
This emergency-oriented organization helps individuals, families, and communities cope with crisis. In case of death there are services to members of the armed forces and their families. For the child who has sustained a loss and does not know how to fill his or her free time the Youth Service Programs have accommodated more than six million young people in worthwhile programs.

Big Brothers of America
220 Suburban Station Building
Philadelphia, Pennsylvania 19103
With more than 235 local member agencies, the Big Brothers has helped thousands of boys who have no father with whom to identify.

Big Sisters
220 Suburban Station Building
Philadelphia, Pennsylvania 19103
The group is especially recommended for the widower who feels that his daughter should have the companionship of an older female volunteer.

National Foundation for Sudden Infant Death
1501 Broadway
New York, New York 10036
Sudden infant death syndrome (SIDS), also known as "crib death," is a disease that causes about 10,000 infant deaths annually. Local chapters respond to such painful questions as "Was it my fault?"—"Did my baby suffocate in its bedding?"—"Could it have been prevented?" In addition to intervening on behalf of stricken parents, most SIDS chapters offer professional counseling services for adults and children.

N.O.W. National Office
5 South Wabash, Suite 1615
Chicago, Illinois 60603
For the widow or widower with a child, the National Organization for Women has created high quality developmental child care programs. "The centers are available to all citizens on the same basis as public schools, parks, and libraries; adequate to the needs of children from preschool age through adolescence as well as to the needs of their parents."

Parents Without Partners
7910 Woodmont Avenue
Washington, D.C. 20014
An international nonprofit, nonsectarian organization with a membership of 80,000 in over 600 chapters concerned with the welfare of single parents and their children.

The Society of the Compassionate Friends
Post Office Box 3247
Hialeah, Florida 33013
An international organization of bereaved parents who have been through their own time of loneliness and isolation, and seek to help relieve the mental anguish of other families whose child has died.

United Way of America
801 North Fairfax Street
Alexandria,Virginia 22314
The Information and Referral Service helps bereaved parents and children find an appropriate agency. It could be a family service association, a children's camp, a Big Brothers or Big Sisters organization, a mental health facility, a child guidance clinic, or a social service.

Physicians

The family doctor may know the patient through years of personal medical service and has a unique opportunity to observe physical and emotional health. More important than possible medicines prescribed are the insights offered by the family doctor. For information, write:
American Academy of Family Physicians
1740 West 92nd Street
Kansas City, Missouri 64114

or

The American Medical Association
535 North Dearborn Street
Chicago, Illinois 60610

Psychological and Psychiatric Services

Below are three major national psychological and psychiatric associations with accredited professionals and services:
Psychological: American Psychological Association
1200 17th Street, N.W.
Washington, D.C, 20036

Psychiatric: American Psychiatric Association
1700 18th Street N.W.
Washington, D.C. 20009

American Psychoanalytic Association
1 East 57th Street
New York, New York 10022

SCHOOL COUNSELING DEPARTMENTS

When a death occurs, it is suggested that you call your children's school counseling service. The school environment often becomes the focus of children's grief. Most communities have a coordinated counseling service for students from kindergarten level through high school. Counseling is the core of any guidance department and can be an invaluable resource during a child's crisis.

WIDOW-TO-WIDOW PROJECTS

Emotional breakdowns among widows, especially in younger age groups, present a substantial problem that few in America are trained to prevent. Recognizing the special needs of the newly bereaved, Dr. Phyllis R. Silverman, psychiatric social worker, and Dr. Gerald Caplan, of the Laboratory of Community Psychiatry of Harvard Medical School, started the Widow-to-Widow Project in 1967. The emphasis is on self-help groups in which the primary caregiver is another widowed person. The concern and goal is to stimulate programs of preventive intervention. The program has grown nationally; the following are but a random sample:

Connecticut Council- Widows Widowers Associated
60 Lorraine Street
Hartford, Connecticut 06105
With other nonsectarian chapters in Norwalk, Waterbury, Bridgeport, New Haven, and Danbury, their purpose is "to bring together the widowed in fellowship, to help them find a new way of life, to assure them that they are not alone, and to develop a public awareness and recognition of the needs of the widowed." Their motto is "Sharing by Caring."

Family Service of Westchester, Inc.
470 Mamaroneck Avenue
White Plains, New York10605
This nonsectarian agency has developed the Widow and Widower Club with membership for Westchester County. Coordinated by a trained social

worker, the emphasis is on individual counseling, small discussion groups, community education, and an outreach program to help the newly bereaved.

Widows Consultation Center
136 East 57th Street
New York, New York 10022
This center is a nonprofit, nonsectarian agency offering information, counseling, and advisory services to widows on an individual or group basis. "In addition to coping with grief and loneliness the widow may have to adjust to a new and difficult role—that of the single parent. She has to accept the weight of added responsibilities while overwhelmed with feelings of dependency and of fear of being a burden to her children. She may feel neglected or may look to her children for emotional support they cannot give."

Widow to Widow Program
69 Summer Street
Havervill, Massachusetts 01830
The program is based on the premise that another widow is the best person to reach out to a bereaved woman. Regarded as an intervention service, volunteers are also especially interested in reaching out to children.

Widow to Widowed Program
Needham Community Council
51 Lincoln Street
Needham, Massachusetts 02192
Patterned on the program of Harvard Medical School of Community Psychiatry, the Needham program is also a self-help approach in preventive intervention. Trained widowed men and women, offering support in adjusting to their new life on a one-to-one basis to recently widowed men and women.

Widowed to Widowed Program of San Diego
6655 Alvarado Road
San Diego, California 92120
Through this program trained "widowed visitors" contact and offer emotional support to the newly widowed. A 24-hour hotline together with ongoing classes and problem-solving discussions are offered to the bereaved and their families.

For further information, consult:

Dr. Phyllis R. Silverman
Laboratory of Community Psychiatry
Harvard Medical School
58 Fenwood Road
Boston, Massachusetts 02115

Summary

1. The "sick role" gives one the right to be exempted from "normal" social responsibilities and to become dependent upon others.
2. The bereavement role is a temporary role.
3. Abnormal bereavement behavior is preoccupation with the death of the loved one and refusal to attempt returning to normal social functioning.
4. The grieving process is similar to the dying process in that it is a series of behaviors and attitudes related to coping with the stressful situation of changing the status of a relationship.
5. It is important in grieving to let feelings emerge into consciousness and not be afraid to express feelings of sadness.
6. It is not uncommon to be unsure as to how to act around a newly bereaved person.
7. To have a properly drawn will allows one to determine who receives his/her property.
8. Life insurance needs are determined by the number of dependents one has.
9. Death education not only prepares one to deal with his/her own mortality, but makes one more aware—and hopefully more sensitive—to the needs of others.

Discussion Questions

1. How can one avoid "deviant" or "abnormal" behavior regarding the bereavement role? What are some functions of defining bereavement roles as "deviant" or "abnormal"?
2. Discuss how the seven stages of grieving over one's death can also be applied to losses through divorce, moving form one place to another, or the amputation of a limb (arm or leg).
3. What does Parkes mean by the statement: "The funeral often precedes the 'peak of the pangs'"?
4. What are the advantages of having a will?
5. Who should have life insurance?
6. Why have medical and theology schools not traditionally offered courses on dying and death?

7. Why is death education important?
8. Discuss why death education should include children and not be limited to adults?
9. What is meant by this statement: "Americans die offstage today."
10. Discuss the pros and cons of crying during the grieving process.

Glossary

INTESTATE: To die without a will.

TERM LIFE INSURANCE: An insurance policy to cover the insured for a fixed period of time (five, ten, twenty years or so). Premiums are usually lower for a greater amount of coverage than other types of policies.

References

Barton, D. 1972. "The Need for Including Instruction on Death and Dying in the Medical Curriculum." *Journal of Medical Education*, Vol. 47:169–175.

Kalish, R.A., and L. Dunn. 1976. "Death and Dying: A Survey of Credit Offerings in Theological Schools and Some Possible Implications." *Review of Religious Research*, Vol. 17:122–130.

Kavanaugh, Robert E. 1972. *Facing Death*. Baltimore: Penguin Books.

Parkes, Colin M. 1972. *Bereavement: Studies of Grief in Adult Life*. New York: International Universities Press.

Parsons, Talcott. 1951. *The Social System*. Glencoe, Ill.: The Free Press.

Robson, J. D. 1977. "Sick Role and Bereavement Role: Toward a Theoretical Synthesis of Two Ideal Types," in *A Time to Die*, pp. 113–120, ed. by Glenn M. Vernon. Washington, D.C.: University Press of America.

Schultz, R., and D. Anderman. 1976. "How the Medical Staff Copes with Dying Patients: A Critical Review." *Omega*, Vol. 7:11–21.

Tandy, Ruth E., and Judy Sexton. 1983. Unpublished survey exploring death education. Texas Woman's University, Department of Health Education. Denton, Texas.

Suggested Readings:

Kubler-Ross, Elizabeth. 1975. *Death: The Final Stage of Growth*. Englewood Cliffs, N.J.: Prentice-Hall, Inc.

An anthology stressing death as an integral part of our lives that gives meaning to human existence.

Parkes, Colin Murray. 1972. *Bereavement: Studies of Grief in Adult Life*. New York: International Universities Press, Inc.

This book is based on the author's twelve years of research on the ways in which men and women react to the experience of bereavement.

Shipley, Roger R. 1982. *The Consumer's Guide to Death, Dying and Bereavement*. Palm Springs, Calif.: E.T.C. Publications.

A comprehensive coverage of material relevant to the consumer. A sourcebook providing information and references to assist individuals in making decisions regarding dying and death.

Werner-Beland, Jean A. 1980. *Grief Responses to Long-term Illness and Disability.* Reston, Va.: Reston Publishing Company.
Topics covered include psychoanalytic and attachment theory explanations for the grieving process, grief responses of patients and their significant others, factors leading to the burnout syndrome in nurses, and nurses' responsibility for seeking and developing their own support system.

INDEX

psychothantic stage (*cont.*)
defined, 135
punishment, 115, 116
Puritan(s), funeral, 265, 266, 267, 302
handling corpse by, 265–266
mourning rituals of, 266–267
view of death, 265
pyre, 251
defined, 258

Qemant, 250, 253

racial differences, in childhood death rates, 182
in infant death rates, 180, 181(*fig.*)
in life expectancy, 9, 11, 14(*tab.*)–15(*tab.*)
in suicide rates, 13
Radcliffe-Brown, A. R., 143–144, 145, 244, 245, 249
reality, perception of, and personal death awareness, 84
Reformed Tradition, 264–267
reforming, 267–269
rehearsal, in stress adaptation, 81
relationships, investing oneself in, and symbolic immortality, 148–151
response of dying child to, 192
religion, as anxiety provoker, 143–144, 145, 249
as anxiety reliever, 142, 143, 146, 249
and death attitudes, 139–171
defined, 170
and funeral homes, 141–142, 303
and funerals, 308
liberal, 276–277, 278
as means of providing understanding of death, 141–146, 147, 161–162, 163
origin of, and death, 140–141
and symbolic immortality, 147–148
and temporal interpretations of death, 146
see also specific religion
religiosity, and death anxiety, 129, 145, 161
and death fear, 129
defined, 170
of older adults, 129
resistance, as adaptive response, 95
defined, 99
resolution, of grief, 306–307
resolution stage, 82
resources, for bereaved, 336–341
denying control of, 50
respiratory distress syndrome, 182
respite care, 211
resurrection of death, in American culture, 289–291
and atomic age, 289–290
and thanatology, 290–291
resurrection syndrome, 40, 85

right to die, 64–67, 69, 86–87
rites of passage, 238, 240
defined, 258
ritual(s), defined, 170, 240
functions of, 240
mourning (*see* mourning rituals)
role(s), bereavement, 327–328
defined, 73
meanings, and dying process, 51–52
relinquishing, by older adult, 127, 128
response of dying child to, 192
sick, 52, 61–62, 327
role expectations, of patient, 52, 61–62
of physician, 60–61
Romanticism, and "dying of death," 270–274
rural cemeteries, 268, 270, 273, 278–279
rural environments, and observations of birth and death, 4, 5, 129

St. Christopher's Hospice, 209, 210, 223
St. Luke's Hospital, 218
Salish Indians, 238–240
salvation, Puritan view of, 265
Saunders, Cicely, 209–210
science, and after-life experiences, 156–157
based on intersubjectivity, 156
defined, 170
and incomplete explanations, 156, 163
scientific naturalism, 274–276
self, death of, and types of death fears, 159–161
sense of, and dying child, 192
self-concept, in adolescent death anxiety, 117, 118
self-determination, and hospice philosophy, 87–88
self-fullfilling prophecy, defined, 44
and medical diagnosis, 27–28
self-utilization, preoccupation with, 124
self-worth, fear of loss of, 85
Semai, 239, 244, 245, 250
sentimentalism and "dying of death," 270–274
separate spheres, ideology of, 269–270, 274–275
separation, 114
sermon, funeral, 267, 272
sex differences, in achievements, in middle-age adult, 124
in life expectancy, 9–12
in modes of coping, 124
in mourning rituals, 241, 242, 244, 245, 271–272
in number of funeral directors, 310
in physician's ability to relate to dying patient, 59
in suicide rates, 13, 16